Merala's Adventures

Scariest
the Best Fastest ↑ Bike Ride

By: Esmeralda Barahona

For my sister, Veronica Lopez, aka Vica,
who gave me my first bike ride!
thanks, Sis, for all the fun childhood memories!
Love you!

this Book Belongs to

_____

"It is a nice day for a bike ride, but I can't reach the pedals," says Merala.

"I will ask my big sister, Vica, to give me a ride on her BIG BLUE BIKE!"

Vica was excited to give Merala a ride.

"Hold on, Merala, hold on!
Here we go! Fast, fast, fast!"
said Vica.

As they got to mean old Mrs. McGee's house, they stopped to see the BIG PRETTY ROSES in her yard.

Merala picked a rose.

But mean old Mrs. McGee did not like anyone picking her roses.

Merala dropped the rose, and Vica began to pedal as fast as she could to get away, shouting, "Hold on, Merala, hold on!"

"Go fast, fast, fast, Vica! Here comes mean old Mrs. McGee to get us!" shouted Merala.

Vica ZOOMED up the driveway and into the garage as they got home.

they were not afraid anymore.
"You are the best,
fastest bike rider!" said
Merala to Vica.

"Yes, I am," said Vica.

Merala kept enjoying lots of fast bike rides with her sister, Vica.

But never again did she pick anyone's flowers without asking for permission first.

FOR MORE READING FUN

WWW.MERALASADVENTURES.COM

Printed in the USA
CPSIA information can be obtained
at www.ICGtesting.com
LVHW051933280923
758962LV00017B/19

9 780615 907239

DZIAŁOSZYCE
Memorial Book

an English translation of

Sefer yizkor shel kehilat Dzialoshitz ve-ha-seviva

Yizkor Book of the Jewish Community of Działoszyce and Surroundings

Project Coordinator: Menachem Daum

Translation Edited and Annotated by Fay and Julian Bussgang

Published by JewishGen, Inc., New York, NY
An Affiliate of
The Museum of Jewish Heritage – A Living Memorial to the Holocaust

First Printing: November 2012

JewishGen, Inc.
An Affiliate of the Museum of Jewish Heritage
A Living Memorial to the Holocaust
36 Battery Place
New York, NY 10280

Printed in the United States of America by Lightning Source, Inc.

Library of Congress Control Number (LCCN): 2012952870
ISBN: 978-0-9764759-8-9: (hard cover: 374 pages, alk. paper)

Original Yizkor Book published by "Hamenora" Publishing House
Tel Aviv 1973

JewishGen and the Yizkor Books in Print Project

This book has been published by the **Yizkor Books in Print Project,** as part of the **Yizkor Book Project** of **JewishGen, Inc.**

    JewishGen, Inc. is a non-profit organization founded in 1987 as a resource for Jewish genealogy. Its website (www.jewishgen.org) serves as an international clearing house and resource center to assist individuals who are researching the history of their Jewish families and the places where they lived. JewishGen provides databases, facilitates discussion groups, and coordinates projects relating to Jewish genealogy and the history of the Jewish people. In 2003, JewishGen became an affiliate of the **Museum of Jewish Heritage – A Living Memorial to the Holocaust** in New York.

    The **JewishGen Yizkor Book Project** was organized to make more widely known the existence of Yizkor (Memorial) Books written by survivors and former residents of various Jewish communities throughout the world. Later, volunteers associated with the different destroyed communities began cooperating to have these books translated from the original language—usually Hebrew or Yiddish—into English, thus enabling a wider audience to have access to the valuable information contained within them. As each chapter of these books was translated, it was posted on the JewishGen website and made available to the general public.

    The **Yizkor Books in Print Project** began in 2011 as an initiative to print and publish Yizkor Books that had been fully translated, so that hard copies would be available for purchase by the descendants of these communities and also by scholars, universities, synagogues, libraries, and museums.

    These Yizkor books have been produced almost entirely through the volunteer effort of researchers from around the world, assisted by donations from private individuals. The books are printed and sold at near cost, so as to make them as affordable as possible. Our goal is to make this important genre of Jewish literature and history available in English in book form, so that people can have the personal histories of their ancestral towns on their bookshelves for themselves and for their children and grandchildren.

Lance Ackerfeld, Yizkor Book Project Manager

Joel Alpert, Yizkor Books in Print Project Coordinator

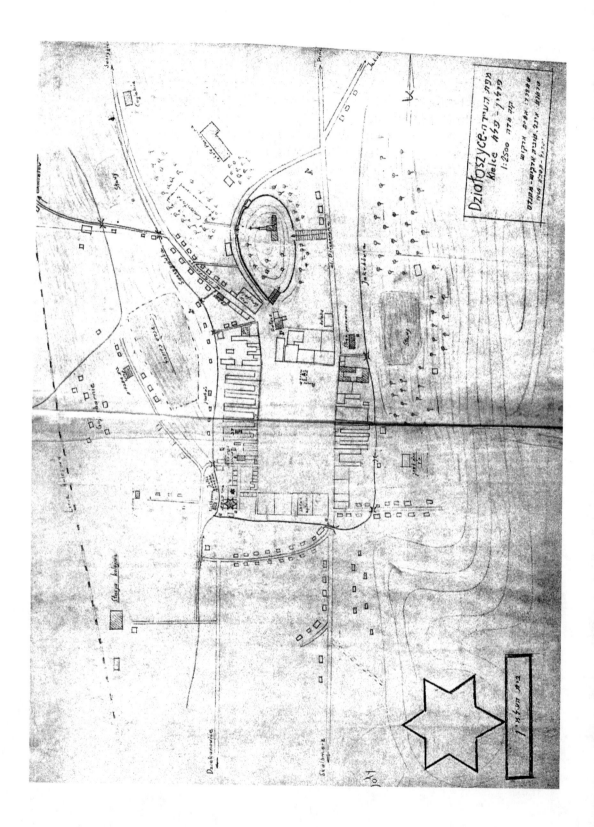

Table of Contents

INTRODUCTION

	Original page #	English page #
Preface and Acknowledgment for the English Edition, *Menachem Daum*	–	7
Guide to English Translation, *Fay and Julian Bussgang*	–	9
Key to Pronunciation	–	10
Foreword to Original Yizkor Book, *Dr. Moshe Bejski*	5	11

PART I: DZIAŁOSZYCE: THE TOWN AND ITS RESIDENTS
BEFORE WORLD WAR I

The Beginnings of the Działoszyce Settlement	11	17
There Was a Town, and Look, She is No Longer, *Izrael Dov Skóra*	16	22
Sources of Livelihood of Działoszyce's Jews, *Shlomo Gertler*	26	33
Grandmother's House (Now in Ruins), *Yisrael Zerachi*	30	36
An Obligation to Remember, *M. Rafali* [*Rafałowicz*]	49	52
The Beginning of the Enlightenment Period in Town, *Josef and Baruch Blat*	56	59
There Once Was A Town, *Chawa Karmioł (Rozenfrucht)*	60	64
From the Mouths of the Elders, *Izrael Dov Skóra*	62	66

PART II: BETWEEN TWO WORLD WARS

Działoszyce and Its Jews, *Abraham Langer*	69	73
From the Old Country, *Chaim Szwimer*	76	75
A Jewish Island in a Gentile Sea, *David Shlomi* [*Szulimowicz*]	78	77
Diałoszyce Jews As I Remember Them, *Yosef Harif (Ostry)*	90	83
Jews with Estates, *Chaim Szwimer*	96	87
Small Businesses in Our Town, *Arje Rolnicki*	101	92
Torah Study and Charity Organizations, *Rabbi Yehuda Frankel*	105	95
The Mizrachi Synagogue, *Joshua Wdowiński*	112	98
The Yavneh School, *Joshua Wdowiński*	115	101
The Hatchyo Library, *Chaja Chaba (Szulimowicz)*	121	104
Hanoar Hatzioni and Its Activities, *Ze'ev Szternfinkiel*	126	109
Hanoar Hatzioni, *Izrael Brandys*	129	113
Hashomer Hatzair, *Moshe Pułka*	135	119
The Gordonia Movement, *Natan Krelman*	138	122
The Agudas Yisroel, *Aryeh Shahar (Lejbl Jutrzenka)*	141	125
Trends of the Zionist Movement, *Naftali Szydłowski*	146	127
Drama Groups and Entertainment Activities, *Shoshana Rolnicka*	152	133
The Flood, *Natan Krelman*	158	140
Grandfather's House, *Chaim Cycowski*	164	145
My Memories, *Menachem Laskier (New York)*	167	148
Memories, *Bracha Pozner (Zając)*	171	151
Memories from the Old Days, *Klara Waks (Kajla Akerman)*	175	155
From My Memories, *Benjamin Włoski*	178	157
Memories, *Majer Cudzynowski*	180	159
Stories from the Past, *Chaim Jakób Kac*	182	160

PART III: CUSTOMS AND TRADITIONS

What the Beit Hamidrash Was, *Hayyim Balitzki* [*Chaim Balicki*]   187   165
Torah and Worship, *Dov Ptasznik*   190   166
Hasidic Shtiblekh, *Aryeh Shahar (Lejbl Jutrzenka)*   195   172
Dedication of Torah Scrolls to the Synagogue, *Josef Kac*   197   175
The Arrival of Shabes in Our Town, *Tova Avni (Szydłowska)*   198   176
Teachers in Działoszyce, *Aryeh Shahar (Lejbl Jutrzenka)*   201   179
The Rebbe Reb Joskele, *Naftali Szydłowski*   204   182
Reb Kalman Dayan, *z"l* , *Alter Horowicz*   206   184
Ignacy Mann—The Rabbi and His Pupil, *Chaim Schwimer*   207   185
The Town Cantor, *Moshe Salomon*   210   187
My Father, the Community Activist, *Moshe Drobiarz*   213   190
From Działoszyce Folklore, *Dov Bejski*   216   192

PART IV: SHOAH AND DESTRUCTION

Days of the Shoah, *Dr. Moshe Bejski*   233   209
The Outbreak of World War II, *Moshe Rożenek*   261   238
Social Assistance During the Nazi Occupation, *Dov Bejski*   267   240
My First Fear of Death, *Avraham Chobeh (Chaba)*   271   244
Jews Repent, *Chaim Icek Wohlgelernter*   273   246
The Horror Has Begun, *David Wohlgelernter*   275   248
The Evil Decrees, *Shalom Szlamowicz*   278   250
Chapters from the Past, *Aryeh Shahar (Lejbl Jutrzenka)*   280   253
In the Polish Underground, *Szlama Leszman (ben Jakób)*   298   269
The Deportations from Działoszyce, Skalbmierz, and Miechów,   304   276
    Abraham Tenenbaum
My Own Experience in the Holocaust, *Dov Bejski*   307   278
All Alone In Hiding, *Eliyahu Rozdział (Raziel)*   324   283
Memories, *David (Gustav) Rajzfeld*   329   288
The Tragedy of Działoszyce, *David Gelbart (Baltimore)*   336   296
Jankielówka and its Jews, *Chaim Fraiman (New York)*   343   301
Years of Pain, *Avraham Chobeh (Chaba)*   349   306
Under the German Boot, *Aszer Rafałowicz*   357   311
I Fainted—and Was a Free Man, *David Rotam (Rotner)*   361   314
My Life Underground with the German Cannibals,
    David Wohlgelernter   365   319
In Działoszyce and in the Camps, *Majer Zonenfeld*   374   325
During and After the War, *Abraham Langer*   380   331
Guide to Town Residents who Perished, *Fay and Julian Bussgang*   –   345
Town Residents who Perished in the Shoah   397   346

INDEX

Guide to Index of Names, *Fay and Julian Bussgang*   –   364
Index of Names   –   365

Preface and Acknowledgments for the English Edition

Menachem Daum

While Działoszyce may have been a small town, it once loomed large in the mental map of Polish Jews. A Działoszyce survivor told me an anecdote about two Jews who once met walking on a road, and one asked the other, "Where are you traveling?" "To Krakow," came the answer. "Never heard of it. Where is this place Krakow?" "It's a town not far from Działoszyce." "Ahaa!" the other answered with sudden recognition. But today Działoszyce has become a Jewish ghost town. Catholics live in the town, but Jewish ghosts still hover all about.

Before the Holocaust, about 6,500 of Działoszyce's 8,000 residents were Jewish. Fewer than 200 survived the war. A few weeks after being liberated, about fifteen Jewish survivors returned to their hometown. On June 15, 1945, Polish partisans warned the Christian residents to say indoors. That night they threw grenades into the house in which the returning Jews were staying. Four survivors were killed, and the rest fled for their lives. Since that night, no Jews have returned to live in Działoszyce.

Afterward, during Poland's postwar communist years, the history of the town's Jews was largely eradicated. Almost all physical evidence of the town's 350 years of Jewish history was destroyed. Vandals reduced its once magnificent synagogue, which survived the war intact, to a graffitied and roofless ruin. Every last tombstone of its Jewish cemetery, even the cemetery wall itself, was carted away for use as building material.

With almost nothing left of Jewish Działoszyce, a number of survivors undertook the sacred task of at least saving the memories of their beloved town. The Yizkor Book they produced gives us a glimpse of the vibrant day-to-day life that Działoszyce Jews lived for many years before the Holocaust. It also preserves the heroic stories of the mutual aid and spiritual resistance that Działoszyce Jews engaged in once the war broke out.

The authors of the Yizkor Book may have passed on, but they certainly hoped their words would outlive them and continue to inspire many generations to come. It is to honor the Yizkor Book's authors and to fulfill their intentions that a number of Działoszyce descendents have made this book available to English speaking readers. The translation from the original Hebrew and Yiddish into English was generously funded by Steven and Renee Adelsberg, Eli and Laura Epstein, Carl and Blossom Fraiman, Joseph Fraiman, Mark and Anita Sarna, Joseph and Marina Sarna, and Ted and Evelyn Weinberger. With their assistance, a number of translators were then engaged to work on this project.

As a labor of love, Fay and Julian Bussgang then stepped in and devoted themselves to the task of editing this book. Their editing was sorely needed as there were many inconsistencies in style and approach taken by the various translators. Fay and Julian made sure that the narrative was clearly presented and flowed smoothly. They used numerous resources in print and on the Internet to verify facts and spellings of names, places, and organizations and added explanatory footnotes. Julian, who was born in Poland and whose grandmother, Etka Spiro, was from Działoszyce, translated Polish words in the text. Fay compiled an index of all the names that appear in the book, so that future generations could find relatives without difficulty. Photos already scanned by the New York Public Library were enhanced by Michael Shade, with help from Larry Gaum and Sharon Grosfeld. The book cover was designed by Nili Goldman. The synagogue picture on the front cover is by Charles Burns. The town scene on the back cover is courtesy of Tomasz Wiśniewski.

This whole undertaking would not have been possible without the vision of the staff of JewishGen, which created the Yizkor Book Project, ably managed first by Joyce Field and then by Lance Ackerfeld. The Yizkor Book Project has encouraged the translation of countless memorial books from destroyed communities and offers a means for the public to have access to these translations by posting them on the JewishGen website. JewishGen's new initiative, Yizkor Books in Print, headed by Joel Alpert, aims to facilitate the publication of fully translated books and is a significant addition to the Yizkor Book Project's initial mission.

On a personal note, my father-in-law, Chaim Federman, and his two brothers were hidden for 28 months on a farm near Działoszyce. Their heroic rescuers, the Matuszczyk-Mucha family, have been honored by Yad Vashem. Their story has been told in the film *Hiding and Seeking*, which I had the privilege of showing to Działoszyce's high school students. Many of the students now realize that to know their own local history, they have to learn the history of the Jews of Działoszyce. It is my hope that this Yizkor Book will help heal the lingering wounds of the Holocaust and contribute to Polish-Jewish reconciliation.

Menachem Daum, Coordinator of the English Edition

Guide to the English Translation

It should be noted that this published English language edition of the Działoszyce Yizkor Book is not identical to the translation that was posted previously on the JewishGen website. Some changes in spelling have been made to assure internal consistency, and certain editorial changes have been made to conform with current publishing guidelines.

Many Polish or Russian words that appeared in the original text, as well as many familiar Yiddish words, have been retained to give a flavor of the language used by the Jews of Działoszyce. The spelling of Yiddish words used here is, in general, that recommended by YIVO Jewish Institute of Research. Words that appear in parentheses are part of the original text, while translations or explanations that have been added by the editors are placed in square brackets. If a word is familiar or used frequently, the translation may be given only the first time it appears in a section.

Transliterating names and surnames from one language to another is a difficult task. Moreover, in the case of Jews from Poland, the names have passed through several language changes over time, making it particularly difficult to ascertain the "right" spelling—if one exists. For the most part, names in this book have been spelled as they most probably were in prewar Poland. This was done in order to make it easier for researchers to trace their ancestors back to Poland and find official records there. However, postwar spellings of names, if known, were used for authors of chapters and in identifying postwar pictures.

As is the custom in Poland, the feminine surname endings "cka" and "ska" have been used for women (Rolnicka, Wdowińska) rather than the masculine surname endings "cki" and "ski" (Rolnicki, Wdowiński).

When looking for names of relatives, it should be kept in mind that people may have been referred to in several ways: by their given name plus their legal surname, by their given name plus their profession, by a nickname, or as the son or daughter of someone. Thus the same person may appear in different places in the book under different names.

A simplified key to the pronunciation of Polish names is displayed on the page that follows; an Index of Names of the people mentioned in the book has been added to the end of the volume.

We apologize in advance for any inadvertant errors.

Fay and Julian Bussgang,
Editors of the English Edition

Simplified Key to Pronunciation:

Most letters in Polish are pronounced similarly to their English equivalents except for the following, whose approximate English equivalents are given:

ą = on [nasalized] (om before b/p)

ę = en [nasalized] (em before b/p)

c = ts

i = ee

j = y

ł = w

ń = n as in onion

ó = oo/u

w = v

y = i as in fit

ch, h = h as in Helen

ć, ci, cz = ch

ś, si, sz = sh

ź, zi, ż, rz = zh

prz = psh

trz = tsh

Foreword to the Original Yizkor Book

Dr. Moshe Bejski

..."And I will take you one of a city and two of a family"... Jeremiah (3:14)

But for our town, even this macabre saying did not materialize. When the Holocaust subsided and its surviving remnants had been traced throughout Europe, it was discovered that in a few families, a lone survivor remained. In most, no one had been left alive; the whole branch had simply been wiped out, leaving nobody.

It is doubtful whether after the Holocaust someone could harbor the notion of resuming life anew on the ruins of Jewish Działoszyce. If a few rescued "embers," drawing upon the last of their strength returned, deluded into hoping that perhaps some of their dear ones might be still alive and that here was the natural meeting-place for a gathering of this sort, they encountered the refusal of the anti-Semitic Polish population to accept the idea that such Jews intended staying longer—until they could recover. The Poles resolved that not a single one of these wretches would cross the gates of the town. With a pogrom, they finished off the work of the Germans. Those who were able to escape the axe or the gun fled in the thick of darkness, so long as body and soul held together. Broken, exhausted and ill, the few survivors dispersed in all directions, facing every evening the recurring problem of finding that night a stone upon which to lay their head.

And the town of Działoszyce remained without any Jews—this time forever!

One generation and more went by. Most of us who chanced to be saved from the hellish Nazi horror have concentrated here in the State of Israel where, within the framework of national resurrection, we built our homes, set up families, and begot children. Others among us dispersed to the four corners of the globe, wherever relatives and kinsmen abroad helped them to emigrate and strike new roots in a foreign land. And although but a few of us were left after the Nazi sword had decimated us, the biological processes did their part, and our fellow townsmen also went the way of all flesh. At the early commemoration ceremonies we hold here to bemoan our sacred dead, we call up the memory of those among us who in that same year passed away—and who, to our great sorrow, are many—and when this present generation will come to pass—this generation born, grown, brought up and who lived in the town of Działoszyce—then the memory of that sacred community may, Heaven forbid, vanish altogether, as did most of the Jewish population.

The original Działoszyce Yizkor Book had a small English section with nine articles parallel to but not identical to chapters printed also in Hebrew or Yiddish. Rather than having these nine Hebrew or Yiddish chapters retranslated, since an English version already existed, this publication has simply incorporated the English version of these chapters as they appeared in the original book. This "Foreword" is one of the nine chapters and is reprinted from pp. 3–6 of the original English section, with minor changes, primarily to standardize spelling and punctuation.

Our children were born in this country. With their mothers' milk, they did not suck the tradition of the small Jewish town in the Diaspora. Not only are they unable to enunciate the name of their fathers' native town, but, moreover, they tend to reject the customs, the traditions that nurtured their parents. Under ordinary circumstances, this is the natural phenomenon of the clashing respective cultures of fathers and sons—which, in view of the changes that affected the people of Israel in its homeland, are here all the more so. It is the same with our fellow townsmens' children who were educated in alien countries, where assimilation draws the young generation further apart from the traditions of its parents.

Maybe our town Działoszyce was not very different from hundreds and thousands of other Jewish communities in Eastern Europe. It is true that the special character of many of the small Jewish towns was common to most such settlements—similar ways of life, institutions of the community, livelihood, and even poverty. In each small town, there were the usual associations for visits to the sick, provision of dowry to needy brides, deeds of charity, and the like. The *besmedresh*, the *shtiblekh*—synagogue houses of learning—the yeshivas, differed only on the outside. Inside, in their contents and the spirit that permeated them, they were as one, to the point that sometimes even the prayer melody and study came forth from one rabbinical court.

It is not necessary to search for the distinctive traits of our town Działoszyce in order to justify in this Yizkor book the chapters of reminiscences and way of life, because although to all intents and purposes our town may have looked like numerous other communities, and although it is not within our hands to glorify and extol it and sing paeans to its unique greatness—it was our town that was and is no more!

For hundreds of years it throbbed with a bustling Jewish life, one generation passing on to the next the flame of Jewish tradition and the yearning for salvation and deliverance. Except for us, nobody can tell about its sages and rabbis, about the ordinary, humble Jews who, for six days of the week, ran hither and thither among the peasants but, on Friday, hastened to their homes to await in reverence and awe the Shabes Queen; about the porters who all day long stood in the marketplace, murmuring one hundred and fifty psalms while waiting (often in vain) for the half *złoty* payment for unloading a crate, so that they might be able to purchase a loaf of bread; about the yeshiva students who spent their nights as days over their Talmud but did not always manage to provide for their fare at the table of the rich.

And who, except us, will remember the terrible days of the Holocaust when, despite the inhuman suffering and persecution, faith did not waver nor hope falter, even when the townsfolk were driven to the unknown, on the way from which there was no return. Most of our martyred townsmen had not even a Jewish burial, and their place of interment is unknown. The old cemetery was completely destroyed by our Polish neighbours, intent to erase memory and vestige of Jewish Działoszyce. And we cannot even place a tombstone over our fathers' graves.

*

Although to all appearances, we the surviving remnants are living our renewed life—we are nonetheless bound with the innermost fibers of our souls and heart to all that is dear to us from our childhood and our past. And so that no town and mother might be forgotten in Israel, so that a memorial might be erected to the sacred community and its martyred members, to these ends are the chapters of this Yizkor—In Memoriam—book dedicated.

Unfortunately, and most sorrowfully, we are but a pitiful few. And because of the Jewish town's destruction down to its very foundations—and the destruction of all that was connected with the Jewish community—sources and material are scarce. Were they to be found, they could have enabled an extensive picture of the community. This is why we must restrict ourselves to these chapters of memories and events, as they were recorded and evoked by those who chose to put them in writing.

Be they blessed, the friends—particularly Mr. Dov Bejski—who saw it as their sacred duty to work for the perpetuation of the memory of our community and ceaselessly labored until they attained their aim.

M.B. [Dr. Moshe Bejski][1]

---

[1] Dr. Moshe Bejski, whose life was saved by Oskar Schindler, became a prominent citizen in Israel after the war. He was a Supreme Court justice and also chairman (1970–95) of the Commission of the Righteous established by Yad Vashem.

Part I

Działoszyce: The Town and Its Residents Before World War I

The Beginnings of the Działoszyce[1] Settlement (pp. 11–15)

Many generations ago, when the great territories of Poland were under the power of the first Polish monarchs, dense forests covered the land and were full of all types of animals of prey. In those days, as it was in the area in which the Działoszyce of today is located, the land was all covered with trees and forest. In the thicket of these dense forests, prominent knights and, frequently, his highness the king himself and his entourage would organize hunts of wild animals. As was the tradition in those places designated for the hunt, the knights would station many of the soldiers, whose role was to locate the resting place of the animals, in shacks with raw wooden roofs. For the most part, these settlement places were located along the edges of a small river and served the hunter-knights as places to rest. A comfortable place to rest was the plain that spread between two small rivers, which joined together when they reached the plateau covered with meadows and poured into a larger river, the Nidzica River.

Upon the banks of these small rivers, about nine hundred years ago, the owner of the lands and estates of those days established a forest guard post. As the years passed, these first settlers flourished, building huts and creating a permanent settlement that they named Zalesice, i.e., "beyond the forest."

Because Zalesice lay next to the king's main road, which led from Kraków through Proszowice and Skalbmierz to the town called Wiślica, the settlers grew in numbers there. And already in the twelfth century, the temporary settlement turned into a large village of noblemen. At the beginning of the thirteenth century, the bishop of Kraków, Iwo Odrowąż, who was known as a builder of many Christian churches in his district, built in Zalesice a stone church named for the Holy Trinity. Over time, ownership of the place changed hands many times, until it belonged to the family of knights of the house of Działosz, from which comes the name that has been used from then until today—Działoszyce.

The owners of Działoszyce, in those days, followed the example of the king's representatives, who extracted great sums from the royal villages and towns. They, too, allowed migrants who came from different parts of the country to settle there. In the days of King Casimir the Great, who reigned from 1334 to 1367, Jews, who were known since the days of the founding of the Polish monarchy as traveling merchants, were also given permission to settle in the town.

Działoszyce's convenient geographic location allowed it to develop commerce with neighboring royal cities—Skalbmierz, Proszowice, and Wiślica. The fact that the town's owner reduced the resident's tax burden, in contrast to the royal towns, further assisted the development of commerce. Because of this, Działoszyce became in a short time a town with a Jewish majority, which engaged in commerce and worked as skilled labor. The Christian minority worked in agriculture and in certain skilled areas such as barrel making, pottery, and woodworking. Then, when the makeup of the population stabilized in

---

Information for this chapter was taken from the Polish pamphlet "Fifty Years of the Voluntary Fire Brigade of Działoszyce," 1958. (Author's note)

[1] The Yiddish name for the town was Dzialoshitz.

the town, the owners of Działoszyce petitioned the king to grant municipal rights to the town.

According to old municipal documents, it appears that the first decree granting Działoszyce status as a town was given on August 23, 1409. It was given by King Władysław Jagiełło to the owner, Michał Bogumiłłow, in a ceremony that took place in the new town of Chorzów. This status was confirmed later by King Zygmunt I in 1520 at the request of the owner of the town, named Ostroróg. The king allowed him to collect bridge tolls in the amount of two rubels (the currency of the period). Additional authority was given by King Michał Korybut, in the first year of his reign, and also by the last Polish king, Stanisław August Poniatowski, in 1786. Permission was given to the owner, Piotr Orzowski, and since then, the number of market fairs grew from six to twelve a year, and weekly market days were established. An old document that was found in the municipality's archives in 1820 includes a historic description of the town of Działoszyce, written by the mayor, and a discussion of the town's municipal decrees that were granted to the town and which are mentioned above. The mayor reports:

> All of these decrees went up in flames, and only the decree that was granted by King Michał Korybut on September 15, 1706, to the town's owner, Jan Stradomski, based on the king's previous known decrees, was found in the town's possession. In addition, the professional unions of skilled workers (the guilds) had special decrees of their own that were granted in the first year of the same king's reign. They serve as evidence of the special decrees that were given to the town…

The fate of this official document was like the fate of its predecessors; it was lost later on but receives its authenticity through a declaration from Szymański, the district commissioner in the town of Miechów, which was put into the appeal protocol of March 16, 1822. It reads:

> The town of Działoszyce, which sits in the province of Kraków, district of Kielce, suffers from neglect, because its owners are concerned only with the well-being and growth of the churches and refuse to relinquish them [the taxes], not even a portion, for the good of the town. Moreover, with determination and, occasionally, by exerting pressure on the town's residents, they find new sources of income every time…

The town does not possess the original decrees that were granted to it. Whereas they were in the possession of the owners and were not returned to the town, they were destroyed in the many fires that came one after another.

The town of Działoszyce sealed its documents from 1553 with a round seal with the town's symbol in the middle. It had a lion leaping behind a wall, and around it was an inscription in Latin reading: "*Sigil Oppidi* [Seal of the Town] Działoszyce." But on documents from 1775, which are preserved in the National Museum in Kraków, the seal has an elliptical shape, and two lions, intertwined by an ornament ending in bourbon lilies, were added to the sides of the original symbol in the middle of the seal. From 1917 until September 30, 1939, municipal documents were stamped with an identical seal with the addition in the Polish language of "Municipal Council of Działoszyce."

Many changes, for the better and for the worse, occurred in Działoszyce during its long history and even in its more recent past. The years of the Russian occupation can be termed "the good period." The town's Jewish population reached 75 percent of the total population. It quickly became affluent through commerce and a variety of businesses.

Later, during World War II, in 1939, the Germans exterminated more than 10,000 Jews and destroyed most of their homes. Of the Działoszyce population, which numbered more than 12,000 people,[1] fewer than 2,000 Polish residents remained, and they were not well-to-do.

Following are the most important events in the history of the town of Działoszyce:

1) Great fires in the town occurred in the years 1668, 1732, 1846, and 1902, in which nearly every residential structure in the town, most of which were built of wood, became fireballs.

2) Visit of the leader of the people, Tadeusz Kościuszko,[2] in the town during its days of naiveté. This was in 1794, when he marched at the head of the Polish rebel army to the battlefield at Racławice.

3) 1907, the year in which the Russian occupation government allowed the organization of volunteer firefighters.

4) Bloody riots of the town's and the area's Polish population against the Austrian and German armies, who, in a treaty known as the Treaty of Brest-Litovsk [1918], created the fourth partition of Poland. They appropriated the Polish territories of Podlasie, Chełm, and Lwów. In riots in the newly formed country, Ukraine, three people were killed and five injured from the bullets of Austrian soldiers.

5) On October 15, 1922, the statue from a memorial for Tadeusz Kościuszko, which had once stood in the market square, was discovered. The memorial had been created by a local group of supporters of Polish education with monies collected from residents of the town. One by the name of Winarski, one of the veterans of the Polish rebellion of 1863, had removed the statue.

6) Laying of the corner stone of the school's large building occurred on June 21, 1930. The construction was financed with municipal funds. Because of the economic crisis that engulfed the country, construction ceased halfway through, and the school was completed only in 1957. The new structure housed two schools, one with seven primary grades and one for high school.

7) The great flood engulfed the town on May 22, 1936. During the storm, a cloudburst, which occurred at six o'clock in the evening, brought great amounts of water to the rivers that traversed the town. The water flooded about two thirds of the town and reached the roofs of single story houses. In the raging torrents flowed corpses of people, cattle, and other animals. Many telephone poles and uprooted trees, as well as household items and parts of buildings that had collapsed like playing cards, were swept away in the great waters. The flood and its spreading waterfalls took the lives of more than ten people, among them six residents of Działoszyce. Twenty-eight homes were destroyed and about 130

---

[1] During the war, the Jewish population of Działoszyce increased temporarily, first, due to an influx of refugees, and later, because several thousand Jews from other communities were forcibly settled there.

[2] Polish leader of an armed insurrection against the czar in 1794.

buildings suffered severe damage. A committee of ministers, headed by Marian Kościałkowski, the minister of social welfare; Mr. Dziadosz, governor of the region of Kielce; and Karol Winiarz, head of the *powiat* [county] of Pińczów— accompanied by a large contingent of Polish newspaper representatives—visited the town.

8)   The difficult fate that struck the town during World War II. During this period, German planes bombed Działoszyce three times—on September 3, 1939, August 5, 1944, and January 19, 1945. During the whole period of the war, the occupation forces created great difficulties for the town's residents. They conducted surprise kidnappings in the middle of the street and sent the kidnapped to forced labor in Germany or to dig trenches. They captured hostages, who were under constant threat of being found and shot to death, exiled dozens of residents to concentration camps, and used other means of oppression. The greatest and most overpowering disaster, which caused the downfall of the town, was the mass extermination of the Jewish population in 1942. Of the 10,000 Jewish residents of the town, 4,000 were shot and murdered, and the rest were sent to extermination camps. After the mass destruction of the Jewish population, houses were also destroyed. Bad management of the town's affairs after the war and other factors brought about the complete ruin of the town.

The German government of terror did not have the power to suppress the noble patriotic sentiments that pervaded the town's Polish residents. A significant part of the Polish youth in Działoszyce belonged to underground resistance organizations during the occupation. On July 25, 1944, an armed rebellion, which encompassed Działoszyce, Skalbmierz, Kazimierza, and Proszowice broke out. In this uprising, the youth took a large guard post of the German gendarmerie in Działoszyce out of commission. Also, several armed struggles with the enemy ensued; each of these operations against the German occupation deserves a more detailed description.

The Town and Its Residents

The town of Działoszyce sits on a plain surrounded by mountains. It lies on agricultural land of 200 hectars [494 acres], which has remained a constant since the founding of the town. Two small rivers cross the town: the Sancygniówka and the Jakubówka, which previously was called the Dzierążnia. At the edge of the town, on the south side, these rivers join together and flow, one kilometer further, into the Nidzica River.

In the times of the monarchy, Działoszyce belonged to the Kraków province and the Miechów *powiat* [county]. After the partition of Poland and the annexation of this area during the Russian occupation, the territory became part of the Pińczów *powiat*. During World War II, once again, Działoszyce was within the borders of the Miechów *powiat*, but from January 1, 1956, the town became part of a newly created *powiat*, Kazimierza [with Kazimierza Wielka as the county seat].

In 1820, the town had 1,692 residents; among them 420 were Christian and 1,256 were Jews. The Christians worked in agriculture and crafts; most of the Jewish population engaged in commerce and a minority of them in crafts. One hundred years later, according to a census conducted on September 30, 1921, the total population of Działoszyce numbered 6,765 persons; among them, only 1,127 were Christians. This relative proportion of Christians and Jews remained steady until the complete destruction of Działoszyce Jewry in 1943.

The residents of the town, who previously had been serfs of the noblemen and estate owners, acquired fields, gardens, plots of land, and buildings over the years. Although these provided them with places to live, they were forced to pay heavy taxes to the landowners. From a small village, the town grew, in 1820, to include 118 houses. Only eighteen of the houses were built of brick and stone.

One hundred years later, in 1921, Działoszyce included 494 residential homes, which included 1,313 apartments. In 1928, the number of houses reached 510, 75 percent of which were made of brick and stone. In the market square and its neighboring streets, there were also houses of two or more stories.

During the last century, the roads and several of the town streets were paved with stones. Today, there are eleven streets in the town center, all of which are paved.

An intercity highway, built in 1937, runs through the town, connecting Kielce with Kraków by way of Pińczów, Działoszyce, Skalbmierz, and Koszyce. Beginning in 1957, this road was paved with asphalt.

In 1916, the conquering Austrians built a narrow railway (*kolejka*) that ran from Charsznica to Kocmyrzów, passing through Miechów, Działoszyce, Skalbmierz, and Kazimierza Wielka.

In 1955, this railway was widened, but it still did not reach the normal width of the other railways in Poland. The *kolejka* and the bus services served as good means of transportation for both riders and cargo.

Presently, the following institutions and offices exist in Działoszyce: the office of the head of the local town council, a post office that includes telephone and telegraph services, a train station, two elementary schools, a general high school, a state orphanage, a volunteer fire brigade, a cooperative bank, a parish church, the command post of the civil guard, a pharmacy, a health clinic with two physicians and nurses, a dental facility, a veterinary clinic, a first-aid clinic, a permanent theater, a powdered milk factory, a regional cooperative for helping farmers, a work cooperative for the disabled, a cooperative for porcelain manufacture, a dairy cooperative, and a jointly-owned meat products plant.

Large gatherings, celebrations, games, and various cultural productions are held in the appropriate halls in the orphanage, in Firemen's Hall, in the schools, etc.

One of the architectural achievements in Działoszyce is its large church. It rises skyward over the roofs of the highest homes in the town. The building was built for glory in the Gothic style. The church was built in the thirteenth century by the then bishop of Kraków, Iwo Odrowąż. The tall walls surrounding the church cemetery give it the appearance of an ancient castle from the Middle Ages.

In 1897, a tower and a four-story tall spire were added on the western side of the church. On top, the tower was surrounded by a balcony and covered with a domed roof, like a crown jewel.

Translated from the Hebrew by Roger Kaplan

There Was a Town, and Look, She is No Longer (pp. 16–26)

Izrael Dov Skóra

I think that there is no need to prolong the discussion about the evolution of this place's name from "Zalesie" to "Działoszyce" before it was a town.[1] We have a satisfactory explanation from a priest's notebook, *Działoszyce in the Past and the Present*.

I heard from Mr. Moszek Dawid Pomeranc, *hi"d* [may God avenge his blood], and from Mr. Mendel Frydman, who for many years financially supported the community, that there was in the possession of the community administration a book called *The Community Notebook*. In the book were recorded all of the important events that happened in the town, in general, and to the Jews, in particular, such as the construction of the community buildings, the synagogue, the yeshiva, the *mikve* [ritual bath], the fencing of the cemetery, etc. To my dismay, I never saw this notebook, which might have solved to some degree the problem of the "age" of the community.

Even if we were to go along with the archeologists to set the time for the founding of our community according to old headstones, this method would not lead us to a definite conclusion, since in archeology there is no great importance to fifty or even one hundred years—which is not so for us, when we are talking about a period that includes altogether only three hundred years. In addition, it was known to all that the community was in existence for many years before it had its own cemetery. The dead were transported from Działoszyce to Książ (it is likely that on account of this the Działoszycers called the people of Książ "the dead Książers"). Proof of this can be seen that the Jewish community of Skalbmierz, which was close to our town and had a rabbi, a ritual slaughterer, and a yeshiva, for many years brought their dead for burial in Działoszyce, since they did not have a cemetery of their own.

Over fifty years ago, I listened once to a conversation among some elderly, and they said that Działoszyce had already existed for three hundred years. Of course, they were referring to the Jewish Działoszyce. But one should not attribute much importance to a conversation such as this. Several times I strolled for many hours among the gravestones, in general, and particularly among those in the area that was called the old cemetery. If my memory serves me right, near the entrance there were some headstones that bore the years 547...[1710s] and 549... [1730s] and the entire century of the 5500s [1800s] and onwards. It was said that the date engraved on a headstone there was 5420 [1660]. I do not accept this opinion, since the letters on it were worn down, and it was impossible to ascertain with certainty what the date was.

(When I served in the Polish army in Kraków, there once was a special play for soldiers called *Kościuszko Near Racławice*. In this play, they showed how they caught a spy—obviously he was a thick-bearded old Jew—who was brought to Kościuszko for interrogation. "Where did you hear that the musicians were coming?" Kościuszko asked Szoel, and the "spy" answered, "This is what Jankiel from Działoszyce told me.")

---

[1] In other chapters, the town's beginning name is given as Zalesice.

I recall this story to prove that even non-Jews in the area knew of the Jewish Działoszyce.

In general, one can assume that the community of Działoszyce existed for about 260 to 300 years, from the time of its founding till its destruction on 21 Elul 5702 [3 September 1942].

My Dear Little Town

My town, the dear little town of Działoszyce, with sacred trembling, with awe and reverence, I return to you, to you as you once were, Działoszyce, full of life, full of joy and delight. I loved you from the depths of my soul, and if sometimes I left you for a short or long time, I immediately was filled with longing for you. There I saw the first light of the world; I breathed the air of the world for the first time. Oh, how pretty you were, even during your sadness! Yes, there were within you sometimes sad days, but, nevertheless, your grace and beauty never left you.

In the days of my wandering, when I was in foreign lands, in other cities, my desire was only for you. The yearnings gnawed at me. At every turn, I saw in my visions and thoughts Shabes and the holidays that were your wings. On Friday afternoon, the "extra soul" was already sensed,[1] the long siren that was sounded from the *mikve* [ritual bath] was the prelude to the symphony whose name was "the Shabes Queen." The awakening from above ruled over all. "It is getting late," the neighbors all rushed each other. "They are already sounding the siren from the ritual bath, and I still have so much to do." The housewives complained while hugging each other, and immediately I saw Jews returning from the ritual bath, their beards wet, dripping with water, their faces red from the *shvitz* [steam bath], rushing to get home. After all, Shabes was not given just for eating. It was necessary to change clothes and wear Shabes clothing, to recite "a Jewish word," the Song of Songs, and to read the weekly portion, twice in the original and once in translation.

Suddenly, the voice of the synagogue caretaker was heard,"*Licht tzinden*" [Kindle the lights], and the streets were filled with Jews dressed for Shabes, going with their children to the synagogue, with their prayer books in hand. Among them, one Jew was seen carrying a hammer and nails rushing to return home. This was the Jew who checked to see if the *eruv* was in place,[2] so that it should not fail, God forbid, causing one to desecrate the Sabbath by carrying some object that is forbidden to be carried on Shabes if the *eruv* is not in order. There were instances that the caretakers in the synagogue would interrupt the prayers in the middle, pound on the Torah reading table, and announce: "By the rabbi's word, it is forbidden to carry any object." Immediately, the children's ears perked up, because only they were allowed to carry the prayer shawls and prayer books home.

In all of the windows, candles flickered. Within a moment, each woman was transformed from a simple woman into the wife of a king, the Shabes Queen. The entire

---

[1] It was believed that those who observed the Sabbath were infused with an "additional Sabbath soul," an extra dimension of spirituality.
[2] An *eruv* is a fence—either real or symbolic—that surrounds an area, permitting the carrying of an object on the Sabbath within its boundaries.

atmosphere was full of light, and the savory smell of Shabes foods filled the house. The prayers welcoming the Shabes were concluded. The fathers returned home. The tune of "Shalom Aleichem" was heard from every passageway. Next came the *kidesh* [blessing] over the wine. All would get up from their places to listen and to sip from the cup. Between each course, ritual songs were sung by the fathers and sons, and so it was during all of the holidays, the holidays of Israel, each holiday with its own beauty.

Pesakh [Passover]

Already a few weeks before the arrival of the Festival of Freedom, the Festival of Unleavened Bread, one could discern that something unexpected was about to happen. The tailors, the shoemakers, the hat makers, the shopkeepers, and most of all, the bakers, beamed with excitement. They all prepared for the season of the festival, which was rapidly approaching. Your heart was gladdened when you passed the bakery and smelled the scent of the fresh *matse* [unleavened bread] and you heard the sounds and laughter of the workers who kneaded the *matse* with rolling pins on clean smooth boards. The special "trusted one" walked around, searching—in fear of finding leavened bread that, God forbid, might have formed if a piece of dough had stuck to the rolling pin or the boards upon which the *matse* was rolled.

For a week or even more, you did not see a man or woman, boy or girl, wandering aimlessly in the street as in all of the other days of the year. They all went in rapid steps with empty baskets in their hands for shopping and full baskets and various heavy packages after shopping. Standing and engaging in idle conversation was not an option. Even from the most verbose women, one could hear a sentence in only one intonation: "Oh my poor head, I have so much to do, and I haven't done anything yet."

And the ceremony of the Seder night![1] An entire book could be written on this alone! The sanctity of the holiday could be seen on everyone's faces. Everyone beamed with happiness and satisfaction, especially the children. They appeared to be the most overjoyed. They enjoyed every detail that appeared before their eyes—their father wearing the *kitl* [robe], the pouring of the wine, the asking of the four questions, the reciting of the Hagada [story of Passover], and the tasty foods. What a symphony of joy and gladness! And so it was on all of the fantastic holidays, each holiday with its myriad of customs. This one article is too brief to describe all of this. Many different memories appear and come to mind. Have compassion for yourselves, Jews of Działoszyce, regardless of status, rich and poor alike. Women of Israel, precious and modest. When our elders enumerated your praises, they said, among others things, that you were demure. This becomes obvious when one approaches to talk to you, so honorable.

I have mentioned just in brief all that has occurred around me when I recall your memory, "Działoszyce from above." Yes, "Działoszyce from Heaven!" For what is there for me with the "Działoszyce from below," the "Działoszyce from Hell" that I saw, for the last time, in the summer of 1946? I traveled to the town with a few other people in a transport truck, for business matters. We stopped in the middle of the town square, and I

---

[1] The Seder is a ceremonial meal on the first (and, in some households, also the second) night of Passover, in which the story of the exodus from Egypt is read and special foods are eaten.

remembered something. And this incident that I recalled, I want to relate, because it was connected to the "handshake" that was forced upon me.

It was Wednesday morning, 21 Elul 5702 [3 September 1942]. Działoszyce was surrounded by German soldiers and their accomplices, the Polish police. From all sides the echoes of shots were heard, and the members of the Jewish police reported in their "professional" jargon: "There are already victims." I went to my mother's house to learn what had happened. There in the courtyard I met my father-in-law, Reb [title of respect] Mendel Zonenfeld, *hi"d*, who came to find me and to seek advice on how to hide. Some other people came. Everyone approached me and asked for news.

Suddenly, one of the neighbors left the house with a bottle of something to drink and some small glasses in his hands, and it was Reb Lejbuś Ptasznik, *hi"d*. In an excited voice, Reb Lejbuś called to all of us, "Gentlemen, let's have a drink," so everyone drank. Knowing the situation well, I did not want to drink. But Reb Lejbuś wouldn't let me be, he forcefully shoved the cup into my left hand and took my right hand with his other hand and said, "Know, son of Israel, I am taking from you now 'a binding handshake.' You are a young man, and you will remain alive. You must promise me that you will visit my grave and tell me, 'Hitler suffered a black end.'"

Of course, I admonished him, saying that as a religious Jew, he must live with confidence. I reminded him of the [Talmudic] saying, "Even with a sharp sword placed at a man's neck, one should not give up on Divine mercy." "Yes, yes," he answered me and continued holding my hand, until finally, I promised him what he wanted.

Now [1946], standing next to the truck, I also recalled that this Reb Lejbuś, who had no children, had said several times in conversation with me that he and his wife, in his opinion, were "unable to cope," and that she could not manage without him, and the two of them should die on the same day. And his prayer for this was answered. The two of them were murdered together with 1,645 other holy souls of our town, on 21 Elul 5702. (One of the Jewish policemen told me that he was present at the place when one of the senior officers of the Gestapo gave the order to stop the "action." The account from those who did this work was that 1,645 individuals were annihilated.)

I left the truck and went by foot to the area of the trench. I approached the mass grave that was already covered with grass. I recognized the place. It was a large grave, thirty meters long, and in it, eight hundred murdered people were buried, and I said, "Lejbuś, son of so-and-so, a holy and pure man, like the rays of heavens shine! I come today to keep my promise that I made to you with that handshake, and I am here to tell you that Hitler, the mass-murderer of all times, and those who helped him have been defeated and met a black end." After saying these words, I felt very, very bad. It seemed to me that it was not my mouth that said the words, but rather I heard them from the side, as if someone else said them. My heart beat like a hammer, and in my ears I heard noise. Dizziness came over me, and I thought that I would collapse. I regretted not telling my friend where I was going. When I returned, they knew that something happened, like some robbers had jumped me. I didn't tell them. I told them only that I just didn't feel well.

At the same time, I began to understand that actually there are two cities with the name Działoszyce, one, "Działoszyce from Heaven," which remains free in my memory and in my heart and which I will miss until my last breath, and the second, "Działoszyce from Hell," which all of us who were born there loathe now—and it shall be cursed together with the unclean who are there, who stood against us and rejoiced at our expense when the town's children, founders, and builders were murdered. Shame on you, you banished town, who hid the blood of its holy and righteous sons and daughters! May God's fury and anger be upon you until your destruction under the heavens.

Działoszyce was a holy community. A town within the nation of Israel that is no more.

Adas Yisroel Synagogue

The exact date on which the construction of the synagogue began is not known. It is said that the laying of the foundation and walls took a few years. On the western wall, up above, from under the roof, was a caption in large printed letters,[1] engraved "תדיר," which symbolizes the year 1854, i.e., the year in which the building of the wall was completed. On the other side of the building, on the eastern side, in the same place up above was a circular window that had windowpanes with Jewish stars in the middle. A bit above that was a stone upon which was written in large protruding letters: Adas Yisroel Synagogue.

I heard many times from the elderly how a young man and an old man volunteered as assistants to the builders and specialists who were brought in from outside, most likely from nearby Przymiarka.

The ceiling was made of wooden beams by an artist who, before he began his work, first made a miniature scale model of the ceiling. They say that when he showed the model to the architect, the architect liked it so much that he kissed him on the forehead. And really, it was a very imaginative piece or work. The ceiling, looking like the sky, had tens of thousands of kilograms of blocks of wood built into it. It looked as if it were hanging from nothing. From the southern side, on the first wooden beams of the ceiling, lay a metal plaque, and upon it in very large letters was written: "The work of my hands for glory, which God granted me to build the house of God, Kalonymos Kalman Zylbersztajn from Chęciny, by the power of God." This caption showed that the building of the ceiling was completed in 5616 [1856].

The painting and drawings were done in part on the beams and in part on metal plaques. All of the background was done in light blue, with stars of gold spread all around. On the uppermost side, all around, were twelve pictures, and upon them were the signs of the zodiac, according to the months of the Jewish calendar: for Nissan—Aries, for Ayar—Taurus, for Sivan—Gemini, etc. All of this was on the beams. From below were twelve wonderful pictures, drawn on metal, symbolizing the twelve tribes of Israel with their standards, according to the order of the blessing of Jacob, our father, as in the Torah reading "*Veyechi*." There were three pictures for each side, and underneath each picture, for each tribe, his [Jacob's] blessing for that tribe, such as, for Reuben: "Reuben, my eldest, you are my strength and my firstborn," for Simon: "Simon and Levi, brothers, instruments of cruelty are their birthright," and so on. Around each picture, in a mix of

---

[1] I use the word "was" because despite the existence of the building, the synagogue itself has ceased to exist. (Author's note)

colors, wonderful flowers were drawn that after one hundred years still looked fresh as if they were picked from the garden just today.

In the four corners of the hall, above, at the edge of the ceiling, there were four drawings in a large formation. A picture in each corner. In the southeast corner, the figure of a deer; in the northeast corner, a figure of a lion; in the northwest corner, a figure of a tiger; and in the southwest corner, a figure of an eagle. Under each figure was a saying in the original language from *Ethics of the Fathers*. But one had to read the saying according to the order of the tractate. Next to the eastern wall, you had to stand facing the entrance, looking upward, and begin reading from the side of the northwest corner, where the tiger was, and continue to the left: "Be strong like the tiger, and light like the eagle, and swift like the deer, and brave like the lion." Below, under the saying, "Be strong like the tiger," in small Yiddish letters was written: "Hilhin made these drawings." It was possible to read this only when standing on the other side of the corridor in the women's area. It was said that once in the 1880s, an old man, leaning on his cane, entered the hall of the synagogue, looked upward, and began to weep. The man said in German, "Oy, how beautiful it still is!" He threw inside a coin of ten kopeks and went on his way. This man was Hilhin, the artist.

Unfortunately, I have no information on the artist or artists of the Holy Ark, which was the glory of the synagogue, or who prepared the multi-faceted piece, so I don't know when it was made. I spoke once with Szmul Czosnek, a native of our town, a businessman and one who understands a great deal about art and artifacts, and he told me that the Holy Ark in the synagogue in Działoszyce was the product of very careful and thoughtful thinking and that those who made it knew what art is. This he said also in relation to some of the ceiling drawings.

Above the sill atop the entrance, there was a space. Inside the space, there was a stone sign engraved with the names of the "committees" that were involved with the establishment of the "small sanctuary." About twelve names appear there, but I remember only a few of them: two by the name of Moszkowski, Reb Dawid Wdowiński, Przeworski, and I think also Rzędowski.

The *bime* [platform], which was for the reading of the Torah, sermons on Shabes and holidays, various community announcements about upcoming weddings, and all sorts of government announcements, was, as in most Orthodox synagogues in Poland, in the middle of the room. It was ninety centimeters high and had two sets of stairs, one on the northern side and another on the southern side. Every Shabes evening, the prayer leader welcomed the Sabbath on the *bime* and intoned the "Bar'chu" prayer [a call to prayer]. The rest of the prayers took place in front of the reader's stand, on the right, before the Holy Ark. And if there was a guest cantor, whether on Shabes or a secular day, his voice was heard from the *bime*.

Among the regulations which the synagogue founders established was the rule concerning the first prayer service, whether on Shabes or a secular day—that one must pray using the Ashkenazi ritual rather than the Sephardic ritual, which was different from that of the Ashkenazim. And most important, those who prayed took care not to say, "*V'yatzmach purkaneï*" (as is the custom of the Sephardim) in the *kadesh* [mourner's prayer], which is said before the service, during the service, and after the service. More than once, someone came to the reader's stand, made an error, or did not know about the prohibition, and said, *"V'yatzmach purkanei."* A great uproar would break out at that moment, and those praying would yell and bang on the lecturns, and the service would stop for a while. The prayers would then be completed by someone else. This was proof of how strong this war was that was occurring at this time among the Jews of Eastern Europe between the Hasidim and their opponents. It didn't stop in Działoszyce, in as much as the lay people stood for the most part on the side of the opponents. Things got to the point where those who considered themselves as "better" people saw those praying in the synagogue as inferior and thought it less honorable to pray together with them. Nonetheless, this didn't prevent them from contributing money when needed.

There is not much to add regarding the "annex" to the synagogue on the southern side, which was called by the name "the women's synagogue." It was a one-story building and was built as a place for women to pray. It was a hall with benches, with four windows looking into the large hall, so that they would be able to hear the congregation. In the entrance to the building, above the sill, one could see a stone engraved with the full date 5639 [1879]. That indicates that this "annex" was built twenty-four years after the construction of the large building had been completed.

I saw Adas Yisroel synagogue for the last time in the summer of 1947. The *bime* had completely disappeared; only one piece of wood hanging on the wall remained from the beautiful Holy Ark. The hall itself had become storage for coal, cement, and building materials. Its entrance was widened so that horses, hinged to carts, could enter! But the ceiling remained in all its splendor.

Khevres [Societies]

In our town there were different societies, a society for everything, each with its own name and function. The incentive to establish each of these societies is, as is known, the natural human inclination to live a communal life. In addition, there is also the factor of the feeling that developed, especially among Jews, who are known as a people of mercy, who are children of the merciful. During their many and long sufferings, they learned to help their brethren.

What follows are the societies that existed in Działoszyce: Biker Khoylim [Visiting the Sick], Lines Hatsedek [Sheltering the Righteous], Nichum Aveylim [Comforting the Mourners], Ner Tamid [Eternal Light], Shomrei Emunah Yisroel [Guardians of the Faith of Israel], Kinyan Sforim [Acquisition of Religious Books], and Khevre Kedishe [Burial Society]. True, I don't have detailed information and dates of the founding of each of these societies that I have mentioned here, but I know very well about all of the societies' existence, their activities, their mission, and function. Here I must point out that Działoszyce, in contrast to other towns, did not have societies named "Escorting the Bride" and "Carriers of the Bed." This is an amazing thing, that in all the years of this Jewish town's existence, there was no initiative to establish these societies, even though, with regard to keeping these *mitsves* [commandments], the Jews of Działoszyce were no exception. They kept these *mitsves* according to Jewish law but not to the point of establishing special societies with those names.

Every society had its own director who was elected to the post once a year during *khalemoyed* [intermediate days—between the first and last days of the holiday] of Pesakh or Sukes. Only a few of the members knew the bylaws and rules, which were detailed in the society's notebook, written by someone who was literate. It also told who spearheaded the idea to found the society, with that person's name inscribed during the first general meeting for future generations to remember.

The main thing that drew the society members and bound them together was, of course, the yearning for communal living. This was expressed very well in the annual meeting, during which a blessing was said. Many of the *kdushes* [collations], which took place, related to the function of the society and matched the weekly portion. For example, the *kidesh* of the Biker Khoylim [Visiting the Sick] Society took place on Shabes "*Veyechi*," which tells of Joseph coming to visit his father, Jacob, after Joseph was told that his father was sick. The Nichum Aveylim [Comforting the Mourners] Society organized the *kidesh* on Shabes "*Acharei mot* [after the death]"; Ner Tamid [Eternal Light] Society on Shabes "*Beha'alotecha* [setting up the lampstead]"; Khevre Tehilim [Society of Psalms] on the second day of Sukes, which is according to tradition, the memorial day for King David; and the Khevre Kedishe [Burial Society], on the holidays on which memorials for the dead are held, that is, "*Shmeni Atzeret*," the last day of Pesakh and the second day of Shavuos.

The name of each society told of its function; every member of the Psalms Society knew that upon his joining the Society, he took on the responsibility to always recite Psalms, whether he was doing so individually or communally. According to tradition, the recitation of Psalms saves you from all harm and evil. There is a story about a town that burned completely. The rabbi of the town came and told his people that in his dream he encountered a man who had recently died who told him that he used to recite twice daily all five sections of Psalms, and that this had protected the town as long as he was alive.

They routinely recited Psalms on Shabes in the synagogue minyan [quorum of ten needed for prayer] in the morning, before "*P'sukei D'zimra*" [morning psalms] and morning prayers, and in the afternoon before the afternoon prayers. Also in the middle of the week, if some sick person or a woman having difficulty bearing children was in the town, they turned to the Society director, and he would immediately "organize" a minyan of members to recite Psalms. The *kidesh* organized by the Society, as mentioned above, took place on the second day of Shavuos and on the Shabes on which the reading of one of the five books of the Torah was completed. This was so, because, after reciting each book of Psalms, which as we know number five, we say "*yehi ratzon*" [may it be God's will], and then we say, "by virtue of the first book in Psalms, which is paired with the Book of Genesis," etc.

Shomrei Emunah [Guardians of Faith]—as to where this name was taken from and what the Society members intended to do, this I would not have known had it not been for what is written in Samuel II (20:19) "…faith of Israel" or Isaiah (26:2) "guardian of the faith." Here too, the members were lay people, members of the congregation. They themselves interpreted the words "Guardians of the Faith of Israel" (such was the Society's full name) to mean that the Society members had to make sure that there would always be a minyan in the morning and in the evening in the synagogue, especially on the coldest of days in the winter, and that people would not converse or talk during prayers or the reading of the Torah and would answer "Amen" when required. There were those who understood "Guardians of the Faith" to mean to remember to answer "Amen."

Biker Khoylim [Visiting The Sick]

This was a humanitarian society that was very popular among the population. Even though its main goal was to visit and to spend the night with the ill without exception, whether rich or poor, in fact, its attention was focused mostly on the ill who were poor. Society members made sure to send them a medical practitioner (*felczer*) or a doctor and to buy medicine. The Society had an agreement with the town pharmacy that with a note from the *gabe* [treasurer/trustee], the medicine would be given to whoever came to pick it up. Similar agreements were also made with certain stores and milkmen.

Every neighborhood belonged to this society, and no one (of course, whoever was able) failed to contribute to and support it. And in almost every home, next to the "*Meir Ba'al Ha-Nes*" [Meir, the Miracle Worker] charity box, hung a "Visiting the Sick" charity box, which had written on it, "For the ill of our town."

Nichum Aveylim [Comforting the Mourners]

This was also a humanitarian society, but its activities were limited to only being concerned about mourners who were poor (the rich were not in need of it) and to call people to pray in the morning and in the evening at the home of the mourner, as well, and mainly, to contribute a great deal to the mourning family during the *shiva* [seven days of mourning], so that they would not go hungry. Until this day, it is hard for me to understand why only tailors belonged to this society. It is worth noting that there were many people who were members of all of the societies at the same time.

Ner Tamid [Eternal Light]

This was a small and lesser known society whose members were bakers or children of bakers who maintained the tradition of their fathers who were bakers. The intent, as a society, was to locate "fuel" for the light of the lamp that hung on the right side of the entrance to the synagogue. It seems that the members took the name "Eternal Light" because they worked next to the parafin fuel, which kept the baking ovens forever lit.

Kinyan Sforim [Acquisition of Religious Books]

This was not a society in the normal sense. It did not have members and did not hold membership meetings. The only thing that is well known about this society's activities is that from time to time, two boys from the *besmedresh* went from house to house of those who prayed or the well-to-do and collected cash contributions to buy books, mostly religious books, to be used by those studying in the yeshiva. The receipt was signed with the seal: "Society for the Acquisition of Books."

Lines Hatsedek [Sheltering the Righteous]

Since this Society was established during the smallpox plague, I will devote to it a few words in the chapter "Between the Two World Wars."

Khevre Kedishe [Burial Society]

If each one of the societies mentioned above, operated according to rules in its own framework, then, in relation to the Khevre Kedishe, I would like to extend a bit the discussion about its far-reaching and varied operations.

In accordance with its rules, this society had to meet its obligation regarding those who had passed away. Its members were concerned with arranging the ritual purification and, afterward, giving the dead a Jewish burial according to Jewish law. But it did not stop with that. We must remember that we are talking about a period in which there was no other organized community organization that had funds, officials, and workers on the payroll. The Khevre Kedishe, before the existence of democratic community committees, was made up only of volunteers, who saw their operations as holy work and a great *mitsve* [good deed]. We learned in the Baraita:[1] "And these are the things that man eats of their fruits in this world and their true essence is saved for the world to come...and to accompany the dead." Because of this, the Society was also called by this name: "Society of True Charity."

It wasn't easy to get accepted as a member of the Khevre Kedishe. There were very strict rules and different regulations and even personal commitments. First of all, every candidate had to be courageous, learned, God-fearing, and of good behavior. In the first three years of his membership, he was called by the name *meludash*. I heard from Reb Moszek Dawid Pomeranc, one of the well-known activists in the Khevre Kedishe, that the name *meludash* was taken from the Polish word *młody*, that is, young. During this period, he had to fill different simple roles like calling the meeting to order, collecting money from the generous, making sure that the halls were ready for the meetings, gathering food and drink for the *kidesh*, which was held a number of times each year, etc. After this period, he was allowed to stand and "assist" those engaged in purifying the deceased. Then the chairman would see if he was up to the job. And only after he was found to be fit for it, he was registered as a voting member in meetings for electing the chairman, on Tu B'Shvat [holiday for planting trees] or the first night of Pesakh.

Other than the main task of "accompanying the dead," the Society filled additional important roles in community life. And in many instances, the same importance was given to working with those who were alive as with those who were dead. Accordingly, we are speaking here about an earlier period when there was no organized community with budgets and tax payers, and all the income and expenses of the community were managed through lists drawn up by the heads of the community. And if it happened that someone did not want to obey the community or did not want to participate in the tax collections, for example, the collection of *matse* money before Pesakh, or the buying of articles of clothing for poor children before winter came, it was sufficient to say to this recalcitrant that the Khevre Kedishe would be notified, and he would immediately return to his good ways. And if he, nonetheless, did not give in to this threat, he was immediately invited to a meeting of the Khevre Kedishe with a warning that if he did not come to the meeting, "it will be recorded in the Society's notebook." And this person knew what was meant by this threat that "it will be recorded in the Society's notebook."

---

[1] The Baraita is a collection of ancient oral traditions of Jewish religious law not included in the Mishne.

This Khevre Kedishe notebook was the whip of fear and awe on the rich and the tightfisted. They knew that if they did not give of their own good free will what was asked of them, and if it was recorded, then the day would come when they would have to pay many times over. And if they themselves did not pay, then their heirs after them would pay hard cash. In cases like these, the civil authorities could not intervene. They could ask the Khevre Kedishe for a burial spot (as they called it then "a plot of ground") for the deceased in the cemetery, but they (the authorities) could not determine in which place in the cemetery the grave would be dug. Also, the Khevre Kedishe was not obligated to provide the gravedigger. It was said that once a rich miser died, and the Khevre Kedishe demanded a large sum for the plot. They [the relatives], of course, refused to pay and turned to the authorities. And after three days had passed, the sons brought an order from the regional officer to the Khevre Kedishe. They were prepared themselves to dig the plot. The Society allocated a spot at the end of the cemetery near the fence. But they did not agree to this because of the shame this entailed, so they gave in and paid the full amount that was demanded.

As I said, the Khevre Kedishe, because of the conditions of the time, was a very necessary institution in public life. There was good reason why people said that the Khevre Kedishe did more for the living than for the dead. I mentioned above the invitation to arbitration. Many arbitrations were established in the Society, and in such matters, the Society was a kind of "Supreme Court." There were instances that a Jew, either due to neglect or a lack of means, lost [his case] in the legal system and in the rabbinical court, but everyone knew that this man was right, and it was very distressing to him. Left with no other choice, the man turned to the Khevre Kedishe and requested arbitration. No one ever questioned the decisions of the Society. And that is because the verdict was declared only after investigation into and discussion of the matter with the help of experts.

After the establishment of a democratic society, the importance of the Khevre Kedishe diminished in our town. Many arguments broke out between the Society and Icek (Icze) Rubin, the head of the community, who founded and set up "his own" Khevre Kedishe. And so, two competing societies were established in the town. Of course, after Icze Rubin left, his society was dismantled, and only one society remained in the town. But, because of the new conditions of life, the Khevre Kedishe ceased being what it once was.

Translated from the Hebrew by Roger Kaplan

Sources of Livelihood of Działoszyce's Jews (pp. 26–29)

Shlomo Gertler

The soil of Działoszyce and that of the area both near and far from Działoszyce was known as being very fertile. It has always been used as a source for rich crops and supplied all sorts of produce, vegetables, and fruits, such as wheat, rye, barley, beans, eggs, butter, domestic fowl, calves, and other animals, especially pigs, as well as onions, garlic, cucumbers, and more.

The countryside around Działoszyce served as an important source of income to the Jews of Działoszyce—the merchants, shopkeepers, craftsmen, and the traveling tradesmen who would buy their goods.

This area was populated with many villages and farms. Most of the villagers were peasants, who worked small plots of land, and small and mid-sized farm owners of areas of around 200–300 *dunam*s [50–75 acres], but not more than that. Every producer of crops dealt with the Działoszyce merchants and tradesmen. Owners of large farms, which occupied 400–600 *dunam*s [100–150 acres] or more, used to sell the crops from their farms to wholesale merchants in larger cities.

The Jewish population of Działoszyce, like the village residents, was divided into classes. There were the peddlers who bought the crops of the peasants' fields, middlemen and agents who purchased the agricultural output from the middle-sized farms, and large merchants and wholesalers who did business with the large estate owners and bought their various agricultural products.

It can be presumed that every village or group of neighboring villages was linked by regular tradesmen who would visit these villages, and the villagers would distribute their different goods through them. These tradesmen were called *dorf-geher*s [village trekkers].

In our town, there were a few hundred tradesmen who would go to the peasants' homes of the type I described, and they made their living through small-scale trading of agricultural products.

Every respectable estate owner had his own middleman who was usually a Jew and who arranged all of the matters for the *paritz* [nobleman], especially the distribution of farm products.

Twice a week (Tuesday and Friday afternoon), there was a market in Działoszyce. Villagers from all over the area use to come to these fairs, bringing their carts full of things for sale.

About 100–120 shops and stalls were in the market, and everyone made good money from those who came to the fairs. Every market day, they made enough money to last half a week, at least.

The villagers would bring to town all kinds of farm-based produce—beans, cheese, butter, and all types of vegetables. They would then buy the things they needed such as kerosene, salt, clothing, boots, sickles, grinding stones, hardware, and such.

As I have stated above, about 300–400 Jewish families made their livelihood from the trade in agricultural goods from the villages in the area.

The agricultural products that were bought were only partly used by the local population; the rest were shipped to other areas where there was great demand for them, because these areas were densely populated and because their land was poor and not productive. The places where Działoszyce's agricultural products were sent, and the areas around them, were Sosnowiec, Będzin, Dąbrowa, Zawiercie, and the coal mine area.

Działoszyce was some distance from the main line of the Charsznica-Jędrzejów railroad.

Buying and transporting agricultural goods employed and provided a living for fifty to sixty families, the heads of which worked as wagon drivers. They would travel in their wagons every day from Działoszyce to the towns of Charsznica or Jędrzejów, carrying their produce along the way and bringing back different industrial goods, such as coal, items made from steel, dry goods, salt, kerosene, and other goods for household use that were in demand in Działoszyce and the area.

Some of the agricultural products were processed right on the spot.

In Działoszyce, two plants produced cooking oil. The raw material for this was the byproduct of vegetables from which oil and cottonseed were produced. These were returned to the different villages as processed products—oil for cooking and lighting, and cottonseed for eating and for feeding domestic animals.

Dozens of families made their living from industry and trade.

In addition, Działoszyce lay in the area bordering Galicia, which belonged to the Austro-Hungarian kaisers [emperors]. The border also served as a source of income for dozens of families of smugglers and border thieves.

They used to transport cargo that came through Russia to the the city of Kraków, and then it was illegally smuggled via the "black" border or the "green" border.[1] These goods included mainly ostrich feathers and real and artificial coral. With regard to the "black" coral, a special profession began to develop, which was the threading of coral beads to make necklaces. About half the women of the town and their children worked in threading this coral.

From Austria, it was customary to smuggle all sorts of natural and artificial coral, packed unthreaded, in boxes. In Działoszyce, they used to work in the threading, keeping up with the demands of the great Russian market.

Dozens of families dealt in the sale of coral in Greater Russia, and these families traveled great distances. The traveling agents focused mainly on Ukrainian cities, but there were those who went as far as Siberia.

They would leave Działoszyce a few days after Pesakh. They spent a full year in Russia, and then on the eve of the first Pesakh seder, they would return to their homes and their families. During the year, shipments of coral would be sent in accordance with the agreed upon destination, and the purchaser would pay the price of the coral upon receipt of the shipment. But, as mentioned above, about half the women in the town and their children made their living by making coral necklaces all year round.

The areas around Działoszyce were blessed with an abundance of water, which flowed in rivers and streams. This brought about the establishment of many flour and

---

[1] The "green border" refers to areas in the countryside where the border was not patrolled and could be easily crossed. The "black border" perhaps refers to black market activity.

barley mills. In the town itself and its environs, two large flour mills operated, and in the nearby vicinity, there were another five or six mills.

All of these mills were managed or leased by Jews.

Each week, large shipments of flour, weighing hundreds of tons, were shipped to Dąbrowa and Sosnowiec. All of this was in addition to the flour that the town itself and the surrounding area needed. The Jews handled all of the flour business, of course.

Dozens of families residing in the town of Działoszyce and the area were connected to the industry of the land. Among the well-known owners of estates were the Szental, Spiro, Szwimer, and Moszkowski families; and among the farmers of smaller plots of land were the families Łaznowski, Owsiany, Lewkowicz, Zelig Glejzor, and others.

There were two banks in town that handled all of the town's trading business. They had links with other banks that were in the cities and that had commercial ties with Działoszyce.

Dozens of craftsmen's (tailors, sandal-makers) workshops operated within the town. They supplied the clothing and shoes needed for stores and businesses in big and small towns throughout Poland. A few workshops also were involved in the production of harnesses, tethers, saddles, and reins for export.

The Gertler Family, *z"l*

Even the chicory factory, which of course belonged to a Jew, was on the edge of town, close to Łabędź. A number of families made their living working in this industry, producing chicory—supplying the raw materials and selling the finished product.

These are the types of sources of income for the Jewish population in Działoszyce during World War I.

Of course, I did not see with my own eyes all the things that I described above. But I know very well about them, because I stayed in constant touch with Działoszyce by way of the town Charsznica, which was on the railroad line and was the gateway to the great wide world.

Translated from the Hebrew by Roger Kaplan

Grandmother's House (Now in Ruins) (pp. 30–48)

Yisrael Zerachi

The Betrothal

The cradle of my grandmother's family was a poor and remote Polish townlet that bordered on a murky river. In the spring, as the snow melted, adding to the flow of water in the valley, the river became somewhat more powerful, moving with increased vigor. But during the rest of the year, it moved sluggishly, like someone with plenty of time but little energy. The townspeople would carry their pails beyond the populated area in search of unpolluted water. Their houses were in disrepair, plagued with rot, falling plaster, and sinking foundations. Grass grew in the cracks of the crumbling rooftops, and when goats climbed up to feast on this greenery, the local children chased them with unrestrained fury.

The Jews of the town sustained themselves with difficulty. As there weren't enough of them to support each other, they spread out to the neighboring countryside—the landowners' estates and the farms—buying wheat, selling shiny buttons and spools of thread. A plump young calf or a dozen fresh eggs might come their way, for which a customer could be counted on to pay well.

Just as the river followed its own course, so each family had its own means of livelihood. Grandmother's household traded in leather. Her father used to buy his wares from the animal skinners, deliver the leather to the tanner in town, and then bring them home—fine skins that filled the air with their strong smell—to sell to local merchants and shoemakers.

My grandmother, who was the youngest daughter, stayed at home. As she was born the day before Purim, she was given the name Ester. She grew into a beauty, her face round and fresh as an apple, her eyes crystal-clear, understanding everything. Even before she was of age, her father began looking for a suitable match. But her mother would scold him, "Is there no room in the house for the girl? Why do you want to send her away? She is still a child." Her father would mutter into his beard and wink at the girl, as if to say: a father knows his daughter's heart.

Before long, Reb Ze'ev, the girl's father, went to celebrate Shavuos with his *rebbe* [Hasidic rabbi], as was his custom. He conveyed to the *rebbe* what was in his heart, that his daughter Ester'l, may she live long, would soon be "of age" and that in order to fulfill the *mitsve* [commandment] of arranging her marriage, it was his task to find her a proper mate.

The *rebbe* offered him his frail hand, saying, "Blessed be the maker of matches."

At this point, many other followers arrived, from near and far, to see their *rebbe*'s face and warm their souls in his light. Among them was Reb Izrael Zerach, a man of property and a military supplier to the czar. His beard was neatly groomed, his bearing

---

Although no surnames are used in this chapter, it was possible to infer from documents available through JRI-Poland that the grandmother was Ester Najman and the grandfather, Jonas Gertler.

erect. He had access to high officials, lived lavishly, and was generous. He would often bring his grandson, Jonas, with him—a shy, submissive boy who approached the *rebbe*, his eyes agape with wonder, his heart pounding wildly. Reb Izrael Zerach confided to the *rebbe* that he was hoping to find an appropriate match for his grandson. Eliasz Gabriel, the boy's father, was incompetent, and he was the boy's guardian. It was not wealth he was seeking but a good name, a chaste and virtuous daughter of Israel.

The *rebbe* squinted and said, "Blessed be the maker of matches…"

At the end of Shabes, when the followers were ready to take leave of the *rebbe*, Reb Szymon-Ze'ev and Reb Izrael Zerach were called in to see him. Shortly thereafter, the betrothal was announced; the young groom, Jonas, son of Eliasz Gabriel, son of Izrael Zerach, and the chaste bride, young Ester, daughter of Reb Ze'ev, were promised to each other!

It was a joyous night throughout the *rebbe*'s court [circle of followers]. Those who had already harnessed their horses now loosened them. Those who had taken up their traveling gear set it down. Reb Izrael Zerach presided over the celebration, displaying his power and wealth. Wine cellars were emptied; the town's oven could not provide enough honey cakes and fragrant *challah* [braided holiday bread], so messengers were sent to neighboring towns to fill the gap.

Only one person did not participate in the celebration, not even dipping his lips in the wine. He stood in a corner, frightened and bewildered, unable to understand how he had fallen in with this raucous crowd. This was Jonas, the prospective groom.

The betrothal was celebrated into the morning hours. Then the Hasidim began to disperse and return home. Reb Szymon-Ze'ev, father of the bride, finally set out, arriving home after midnight. Full of joy and good feeling, he awakened his daughter and declared, "*Mazel Tov* [Congratulations], Ester'l. You've been betrothed, with God's blessing. You're betrothed, my child."

The Wedding

On Sukes, the groom, young Jonas, then about 14, came to spend the holiday with the family of the bride, the maiden Ester. He arrived with his teacher and stayed in the home of the *dayan* [rabbinic judge], as it would not be proper for him to be under one roof with the girl. Reb Szymon-Ze'ev, his prospective father-in-law, walked to *shul* [synagogue] with him, proudly, as if he were a rare and precious *esrog* [type of citrus used in Sukes celebration].

The bride's friends plagued her with questions. "Nu, Ester'l, have you seen your bridegroom yet?" She answered calmly, though her heart was pounding. "What's the hurry about seeing him? In any case, he'll be my husband."

Nonetheless, she allowed herself to be dragged into the adventure and, along with her friends, she ran past the courthouse where the guest was staying and even peered into the window. Seeing only the vague image of a boy bent over a page of Talmud, she wasn't satisfied and watched for him again toward morning. When she spotted him, marching to *shul* to pray, flanked by her father and his teacher, she jumped up and fled. She didn't leave her house the rest of the day, saying not a single word, not even in reply to her taunting girl friends.

Once the wedding day was set, the boy went home, but Satan intervened, and a heavy shadow descended on the bride's house, postponing the event. Reb Szymon-Ze'ev, the bride's father, died prematurely, leaving his wife with the burden of supporting the family. The wedding was put off from year to year, until relatives intervened. They all agreed that the marriage could no longer be postponed, that the girl, though physically small, was of age and should be married. The widow relented, and a wedding date was set.

The groom's family arrived—his father in a shiny silk cloak, his mother with an elaborate embroidered head-dress, and the grandfather, Reb Izrael Zerach, purveyor to the czar, in a stylish garment of a rare dark fabric and soft leather shoes that squeaked as he walked. Uncles and aunts arrived in festive clothes, and children, whose round black hats glowed with newness. The large entourage settled itself once again in the home of the *dayan*.

The widow went to welcome them. When she saw the groom, a lad whose beard was beginning to grow in, now much taller and with a strikingly obtrusive nose, she greeted the party wanly, ran home to her expectant family, and began to wail, "They've switched grooms on me!"

The assembled relatives were bewildered. What is she talking about? But she persisted. "Do they think they can abuse me because I'm a widow? Because the girl's father isn't alive to protect her? Is this the delicate boy with the soft eyes and gentle face that my husband, Reb Szymon-Ze'ev, may he rest in peace, chose as a groom for his daughter Ester'l? This can't be! Is there no one who will rise to the defense of an orphan? I won't go along with this!"

What a commotion, everyone talking and arguing. One relative remarked that such things do happen, as in the case of Laban, the Aramean.[1]

Another said that from the start he hadn't approved of the boy but, for the sake of peace, had remained silent. After a while, the more agitated voices subsided, and more considered ones were heard. "Let's ask those who knew the boy when he was here years ago!"

The bride's mother agreed on one condition: her older sister, Brajndla, must be the one to be consulted. In the absence of the bride's father, she would trust only her opinion.

It began to rain, so Aunt Brajndla put on her heavy boots, took her spectacles, and prepared for the journey. Magda, the gentile servant, who was like a member of the family, sharing its joys and troubles, took up a heavy wooden lantern, set a candle in it, as it was by now nightfall, and set out with Aunt Brajndla.

The delegation arrived at the home of the *dayan*. Brajndla put on her spectacles, took the lantern from Magda, shining it on the groom's face as she turned the baffled fellow around and around. She listened to his voice and checked his skin. When she returned to the bride's home, she delivered her verdict to those who were assembled there, waiting with bated breath. In a firm and measured tone she proclaimed: "No! He is not the same young man; he is not the chosen groom!"

---

[1] Laban substituted his daughter Leah for her sister Rachel as a wife for Isaac.

Once again, the bride's mother began to wail. "Isn't that what I said from the start? Didn't I know it right away? A blind man would be able to tell! Because I'm a widow, is it all right to spill my blood?"

At the *dayan*'s house, there was great confusion. The family was waiting to be called to the wedding ceremony to no avail. The guests didn't understand the delay nor did they know the meaning of the odd visits by the relatives of the bride. The evening passed with no celebration. The guests' faces fell.

After a while, they became aware of the rumor that was circulating through the streets, stirring up the entire town. An incredible tale: the groom of Ester'l, daughter of Szymon-Ze'ev, may he rest in peace, was replaced by another young man!

And when this became public, the town's dignitaries, led by the rabbi, began to deal with the error. Reb Izrael Zerach swore that he had no grown grandson from his son Eliasz Gabriel other than Jonas, the groom, who was here before their eyes. How could anyone claim that he had been switched? The bride's mother was called to the home of the *dayan*, and everyone began to plead and coax her with words sweeter than honey. "What could she have in mind? Such a clever and respected woman; she is mistaken. The true groom is right here, Jonas, and no other. Heaven forbid. The boy has merely grown in the interim and has become, no evil eye should harm them, an adult. What would be the point of switching grooms? She is a smart woman, and, surely, she can see her mistake."

Several townspeople even testified that they recognized the groom as the one who had come some years back, Ester'l's true groom.

Slowly, the widowed woman began to feel more confident, and, after midnight, she finally agreed to go ahead with the wedding.

The delayed celebration was under way. Musicians and singers began to tune up; cooks became busy in the kitchen as tables were arranged for the feast. The groom was led to the bride's home along with his entire entourage. A jeering voice was heard from a member of this party, as the bride was led in to sign the *ketuba* [marriage contract]. "Is this the bride? She probably doesn't know how to sign. She's tiny as an olive." To which the girl retorted, "Large coins are made of copper; a *dinar* is small but of gold."

The bride allowed them to scurry about in search of a pen and ink, which had not been prepared in advance. When, still hesitant, they offered her the quill, she rejected it, declaring, "I have my own; I don't need yours."

To everyone's surprise, she reached into her bag and produced an elegant quill along with a small bottle of ink. She opened the bottle, dipped the quill in the ink, and signed her name in large clear letters, like a string of pearls.

Her mother's eyes glowed with hidden pride, and the groom's family was also pleased. The groom, flushed with embarrassment, hid his face in the document on the table.

It was a wild wedding, such as the town had not known for a long time, and it was remembered for many years.

A Livelihood

Years passed. Many children were born to the young couple, but their situation was always precarious. Both of their families had been well off but were now in decline. In one case, because of the father's death, in the other, the grandfather's death. Trading in leather was no longer profitable, and the estate left behind by Reb Izrael Zerach diminished with time. The young student, Jonas, and his wife, Ester'l, had to devote themselves to supporting their household, like everyone else in the town. As their family grew, so did their poverty. The young father was compelled to abandon his studies and to work for a livelihood. Being a novice in the ways of commerce, he entered into a partnership with a bright but crafty fellow, whose strategy was to have one of them invest the capital and the other to collect the profit. This partnership was not successful...

Grandmother's brother, Reb Moszek, intervened. Known as "Moszek the Terror," he could not stand by in silence as his innocent brother-in-law was cheated. In his youth, he himself had strayed from the proper path, gambling away days and nights, bringing sorrow and shame to the family, heartbreak to his mother. He would sometimes appear in the morning carrying a chest filled with valuables given to him by friends who couldn't pay their gambling debts. His mother would scold him harshly, even lock him out of the house. But he always found a way in. It was even reported that he had been involved in a love affair with a young woman, that after she was married to someone else, he wrote up their story, and his manuscript was passed from hand to hand and read by the doctor, the pharmacist, and the local lawyer. He had golden hands, endless skills. He once drew a menorah and wrote the entire scroll of Ester on it. This same Moszek was totally transformed after his marriage to a chaste young woman. His beard grew, his body filled out, he gave up gambling and licentiousness, began to deal in commerce, and even found some time for study. He was known for acts of charity and generosity. Before long he gained a reputation as an upstanding Jew with a sharp mind and experience in the ways of the world, so much so that people began to consult him about their financial affairs and disputes.

This Moszek, seeing his brother-in-law's troubles, said to him one day, "Jonas, it seems to me that you were not destined to be a merchant. Why torture yourself? Even if it is the way of good men to accept suffering, which is known to purge the soul, they don't tend to pursue it. There are many ways to serve God faithfully. And you, after all, have a wife and small children."

The young student looked at him sadly and said, "What can I do? I don't have the strength to bear my suffering. But what is there for me to do? Give in to despair?" To which his brother-in-law responded, "Was that my suggestion? I, myself, in my youth, had days when I didn't know how I would extricate myself from my difficulties. And it's no secret; one has to wake up and take action. With God's help, I abandoned my wanton ways and achieved my present position. If I have accomplished this, why not you?"

"What more can I do?"

You should leave this town. As the saying goes: "Change of place, change of fortune." Find work that offers you steady pay. You won't be dependent on trade where the profit is sometimes high, sometimes meager. And there are those for whom it is always meager."

The young student pulled at his beard, his eyes flaming with emotion. "Where can I go?" To which Moszek responded, "I'll take care of that, if you agree!" "In the name of my love for my family, I agree!" They shook hands, and nothing further was said.

In less than a month, a situation was found for Jonas far beyond the town limits. When his brother-in-law gave him the news, he said to his wife, "I'll go first. Maybe the place will be hard to live in. Why should we both suffer?" She answered, "Whither thou goest I shall go. I'm no better than you. And I may be able to help."

They prepared for the trip. On the appointed day, they loaded their belongings onto a wagon, settling the children among the packages. They took leave of the family and set out with Magda, the servant girl, who walked alongside the wagon for a while, making sure the ropes were secure and reminding the children not to cry or be a burden to their mother. When the wagon was some distance from the town, warm tears began to fill Ester'l's lovely eyes, flowing relentlessly down her cheeks. She was leaving her parents' home for the very first time, the humble wooden house at the edge of a modest stream, its interior suffused with warm, caressing light.

After a day's travel, they reached their destination: a grain mill situated in a grassy valley, beside a powerful steady stream whose waters powered the wheels of the mill. There was no sign of habitation, apart from a single house, and no trace of Jews in the entire area. The mill belonged to a *paritz* [nobleman], who owned property and leased it to Jews. They, in turn, hired my grandfather to be treasurer, secretary, and miller—in charge of the entire operation.

This is how my grandparents' new life began. They—Jonas, the student, and his wife, Ester, were still young.

The Pains of Parenthood

Here, in their new home at the mill, young Ester's qualities and pleasant ways became evident. She understood how to meet her husband's needs, smooth his rough edges. He, who was not accustomed to being in public, was suddenly successful in his affairs—knowing when to be tough and when to be gentle. It was, in fact, his wife who counseled him, with her intelligence, and was a source of strength to him.

Though this new work was not rewarded lavishly, there was now food on the table. Jonas's gentle temperament, integrity, and honesty made him easy to get along with and widely appreciated. There were fewer financial worries, but other worries took their place. There were almost no Jews in the area, so the oldest boy, Szymon-Ze'ev, could not study Torah. He had already learned to read Hebrew but was beginning to forget what he knew. How could his parents allow him to be deprived of study? Yet, for the boy, the new town was a treasure, an unexpected find. Broad meadows, cool springs, and a rushing river unlike the muddy one of his birthplace—can one make light of all these riches? The boy would leap like a goat, swim in the river, and sun himself, just like the children of the neighboring farmers. His father was horrified when he saw this; would his firstborn son grow up coarse and vulgar like them? This could not be! At night he would share his concern with his wife; the other children were still too young to worry about, but what would become of Szymon-Ze'ev?

One morning, he took a break from his work at the mill, tied his horse to his wagon, and brought his son back to the town of his birth, to Grandma Dina, Ester'l's mother, so he could study with Jews rather than spend his time with the local boys.

At first, the boy enjoyed the change; living with Grandma rather than under his parents' watchful eyes, going to Reb Kalman's *kheyder* [small Jewish religious school] to study, getting pocket money every week—what more could he ask?

The pocket money was especially precious to him; nothing was as sweet. What could it not buy? Bagels, immersed in boiling water, then baked, a giant pear, dripping with nectar; but most wondrous of all was shopping in Reb Mendele's fragrant store. The *kheyder* boys would cram into this narrow, dimly lit space, filled with the perfumes of Eden; there they reached into crates of rare fruit, boxes of raisins, and fig rolls, but the main object of their desire was a glistening carob. Its enticing scent caressing their nostrils, they checked to see if it was wormy as they haggled over a price. They were about to drop their coin into Mendele's wooden money box, when the boy Szymon asked one final question, "Is this carob truly from Eretz Yisroel [the Land of Israel]?"

At this point, Black Laja, Mendel's nasty wife appeared and yelled, in a voice with the power to bring death to the living and life to the dead, "Imagine, for a few dingy coins they expect carob from Eretz Yisroel. Get lost, you hoodlums, before I get my cane and chase you."

They left the store without making their purchase, with money in their pockets and the scent of carob on their fingertips.

It wasn't long before the boy began to reject his new life. Grandma Dina turned into a tough woman, strict with her grandchild, raising her hand to him for no reason. Why was she angry? Because of the pocket money! She changed her tune and stopped giving the boy his allowance. "You don't need pocket money," she argued. "You want a pear, here's a pear! Nuts? have some nuts! Show me a single store where, for a copper coin, you'll get such a big pear or a handful of nuts like the ones I give you. Silly boy, do you think Mendel will give you anything like this?"

But the boy did not relent. He wailed, "I don't understand, Grandma. All the boys get money, and what's the point of getting nuts instead?"

Grandma insisted. Whatever he would like to buy, she would give him, but she would not give him a single penny!

The boy suddenly remembered his parents and the grassy meadow in the country, the mill, and the rushing stream. His head was filled with longing. Now, when his father came to town on business, the boy clung to his father and went everywhere with him. And unbeknownst to Grandma Dina, his father slipped him some pocket money. He then took leave of him, sadly, regretting that he was leaving the child in exile.

The boy began to neglect his studies. He began to dislike his teacher, Kalman Kalonas, and to slip away from school. The assistant would chase him through the alleys, sometimes even over the low rooftops and force him to return. Uncle Moszek tried to influence him, but to no avail. His grandmother appealed to his conscience, in a tone at once coaxing and menacing—invoking ancestors, distinguished in learning and wisdom— but without success. When she realized that her words were having no effect, she took action. Grandma Dina was a fierce woman, and she decided to break the boy's will.

Once, when the assistant teacher came with the "good news" that Szymon-Ze'ev had, once again, failed to come to school, she hired a porter to find the boy, tie him to his back and deliver him to school, like a sack of potatoes. She agreed on a sum to be paid upon delivery.

It was a long time before the boy was found. He was caught, tied up, as instructed by his grandmother, and delivered, like a fattened calf, to school. In response to the boy's shrieks, crowds gathered and accompanied them all the way. The porter, after fulfilling his mission, went to collect his pay. As Grandma was reaching into her apron pocket for the money, the boy appeared, having managed to escape from school yet again. He was sobbing violently. Grandmother left the money in her pocket and shouted at the porter, "What's this all about? Why should I pay you when here he is?!" To which the porter answered, "What's that to me? Is it my affair? You hired me to carry merchandise from one place to another, and I did. Now give me the money!"

But the woman refused. Until the boy was back in school, she would not agree to pay a penny.

The boy enjoyed this negotiation and stopped crying so he could hear the argument. They finally compromised and settled for half the sum. But this was the boy's last day in town. The next day he was sent back to his village with a farmer who had brought flour from the mill and was returning with an empty wagon. He dreaded the meeting with his parents. This was not how he had pictured his return.

It was a sad day when the boy arrived. His parents were heart broken when they saw their child sent home by his grandmother. And the boy, as if suddenly transformed, begged his parents to send him back to the town. He promised that he would study diligently and not cause any more trouble. But he was not sent back. From their meager resources, his parents set aside some money and found a teacher who would come to teach him in the countryside.

A Guest Arrives from Nearby

One day, a young, rather odd-looking man arrived on the evening train. His young face, almost childlike, was adorned by a light, silky beard. He wore a large broad-brimmed hat and a flowing black cape that flapped in the wind as he walked. His shoes were worn, their soles almost non-existent, and barely a trace of heels could be seen. He carried a small bag and, with a firm step, as if the path was familiar, he turned toward Grandmother Esterl's house. He opened the door calmly and seated himself at the large dining table. At that moment, there was no one else in the room, but soon, the littlest girl came in, and, startled by the sight of the stranger, she ran to call her father. Grandfather's eyes were no longer very sharp, so that when he entered the room, he didn't recognize the stranger but simply greeted him politely. The guest extended his hand to Grandfather and said nothing. Grandfather was uncomfortable, not knowing how to begin a conversation with this stranger, yet hesitating to ask what he wanted. As it would not be very welcoming to ask the guest why he had come, Grandfather nodded in response and went to call Grandmother.

Grandma came into the room, bewildered, having already heard about the odd guest. She approached him, looked into his eyes and cried, "Why it's Szlama. May evil overtake my enemies, have you lost your mind? Why are you wearing a Purim costume on an ordinary day? What is this?!"

The guest smiled broadly, fell into his mother's arms and kissed her. Everyone crowded around and began to laugh heartily. The little girl hadn't recognized her brother, and now she was crying. Grandfather laughed good-naturedly. But Grandma shouted,

"Go right to the barber, and get rid of those clothes. Did your brothers send you to the city so you would come back dressed like a priest?"

Uncle Szlama tried to explain to Grandmother that he couldn't possibly give up the black cape or the beard he had been grooming for months. And he tried to explain to his brothers that his clothes and beard were not frivolous but related to his faith, as it were… "Just what sort of faith?" his brothers asked, grinning. The young man's face turned serious as he responded, "If you don't laugh, I'll tell you."

They promised, and he answered gravely, as if revealing a cherished secret. "Anarchism," he whispered, as if mouthing the ineffable name of God. "I plan to translate Krapotkin [a Russian nihilist] into the holy tongue. "This was received with laughter and confused chatter. His brothers looked at him as if he had lost his mind. "Who is this Krapotkin whose teachings you mean to translate? Is he a descendant of the Kotzker [from Kock] *rebbe, z"l* [of blessed memory]? Who is he? It turns out that our Szlama, son of Reb Jonas and Ester'l, is an anarchist?" They sighed and laughed as hard as they could.

The guest was offended and retorted, "I thought you would laugh, but you promised not to." They fell silent, and he began to explain to them about private property, resisting authority, love, marriage—the entire catechism on one foot. He spoke about the struggle between the rich and the poor, argued that poverty was not a thing to be ashamed of— until his throat was sore.

Grandma, feeling sorry for her son, interrupted him, "True, poverty is not a disgrace, but is it something to be proud of? As for the beard, let the boy be. Tomorrow he'll go to the barber and put an end to it. Meanwhile, come into the kitchen and have some meat dumplings, the kind you love. Unless anarchists are not allowed to eat such delicacies."

Grandmother's face was aglow with love, which influenced the rest of the family. The storm subsided, and they all escorted the guest into the spacious kitchen and joined him for a meal. They devoured the dumplings, for which Grandmother was famous, stared at his thin, well groomed beard, their laughter replaced with warm smiles and a sense of well-being.

The young man stayed at home for a while. He took off his cape, folded it with religious fervor, and placed it in his bag. Chaim-Ber, the family shoemaker, replaced the heels on his worn shoes. Even Grandmother had no impact on his beard.

Zoszka, a young gentile girl from a poor village adjoining the train station—ten meager huts, their foundations sinking into the ground and their roofs covered with black straw—worked in Grandmother's house. The poverty in this remote village was overwhelming; its men worked at the station loading and unloading freight for grandfather or for Reb Mordka's warehouse. The young women did housework for Jews by day; some of them spent their nights at the train station. They often returned home with swollen bellies, remaining there until they were fit to work again.

This Zoszka, who worked for Grandmother, was a hefty young woman. The wooden floors groaned under her weight, and the glass objects in the pantry rattled gently when she walked by. When she washed the floor, she would roll up her skirt, tucking it under the belt that circled her waist. Her full, powerful thighs, tanned by the sun, would show through the simple homespun cloth.

It was rumored that this young woman's behavior, though she worked for Ester'l, was not altogether proper. When the young man in the cape arrived, talking of freedom in government and freedom in love, the rumors became more intense. When he retrieved the cape from his bag, as it was time for him to return to Kraków, and Zoszka's belly, in the meanwhile, had begun to swell, the gossips observed, "Isn't this what we predicted? Wait and see, Zoszka's baby will be born with a cape on its shoulders."

My grandparents were too innocent to pay attention to this talk. It may even be that it never reached their ears. But, as Zoszka's body grew rounder, Grandmother scolded her harshly, "Why did you get yourself in such trouble? Were you missing anything here? Now go away; there is no room for such behavior in this house!"

The girl cried and pleaded. It was not her fault if her young blood cried out for a man, and they, the men, were vying with each other for her favors. She begged her mistress to allow her to stay. She had nothing to live on, and who would hire her now?

Grandmother stood firm and sent the girl away. But the next day she filled a basket with provisions—a sack of flour, a bottle of goose fat, some meat—which she gave to her young daughter to deliver. "Take this basket to Zoszka," she said. "She's sick. But don't get involved in conversation, dear, because you could catch her sickness. Leave the basket at her door and hurry back home."

Grandmother, with her heart of gold, sent food to Zoszka throughout the pregnancy. After the birth, she even cooked her a chicken soup, grumbling incessantly about the girl's immoral behavior... I don't know whether Zoszka's child was born with a cape on its shoulders. I know only that from then on she used to come to Grandma's regularly to do the laundry. She often disappeared for a while, when her belly began to swell, and returned to the mill some months later, pale and feeble.

Returning to the Ancestral Home

The road extended over hill and dale, through dense forests, across crumbling bridges. Finally, the stumbling wagon reached the outskirts of Grandmother's town. The old mare, its strength giving out, plodded along sadly. The passengers, almost breathless from exhaustion, sighed and groaned dejectedly. The children wailed, but there was nothing to offer them for comfort. All the food had been eaten, leaving nothing but hope to sustain them. The mustached driver was cursing his horse, the passengers, and even himself, spitting in anger and rage. Only Grandmother was wondrously calm. As the wagon approached the outskirts of town, she began to call out the name of every familiar path, each field and hill—this was where she used to walk when she was young.

They finally arrived at a stream. The horse began to drink thirstily; the driver got down and unharnessed the animal. Then, when the horse finished drinking, they crossed the stream, the water lapping noisily at the wheels of the wagon. They entered a small valley that separated the riverbanks from the gentile cemetery. Its tall trees rustled in the wind. This valley was the scene of an annual fair which, in Grandma's youth, was a festive and noisy event. The village children would gather there, play an endless variety of games, ride colorful wooden horses, buy kites, paper birds, candy on a stick, all sorts of confections, and sweet fruit drinks. Her husband, when he was young, used to love the bustle of the fair. Her children, young and old, used to spend endless hours there. However, these young grandchildren of hers knew nothing about it.

At last, one could see smoke rising from chimneys in the town. Eager eyes fixed themselves on a transparent cloud that trembled in the air. The scent of cooking wafted their way, as if the warmth of home was rising to greet them. Any minute now… they would soon be there. But what was in store for them now in this remote Jewish town?

The travelers got out of the wagon to lighten the old mare's load, walking slowly toward the outlying houses. When they reached the first alleys of the town, a confused scene unfolded: hundreds of refugees from near and far—from regions already affected by the turmoil and from areas it was about to overtake—seeking refuge in this remote corner, hoping it would be spared. Entire families, young and old, camped in the streets with their bags. As there was no housing for them, they claimed a spot in any available corner, in vacant lots strewn with trash, in the ruins of crumbling buildings. The town was dying under the burden.

The main concentration of people could be seen beside the lazy stream, in the square that stretched between the butcher shops and the old synagogue. With difficulty, the wagon made its way through the mass of people and bundles, reaching the end of the encampment, where children dozed in their parents' arms, old people sat and argued, women tried to find food or sat with their eyes fixed desperately on the ominous horizon.

A noisy commotion was heard from beyond the synagogue where a crowd had gathered around a small, frail Jew with disheveled hair, his *peos* [sidelocks] rocking wildly, his black hat slipping down his back, his entire appearance bedraggled and confused, as if he had escaped some great calamity. The wagon was forced to stop before the crowds that blocked its way. Its occupants watched as the strange fellow climbed onto a pile of rocks. His fiery words stirred the hearts of his audience. He waved his hands to and fro; his eyes blazing with an alien fire as he spoke the fierce words that seemed to inflame his throat: "A holy people, a tortured people, how can I comfort you? From whom can I demand recompense? When will the fury relent? Is this how You reward Your people, Israel? You have spilled its blood, violated its honor. How long? Until when? Entire holy communities are torn apart, destroyed, slaughtered. There is no justice and no judge."

The meaning of these words was soon explained. There was no one in the village, either among its inhabitants or the refugees, who didn't know this man. He was an observant Jew, a teacher, who was as careful with minor commandments as with more serious ones, the scion of a fine family that Grandmother knew well in her youth. This was a man who had deprived himself of all luxury, devoting himself to lamenting the destruction of the temple. On Shabes, he didn't so much as speak to his family. And from sunset on Shabes eve until the three stars that signified its end, he didn't utter a sound other than prayer and penitence. He was a fervent Jew, ready to sanctify the name of his God in public. When calamity struck, destroying Jewish settlements in adjacent lands, when Satan's hand was extended over the entire state to destroy and annihilate, he was transformed by grief. He began to rant against heaven, violated the Shabes in public, called people together to listen to his raging, horrific orations.

The wagon began to move again, wending its way through the crowd, the alarming words they had just heard echoing in their ears: "Woe unto the ship that has no captain and woe unto the ship whose captain You are. Is this how you redeem the blood of the persecuted?" Those who heard his words nodded sadly and shrugged their shoulders in sympathy. "May the Lord have pity on him. This pious Jew has lost his mind from so much suffering and pain. May God forgive him."

When they reached the other side of the square, they caught sight of their small ancestral home. It looked even more forlorn and modest, having sunk ever more deeply into the ground, its frame in total disrepair. Yet the distant shadow of the past cast over it an aura of love, charm, and longing—like the longing for a distant childhood. This humble house was now a rare refuge, the fulfillment of a long dream, the most beloved, most precious of houses.

They stood before it in deep prayer. When the wagon came to a halt at its doorway, their eyes were misty. Grandmother's legs began to falter, and it was necessary to support her and all but carry her inside, where she was welcomed with a burst of activity and excitement. Some of Grandmother's children, driven by fear of the encroaching enemy, had already assembled here. When the men left the centers of commerce during the first days of the catastrophe, they decided to return to the shelter of their ancestral home. Though they had each followed a different road, they were reunited, without having made such a plan ahead of time. Now their wives and children, along with Grandma herself, joined them. In the midst of the terrible events, was this not a happy occasion?

As soon as she arrived, Grandma felt weak and had to get into bed. Her legs were swollen, her entire body painful. The wanderers no longer needed her to cast her protective spirit over them. She could rest. This small, aged woman, this valiant Jewish mother, having collected her dispersed family, could finally rest.

When the children fussed over her and tried to relieve her discomfort, she would dismiss them with a gentle sigh. "It's all right, children. It's all right. Don't worry about me, my dears. I don't need anything more. I'm home again, back home, like in the past, so many years ago. Don't worry about me. Am I a young woman? I'm almost eighty; I ask only that I be allowed to reach eighty…"

Chaos

The joy in the old house was short-lived. It was soon replaced by terror. The enemy's heavy equipment advanced steadily, tightening the noose around the entire country. Jews were trampled and abused in all the lands of conquest. There was no escape from the airplanes that circled everywhere. Even the skies of the village began to thunder. No lights were lit at night for fear of the airplanes, but by day the sun provided light for the demons of destruction. Meanwhile, there were heart-rending rumors. Warsaw was besieged; German tanks decimated the cavalry regiments that defended the city. Acts of heroism and despair were recounted again and again—how Polish and Jewish soldiers, armed only with swords, rose up against the tanks only to be crushed, falling like grains of sand… The Hel Peninsula, a fortress on the Baltic Sea, surrendered. When, after a bloody battle, enemy soldiers entered the fortress, they were stunned by the courage of the defenders. There were no armed men left; they were all dead or fatally wounded—a handful of fighters wanting only to die.

One day, the village was shattered by the sound of a powerful explosion. Many houses were destroyed. The sturdier ones survived, though all their windowpanes were broken. Everyone thought the end had come. But the sound was not repeated. It was later discovered that a nearby junction, rarely used as it was in such disrepair, had been bombed. An entire refugee family, camping close to that spot, was destroyed. It wasn't even possible to bury their remains in the proper Jewish way. There were constant upheavals. The refugees began to run again, but where was there a safe place? Slowly, the panic subsided.

But no attack from above could match the fear that came with the news that the German army was approaching. Many refugees resumed their wandering. The village was divested of its first round of refugees, but newcomers replaced them. Regiments, defeated by the enemy and now in flight, began to occupy the abandoned houses; and recruits, who had not yet been mobilized, wandered about like lost souls. Husbands searched for their wives, desperate parents searched for children lost in the confusion.

As the enemy approached, those men who had not already fled, left for the interior of the country, which continued to hold out. The male members of Grandmother's family decided to leave the danger zone, and, once again, they took leave of their loved ones— the second such parting since the terror began. This time they took their grown sons with them. First in the procession was Uncle Szlama with his oldest son. He kissed his wife, then Grandma and the others, and went off. Uncle Henie walked along with him for a while, but then they parted ways, as Szlama had a Polish friend, a town official, whom he wanted to see before leaving. When he found his friend, the fellow seized him and declared, "*Panie* [Mr.] Salomon, my dear *Panie* Salomon; I've been struggling all day— to leave or not to leave. My family holds me back. But I myself… I can't bear to see the swastika in our sacred land. I would rather die. Now I know what I'll do. I will go with you. Wait just a minute. Wait for me, my friend."

His family surrounded him and began to wail. But he ignored them, turning to Szlama. "My dear friend, wait. We'll go together. We will flee from our misfortune. Don't we have the same fate? The destruction of your temple so long ago is like our terrible destruction now. Because we hated you… How did we treat you? With hatred? Envy? Murderous rage?! This is the day of reckoning. Our plight is the same as that of the Jews. Our beloved Polish homeland is being trampled by the Krauts [Germans]."

He fell on the neck of Uncle Szlama, his shoulders trembling as he wept. Beyond the window, the dirge of that mad Jew could be heard, bemoaning the destruction of the people of Israel; while, here, the Pole was lamenting the destruction of his people. Only Uncle Szlama's soul wept, secretly, for both losses.

Less than a week after the men fled the town, German regiments approached. First, they appeared on motorcycles. Then came tanks, followed by a mass of troops. Their air force provided cover, for which there was little need, the spirit of the town's defenders having already been broken. No one dared resist the enemy. Deadly terror overcame the town. The people stayed in their houses, crowded together and densely packed, not daring to stick their heads out.

Soon there was no more food. A few daring individuals ventured out, submitting to the yoke of the cruel conqueror, exposing their souls to scorn and humiliation. The ironclad steps of German soldiers, messengers of Satan, echoed everywhere, spreading terror throughout the town.

At first, the family tried to hide the arrival of the Germans from Grandma, who was sick and bedridden. But, though she hadn't been told the news, she asked, "Are they as cruel as their leader? Have they not a single spark of soul? After all, don't they have wives and children at home? Is there no God in their hearts?" The family was silent.

As soon as the Germans took charge, a Polish mob, led by seasoned rioters, began to seize and plunder the meager property of the Jews, attacking, wounding, smashing windows, inciting the neighboring peasants, inviting them to bring their wagons to town and fill them with loot. Screams were heard in the alleys as rioters with axes broke down the doors of Jewish stores. There was total license with regard to Jewish property, a gift from the Germans to the Poles, whose homeland they were trampling—a soulless people who leaped at this bargain, unleashing their rage and fury, behaving like vicious animals.

Finally, the Germans put an end to the riots so they could get on with their program. The old synagogue was turned into a stable. Aged Jews were forced to groom the horses. Many of the young people were imprisoned. No one knew their whereabouts. Special laws were enacted, excluding Jews from the human community. They were forbidden to leave the house after sunset under penalty of death; they were ordered to salute every German soldier and make way for him; they were not to walk on the sidewalks. There was to be no contact between Poles and Jews; property was being confiscated.

And then this happened: One night some carousing German soldiers got drunk and began singing blood-curdling songs about the Jews. When they were thoroughly intoxicated, they began waving their weapons at each other, and, in the course of their horseplay, a shot was fired, injuring one of the soldiers. The rumor went out, instantly, that the wretched Jews had struck a German soldier. And there were even some Poles who attested to this. A few leading citizens were summoned by the military governor. What transpired is unknown. But when they were released, crushed, and humiliated, the crowd of Jews was informed that this time they would be pardoned and merely required to pay a ransom; but, should there be a second offense, the town would be razed and not a single Jewish soul would remain.

The fine imposed on the impoverished community was beyond its modest means. Money, jewelry, and provisions were collected and delivered to the authorities. But was that enough to satisfy the appetite of the new rulers and to assuage their anger? Not a day passed without incident. The lives of Jews were in mortal danger.

One comforting possibility remained; the forces fighting in the eastern sector might still defeat the enemy and rout its armies from its border. Every heartbeat was devoted to this hope, which shone like a distant star. Then came the astonishing news that the Russian army was camped on Poland's eastern border. There was great joy in the occupied territories; everyone was eager for the Germans and Russians to confront each other. Hope was ignited even in those hearts that had despaired. Everyone expected the German enemy to be driven out. But then the [Soviet] alliance with the enemy was made public; the unoccupied section of Poland, which had been preparing to defend itself, had fallen into the hands of the Russians.[1] In the light of this news, the last of the freedom fighters dispersed. Warsaw fell; the occupation of Poland was complete—the forces of the Swastika having joined hands with those of the Red Star over the body of Poland, now torn apart and writhing in its own blood.

---

[1] Based on the Molotov-Ribbentrop secret pact between the USSR and Germany, the Soviets entered and occupied the eastern half of Poland on September 17, 1939.

Grandma's family was similarly torn apart. The men were trapped in the area now taken over by Russia, while the women and children remained in the clutches of the Germans. The fate of those who fled is unknown. There was no news from them. A heavy black curtain obscured everything.

Sunset

Winter descended on the town, on all its gloomy dwellings. White snow covered the fields, brightening the blackened roofs and the worn cobblestones. The river froze. At first, it was covered with a thin strip of ice under which it continued its lazy flow. Then, the last drop of water froze, and it became totally still.

Once, on a cold and frosty day, an old woman came to Grandmother's door, her head covered by a woolen scarf as was the way of the local peasants. She entered the house with gingerly steps, leaning on a heavy stick. When no move was made to welcome her, she exclaimed, "What's the matter? You don't recognize old Magda?" Is it for this that she had worked all those years? Only to be forgotten? When she undid her scarf, they all recognized her immediately. This was, indeed, Magda, who had worked in their house so long ago. They bestirred themselves and brought her a chair.

She caught her breath, allowed the scarf to slip down her back, and said, "I heard Ester'l had come to town, and I had to see her. Though I haven't been here in years, I've come from the country to see the girl." She went in to see Grandmother, whom the old servant woman still regarded as the little girl from the ancient house. She threw herself on Grandmother's bed and wailed: "My dove, my heart, are you sick? You're not old at all, my soul... When was your wedding, wasn't it only yesterday? And the mix-up with the groom, remember? I heard he's already dead. May he rest in peace. I remember everything, everything. When did it all happen? Wasn't it only yesterday? My dove, dear heart of mine, I found out that you are here, and I came, quick as an arrow, on my aged feet."

She embraced Grandma and bestowed warm kisses on her cheek. Grandma's eyes blazed with a distant light, warm and excited. The family tried in vain to remove old Magda from the sickroom. Grandmother protested, asking, with her burning eyes, that the guest remain at her side. And Magda murmured repeatedly: "Now that I've come to you, my dove, to my heart, can I leave so quickly? I've brought some food for you, my soul. At such a time, when such villains are ruling the land, who knows—you may need something."

As she spoke, she dug into the recesses of her crude garment and produced a cup of butter and a dozen large eggs, which she placed at the edge of the bed. Then she fell silent, sat on the bed, took Grandmother's pale hands in her own and pressed them tight. The two old women sat together, a remnant of distant times, their hands clasped in silence.

But Grandmother didn't need the nourishment old Magda had brought. She was sinking, the thread of her life becoming more tenuous. Only her eyes retained a faint spark. She worried about her children, scattered in far off fields, wandering in unknown places. They might be hungry; they could have fallen into the hands of the cruel enemy. One night she asked that one of her young grandchildren be brought to her. When he approached, she gave him a finely crafted silver goblet, one of the few objects that had survived the upheavals, and whispered, "When you grow up and go to Eretz Yisroel, give this goblet to Yisrael Zerach [the author of this account], and tell him that it belonged to your grandfather, whose memory is a blessing."

She kissed the boy, who didn't understand her words, and sank back into the pillows.

Purim arrived—Grandmother's 80th birthday. But the time was not suited to celebration, with the enemy ruling one's body and trampling one's soul, the family torn asunder and Grandma herself, like the House of Israel, shrinking. Nonetheless, the plan was to mark the day. As the *Megile* [Purim story of Ester] was being read, in the semi-darkness of the low-ceilinged room, Grandmother's heart began to falter, and she no longer understood what was going on around her.

The following day, her simple, innocent soul, the soul of a precious Jewish mother, continued to fade. Benign spirits arrived to envelop her soul, the spirits of the old homestead to which she had returned to complete the circle of her life. Images from the bright shores of childhood and from the abyss of great sadness were now revived, fluttering before her eyes. What they whispered to the old woman in her last moments is not known...

Translated from the Hebrew by Zeva Shapiro

An Obligation to Remember (pp. 49–55)

M. Rafali [Rafałowicz]

Anniversary

Every year, a gathering of survivors
Come together, to sit, to mourn
The Działoszyce and Skalbmierz
Communities that exist no more.

Every year I will show you around
Around me, my city, so beloved
Everything that no longer remains
There, where my happiness was, it hurts

Among the alleys and bridges
Under which there flowed the streams
And from the river where I drew "our water"
Holy, I cast into the stream, crumbs of *tashlikh*.[1]

Your stream—to return a soul, to quench a thirst
But now, from your days, waters quiver like after a flood.
To visit you, I yearned and what a shame
I won't see you anymore, a real tragedy.

As is the nature of things, we forget things that flow like the distant past, and time goes its own way. As our day of remembrance approaches, which begins a few days before Rosh Hashanah, let us remember and gather even the smallest bits of memories of our town, about the gray days of everyday life, all year long, and also about its wonderful days.

Our city was rich with all sorts of people, from all different economic and social classes. This time, we will try to bring up from the depths of oblivion images of the cantors and congregants during Rosh Hashanah and Yom Kippur, those who once were but are no longer. The cantor about whom we will speak used to pray every day of the year in the *shtibl* [small Hasidic house of prayer] of the Hasids of Trisk,[2] but every year during the Days of Awe [High Holy Days], he would lead the services in the *besmedresh* [Orthodox house of prayer], accompanied by his sons and grandsons. They would stand on each side of the rails of the stairs that led to the Holy Ark. The cantor, standing erect, with his long white beard adorning his face, looked like the High Priest. He would lay out

---

[1] *Tashlikh* is the ceremony of casting bread crumbs into a body of water as if casting away one's sins.
[2] Trisk was the Yiddish name for Turisk, Poland, now Turijs'k, Ukraine.

his warm prayers before the Creator in a pleasant manner like an old hand who had done this many times. When he stretched his hands upward and raised his voice during the *avoda* [prayer service] of Yom Kippur, there was a stillness in the *besmedresh* amid the large congregation. And from the increasing silence arose the eternal tune of "The Priests and the people standing in the Temple Azara[1]...quench the yearning for redemption and kingdom..." The echoes of the prayer leader's voice would float and blend with those accompanying him.

On the side, completely bowed, stands one of the penitent, with tears streaming from his eyelashes and rolling down his face. And his lips say, "Please, *God*, forgive me." He forgets his distress and turns his thoughts away from his personal tribulations. He is caught up in the fast and prayers on the awesome holy day, the Day of Judgment.

Such as these were the congregants and cantors in our town, *hi"d* [may the Lord avenge their blood]. I am sure that some of our friends knew them. They were the prayer leader, Reb Chaim Szaja Kac, *z"l* [of blessed memory], a Hasid who followed the straight path, and the congregant Reb Zalman Majer, the tailor, *z"l*, who was humble and God fearing. There were other good cantors in our town who were appreciated and desired by all, such as Reb Abram Lejb Solny, *z"l*, who was well known for his sweet voice. Echoing in the ears is the sound in the *besmedresh* [house of prayer] of his first *slikhes* [prayers of repentance preceding the High Holy Days], when he would call out, "God instructed us to say the Thirteen Attributes." Reb Abram Icek Zając, *z"l*, a wonderful Torah reader, also led services. Reb Moszek Dawid Pomeranc, *z"l*, led the services in the *shtibl* of the Chęciny Hasids, and Reb Abele Grandapel was the established leader of *musef* [additional morning prayers] for the Chęciny rabbi. There were many more. In general, Działoszyce had a good reputation, near and far, regarding the quality of its cantors.

As all that once was in our small town and is no more passes before my eyes, like a fleeting dream, it is hard for my mind to accept that its human richness no longer exists.

A Day In A Year

Every year I'll see you around me
My town that I so love.
Of all its treasure, nothing remains.

A place where my happiness dwells
Among your narrow alleys and bridges
Under which rivers flowed.

To visit you, I yearned for many years
I will not see you until the end of days.
Every year, a gathering of survivors
Come together, to remember, to mourn
For the Działoszyce community, which is no longer.

---

[1] Courtyard of the Temple where sacrifices were offered.

As I now recall the memories of my dear town where I spent my childhood, when I think about and ponder about this small town of "Poor King Gitar," a great sigh bursts from my heart, because it is no more and has vanished on the altar together with its good people.

I dreamt once of visiting there to see members of my family and all the people of our town. I wished also to lie down on the graves of ancestors, on my mother's grave, may peace be upon her, who died in the prime of her life. (Incidentally, she was a teacher of girls; she taught Russian and Yiddish.) And then came the catastrophe that cut her life short, and I was not able to visit her. My lips are unable to express the whisperings of my heart and bring to mind the memories of the past. Our town was a one-of-a-kind special town, and perhaps, justly so, was called the "mother town" of the rest of the towns in the area. They lived a real Jewish life (*gelebt ein yidishkeyt*). Only now am I able to properly appreciate it, for I was young when I emigrated to Israel. It was at the beginning of the 1920s, and I didn't have the experience to be able to appreciate fully the town and its dear people. A wide variety of all types of different people lived there—the rich, the middle class, laborers, rabbis, rabbinic judges, scholars, craftsmen, storekeepers, and workers of many different kinds. Life was peaceful, natural, without commotion, and far from the tumult of the big city. It was a town that had a wonderful mix of Torah and Enlightenment, and Zionism also held an honorable place in its time. I remember, among other things, among the newspapers that came to our town, there was the first Hebrew paper, *Hatsefirah*, whose editor was Nahum Sokołów. This was about 1910. Other Hebrew periodicals came regularly, too. The Hebrew language wasn't foreign to the Jewish youth in our town, especially to the boys of the *besmedresh*.

I remember once during a Talmud *f*lesson that they found one of the boys had a copy of *Hatsefirah* underneath his book of Talmud. One of the town leaders made a big fuss about it. If my memory serves me correctly, it was Izrael Chaim Szac. From today's perspective, our town held Zionism and Enlightenment in high regard.

I also remember World War I and its aftermath, when we heard the news about the Balfour Declaration and the San Remo Agreement.[1] What a spontaneous awakening and general happiness came over the town and its residents. Everyone in the town gathered together in the *besmedresh*, and there were vociferous speeches by those from Mizrachi [Orthodox Zionist Party] and the Zionists. The speakers were Herszel Moher, Hercel Karmioł, Icek Kołatacz, the Tall Jekl, and others. There was a great commotion; they called this gathering "a gathering to redeem Israel." The gathering was lively, people from every class contributed money, and whoever couldn't give money brought various gold objects. Many removed their own jewelry. Then a committee was formed that gathered all of the property and took it to Warsaw, to the Zionist Center, or some other place. This detail I don't remember exactly.

A committee to purchase land in Eretz Yisroel was also formed. It seems that all of the town's residents wanted to travel to the Holy Land. And thus, after all those years of

---

[1] The Balfour Declaration of 1917 stated that Britain viewed with favor the establishment of a Jewish homeland in Palestine. The San Remo Agreement in 1920, made by the four principal World War I Allied Powers, gave Britain the mandate for Palestine and Iraq.

my living in Israel, I met here a delegation of Jews from Działoszyce. This was in the late 20s, when they came to Israel and purchased farming settlements for members of the Zionist organization. Among those in the delegation were Awisz Grundman, Moher, and others. They came, but I don't know what happened to them.

After the Balfour Declaration, the town's residents joined together to form different political parties: Mizrachi [Orthodox Zionist Party], Ha-Mizrachi Hatzair [religious Zionist youth], the General Zionists, and even the youth of Agudas Yisroel [non-Zionist Orthodox party]. There was a general excitement for the redemption of the Land. And, of course, a variety of activities began in the socio-cultural arena. These activities were fruitful. The result was that the youth began preparing to emigrate to Eretz Yisroel. I was among the first pioneers, who emigrated in the month of May, 1920. We came straight from Działoszyce to Eretz Yisroel. There was no need for visas then, except for identification documents, and when we arrived, there wasn't anything except diseases. Amazingly, I found two people from Działoszyce who came before me. One of them was named Jakubowicz, and the other was the son of a scholar in our town. The two are no longer alive.

This was the account about Zionism in our dear town Działoszyce.

Life in the Town

Now I will dwell a bit on describing the simple Jewish life and institutions—the community, the religious courts, the kosher butcher, etc. Everything is a blur to me, because in 1914, World War I broke out, and I was only thirteen then. I was orphaned then by my mother, may peace be upon her, and I wandered to Olkusz, Kielce, since I had relatives there. One thing I remember now, while writing this, and this has to do with the Zionist youth of the time. This was in 1910 or 1911, when the Zionist organizations decided to hold a memorial for Benjamin Ze'ev Herzl [Theodor Herzl, founder of the World Zionist Organization] in the main synagogue. The rabbi of the town at the time, it seems to me, was Rabbi Staszewski, hi"d. He did not permit holding the memorial ceremony in the synagogue. A great commotion arose, but the Zionists got the keys to the synagogue from Arele, the shames [sexton], and the memorial took place.

As I said, my memory is weak, but what is engraved in my memory is the Jewish life of the town. Every household was a fortress for yidishkeyt [Jewishness]. Here, I remember the different kinds of shtiblekh [small Hasidic houses of prayer] and the highly elaborate main synagogue decorated with wonderful art. By the way, my grandfather had a Stätt (an assigned seat) in that synagogue. I remember that the besmedresh was always humming because of the many people praying and studying Torah. They took a brief break only for lunch.

I have a vision of our town after lunch in the summer, from my time, of course. People used to go out a bit shpatzirin (to stroll) and enjoy the smell of the fields. There were those who walked to the stara rzeka [old river] and to Chmielów to Anka's. Among those walking were also the students of the besmedresh, dressed in shortened frocks. There were also some young people of this type, progressive youth, caught up in the Enlightenment, who took with them bikhlekh [booklets] by I. L. Peretz and other books, even some by the French author Michel Mufson. And mothers with their little children came out into the streets; they went out to buy themselves egg bagels and small matses. I particularly recall the different names of things in Yiddish, because all of this is fixed in my memory as such. Before evening, of course, for the afternoon service—all of the workers, craftsmen, sellers who stood in the market with their *shtekelekh* [small sticks (small items to sell)] left and went to pray at the afternoon and evening services and to hear a sermon, if by chance a preacher had come to town.

On Thursday afternoon, people began returning home again, among them my father, *hi"d*, who made his living in the distant and nearby towns in the area. They would return also from the market in Skalbmierz, the sellers of cattle, feathers, leather, and more. Housewives prepared for Shabes. This was on regular weekdays. Friday afternoon, before Shabes, the preparation became very serious. Everything was done at a fast pace. Housewives cooked and baked for Shabes. On Friday afternoon at one o'clock, the shrill of the siren was heard, a signal that it was time to get ready to go to the bathhouse. Who didn't go to the *mikve*? It seems to me that no one from the town was absent. In particular, no one missed going to the steam bath. The Jews bathed, sweated, and appeared really like "the herd that slipped down Mount Gilead." Everything was done to honor the Shabes. The flow of people to the synagogue on Friday evening at dusk was a sight to be seen. The old and the young went as one. Whoever hasn't seen Shabes evening in Działoszyce has never seen anything so amazing in their life.

To everyone, whether rich or poor, the holiness and restfulness of Shabes were well known. Everything shone brightly, the *kidesh* [blessing over the wine] and the songs burst out from every house and courtyard. Hasids, on Shabes night after eating, went to the communal table of any Hasidic *rebbe* who happened to be visiting our town. They went to hear Torah from his lips. They also went to the local Hasidic *rebbe*, Rabbi Epsztajn, *hi"d*, the son of the *rebbe* from Neustadt, the grandson of "the Good Jew" and brother-in-law of the Hasidic *rebbe* of Komarno, *zts"l* [may the memory of a righteous person be blessed]. In our town, there were very active Hasidim. They would travel to visit Hasidic *rebbe*s, and these *rebbe*s would also visit Działoszyce frequently. The *rebbe*s Reb Motele, Reb Nachumcze, Reb Mojsze Lejbele, and Reb Jakób Lejbele were the Hasidic *rebbe*s of the Trisk lineage. Among those who lodged with my grandfather, Joel Kołatacz, *z"l*, was the *rebbe* from Pińczów and also the *rebbe* from Chęciny, as I recall. My father was also a Chęciny Hasid, and when I was a youth, I traveled with him to visit the *rebbe*s.

Up to here is the chapter on Hasidism.

A Shabes morning

On Shabes morning, I don't think there was another place where Shabes was felt like it was with us. Peace and calm hovered over the town. The streets and the alleys were empty. Only the flow to the synagogue continued. It was possible to see only the janitors sweeping the sidewalks and nothing more. There was complete quiet. After prayers, again the same picture was revealed—*kidesh*, a meal, songs, etc. And sleeping on Shabes, that was such a pleasure! Even about this, they were adamant. After they got up from sleeping, there were those who went to visit family or went out for a walk. But most went to the *besmedresh* to study "Ethics of the Fathers" or to hear a sermon. After that, of course, came the "third meal" and again songs, evening prayers, lighting the Havdole candle [signifying the end of Shabes]. Life went from a holy pleasantness to the non-holy, to work and to toil.

My Town

Stormy waves wash over you.
I yearned for you
Cruelly, your roots were pulled out
And I won't be able to see you any more.

From your springs, the saturation of man
Great waters surrounded you
Which transformed into rivers of blood.

Your treasures are forever hidden.
Desecrated are the synagogue and the study house
Ohhh, God, don't be silent,
The cemetery was desecrated at the hands of the cursed Nazis.

My mother's name was erased from her gravestone
It was destroyed and silenced, and left for ruin
Mother, your disgrace I will remember.

The cemetery of all generations
Gravestones are bent over the rib of the oak.
Dwellers of dust, great ones of the caves,
Have been uprooted at the hands of foe, the great disaster.

Gazing at me during my sorrow,
Demolished and destroyed
Is the *ohel* [structure over grave] of Reb Yossi,
May he be exalted and praised.

About my grandfather Reb Jakób Rafałowicz, *z"l*

It is my wish to recall pleasant memories, from my days of youth, about my grandfather Reb Jakób Rafałowicz. Although I walked alongside him for only a short while, memories remain with me of his honest and worthy behavior. A few memories deserve to be re-awakened in my heart while I recall his image. I cannot forget the pleasure that I got from traveling with him to the Chęciny *rebbe*, and the experiences of that Shabes I have not forgotten. I also remember the elderly Jews of Działoszyce from fifty or more years ago—the witty, the learned, and the strong in their faith. They prayed and studied, hoped, and lived a modest life. They had the Torah, the holy Shabes, and the joy of holidays and festivals. In the midst of all this, the life of my grandfather, *z"l*, was intertwined. Every morning, he was up early to go to the *besmedresh*, and before prayers, he was immersed in the Mishne [Jewish code of law] or Psalms. He sent his sons to study in the Gur [Góra Kalwaria] and Radzymin yeshivas. He gave his daughters to marry into respectable families. His financial situation was fairly stable; he was in the business of trading crops with nearby and distant landowners of the area and was beloved among the circles of businessmen in our town. May his memory be blessed.

God forbid that I neglect to praise my grandmother, Surele. She was a devoted wife to Grandfather and modest in her lifestyle. She reached an advanced old age but was caught by the cursed Nazis, and her fate was like that of all the Jews of Działoszyce, *hi"d*.

In Memory of Masza Rozenblum of the Kołatacz Family

Here, I turn my thoughts to and plunge into the very distant past. My faithful journey, which I made in a cart through dangerous obstacles, from my home to Sosnowiec and from there to the border, on the way to Eretz Yisroel, stands before my eyes.

It was the end of World War I, during clear spring days. At the time, it occurred to her to tell me something, clear and wise, with absoluteness and confidence. She said, in her native tongue, "Motel, you will not go to the Polish army! We will find some way out of Działoszyce and get permission to pass through the passport control station. This shall be!"

And so it was; she arranged my travel with a passport, and I dressed as a girl. We left town in Reb Lejbele Ptasznik's wagon, if my memory is not mistaken, on the way to Będzin-Sosnowiec, in order to pass the border next to Katowice. She accompanied me, together with Grandma Marida Kołatacz, *z"l*. Of course, the route and the disguise were dangerous for the three of us, and that is how we, with God's help, reached the appointed place, the Polish-German border.

From the mists of the past, there is a clear memory of my last farewell. My aunt said to me the following words: "Never regret that you are going away from us. Everything will be for the best, and God willing, we will meet again sometime." Tears were in her eyes because of the great emotions, and as if she wanted to diminish the distress, she added, "After all, you are going to Eretz Yisroel. And soon, we, too, will join you." She always longed for Eretz Yisroel. But she was unable to fulfill her dream. There are those who dream about a nice life, and then fate intervenes, and the whole thing is turned upside down. Such was her fate, my dear aunt.

When I bring to mind her image before me, it is the image that shone from her beautiful eyes, which all the afflictions of time and fate could not remove from her. She hoped and believed in the light emanating from the Supreme Source, and she succeeded in hearing from me how I was managing in Israel but not in seeing me. In the midst of the days of her flowering and her youth, the thread of her life was cut.

For a long time I have wanted to honor you but was unable to do so. Now, I will memorialize your name in the holy book of our town Działoszyce. May your memory be blessed.

Translated from the Hebrew by Roger Kaplan

The Beginning of the Enlightenment Period in the Town (pp. 56-59)

(As We Remember It)

Josef and Baruch Blat

Enlightenment penetrated Jewish homes on the edges of Europe and Poland back in the nineteenth century, but only light echoes of it reached the town of Działoszyce, which lay in a remote corner, cut off from the larger world, without means of transportation, even without paved or unpaved roads connecting the villages in the area. A change in values, which began among Jews all over the world, touched only those certain special individuals who succeeded in leaving the narrow domain of our town and managed to glimpse the changes that were occurring in the Jewish street.

In 1911, about three years before the beginning of World War I, the first sparks of Enlightenment reached our town. A few young men, members of the *besmedresh* [house of study], who, day and night, were immersed in the study of *Shisha S'darim* [the six Orders of the Mishne] and verses, began to glance upon the hidden in the Hebrew secular books of Mapu, Lilienblum, Pinsker, Shedal, Smolenskin, and others. After having a glimpse, an intense hunger for Enlightenment took hold of them; there was a desire by these youth who were thirsty for knowledge to broaden their horizons. Zionism was foremost and naturally an inseparable part of the cultural flow. They wanted to delve into the Zionist idea, the idea of the liberation of their people from its two-thousand-year-old exile to become an independent people settled on their land in Zion. Included in this group of young men were Awramcze Frydman, Aron Blat, Icek Tenenwurcel, Salat, and Moszek Szklarczyk. They were active in the organizing of clubs. Meetings for these clubs took place in our house, because my father, Reb Abram Moszek Blat, was often out of town on business, and there was no one who would interfere with us holding the activities in our large apartment. In addition to the cultural activity, we began collecting funds for the Jewish National Fund [JNF], the fund whose purpose was to redeem the land of Eretz Yisroel from the hands of its occupiers. Members of this group mentioned above placed bowls among the other charity bowls in the synagogues in town during holidays on the eve of Yom Kippur and Hoshanah-Rabah [seventh day of Sukes] to collect contributions of cash for the JNF.

The need for information from various books was felt in the activity of the clubs promoting culture and Enlightenment among the youth. And thus, the idea arose to establish a library, which would acquire books in the fields of science, history, and the *belles-lettres* [literature] and would loan them to the youth whose eyes had just opened and who drank in the words of the authors no matter what the subject. A committee was organized for the task of creating the library. In a similar manner, leaders from each of the many groups in the town were selected. A large bowl, a ballot box of sorts, was placed on the table, and the names of the candidates for the committee were put in the bowl, and I, Baruch Blat, being the youngest, pulled out the slips of paper. And in this way, the first committee of the library was chosen.

Even though those of the old generation, the *shtiblekh* Hasidim [who attended the small houses of prayer], opposed the young people's work in the library, at clubs, and for JNF collections, that didn't stop them; they continued their work with great success.

But in the meanwhile, in 1914, World War I broke out, in which the nations of Europe were thrown into turbulence, and even the Kingdom of Poland, occupied by the Stalinist Russian authorities, was not exempt. Most of the youth hid in various hiding places; some of them were drafted into the army, and the work of the clubs spreading Enlightenment ceased. The group's desire to do something for Enlightenment and Zionism came to a halt; only the great desire of an individual to keep his family whole during this insane period remained.

In 1918, the war ended. Poland became independent. In liberated Europe, many new independent nations arose. On October 2, 1917, Lord Balfour, in the name of Great Britain, proclaimed the historical declaration of the creation of a national homeland for the persecuted Jewish people. Great happiness engulfed world Jewry, and this happiness and joy were felt even in Poland. When the news reached Działoszyce, the rabbi from Kutno, J.I. [Jechiel Isaiah] Trunk, one of the Mizrachi leaders who came to our town, spread the news and declared in a general meeting at the synagogue the approaching of the Messiah and the beginning of Redemption.[1]

Immediately after this, an organizational framework for the Zionist Union was created in the town, and its active members were Icek Kołatacz, Josef Blat, Dawid Skóra, Pejsach Sternberg, Herszel Kopeć, Alter Spokojny, Moszek Groswald, and Dubiński.

The work was expanded. All types of Zionist youth movements were created. Professional associations for workers were established. All of these were the direct result of the initial work on the spread of Enlightenment, which had begun before World War I.

Commerce and Labor

The economic life of the Jews in the town was usually stable. On the one hand, there were the prominent well-to-do Jews, respected businessmen and owners of large estates and mid-sized agricultural land, such as the Szental, Szwimer, Spiro, and Moszkowski families. On the other hand, there were many minor craftsmen who made their living honorably from their work, whatever it might have been. There were never local beggars in town; if beggars happened to appear at doorsteps, they were wanderers who came to the town from other places.

The wealthy Jews used to establish houses of prayer and *minyans* [quorums of ten needed for prayer] in their private homes. The general masses, the small businessmen, and various craftsmen prayed in the *bes hamedresh* and the *beysakneses*.[2] Each group of followers of a particular Hasidic religious leader (*Admor*) prayed in its own Hasidic *shtibl*.

---

[1] The Mizrachi [Orthodox Zionist party] believed that settlement in Eretz Yisroel would be the beginning of Redemption.

[2] According to survivors, the *beysakneses* [main synagogue] was only used for Shabes and holiday prayers and for large assemblies, while the smaller *bes hamedresh* [house of prayer] was also used for Torah study and for weekday prayers. Both were Orthodox, not Hasidic.

Father's House

My father, Reb Abram Moszek Blat, was involved in commerce and in the export of coral necklaces. He used to travel to different countries in Europe to import from them the needed raw materials to create and market the finished product. Many Jews from our town made their living from such a unique light industry. Our brother Aron, the oldest in father's house, used to organize the making of necklaces; he employed many women, young and old, in threading the coral, and afterward, he would send the finished product abroad. They would bring the raw materials from Czechoslovakia and later on from Częstochowa, Poland.

The Grodzisk *Shtibl*

On the first Slikhes Shabes [Shabes before the High Holy Days on which prayers of repentance are recited], about two hundred people used to pray in the Grodzisk *shtibl* [*shtibl* for followers of the Grodzisk *rebbe*]. I remember that close to the *shtibl* there lived a baker who sold fresh hot pretzels at midnight before the beginning of the *slikhes* prayers. And we young people, what did we do? We would lower the sash of the long robes we wore; with joy and happiness, we would thread the pretzels through the sashes, and we then walked toward the prayer house. The many hoodlums who trailed behind us, running in the midst of the crowds there, used to remove the pretzels from the sashes and eat them, until only the empty sashes remained in our hands.

The *shtibl* leader, Reb Arysz, made the arrangements for the *slikhes* prayers, lit many candles, and welcomed Reb Alter Jakób as our *shaliakh tzibur* [prayer leader]. He was gracious, with a pleasant voice, and he would make a plea to the Ruler of the World both in his name and in the name of all of the community. After he passed away, Reb Alter Ptasznik continued in this role in the synagogue. His prayers were very pleasant, even though in regular speech, he stuttered.

After prayers, there was a meal fit for a king, with alcoholic beverages, all sorts of meat, goose, fowl, and more. Whoever didn't partake of this meal missed great happiness in his life.

Baruch Blat's Story

In 1912, a special generator to produce electricity and lighting for the town was installed in the Wdowiński flour mill. Only a handful of rich people in town were connected to the electricity. The electricity did reach the synagogue for lighting. The wealthy Karol Rajzfeld contributed and donated a chandelier that was attached to the ceiling of the synagogue. At the same time, an overhaul of the synagogue was conducted after the prayers. They renovated, plastered, and painted anew the walls with eye-pleasing artistic drawings on the ceiling. At the conclusion of the work, a housewarming with a large public celebration was held.

The great cantor and opera singer from Lwów, a native of our town, Ignacy Mann, was invited to the celebration and performed in a concert of cantorial music. The whole town—men, women, and children—came to see and hear the town's native son at his best. All of the Jewish residents in our town who knew him when he was just a small, miserable two-year-old boy experienced his pleasant and strong voice, the echoes of which reached great distances.

Josef Blat's Story

In 1922, in the month of Shvat, it snowed like it never had before. The snow covered all of the small structures and the roads, reaching one and a half meters or more. I, already engaged, was to become a godparent at the circumcision for my brother-in-law's son, who was born in Charsznica. It was very cold, and to get to Charsznica from Działoszyce, a distance of thirty kilometers, was just about impossible; yet I couldn't refuse this honor, because according to the tradition of our ancestors, the groom is to be the *sondek* [godfather] for the circumcised child of the bride's family.

It got colder in the meantime; barely anyone could be seen in the snow-covered area. Despite this, I went out onto the street and looked for a way to travel. Visibility was impaired, and I was barely able to drag my feet through the deep snow. Suddenly, I saw before me a prominent wealthy man of the town, Reb Szyja Srebrny. And since I had always liked him and it was normal from him to pinch my cheeks, he asked why I was so upset and why I was so surprisingly walking in this horrible weather. I told him what was happening, and with that, I ended by saying that I had to get to Charsznica that night.

And he turned to me, saying, "Don't be so worried, my friend; see, you found me and now you will be able to get there." I could not believe what he was saying. I thought to myself, what kind of crazy guy would take his horses out in this snowy hell? But Szyja Srebrny, who sensed my skepticism, turned to me, stopping me, and said, "Come to the market square at two o'clock, and you will be able to get there."

At the appointed hour, I went out, and I saw before me a winter carriage hitched to a pair of horses that resembled lions. On the carriage bench sat a driver, a mustached non-Jew, with his mustache and even his eyebrows covered with snow. He invited me to get on, handed me a fur cloth and felt boots. I wrapped myself in the fur, I put on the felt boots, which went up above my thighs, and then it became clear to me from what the non-Jew was telling me, that at twelve o'clock midnight, he had to meet the next train from Charsznica.

Srebrny consequently sent the carriage to bring him from the station in Miechów to Działoszyce.[1] And this is how I happened to have this one-time opportunity to travel [to Charsznica].

We left. All around us the road was invisible; there was only snow and more snow. The telephone poles were covered up to half their height. The driver was unable to restrain the horses. They trotted wherever they wanted, and only after eleven hours of traveling, we arrived very late at night in Miechów.

I didn't go to my grandfather's, Reb Jakób Icek Blat, because of the late hour. I went to Reb Dawid Binem's hostel, whose lights shone from it and lit up the darkness on Charsznica Street. The driver sipped a few cups of brandy and happily ate a piece of sausage. I also didn't sit idle, and after a short rest, we were on the move again, and within four hours, we arrived in Charsznica.

---

[1] Miechów was two-thirds of the way to Charsznica.

All the guests who gathered to celebrate the circumcision looked at us as if we were crazy. I myself was very proud of the bold mission, to make a dangerous journey in the snow and all, without being able to see a thing, in forty degree cold, alone, just to be the godfather. What's wrong with that?

Translated from the Hebrew by Roger Kaplan

There Once Was A Town (pp. 60–61)

Chawa Karmioł (Rozenfrucht)

Działoszyce was, at the beginning of this century and until World War I, a small town with a large Jewish population and a few Christians.

Among the Jews, a few wealthy ones stood out, like Moszkowski, Przeworski, Rajzfeld, Spiro, Szental, and other families.

Moszek Szental owned a few estates in the villages, one of them was Buszków Raba and the second was Buszków Zuta. Hundreds of hectares of land belonged to him, as well as horses and work animals, used mostly to work the fields. He also had a flour mill, where area farmers would grind their flour and rye. Moszek Szental had three sons, Gerszon, Arysz, and Szmul, who followed in their father's footsteps but were great misers who loved solitude. They weren't friends with the town's people and lived their lives without being involved in the Jewish communal life or activities.

A short while after the end of World War I, a band of thieves made their way through the area. Headed by the well-known thief, Kuzin, they brought fright and fear among the town's wealthy residents. Alter Szental was murdered in one of the robberies.

During the war, the Russian army didn't make its way to Działoszyce; it was stopped in the area of Pińczów and Busko. The Austrians conquered and held the town. They treated us like family. In their eyes, our place was like a village farm, and they would say that the rolled straw smelled like tobacco. In fact, sometimes we would dry the straw there and roll cigarettes from the straw to smoke.

My father, Reb Szlama Rozenfrucht, whom everybody called "Szlama the Lerer" [teacher], had a school. He would teach Tanakh [Scriptures], Hebrew, nature, math, and more at the school. My father would study by himself; he never finished any schooling, neither secondary nor higher education. All of his knowledge he gleaned from books that he read himself.

Jewish Działoszyce was involved in a wide variety of commerce. Textiles, precious stones, the field's harvest, store supplies, various goods, flour, and eggs. Most of the Jews would wander the villages selling to the landowners different goods and buying from them various crops, chickens, eggs, leather, etc.

In addition, different craftsmen lived in the town—shoemakers, tailors, carpenters, cart makers, and others. Among the cart makers, there were those who would smuggle things that were in demand. I remember three bakers who baked bread, *challah*, and before Pesakh, *matse*, too. They were called Nachman the Baker, Moszek the Baker, and Judka the Baker.

There were also tailors and shoemakers who worked for the landowners in the area, and the landowners would pay them for their work with the harvest from the fields, dairy products, chickens, and eggs.

From among the bead sellers, I remember the Szlamowicz and Blat families. They would bring the raw materials from abroad and employ workers, especially women and young girls, to thread the beads.

A number of fires broke out in the town. The first fire that I remember happening in Działoszyce was in the middle of the nineteenth century, and I heard a lot about it from my parents. The second fire broke out in 1906. The flames began at Nachman the Baker's and burned nearly one half of the town, because most of the houses were built of wood. The fire stopped near Arysz Szental's house; only part of Kraków Street was left unharmed. The third fire broke out during World War I. After the fire, an epidemic of typhus broke out and took many lives.

Now I would like to describe the beginning of the Enlightenment period in Działoszyce. My father, Szlama Rozenfrucht, *z"l*, studied in *kheyders* [small Jewish religious schools], as was the custom. When he was a teenager, these studies didn't satisfy him, so he continued his studies at the *besmedresh* [house of study], and there he immersed himself in studying Talmud and *poskim* [Halakhic adjudicators] with the rest of the Torah students until his wedding. But secretly, without anyone knowing it, he would take a peek at "external" books and thus enriched his knowledge with science and other languages, in addition to the Hebrew language, which he knew fluently.

At the same time, he would read different newspapers. He had a subscription to *Hatsefirah* [The Dawn], which came out in Warsaw and was edited by Chaim Zelig Słonimski.

In the village Dziekanowice, there lived a landowner by the name of Rafał Herc Spiro, who had a son named Szyja and a daughter named Dwosia. My father used to teach them Hebrew and other Jewish subjects, like Torah and Mishne. In the village Buszków, he used to teach the same things to members of the Szental family. And in this way, education penetrated many homes in the town and the area. The habits and way of life of the Jews of the past generation became a bit old-fashioned. Something from the progress and education of the world slowly, slowly made its way into the remote cities in Poland. My father, *z"l*, spread the idea of Enlightenment among his friends. And he had great influence upon such families as Meryn, Rotenberg, Książski and Alter Profesorski.

Finally, I want to describe the activities of the drama societies that operated at different times and in different forms. Usually, an outside troupe of actors would appear in town, but sometimes they included a few residents in their show in different roles. Dawid Skóra was especially active in this field; he excelled in theater more than others, until a much later period. He succeeded in organizing a drama club made up only of town residents. I remember a few shows they put on: *The Jewish Heart, The Jewish Soul, David's Fiddle*, and *Shulamit*. The shows ran in the Firemen's Hall, in Yiddish, and most of the Jews of the town frequented them.

These are the things I managed to recall from my memories about Jewish life in our town, Działoszyce, most of whose sons and daughters, including my family, perished in the Great Holocaust at the hands of the cursed Nazis.

Translated from the Hebrew by Roger Kaplan

From the Mouths of the Elders (p. 62)

Izrael Dov Skóra

When I was still a child, I heard from the elderly different stories about the greatness of *Margrabia* [Margrave, a title of nobility] Wielopolski. What a rich man he was, how he loved Jews, that he had one hundred estates (*sto majątków*). He sold one of them just so people wouldn't say that he had one hundred estates but rather ninety-nine, because that was more modest and sounded better. He hated the *goyim* [gentiles], and when he died abroad, his bones were brought through Działoszyce on their way to his ancestral graves in Chroberz. His coffin wasn't brought to the church, but rather it was placed next to the synagogue. The famous cantor, Majer Ziegelschmidt (whom the wealthy families of the town—the Przeworskis, the Moszkowskis, the Rzędowskis, and others—brought especially from Kraków for this 'joyous' ceremony) recited Psalms, *yizkor* [memorial] prayers, El Mole Rakhamim [God of Compassion], and *kadesh* [mourner's prayer].

They also told me that noblemen, the sons of the *margrabia*, publicly thanked the Jews for the respect they had shown the deceased man.

A few years later, when I was twenty years old, I happened to be in the voluminous library of Władysław Woźniakowski. This *goy* [non-Jew], who was an intellectual man, had a rich library with valuable books. While skimming through some books, I found one thick book that was a collection of periodicals that were published in Warsaw at the beginning of the 80s of the previous century. I found something in it about the incident that happened in Działoszyce that I mentioned above. The article confirmed what I heard from those who were present at the "ceremony," but in a different form, a bit more understandable.

The story is that a few years before the January 1863 insurrection broke out, in 1861, the Russian authorities knew about the restlessness and the Poles' plans to rebel. They tried to prevent it in different ways, and one of them was to appoint Margrave Wielopolski as head of the civil administration in Poland. Aleksander Wielopolski was known as a Polish patriot, a moderate politician who loved peace and was against the rebellion, because he knew that the rebellion could bring destruction and ruin to his country. But the hot-tempered of those days saw him as a traitor.

The appointment of Wielopolski didn't bring any support to the czar, Alexander II, who himself was a moderate man, an exceptional person among all the czars. The insurrection broke out, the margrave fled to Switzerland and died there. When his family, in accordance with his will, brought his bones to his ancestral gravesite in Chroberz, not a single Pole and only a small number of the nobility and family came to his funeral.

When the funeral procession passed through the town of Działoszyce, bells didn't ring, and the Catholic priest refused to appear. Only near the synagogue did the funeral procession pause, where Dr. Steurmark said prayers for the deceased. The first words he said were from Jeremiah 22:10: "Don't weep for the dead, neither bemoan him." And after that came the cantor's prayers and appropriate remarks by those present.

Translated from the Hebrew by Roger Kaplan

The town from Jankielówka – a view from the cemetery

Statue of Kościuszko – Peddlers in the market square

Municipal offices, church in the distance

A view of the town from Woźniakowski Hill

The market square during weekdays

Memorial service by Cantor Reb Moszek Śpiewak

Part II:

Between Two World Wars

The Jews of Działoszyce (pp. 69–75)

Abraham Langer

When I came to the town from Bendin [Będzin] in 1915, it was under Austrian occupation, and the authorities decided to construct a *kolejka,* or narrow-gauge railway. The mud in the streets was replaced by a paved way. The hooting of the first train to arrive from Miechów brought all the town together amid general jubilation. Indeed, riding in a vehicle without horses was a remarkable experience for a long time to come. The Austrians also built a boardwalk the whole length of the Kraków Road to the railway station. Some Jews built coal stores, which had never existed in town before and now provided a living for the cart drivers who delivered coal to the houses.

In those days half the Jews of the town lived off the neighboring villages, which they regularly visited to buy grain, foodstuffs, and milk produce, selling them all they needed. During the war, they traded in food, flour, and buckwheat, which they peddled from knapsacks on their backs, bringing back tobacco and other wares from as far away as Kraków. Cigarette-making, spirits and soap manufacture also began. Some strong-arm young men also engaged in smuggling goods into Galicia. They did large-scale business, earned well, and helped many poor people. They kept an eye open for any mistreatment of Jews in the region and put a stop to it.

The Joint Distribution Committee had an office and provided food and clothing for the needy, besides engaging in general hygienic measures. Its representative was a Jew from Będzin named Weissler. The town was full of refugees with whom the townsfolk lived well. They mutually aided one another.

In 1918, following Polish independence, some rioting members of the Haller Forces (Poles who had returned from the United States) took away Jankiel Skopicki's gold watch and cut his beard off. When Hilel, Jankiel's son, aged eighteen, was informed, he caught them one in each hand and simply banged them together one against the other.

My uncle, Wolf Kuzmer, was a barber-surgeon and what was called a Nikolai soldier (who had served twenty-five years in the Russian army). He was very hospitable and treated a number of diseases. He brought up my sister from the age of eight and married her off in due course. I myself maintained my mother and two sisters and opened my own barber shop.

When Poland became independent in 1918, arms were distributed and Jews received some, but young Polish ruffians attacked them and shot Zalman Cudzynowski. There was a typhoid epidemic that year, and many people died. Both joy and sorrow were widely shared. Bridegroom and bride were conducted in separate processions to the canopy with music, song, and dance. Everybody came. When a Torah Scroll was taken to the synagogue, there were eight days of festivity.

Before the Shavuos festival in 1919, the son-in-law of the slaughterer Moszek Benjamin committed suicide because he could not bring himself to learn the slaughtering trade.

This chapter is reprinted from pp. 20–22 of the English section of the original Działoszyce Yizkor Book, with minor changes.

Founders and members of the Khevre Biker Khoylim, Nichum Aveylim (society for visiting the sick, consoling mourners) were: Aszer Moszenberg, chairman, Herszel Skóra, Bencion Bejski, Josef Kamelgarten, Zyskind Jakubowicz, Benjamin Pińczewski, Malc, Koźma, Josek Bratkiewicz, and Chuna Edelist.

There was a cloudburst and a flood in 1936, beginning one Shabes afternoon. The town was cut off for eight days. Many houses were simply washed away, and my aunt, Uncle Wolf's wife, was drowned. The Polish Government granted loans to rebuild the destroyed houses.

Icze Rubin, the Jewish deputy mayor, was a handsome, elegant Gerer Hassid. He had a *mezuze* on his official door and told Jews not to remove their hats when they entered the municipal building. His home was always full of people who came for advice or favors. He was the warmest and most cordial person I ever met. When regulations requiring lavatories and dustbins were issued, he provided them for the poor folk and took the money from the rich. Once I complained to him that the police were troubling me. He advised me to collect the money for a fine, and he accompanied me to the district offices in Pińczów. The road was blocked, but he insisted on his rights as mayor of Działoszyce, and we were allowed to pass. In Pińczów he reported the misbehavior of the police. The fine was returned, and the police were instructed by telephone to leave me alone.

There were four Jewish councilors—Aszer Moszenberg, Herszel Skóra, Bencion Bejski, and Aron Retman—who always protected Jewish interests and saw to it that no harm was done to the Jewish inhabitants.

There was also a Gmiles Khesed Fund [interest free loan fund] which gave loans without interest. The Jewish firemen were: Lejbele Ptasznik, Majer Kompot [Kamrat?], Joska Bratkiewicz, Hercke Czosnek, Izrael Juda Prasa, and Izrael Jakób Waserman. When a fire broke out, the latter would blow a resounding blast on his trumpet. But if anyone asked him, "Where's the fire?" he would answer, "That's my affair."

From the Old Country (pp. 76–77)

Chaim Szwimer

Bandits rob the town. A Jewish self-defense organization is established.

It was in 1918, several weeks after the liberation of Poland. Gangs were organized in the region of Kielce that attacked landowners and their estates, robbed people on the roads, and sometimes also killed them.[1] Many people became the victims of these gangs, both Jews and non-Jews. In our area, people even knew the leaders of these robbers. But the worst gang was that of the bandit Kazun. Various legends were told about him. One said that he was a patron of the poor; he took from the rich and divided it up among the poor; a second said that he was literally a person who could transform himself—a person with seven faces. He couldn't be caught because he changed his outer appearance over the course of months, and because of this, the police had shot and killed not an insignificant number of people. As soon as they saw a suspicious looking person, they shot him, not wanting to meet up with the live Kazun.

Kazun, however, stood up to them, and in a short time shot quite a number of policemen.

It was an evening in the fall. The stores were already closed. Here and there, a restaurant and a butcher shop were still open. The street lamps burned with a weak light as they do in a small town. The streets were empty; one rarely saw a person pass by. Suddenly a noise was heard, and, as if from under the earth, several wagons with bandits arrived. They made a circle in the market square and opened fire from the wagons, so that the whole town resounded with the shots. There was terrible panic. The few people who had just been in the street fled and looked for protection somewhere.

The wagons placed themselves in the middle of the market square. The bandits jumped down. And one of them called out in a loud voice, "*Biedni ludzie, schodźcie się!*" [Poor people, come unite!] At this invitation, all the Polish janitors, butchers, underworld characters, and crooks who carried knives came out and went with the gang to plunder.

Szymon Kołatacz was the first to be robbed. They took whole wagons of material from there. Then they went after all the rich Jews, robbing the stores and the apartments, all within a few hours.

I was standing in the house of Mendel Frydman; a little further down, several people ran out into the street yelling, "Bandits! Murderers!" They thought that with their yelling they would frighten Kazun. In response, the bandits opened fire. The people quickly fled. Soon a victim fell, a water-carrier who was standing perhaps a meter away from me. She did not even manage to let out a groan. The bullet hit her right in the head.

---

[1] After World War I, Poland, which had been previously partitioned among Austro-Hungary, Prussia, and Russia, was reconstituted as a nation. It evidently took awhile for the new government to gain firm control.

As I was going home at three o'clock in the middle of the night, I saw many stores that had been robbed. In the store of the Cukierman brothers, everything had been emptied out. Only remnants of valuable materials were lying about on the street.

The next day, the police, which had only recently been organized (for the most part, they had little worth, because every day, policemen would shoot one another, being unable to handle their weapons), together with the Jews of the town, looked for the stolen merchandise, but barely anything was found.

Right after the attack, a Jewish self-defense organization was formed; it obtained a few guns. While they were walking with these guns, which they had just received and had not yet managed to load, Poles shot at them and seriously wounded Zalman Cudzynowski, who lay in a hospital in Kraków for two weeks and then died.

And thus was founded and dissolved the Jewish self-defense organization in Działoszyce, which existed only for minutes. Some time later, when the police were better organized, they fought against the gangs.

Kazun, the leader, was killed. People said that he had been wounded in Radom, and a Jewish doctor who had been treating him turned him over to the police. Somebody else said that a policeman shot and killed him at the Skarżysko train station, shooting him through both pockets of his military coat with two revolvers.

Thus ended two legends, the legend of Jewish self-defense in Działoszyce, which cost the town four victims, and the legend of the bandit Kazun, who cast fear on the surrounding population, in general, and on the Jews, in particular.

Translated from the Yiddish by Sheva Zucker

A Jewish Island in a Gentile Sea (pp. 78–86)

David Shlomi

Between the two World Wars, Działoszyce was a country town in the Kielce District, without famous rabbis or wealthy men or outstanding leaders—just a small Jewish center where people made a living and lived a decent family life. They depended on the surrounding peasants who came to market on Tuesday and Friday. On Monday morning many Jews set out for neighbouring markets and fairs and came back on Thursday evening to prepare fresh goods and spend Shabes with their families. Wholesale textile and leather merchants sold their goods to retailers, stall-keepers, tailors, and shoemakers over the weekend. But the craftsmen were hard at work all week long: Tailors, shoemakers, metal workers, hatmakers, bookbinders, bakers, tinsmiths, goldsmiths, barbers, etc. There was usually plenty to do, but it was hard to make a living for the pay was low. The tanners had a workshop and residential quarter on their own. Shoes were manufactured chiefly for Upper Silesia. There were soap makers, stocking makers, oil makers, etc. Some 85 percent of the population were Jews, and most houses, shops, workshops, and factories belonged to them. The non-Jews lived on the outskirts and were mostly craftsmen, local or government officials. But the town was administered by Poles, though there were several Jews on the Town Council; the deputy mayor was a Jew, and there were many Jews in the Volunteer Fire Brigade. Most of them were highly observant, and the rest lived according to tradition. Only a few of the younger generation were affected by heterodex or modernist ideas.

Conflict of Beliefs and Opinions

As elsewhere in Poland, much of their spare time was spent on the internal conflict of beliefs and opinions. Here the war was waged between Hasidim and Zionists. None of the various other groups were represented, except by two Communists, one of whom went to Russia and was apparently liquidated in due course, while the other came to pray in the synagogue at the festivals. The observant were of two kinds. Some spent all their time at prayer or study of the Torah, while others made it their business to combat all Zionist activities on account of their secular character and their desire to set up a Jewish State in Eretz Yisroel before the Messiah had come. These were mostly Gerer [Góra Kalwaria] Hasidim and members of Agudas Yisroel [non-Zionist Orthodox Party]. Their political opponents were the Zionists and Mizrahi members [Orthodox Zionist Party].

The Zionists were young and youngish people who set up a Zionist group immediately after the Balfour Declaration (Szlama Gertler, Icek Kołatacz, Hercel Karmioł, Josek Alter, Josek Targownik, Josek Tauman, Izrael Ber Skóra, etc.). They had a club in the Talmud Torah Building where there was also a Public Library, and in it they

---

This chapter is reprinted from pp. 9–13 of the English section of the original Działoszyce Yizkor Book, with minor changes.

held meetings and discussed Zionist and Jewish developments. They also conducted their specifically Zionist celebrations and activities.

The Mizrahi and Tseirei Mizrahi [Mizrachi Youth] were also represented, the leaders of the former being Pejsach Sternberg, Bendet Majerczyk, Herszel Moher, etc. For the greater part of the year there was an armistice between the Hasidim and the Jewish Nationalists. Debate became fierce only on certain occasions. Thus the Hasidim objected to the Memorial Service for Herzl in the Synagogue, and there were lively election campaigns for the Polish Sejm [lower house of parliament] and Senate and the local Community Council, for which the Aguda and the Zionists presented lists of their own.

The Younger Generation emerges

The younger generation emerged on the scene in the later 20s, following an abortive attempt to establish a scout movement some years earlier. In 1927 the pupils of the Yavneh Hebrew School set up a society to foster Hebrew as a living language. A branch of the Hashomer Haleumi was founded in 1928 as a national Zionist scout movement, as against the already Socialist and Marxist Hashomer Hazair. The founders were: Moszek Szwajcer, Moszek Cukierman, Moszek Wdowiński, the late Josek Brandys, Nathan Szternfinkiel, the late Aron Wdowiński, the writer, etc. In due course it came to be headed for many years by Ze'ev Szternfinkiel, the late Josek Szulimowicz, Dov Bejski, etc. One of its first steps was to set up a choir. Following a visit by a Hashomer Haleumi leader, it was decided to join the latter, but the local group soon separated again. In due course the name Hashomer Haleumi was changed to Hanoar Hatzioni. The youth movement served to maintain the Zionist spirit at a time when older Zionists were inactive for various reasons.

The Hanoar Hatzioni was very active in the 1932 Polish general elections, when the leaders of Agudas Yisroel chose to support Piłsudski and his followers, whereas the Zionists remained opposed. Zionist electioneering material sent by post failed to reach the town, and police pressure was applied and seemed to deter the older Zionists. However, an election committee of young people was set up, electioneering material was locally printed, and placards were prepared by hand. Finally, most of the local Jewish population voted for the Zionist list.

The Halutz Movement was strengthened by the growth of anti-Semitism and the difficulties of finding employment. There were two *hakhshara* (training) centers in Działoszyce. The Hanoar Hatzioni center was on the estate of the Zionist Spiro family and was agricultural. The other was set up by the Gordonia movement and its members took on work in town, as was then the practice in urban *hakhshara* centers.

In 1933 the late Josek Brandys, Moszek Wdowiński, the present writer, Bella Bursztyn and Necha Brener, leaders of Hanoar Hatzioni, proceeded on *hakhshara* and were followed by members of other youth movements which had meanwhile been set up. These included Hashomer Hatzair, Gordonia, Betar, and the General Zionist Youth.

Life and Living

Besides the struggle for a living and the conflict in beliefs and attitudes (largely a conflict between fathers and sons), daily life was lived to the full in accordance with

Jewish tradition, which encompassed everybody. The year was marked by the Sabbath and the periodicity of the festivals, when the families dispersed all over Poland returned home. Weddings were usually held on Friday afternoon in the square between the synagogue and the Beit Hamidrash [house of prayer/study], bride and bridegroom being brought in two separate processions accompanied by the local musicians—Lokaj the tinsmith and his children, each playing a separate instrument. They were also the orchestra for youth parties and amateur and professional troupes.

In winter a *maggid* or preacher appeared to describe the battle of good and evil, the reward of virtue and punishment of wickedness. Sometimes an outstanding *khazn* or cantor would lead the prayers. A Hasidic *rebbe* might come to town to visit his group of followers. (Działoszyce actually had its own, Rabbi Lejzor Halevi Epsztajn, most of whose followers lived in neighboring villages). Sabbath and festivals were celebrated as they had been for centuries. On Sabbath morning children brought steaming jugs of tea and coffee and *cholent* [dish of meat and vegetables kept warm from previous day so as not to cook on the Sabbath] from the bakeries, where they had been put in the ovens the afternoon before. The Khevre Kedishe or Burial Society was something like a Masonic Order; and whenever Icekl the gravedigger was asked how business was, he would answer, "Poorly, very poorly of late."

The young people developed their own Zionist, sport, theatrical, and literary activities. A cinema had opened in the early 20s but soon closed again. Traveling Yiddish theatrical troupes were regular visitors. The local amateur theater was largely the offspring of Jakób Leszman, a private teacher. There were annual balls, Keren Kayemet bazaars, etc. On Sunday mornings villagers in vast numbers came to prayer in the ancient church, but by afternoon the town was Jewish once again.

The Calm before the Storm

I went to Eretz Yisroel in 1934 and returned for a visit in 1938. It was a very disturbed year on the international scene, and Poland was becoming more actively anti-Semitic. The town was almost without adolescents. Young people had moved elsewhere, particularly to the towns of Upper Silesia, but otherwise nothing had changed and the inhabitants were almost entirely unaware of what was going on in the larger world. The Zionist movement and its youth movements seemed to have gone to sleep. Nobody had heard of the "illegal" *aliya* to Eretz Yisroel. But after Munich,[1] when Poland demanded the ceding of the Teschen [Cieszyn] district by Czechoslovakia, the town became excited for a little while until the latter gave in. Then the town returned to its former tranquility. It was the calm before the final storm.

---

[1] The Munich Agreement in October 1938 appeased Hitler and permitted Germany to annex the Sudetenland from Czechoslovakia. At that time, Poland took over the other half of the city of Cieszyn, which, after World War I, had been divided between Poland and Czechoslovakia (and is again today).

Caption in photo: Members of Hechalutz Haklal-Tzioni
Działoszyce, Lag Ba'Omer, 5693 [May 14, 1933]

Betar in Działoszyce
Caption in photo: Brit Trumpeldor, Działoszyce branch.

Members of Betar in uniform

Movie Day for Keren Kayemet L'Yisrael [Jewish National Fund], 1927

Appeal from Nichum Aveylim Society

Hebrew Text: Mazel Tov! We, the treasurers of the local Nichum Aveylim Society appeal to the newlywed Mr. Juda Lejb Zohn to assist us in this holy endeavor and make a tithe contribution to the best of his ability and free will to the Nichum Aveylim Society. May justice walk before him, and in the merit of this charitable contribution, may his marriage succeed for many many years to come.

Treasurers: Henoch Zohn, Lejb Icek, Szmul Rodał
Bookkeeper: Icek Rafałowicz,
April 15, 1934, Działoszyce

A group of young people in Hanoar Hatzioni

Diałoszyce Jews As I Remember Them (pp. 90–95)

Yosef Harif (Ostry)

I was never in Diałoszyce, and yet I see the town before my eyes. First of all, somewhere in one of my documents, it says that I am a Diałoszycer, although I was actually born in the village of Piotrkowice in the Miechów district. Ah well, anything is possible when it comes to those times. Certainly, there must have been some sort of reason for it.

My home had a very close relationship to that deeply-rooted Jewish community. My father, Reb Izrael Wolf, *z"l*, was a genuine Diałoszycer, and my grandfather, Reb Moszek Ber, *z"l*, never left Diałoszyce. Also my mother, Chana Ruchl, *hi"d* [may God avenge her blood], had a close relationship to Diałoszyce because of Aunt Jentla, her oldest sister, *hi"d*, who was the wife of Reb Abram Wdowiński, *z"l*, the owner of the mill and the electric plant. These close relatives linked us firmly to the town, and Diałoszycers were also frequent guests at our home in the village.

Those whom I remember the best, who have become engraved in my memory, are the village trekkers. Almost every week they came to us, sacks tied over their backs. They wandered through the villages, buying whatever they could—skins of rabbits and hares, feathers, wax. Sometimes God sent them a real find, a fox, and once in a great while, a silver fox, a marten (a kind of predatory animal), or a skunk.

Wintertime these rare animals were of very great value, because their furs were stiffened by frost and snow, no hairs had fallen out, and they had a nice sheen. They also bought heavy cattle hides and dragged them along with them. They worked hard, and it took its toll on them. They were accosted by barking dogs whenever they entered a village and chased them away with their gnarled sticks.

At our place, at the home of the only Jewish family in the village, they [the village trekkers] rested, ate a warm meal, and spent the night on spread-out bundles of straw covered with sheets. Lying under bedding and furs, they rested their bones until the next day, until new toil began.

In the evening, as soon as they crossed the threshold of the house, they placed themselves with their faces to the East—to Jerusalem, and prayed with all their hearts.

The winter nights during Hanukkah have especially found a place in my memory— the frost crackling, the stove burning, and, after evening prayers, their passionate *Vehu Rachum* [And He is merciful] still echoing in the room. Everyone cut a potato in half, bored out little holes, and stuck candles in them to light for Hanukkah. Festiveness spread over the house, faces were shining, we made a *Shechechiyanu* [prayer of thankfulness] over the miracles of bygone days and for the miraculous years lived through *biyamim haheym* [in those days].

We washed up and sat down to a delicious dinner—potato soup with flour and *griven* [cracklings] from fresh goose fat being prepared for the coming Pesakh—and topped it off with lungs and liver that my father brought from Słomniki in honor of Hanukkah and in honor of the guests. Awramele, the youngest in the crowd, a silent type, would help peel potatoes, a happy smile on his face. A delicious smell of Pesakh *schmaltz* [rendered fat] spread over the house due to the *latkes* [potato pancakes] that were being served at the table. The crowd sipped hot tea, which they drank with a cube of sugar, and started to play *kvitl* [a card game].

I used to gaze intently at these people, and they remain before my eyes, as if alive, to this very day. Even today I think about their fate, about how they carried those big, heavy packs over their shoulders—days, weeks, and years; many of them were then already fairly old. In a separate little sack of coarse white linen, they kept a homemade loaf of Działoszyce bread and a few onions.

And here they are, floating up in my memory. One of them, Reb Moszek Szmul, a solidly built Jew with a blond beard framing his face, was a joker. He would call potato soup "a bit of watery stuff." Starving after a long day, he would eat his soup with piece after piece of bread. My mother would usually add more and more of the steaming hot delicious dish. After he had eaten and said the grace after meals, he would roll a cigarette of cheap tobacco and, content, he would blow the smoke out through his nose.

It sometimes happened that my father would talk to him about his brother who had passed away; my father had a lot of heartache over this incident. This was the story. Grandfather Moszek Ber had a small child, a boy, who died. Apparently they had forgotten to register this fact. And when it came time for the draft, *Fonye* [derogatory term for the czar] demanded that the dead boy sign up. He suspected that the boy had gone away, across the ocean, and he demanded a fine of 300 rubles. Since Grandfather didn't have the money, they went after our store, because my father was the oldest son in the family—that's how it was according to the Czarist laws. Quite often they would come and make a *zajęcie* [confiscation] for the fine.

Whenever the enforcers showed up in the village, we had to clear out the better, more expensive materials—until my father's relative, Reb Szymon Kołatacz, *z"l*, intervened, being close to the officials, and for a secret bribe had the evil decree revoked.

Moszek Szmul's son, Gerszon, had an easier way of making a living; he had a horse and cart and bought up scrap metal. He was also like a member of the family.

Jankiel Święty [the saint] had reddish cheeks, as if they had been frostbitten. A round grey beard, on one eyebrow a spot shaped like a small *latke*, he looked like a holy man, always with a cheerful face. His expression would change according to his mood. When he spoke from the heart, a tear appeared in his good eye. The gentiles also held him in high esteem, because he spoke Polish so well.

Reb Izrael Lejb Ostry was a very pious, God-fearing man. He was my father's cousin and a scholar. Only rarely did a smile appear on his face. He had the face of a monk— thin, skin and bones, a tiny little beard on the tip of his chin. We suspected him of perhaps, God forbid, pasting his beard to his chin with soap. His slightly curly *peos* [sidelocks] covered the bareness of his cheeks.

He took little part in the conversation or joking around. But nonetheless, he was a wonderful storyteller about "good Jews"—stories of Hasidic *rebbe*s, miracle workers, about the Besht [Baal Shem Tov] and the *rebbe*, Reb Ber, about the miracles that took place in the days of Hanukkah, about Reb Nachman of Bratslav and his longings for the Land of Israel. He accompanied each story with a sigh, and ended it like a prayer with *"V'li'Yerushalayim ircha b'rachamim tashuv"* (and to Jerusalem, Your city, You shall return with compassion). His eyes were filled with tears, and there were also tears in the eyes of my mother and of us children.

Mother again served hot tea, and it seemed as if the Besht himself, may his blessings be bestowed upon us, was speaking directly from his mouth.

He would get out of bed before everyone else, recite his daily Psalms with ecstasy, look into a holy book, and hum a quiet *niggun* [melody without words]. The spare light of a kerosene lamp cast a pale pink glow over his face. He rocked back and forth, casting a shadow on the wall that I used to stare at.

It was certainly hard for him to drag the heavy sack on his shoulders. And maybe even heavier than the sack was the sorrow of the Jewish exile.

To this very day, I do not understand how he communicated with the peddlers, traded his wares, and sustained the members of his household; maybe he was helped by the great faith that he carried in his heart.

Reb Dawid Brojgies, a cheerful Jew who rhymed more than he spoke, held a very special place in our house. At the time, he lived in Łódź, but he considered himself a Działoszycer. He was a frequent guest in our house; he had been our father's friend from *kheyder*. In his younger years, he had been a jester, and in his old age, he would carry around a little bottle of animal bile with which he'd remove stains from clothing. It was such a bitter way of earning a living. He would arrive in a village around Shavuos [holiday commemorating the giving of the ten commandments], and stay until after Sukes [Feast of Tabernacles]. On Simkhes-Toyre [festival marking the completion of the cycle of reading the Torah], he would delight our village minyan [quorum needed for prayer], pearls literally flowing from his lips; he had rid himself of all his worries. On the night of Heshayne Rabe [last day of Sukes], he became a very different person. He recited *Tikun*, the night liturgy for the holiday, in the *suke* [booth] almost the whole night long, humming a sad melody by the dwindling light of the Yom Kippur candle.[1]

These are just a few of the people whom I recall.

At our place they also used to tell various stories about people from Działoszyce. About the *gvir-adir* [very wealthy] Przeworski, they said that at his place, people used to eat livers of fattened geese even in the middle of the week.

It became very lively in the house when Grandfather Reb Moszek Ber, *z"l*, came to visit. He used to come during the winter; it was freezing outside and birds were literally falling in the middle of their flight. After crossing the doorstep with a jolly *"Gut Helf!"* [Good Day], he took the bundle off the stick that had been slung over his shoulder, speaking a bit hastily because he wanted the bagels to arrive warm. His beard and mustache were covered with ice and downy snow, and the bagels were actually warm— real Działoszyce bagels, braided and boiled, sprinkled with poppy seeds, browned to a golden shine. We merrily crunched them between our teeth.

Grandfather would tell us a great many stories, and we would ask for more and more. He got up early in the morning and recited Psalms for a long time, and he used to stay with us for several days and leave a sense of longing when he left.

Grandfather passed away at a very old age. It was a Friday night. Friday, during the day, he went to the cemetery to visit the graves of his ancestors, and looked at the "plot of

---

[1] It was customary to stay awake all night on *Heshayna Rabe* and recite the *tikun* [healing] service and other prayers.

land" that he had provided for himself near the grave of one of his brothers who had died a martyr's death (*Kidesh hashem* [sanctifying God's name]).

Grandmother Rywka, from my mother's side, lived with us for many years. When we left the village, she went to Działoszyce and stayed with Aunt Jentla. We moved to the city. Living in the village was hard for a Jew, and the only Jewish light, in our village hut, was extinguished.

The first time I ever saw Aunt Jentla, I was a boy of ten. Coming home one time on a summer's day from *kheyder* at lunchtime, I met a dear, distinguished guest, Aunt Jentla, a tall, well-dressed woman, who gave the impression of being a noblewoman—rich clothing, a hat with an ostrich feather, and a wig that had grey hairs woven into it. Ever since her son Hercke, having fallen through thin ice, had drowned at the Bydlin mill near Wolbrom, which he leased, the deep sadness never left her face. Aunt Jentla would send descriptions of Japan, in notebooks with yellow covers, to my mother in the village.

Incidentally, we had some sort of connection with Japan. Uncle Josel, *z"l*, had served in the Russian army near the Japanese border, and when the Russo-Japanese war broke out, he crossed the border into Austria.

I never had the opportunity to see Aunt Jentla's home, but I imagined it for myself as a rich patriarchal home, a home rooted in children and grandchildren, something like what you would find among our biblical ancestors, full of primeval *yidishkeyt* [Jewishness]. I watched Aunt Jentla very closely when she was at our house. My mother told me to go back to *kheyder* and say good-bye to my aunt. Aunt Jentla took me by the hand then and said, stroking my head, "Let him take a good look at me; perhaps he will never see me again." She was right. I never did see her again.

Amid the devastation in the Nazi deluge, the home of Uncle Abram and Aunt Jentla, built by them with so much diligence, was also destroyed. The well-established house that had been filled with warm *yidishkeyt* was annihilated.

Aunt Jentla, was taken away by the Nazis when she was past ninety, with her full wits about her and with all her charm radiating from her. In her hand, she held a newspaper. She could not bear not to be looking at something. Together with other elderly men and women, she was taken to Wolbrom.

Yes, even now stories of Działoszyce appear before my eyes. There were times when this town even had a Jewish mailman.

Here I have only noted a few of the people that have been preserved in my mind, from my childhood in the village—until Jerusalem. People who were annihilated as they were longing for redemption, with their faces to the East, their gaze turned toward Jerusalem.

Translated from the Yiddish by Zulema Seligson

Jews with Estates (pp. 96–100)

Chaim Szwimer

Over one hundred years ago, a decree was issued, signed by the czar that stated that all Jews involved in farming would be exempt from military service. During those times, it was a major problem if one got drafted and became a soldier in the Russian army. The service lasted dozens of years, and there was a grave danger of assimilation and conversion.[1] The Jews heeded this decree and started to settle their children to work the fields. Around Działoszyce there were thick forests (hence the name of the town); they started preparing the land for agriculture. At first, they named the place "Zalesice," which means "beyond the forest."

After they cleared away the trees, the agriculturally prepared land was offered for sale to the highest bidder. Several Jews acquired parts of this land. The area was called Łabędź (a swan), and on it was established a Jewish agricultural community. With the establishment of this settlement, there was a sizeable number of Jews who worked the land and cultivated their fields with loving care. Among them were my father, Szulim Szwimer, his brother, Dawid and Judka Przeworski from the Lorja family, a few sons from the Paszkowski family, and others. Things were running well for dozens of years. Afterward, the wealthy sold their estates, since from the outset their motivation was to avoid the draft. As a result, the settlement became impoverished. In spite of all this, a few families still remained, the offspring of the original settlers, and continued living there until the outbreak of World War II.

I remember well one Jew with an interesting personality whose name was Herszel Kołatacz. On each and every Thursday, he used to go from house to house and collect funds for the poor in his town, and in each house, they would give him a generous donation.

The entire area was uncultivated and inhabited by a large variety of wild animals—wolves, foxes, and others. This was after they bought their properties. My grandfather, z"l [of blessed memory], related to me an incident that once, at night, while he was grazing his horse in the meadow, he very suddenly saw a wolf from afar. He barely managed to mount his horse and escape with his life. During this entire night, the horse was shaking and shivering from fright. Another time, a wolf preyed upon his dog, which was tied to a chain in the yard of the house. In the morning, the only memento left was the steel chain.

One time a woman was returning from Działoszyce to Łabędź carrying a basket of produce that she had bought. A wolf she encountered was following her, and every so often, she would throw him something from her basket. When she arrived at her home in Łabędź, she realized that by then her basket was empty. But the most important thing was that she had returned safely.

---

[1] During the reign of Czar Nicholas I (1825–55), youngsters were drafted at a very young age and required to serve in the army for twenty-five years. There was a great deal of pressure on Jewish conscripts (called Cantonists) to convert to Christianity during their time of service.

Such were the memories of the Jews living in Łabędź, which they used to relate as they gathered at the home of my grandfather.

The wealthy Jews who had sold their properties in Łabędź still remained committed to agriculture. However, almost all of them had switched to acquiring a very vast area of fields, where each was spread out along thousands of morgens.[1]

In any event, in Łabędź, there was a concentration of Jewish landowners in the area.

After this original edict regarding military service was eliminated, in 1864, the Polish landowners had to pay higher wages to farm laborers. This forced many of them to sell a portion of their land, if only to be able to continue their lavish lifestyle that required large sums of money.

Initially, they borrowed money from their Jewish lenders, but when it became apparent that they wouldn't be able to repay their loans, they would agree to turn over a portion of their property as compensation. As a result, many Jews became landowners of large properties.

Some of these [Jewish] landowners decided to divide these huge estates into smaller portions and sell them to the peasants, who were hungry to acquire land. They gave them terms of installment payments lasting long periods of years. These promissory notes were then kept in the banks, and as a result of this, they received large amounts of money. With this income, the [Jewish] landowners went out and bought huge properties from Polish landowners.

A great many of these real estate dealers became landowners themselves and got tied to a rural way of life in which their main occupation consisted of farming. They then transferred over their holdings to their sons and sons of sons until the outbreak of World War II—which caused the destruction of everything.

The original landowners, who did not possess the necessary expertise to work the land, employed the help of a manager to oversee the operations of their fields and properties. Their children, afterward, came to learn the trade and were thus able to continue being involved themselves with the cultivation and enrichment of the land. So came into being, in the areas surrounding Działoszyce, a type of Jewish landowner who was no different in his makeup from the Polish landowners, one who was able to run his estate on his own.

The numbers of Jewish landowners in the vicinity of Działoszyce, as well as those Jews who themselves were involved in farming, was quite large, so much so that I couldn't even begin to list them by name. I do know, however, that among the initial Jewish landowners was someone by the name of Moszkowski, a very wealthy Jew who left two sons and two daughters. One of these daughters was the wife of Dr. Edelman. The two brothers, Bernard and Zysza Moszkowski, within a short period of time after their father's demise, lost all of their possessions and properties and were forced to live on handouts from their wealthy relatives. They say that Bernard Moszkowski owned one of the big flour mills. Once a salesman came to him and offered him sacks, along with needles for sewing them. The mill owner bought from him needles worth a few hundred rubles, while he could have bought enough needles for the entire year with one ruble. He was impressed by the wholesale price the salesman offered him for the goods and his

---

[1] One morgen equals about two acres.

promise that the bigger the order, the cheaper the price. So he bought a large stock of needles that was enough to last him for several hundred years. And with this type of logic, more or less, they ran the entire business.

The brother of Bernard Moszkowski, by the name of Zysza Moszkowski, was the owner of a large manufacturing plant that was built near Łabędź in the larger town of Czarnocin. In his later years, he lived in Warsaw. There he owned several big houses. His two sons ran Łabędź and the town of Czarnocin. Józio [Józef] and Marcel Moszkowski were both assimilated Jews. Józio's only daughter married a *goy* [gentile] and, as a result, both her father and mother converted and became Christian.

The same fate met up with Marcel. He married a Christian woman and converted as well. He lived in Czarnocin. In the eyes of Hitler, however, he still remained a Jew. He had to escape from his comfortable home and wandered around with a group of Jews hiding from the Nazis. His wife left him and lived with a German Nazi and didn't want to know him anymore. The Jews with whom he was hiding from the Germans reminded him very often of his having been a traitor to his people, and while exchanging words, told him that from his family name of "Moszkowski," all that remained in the end was "Moszk [Moszek]."[1]

In Dziekanowice were the properties of very prominent Jewish families, the families of Aszkiel and Spiro. These families represented the aristocracy among the Jewish real estate property owners in the area. For many, many years, they inhabited the areas surrounding our town.

The Szental family were the owners of great and vast land. The father of the family, Arysz [Aron] Szental, initiated the acquiring of land. He left behind three sons and two daughters who were the proprietors of the entire family estate until the outbreak of World War II. From this entire family, only one daughter survived, by the name of Dania, a scientist in London, and a grandson who lives in Netanya [Israel].

One branch of the Szental family lives in Israel in a place called Karkur. The head of this family is one of the original settlers in the place, from the fourth immigration to the land.

The village of Parszywka belonged in a partnership to Tuwia Meryn and Icze Owsiany. After some time, they sold their joint assets, and the sons of Icze Owsiany bought a parcel that was part of Jastrzębniki, and afterward, land in the village of Dębczyna. They held on to these properties until the outbreak of the war.

From the Owsiany family, only the son of Chaim Owsiany—by the name of Szmul— is still alive, and he lives in Canada.

The village of Jastrzębniki belonged to the Łaznowski brothers. They held on to their property until the outbreak of World War II. The daughter of one of the brothers, Aron, is still alive. She is in the United States. As for the three daughters of the second son, Szlama, all three of them are living in Tel Aviv.

Szyja Herszel Brener owned vast areas of land along with a large flour mill. From this family, two sons are still alive. One of them, Moszek, lives in Tel Aviv, and the other, Binem, lives in America.

The brothers Szwimer owned property in Kościejów. They also dealt in real estate.

---

[1] At one time, names ending in "owski" indicated Polish nobility.

They subdivided their many holdings into smaller agricultural ones. From that family, three girls and a son remain, all of them residing in Israel.

A special type of property owner, and one who worked his land with dedication, was Aron Lewkowicz. He owned fifty acres of land that he cultivated agriculturally. In addition to this, he was a grain merchant. He maintained a very close relationship with all the Polish farmers in the area and was considered one of them. They nicknamed him "Bajka," which means a fable. This nickname sprang from the nature of the Polish farmer, who was full of unrealistic fantasies, and he, Lewkowicz, would listen to all the imaginary tales that his Polish farming peers would relay to him, and he would react with the exclamation, "Fables!" During the last years prior to the war, there used to exist a minyan in his house. All the Jews from the surrounding areas would gather together in his home for a regular minyan on Shabes, Shabes Mevarchim [the Sabbath on which one blesses the new month], and on the holidays. Prayers would take place there.

After the invasion of Poland by the Nazis, he continued living on his land until 1942. At that point, the head of the farmers' council invited him to come over and explained to him that the Poles in the village could not stand his wearing a beard, and if he didn't want them to tear it off, he would do well to shave it off with his own hands. Without a choice, he shaved off the beard that had lit up his face and was a part of his life as a symbol of Jewish pride during a period of fifty innocent years.

From his family, four sons survived, and two grandsons, named Dawid, and Jankiel, the son of Dawid. The latter lives in Bat Yam [Israel]. His three other sons, Michał, Szmul, and Herszel, reside abroad.

Zelig Potok, or Zelig Gluzen, was the owner of fifty acres of land in the village of Gluzy. His daughter survived and lives in Israel.

To the Majtek family belonged lands in one village. Two of his daughters survived and reside permanently in Tel Aviv.

Until the outbreak of World War I, the Jewish property owners were steeped in debt. Only during the war did their revenues increase greatly from their working of the land, and they became very wealthy.

After Poland gained its independence, after the end of World War I, the government began to tax them heavily, with the intention of oppressing them. Because of this, the agricultural workers united and demanded higher wages. One could surmise that the landlords could have survived this double onslaught, the taxes and high wages, if only the work had been industrialized. But in Poland, everything was done manually instead of with machinery and tractors. They could not, in any way, compete with the United States and Canada, where machines did everything. These countries flooded the markets of Europe with their agricultural products and supplied wheat and oats very cheaply, nearly for nothing.

The Jewish farmers bore the brunt of this competitiveness. They sank into deep debt and could not get out from under this situation. This brought the entire agricultural community to the brink of bankruptcy in Poland. When the government realized that the situation was so grave, it hurriedly declared a moratorium to eliminate all their debts. The outstanding payments of the farmers were extended over a longer period of time and given better terms. The Jewish property owners dealt mainly with the selling of parcels of land to small farmers, who then owed them large amounts of money. Thus the owners remained without any liquid flow of money and without any cash. All this, while on paper, they possessed such great wealth that one couldn't even put a value on it.

In 1942, after the Nazis got organized in their occupied country, they liquidated all Jewish-owned properties and appointed managers instead. The property owners were chased out from their villages to the towns, poor and poverty stricken, without any possessions, persecuted, hunted, and oppressed until the final expulsion. All of them perished together with their brothers, the Jews of Działoszyce.

Translated from the Hebrew by Zeva Shapiro

Small Businesses in Our Town (pp. 101–4)

Arje Rolnicki

As you know, there were no extremely rich people in Działoszyce. The few landowners in the area could be counted on one hand. I intend to describe only the small businesses and will not deal with the large textile shops or the wholesale grocers, such as Icze Majer Waga, Abram Dula, Jekutiel Płatkiewicz, Mendel Wdowiński, Pleszowski, Szwajcer, and the like. Or Richter's fabric store, which, earlier on, was located on one of the major corners. The wholesale grocery trade was dominated by Reb Eliasz Rolnicki, *z"l*, while Pinkus Formalski had the dry goods store. I still remember Szmul Jutrzenka's store as well as Izrael Wajnsztok's, along with those owned by gentiles—such as Paweł Książek and son, Kabziński, and Zwoliński, who was also the mayor and had a monopoly on cigarettes and tobacco.

Even before World War I, the merchants of Działoszyce were surprised to learn that a Jew, one Pejsach Sternberg, had succeeded in getting a permit from the authorities in Warsaw to sell drugs and various pharmaceuticals.

There were various other stores in the market area: Epsztajn's liquor store, the Cukierman brothers' dry goods store, Tauman's tobacco shop, the stores of Tuwia Meryn and Moszek Laskier that sold iron products, and those of Lejbuś Brandys and Smolarczyk that sold hardware. Mejlech Blat, Majer Szulimowicz, Josek Judel Mandelbaum, and Drobiarz all dealt in processed leather goods. The housewares and glass products store belonged to Joska Tajtelbaum. Mendel Frydman (little Mendele) and Aron Baum sold plate glass and paint. There were other stores on the market square that sold a variety of commodities, brought in mainly by farmers from the surrounding area.

There were several merchants in Działoszyce whose main business was to acquire produce from neighboring villages and market it in town. This trade took place as follows. Peddlers made their rounds throughout the countryside, buying feathers, rabbit skins, whatever came their way. They returned to town after five days, on Friday, in time to deal with the wholesalers to whom they were connected. Sometimes, the wholesaler underwrote a peddler's travels for a week or two, advancing him some money until the next Friday, when they would settle their accounts. The peddler was often pressed to settle for a minimal profit, hardly enough to support a family. But, as he was offered on the spot an advance on the sales of the coming week, he spent Shabes resting and on Sunday, shortly before dawn, set out on his rounds once again. The financial condition of the wholesalers, in contrast to the peddlers, or, as they were called in Działoszyce, the *dorfs-loifer* [village trekkers] was pretty stable. There were even some fairly wealthy individuals among them. In this connection, it is worth mentioning Moszek Nifkier, whose feather exports extended as far as Germany. He eventually opened a feather-cleaning factory in Upper Silesia. Moszek Waga also dealt in feathers, though on a much smaller scale. (Earlier on, Abram Profesorski was in this same business.)

Since the surrounding area was totally agricultural, the farmers used to bring their produce to town on market days. A significant number of Działoszyce's Jews traded in farm produce, mainly field crops: wheat, rye, barley, oats, and products such as eggs, poultry, butter, vegetables—whatever could be stored and sent to the big cities and industrial centers. Most of the farmers had connections with a particular merchant on whom they could count to buy their goods. Despite this fact, hordes of peddlers and traders would overwhelm the neighboring villages, swooping over every farmer's cart, vying over the goods, and competing for them. The farmers would bargain over the price of the eggs and wheat they were carrying. Trade with these farmers was the major occupation of our small-scale merchants.

There were also several horse traders in Działoszyce. True, the main horse markets were located in Skalbmierz, Miechów, and Proszowice, and traders from Działoszyce participated in those markets as well. These traders would set out to the market with a cart pulled by two handsome horses. Those animals that were being offered for sale were tethered to the back of the cart. When they reached the market place, all of the horses were sold—at a significant profit, of course—and replaced by others. When business was good, the new horses were sold as well, so that the dealer sometimes had to hitch a ride home.

At the end of the summer, when the harvest was over, the farmers tried to dispose of their aging horses rather than having to feed them all winter long, knowing they would not be able to do much work in the spring. The horse traders bought these aging horses, too. More than once it happened that they bought back a horse that they had sold the farmer a few months earlier, its teeth having been sharpened, and its coat groomed to make the animal appear younger. These horses, everyone agreed, were not suitable for work and would be killed off before long. The unfortunate animals, frail and limp, were led to a valley near Działoszyce, where they were killed and then skinned. As it turns out, the dealers made a handsome profit on their carcasses.

The *balegole*s [wagon drivers] were a special economic class with an important function and a distinct character. These drivers, in all weather—winter, spring, summer, even the rainy and often-frigid Polish autumn—spent their nights hauling goods over the winding, unpaved roads that led to the big cities. The main road led to Kraków and to the Zagłębie [coal mining] area. The Smolarczyk family lived near the main road and were the principal wagon drivers. Their lives were very hard. The wagons and horses they drove belonged to someone else; they were hired as day workers. The trip to Kraków usually took an entire night. In the morning, the horses rested. The wagons were re-loaded in Kraków, and, at nightfall, the drivers would set out on their return trip. Their lot was difficult, their livelihood hard-earned, but their honesty and decency were exemplary. The merchants preferred to entrust their goods to them for transport, although there was also a train in the region that carried freight from town to town. On gloomy autumn nights, in relentless rain, when the darkness of Egypt seemed to overtake the world, these drivers, perched on the platforms of their slow-moving wagons, and tightly wrapped in their warm coats, would loosen the reins to allow their horses to proceed at their own pace.

All the usual occupations were represented in Działoszyce. I do not mean to list and detail all the different trades that were represented. Someone will probably emerge to properly describe their lives. Still, it is hard to move on without mentioning the porters, who were tightly linked to the activities of the merchants of Działoszyce, depending on them for their meager livelihood. When a wagon heaped with goods approached, some of these porters would climb to the top, with alacrity, and pass the sacks or the bundled hides to those waiting below, who, in turn, piled the load on their backs and delivered it to the merchant's warehouse. In this overview, we recall their weary faces, shabby beards, heavy clothing, the coarse rope tied to their bodies, and their oversize boots. My heart aches to this day when I recall their toil. This was among the most difficult and back breaking labors, offering meager wages with which one could barely support a typically large family.

There were also bars and restaurants in the town square. The local farmers who came to the town, after concluding their business, were in the habit of "drowning the worm" in drink. They would buy a bottle of whiskey and some herring, while their wives, anxious to get back home, stood by, cursing and urging them to hurry. There were several bars belonging to gentiles: Kulczyński-Ślęzak, Bielecki, and others; for our own people: Goldkorn, Fajwel Pałasznicki, and Chaim Chaba. The villagers were in a state of high excitement, and their money flowed into the hands of the bar owners.

The excitement that we witnessed in our childhood is engraved in my memory and especially connected to market days—Tuesdays and Fridays. The major merchants waited eagerly for these days, which provided a significant portion of their livelihood and were especially important to the peddlers and hucksters. At dawn, they set up their stands, row upon row, each one in its regular spot. Those offering manufactured goods, fabrics, and luxury items were posted near the statue of Kościuszko. A variety of colorful scarves and skirts were also sold in this spot, along with men's shirts, suits, and pants. These sales were real "works of art." In the words of a local proverb, "If the garment doesn't fit the living, it will fit the dead." There were plenty of shoemakers as well. They sold shoes, boots, and rain gear for men and women. There were vendors whose colorful and stylish hats attracted many customers.

The sweets were particularly appealing—fresh cakes topped with sugar and colorful cookies whose taste didn't live up to their looks. There was an array of seasonal fruits and greens—cherries and blackberries in the spring, apples and pears in the summer. All of this activity was accompanied by shouts and exclamations touting the quality of the merchandise. There was wild competition among the sellers. Market days were marked by the neighing of horses, lowing of cattle, bleating of sheep, and billowing dust that covered the town with a thick gray-white mist.

The peddlers of Działoszyce participated in their local market and traveled to adjacent towns. In the summer, this was no problem. Two or three peddlers would set out together. But, in the winter, with snow-covered roads and freezing temperatures, it was still essential to leave home in order to bring in some money. One would see peddlers and vendors, wrapped in blankets and furs, stomping their feet to keep warm. The women could be seen sitting or standing over pots filled with glowing coals in an effort to warm their frozen bodies. These street peddlers were simple, hardy women—but also devoted mothers who left their young children at home to help their husbands eke out a living.

The market was not always a success. On a frigid, stormy day, there were not many customers. Peddlers stood idle, angrily picking at their nails, or chewing on straw from a nearby wagon. Any customer seemed to offer salvation and was besieged with seductive offers to keep the wheels of business rolling.

Translated from the Hebrew by Zeva Shapiro

Torah Study and Charity Organizations (pp. 105–11)

Rabbi Yehuda Frankel

Rabbi Yehuda Frankel

I. The Talmud Torah

When I came to Działoszyce in 1925, the Talmud Torah [free Jewish elementary school] scarcely existed, while the Beit Hamidrash [house of study] was almost empty. I promptly took steps to organize the Talmud Torah, with the aid of Reb Abram Moszek Szenkier, the late Reb Szmul Jutrzenka, and the late Reb Chaim Josek Dziewięcki. Reb Szmul, a Gerer Hasid, not only raised money but recruited others and dedicated himself to the development of this and other Orthodox schools, such as Beit Yaakov [school for girls], etc. Similarly Reb Chaim Josek was dedicated to everything that encouraged the study of Torah and the performance of good deeds and was both personally charitable

This chapter is reprinted from pp. 14–16 of the English section of the original Działoszyce Yizkor Book, with minor changes.

and dedicated to communal welfare. Naturally, they were by no means the only ones. May their memories be blessed.

At first it was very difficult to raise funds for salaries, etc., as the pupils' fees covered very little of the costs. However, the community came to realize the value of the institution, and the community council allocated an annual amount. This was not enough, however, and with the assistance of Mr. Spiro, the landowner of Dziekanowice, we prevailed on the district governor at Pińczów to permit the council to increase its allocation.

Though the general economic situation of the local Jews grew worse, they devoted themselves increasingly to the growth of the Talmud Torah school. Craftsmen, wagoners, small shopkeepers, and peddlers and others who made the rounds of the villages during the whole year all helped. Reb Mordka Icek Staszewski, the town rabbi, was invited to the end-of-semester examinations together with town worthies. This ensured better study and greater general support. The registration of pupils and the fixing of fees, no matter how minimal, at the beginning of the *zman* (semester commencing after the High Holidays or after Pesakh) often gave rise to heart-rending scenes, so poor were the parents. My partner in registration on these occasions was the late Reb Abram Cukierman.

The Talmud Torah provided a living for twelve to fourteen *melamdim* (teachers of traditional Jewish studies) who served as a team of teachers, and whose position was greatly improved by this. Their headmaster was the late Reb Izrael Szlama Landau. We refrained from bringing teachers from elsewhere in order to ensure that the local *melamdim* should have a secure source of income.

II. The Yeshiva

When the boys grew older some went to *yeshivot* elsewhere; but special free courses in Mishna and Talmud were given daily to those who remained in town by Reb Icek Majer Frydberg, the local *shoykhet* (slaughterer), a leading local Gerer Hasid; by the martyred Reb Abram Szenkier; and by myself. Some boys studied in the local Beit Hamidrash under the guidance of Reb Chaim Jechiel, head of the yeshiva, others in various Hasidic *shtiblekh* [small houses of prayer] or in private homes.

In the course of time a yeshiva worthy of the name was established, and a yeshiva head was invited from elsewhere. In due course youngsters came to study there from neighboring towns such as Miechów, Skalbmierz, Proszowice, etc. Special care had to be taken of the latter, board and lodging being necessary for them.

The poorer groups were fighting the battle of economic existence and could not afford to pay for the Jewish education of their children. Hence the communal workers dedicated themselves to ensuring that the poorer children in particular should not be deprived of a Jewish education, in order to ensure the continuity of Judaism and the Jewish people.

III. Beit Yaakov

Reb Szmul Jutrzenka, Reb Icek Majer Frydberg, and others, including myself, also established a Beit Yaakov school for girls and hired a dedicated group of women teachers to bring the girls up in the traditional Jewish fashion. Its reputation spread far and wide through the region, and it was visited by Mrs. Sara Schenierer, founder of the Beit Yaakov Schools. This did a great deal to persuade and convince the outstanding women folk of the community that the traditional education of girls was as important as that of boys.

IV. The Biker Khoylim Society

Special mention should be made of the Biker Khoylim Society, whose purpose was to provide for the needs of the sick and their families. Those who were most concerned with education also dedicated themselves to the *mitzve* (commandment). This society represented all sections of the community. Every night, one of a group of young men, in rotation, would spend the night with a patient in order to enable his family to rest. The Society also paid for doctor's visits and the services of two *felczers* (medical practitioners). Reb Lejbuś Szeniawski and Reb Aszer Moszenberg regularly visited the sick. The Society paid for medicines. It must be remembered that there were no hospitals or nurses in the smaller Jewish towns of Poland in those days.

V. "Purity of the Family"

There was also a special fund which, whenever necessary, paid for the minimal costs of immersion in the *mikve* or ritual bath, in order to ensure that the time-established practices involved in conjugal relations should not be neglected.

Apart from these organized activities, there was a vast amount of private and unrecorded charity. The Beit Hamidrash students and young scholars dedicated themselves, in particular, to helping needy wayfarers and traveling scholars, preachers, etc., doing all in their power to fulfill the commandment of hospitality. All in all, Działoszyce could well stand comparison with far larger Jewish communities.

The Mizrachi Synagogue (pp. 112–14)

Joshua Wdowiński

The Mizrachi synagogue was connected to the Yavneh School.[1] At first, when lessons took place in the women's section of the *bes hamedresh* [house of study], the prayer service was held in two rooms down below, which were right next to the *bes hamedresh*. Upon moving the school to the Targownik house, the synagogue also moved there. In fact, this became its regular and well-known location.

In an old Jewish town with its own traditions even in the realm of synagogues, this was a kind of miniature revolution, to establish a kind of politically affiliated house of prayer. On the one hand, there already was the great synagogue, the only one in which prayers were said in the Ashkenazi tradition, with its regular worshipers, and the large *bes hamedresh* and the small *bes hamedresh* named for Reb Abele. On the other hand, there were the many *shtibls* [small Hasidic houses of prayer] that represented all the different kinds of Hasidic "courts."[2] Naturally, however, the worshipers in the Mizrachi synagogue were for the most part parents of the children who studied in the [Mizrachi] school and those with a Zionist leaning. The youth who did not find their place in the houses of prayer where their parents prayed were also attracted to this special house of prayer. It is worth noting that friendships and groups from among the worshippers crystallized very quickly there.

This synagogue was known for its special atmosphere. Its members, most of whom were lively and active, accompanied the *shaliakh tzibur* [prayer leader] in conducting services. The melodies and songs flowed beautifully, with everyone participating. More than a few of the congregants had pleasant voices, and they regularly sang in the choir, which was conducted by Cantor Zyskind Jakubowicz, *z"l*. The former conductor of the cantorial choir was Reb Szyja Śpiewak [singer], *z"l*. Usually the choir sang on holidays, mostly during the Days of Awe [High Holy Days]. Most of the tunes and melodies were by Cantor Reb Szyja Śpiewak, *z"l*.

Most of the prayer leaders were liked by the congregants, and they frequently went up to the prayer leader's podium on Shabes and the holidays. Among those who went up to the podium, those who stand out, are Bendet Majerczyk, *z"l*; Aron Jurysta, *z"l*, who never once relinquished one "chair" or "fire" in the *piyyut* [liturgical poem] of the *kedusha* [sanctification] on Yom Kippur; Icek Chęciński, *z"l*, who was the *bal hatokea* [shofar blower]; Jakób Szyja Spokojny, *z"l*; Mejlech Bursztyn, *z"l*, Torah reader; Jakób Szklarczyk, *z"l*; Gabriel Edelist, *z"l*, leader of Psalms; Aron Balicki, *z"l*, Torah reader; Wolf Topioł, *z"l*; and others.

There is no doubt that the central personality in the synagogue was Reb Pejsach Sternberg, *z"l*, chairman of the local Mizrachi branch and head of the Jewish community council for many years. His personality overshadowed everyone. On every holiday, in

---

[1] Mizrachi was the Orthodox Zionist political party.
[2] The various Hasidic rabbis throughout Poland had followers, considered members of the rabbi's "court." In each town, the followers of a particular rabbi often had their own *shtibl*.

fact, on every important occasion, his folk-like sermon on current events pleased the congregants, even the youth. Reb Pejsach Sternberg, a renowned scholar, an expert in world literature, who even excelled in his knowledge of chemistry and did business in consumer goods, served as deputy mayor of the town, chair of the Biker Khoylim [Visiting the Sick] Society, and more. All the people appreciated his honesty and simplicity. Unfortunately, there are few among the congregants who are still alive after the Great Holocaust who remember to this day the image of Reb Pejsach, standing before the congregation, draped in a *talis* [prayer shawl] and wearing a black *kitl* [robe-like garment], before reciting the Kol Nidre [prayer on eve of Yom Kippur]. It was his tradition each year to deliver his sermons about current events dressed liked this. In this ritual, he relied on a certain *medresh* [creative interpretation of the scriptures] about the binding of Isaac, and all of the congregants listened, trembling and shuddering. It is amazing to us how he succeeded each year to find new things in this *medresh* and to relate them to the events of the time. Even his waving of the *lulav* [frond of a date palm tree used in Sukes service] deserves special recognition.

Each and every Shabes, there were those who came early in the morning to study the Medresh ein Ya'akov, the weekly portion, or a chapter of Talmud. In the evening, the synagogue served as a meeting place for many people. There were those who came to study, and those who came to delve into a book in the rich religious library there, and those who came just to chat with friends. After evening prayers, the third meal was served, which lasted until the end of Shabes. The tradition was that the reader of the *maftir* [final Torah portion] of that Shabes took care of the salty fish and *challah*. Songs, with everyone participating, were pleasant to everyone there.

Each holiday, celebrations with a reception were held for all the congregants. A few receptions became special occasions of their own. For example, a formal meal, Melave Malka,[1] was eaten after the first *slikhes* [penitent prayers]; a celebration was held on Heshayne Rabe [last day of Sukes], and others. Known well was the Simkhe Bes Hashoeva [celebration of water-drawing at the well] that the congregants would put on in one of the large *sukes* [booths] of the members.[2] At the height of the celebration, friends came for the *hakafot* [dancing with the Torah] on the evening of Simkhes Toyre [celebration at the end of the cycle of reading the Torah]. These dances continued until very late in the night and attracted a great number of participants in addition to the regular worshipers.

Every once in a while the congregants would meet to hear a report by Pejsach Sternberg, *z"l*, following each of his visits to the central office in Warsaw, of what was happening in the Mizrachi movement. The congregants contributed greatly to the national funds—Keren Kayemet [Jewish National Fund] and Keren Hayesod [United Israel Appeal]. It is a bit curious that a lively and vibrant community like this, with an educational institution like the Yavneh School, was not successful in educating the next generation. The Mizrachi movement in town barely even had a youth scout movement

---

[1] Melave Malka is the ceremonial meal on Saturday evening that escorts away the Shabes Queen.
[2] In the days of the Temple, the drawing of water for use in the celebration of Sukes was preceded by all night celebrations with singing and dancing. This custom was based on: "You shall draw forth water in gladness" (Isaiah 12:3).

[Hashomer Hadati]. Very few members went for *hakhshara* [pioneer training] by the movement specifically for emigration to Israel.

At the beginning of the 30s, with the closing of the Yavneh School due to lack of funds, the number of congregants in the synagogue began to dwindle. The main reason for this was the emigration of the town's residents to larger places like Kraków, Silesia, and Zagłębie. This emigration continued, actually, without any break, until the beginning of World War II. From year to year, it became increasingly difficult to maintain the synagogue's many rooms for a small and dwindling community. In the end, the members were forced to give up the idea of an independent synagogue, and they merged with the synagogue of the members of Biker Khoylim, which was in the Jewish community building in the center courtyard. At the time of the famous flood in 1937,[1] some congregants were trapped inside the synagogue and were rescued only by a miracle. One *seyfer-toyre* [Torah scroll] was damaged. The chapel served the same purpose during World War II. With the increase in the flow of refugees from different places to the town, the house of prayer was used to house a few refugee families. A handful of members and regular worshipers continued meeting and holding services there in a private room until the deportations.

Translated from the Hebrew by Roger Kaplan

---

[1] Other authors say the flood occurred in 1936.

The Yavneh School (pp. 115–18)

Joshua Wdowiński

After the establishment of the seven-year elementary school system by the Polish government, the Jews of Działoszyce set up a communal elementary school of their own, which was associated with the Yavneh School system of the Mizrahi [Orthodox Zionists] and provided a traditional Jewish education while satisfying state educational requirements. Its upkeep imposed a considerable burden on the parents and school curatorium [governing board], but it continued to function for the better part of a decade, together with the Yavneh School for Girls, which was set up some years later.

Premises were never adequate or suitable, but there were regular classes, and for some time, pupils received a roll and cocoa at school every morning. The teachers were: Szaja Szmul Hirszenhorn of Miechów (Talmud, Mishna, and literature); Szaja Jonas Przenica (the same subjects); Chaim Jakób Gotlieb (Bible, Mishna, and Talmud), who used the old-style Polish-Jewish pronunciation of Hebrew; Hercel Karmioł (Hebrew literature, grammar, geography, and history); his brother Mordka Karmioł (the same subjects in the lower classes); Mordka Ungier (Bible, literature, singing, and play-production); Szymon Płatkiewicz (in charge of the lower classes, singing, and gymnastics). Hebrew was taught in the correct Ashkenazi pronunciation, which made the study of grammar far easier. Though there was no playground, time was dedicated to drill, singing, and rambles every Sunday afternoon in fine weather. The pupils used to contribute to the Hebrew children's weeklies, which were then appearing in Poland. However, the economic crisis at the end of the 20s caused many families to move elsewhere, and the Yavneh School had to close, though repeated attempts were made by the brothers Karmioł and others to continue it on a private basis. After the outbreak of World War II, Mr. Landau and Mr. Rozenman continued to conduct organized courses in Hebrew for as long as possible.

Teachers at the girls' school were Mrs. Ćwik and Chaim Szlama Rozenfrucht (Shlomo Lehrer), who taught Jewish religion at the government school. They were joined later by Mrs. Chaja Brener, and, in due course, Sura Klementynowska was sent from Wilno [Vilnius].

This chapter is reprinted from pp. 13–14 of the English section of the original Działoszyce Yizkor Book, with minor changes.

Grade seven class of Beit HaSefer Ha'am [Folkshul] (1926)

Students at the Hebrew Girls' School

A class at the Yavneh School

Hashomer Organization

The Hatchyo Library (pp. 121–24)

Chaja Chaba (Szulimowicz)

Działoszyce was not an academic town; there wasn't a single high school in the whole town. Pupils who wanted to prepare for the *bagrut* exam were forced to take the long hike to Miechów or even Kraków.[1] And because the young and intelligent aspired to expand their minds, it was particularly necessary to learn independently. Because of this, it is no wonder that the active Zionist movement in town organized evening seminars, lectures, discussions, etc.

In the area of religious study, the town residents found an abundance of treasures in the yeshivas, in the *besmedresh* [house of study], and the *shtibl*s [small Hasidic houses of prayer], whose libraries had shelves overflowing, for the most part, with religious books. At every hour of the day or night, you could see young men and yeshiva students bent over different books, whispering, studying Talmud [collection of Jewish laws and traditions] and arguing. The spiritual food for general enlightenment was found in the Hatchyo [Ha-t-khih-yo] [a Zionist youth group] library.[2] It would not be an exaggeration if I said that this library was a makeshift university, although there weren't any professors or classroom furniture. The library wasn't just an institution in which one could find a book to read, but it also served as a center for the secular cultural life of the town. In this way, those who were self-taught could find many books of interest. Here, it was possible to express thoughts and ideas during those evening seminars and lectures. Those who were active in the library also organized cultural and educational activities in town.

Even though, beginning in 1919, public education was mandatory, not all of the young people attended public school. Many acquired their basic general education from private teachers. But for those who finished school and those who never went to school—but had the ambition to learn—there was the library, the sole source where they could find what they wanted. True, learning in this manner was very difficult, because students had to independently manage to learn things without the help of a teacher or lecturer. But, because so many aspired to learn, out of necessity, the importance of the institution grew.

With the increase in regular reading habits and the growing interest in fiction, the importance of the library changed. The institutions of culture and entertainment in the town were few; the "movies" hadn't yet come to town, and the amateur theater only occasionally presented a play. The fact that the young people could find popular literature that they otherwise could not have put their hands on was the main factor for the development of regular reading and familiarity with world literature. It would be no exaggeration to say that for most of them, this was their only spiritually uplifting entertainment during the long fall and winter nights. Of course, the youth began reading regularly thanks to the library; and once they got a taste of the library and understood its

---

[1] *Bagrut* refers to the *matura* exam in Poland needed to enter university.
[2] The Zionist Youth organization in Brzeziny, near Łódź, transliterated the same Hebrew word התחיה [Revival] as "Hattechija" rather than "Hatchyo," though the Polish pronunciation is similar.

nature, other entertainment forms and the passing of time by playing cards or dominos disappeared.

I don't know the exact date when the library was established, but it seems that it was toward the end of World War I. The first books were collected from a handful of donors. Again, I don't know where the library was located in its early stages, but I still remember—and I was a little girl then—that the one and only bookcase was transferred from Mr. Hercel Karmioł's room to the front room of the *talmed-toyre* [Jewish elementary school] building. Then began the library's period of great development, thanks to the first people who dedicated themselves to this blessed act. I must recall, in this context, the names of Hercel Karmioł, *z"l*, Icek Kołatacz, *z"l*, Dawid Targownik, *z"l*, Josek Tauman, *z"l*, Dawid Skóra, *z"l*, Herszel Baum, *z"l*; and, those who have been blessed with a long life, Abram Gałązka, Izrael Dov Skóra, and Herszel Horowicz. Of course, there were other involved, but I don't remember their names.

In its new location, the library grew by leaps and bounds; now there was more than just one bookcase that came from a single donor. The number of frequent readers grew on a regular basis, and in order to meet the demand of those thirsty for knowledge, hundreds of recently published books were purchased very quickly. Sources of funding came, first and foremost, from the Histradut [Zionist Labor Federation] budget, which organized a number of events for this cause. On a number of occasions, it was declared that on "flower days" [when flowers were sold to raise money], the proceeds would go to the library. For a limited period, the municipality also supported the library. I must also point out here that there were those from among the Polish-Christian population who used the library.

Such was the situation in the early 20s; just as the Zionist Histadrut expanded and stabilized and the Zionist youth movements from all the traditions were founded, so did the library grow and expand in terms of the number of books purchased and in terms of the number of readers who used it. With the splitting of the Histadrut, in the late 20s, into two different factions—Al HaMishmar [On Guard] and Et Livnot [Time to Build]—the library began standing on its own and became an independent institution.

The work and care for the library was done completely by volunteers from the Zionist youth movement. It was considered an honor and a duty to help young people and adults alike to acquire knowledge in this way. And, it is in this activity that we see the best of the town. Indeed, I cannot help remembering the many founders who were members of the committee elected in 1930, and they are Ze'ev Skóra, *z"l*, the secretary—and it is he who was the true spirit behind the group and the main leader; Szlama Gertler, who died recently in Israel, the chair; the author of this chapter, in the role of treasurer; and among the rest of the members of the active committee were Róża Chęcińska, *z"l*, Witla Cukierman, *z"l*, Icek Szaniecki, *z"l*, and, may they enjoy a long life, Mania Moszenberg, Róża Zonenfeld-Rolnicka, and Ze'ev Szternfinkiel, who was one of the most active.

Among the young people who helped on a daily basis with this work, I must recall, the son of the scholar, Kopel Brandys, and Moshe Bejski—who was just a youngster in those days.

I already pointed out above that the main growth of the library began with its move to its new location. Just as the number of readers increased, so did the number of books increase; on the one hand, with the arrival of more books, the demand for them grew, as did the number of readers. Because the members had such a wide variety of interests in different kinds of literature, the library struggled to fill its shelves with books from all different fields. And, so that the reader could find most of the classics in Hebrew and Yiddish, books from the Enlightenment period were placed next to books of the world's great authors whose works were translated into Yiddish, Polish, or Hebrew. This is to say that the library's collection included books in these three languages. But with time, the Hebrew collection grew. The library served, among other things, as a motivating force for the promotion of Hebrew, not only among the school students, but also among adults. There is no point in trying to list the names of the books and their authors; it is enough to say that those in charge made sure that the reader would find every book in whatever field interested him. It is clear, however, that while the Jewish collection received special attention, the other general literature fields were not ignored.

I would not be fulfilling my obligation if I did not fondly recall my friend, Mr. Eliasz Chaba, who, through his great devotion in the area of bookbinding, ensured that the books were in usable condition. And among the many hands that handled them, there were those hands that regularly worked on them.

If I must speak about the readers, then the truth is that they came from every strata of the population. Here, a school pupil would find whatever book he needed for his studies, the scholar himself could expand his knowledge in a field if he wished, and the lay reader could find here many books for his enjoyment. The special importance of this is that the people acquired regular reading habits, even just ordinary people. For the people pushing their carts, the tailors, and the rest of the craftsmen, a new field of interest opened up— and they, in order to expand their knowledge, came straight to the Zionist youth movement. Even the yeshiva boys, who immersed themselves in their Talmud, couldn't stay away from the library's doorstep. It was sometimes possible to observe a yeshiva student coming to borrow a book and hiding it under his cloak, so he wouldn't be caught red-handed.

Even though the institution was Jewish in its roots and in its essence, its gates were not closed to the Polish-Christian population, and more than a few of them used it. Because it was the only one in town, the Polish language section was not that small.

With time, the main room of the library became a venue for social and cultural activities. Indeed, it was the most appropriate place for evening discussions on literature and the exchange of ideas about what was happening in those fields. Moreover, the room also served the Zionist Histadrut, the Hanoar Hatzioni [Zionist youth]; and later on, the Hechalutz Klal-Tzioni [General Zionist Pioneers]. The library was open to the public for borrowing books three days a week, but readers often remained in the library beyond the regular hours of operation for discussions, debates, and cultural activities, which were organized by the active members and the committee.

Another activity, also connected to the library, was conducting Hebrew language classes there. In this context, we remember Mr. Hercel Karmioł and his brother Mordka Karmioł and Mordka Ungier, who did much in the way of teaching Hebrew to the town's residents. Thanks to them, many people didn't suffer any difficulties, with respect to language, and were able to make a smooth transition when they immigrated to Israel.

However, it appears there may be no special need to glorify and praise a library in a remote town when there were others, some more significant, found in towns all over Poland. And of course, this one was small and had no special importance in contrast to the great libraries found at some of the most famous educational and cultural institutions. Yet, its existence in such a small corner gave it great importance and meaning for the population of this remote Jewish town, which, during those years, sought to find new pathways to new horizons, ideas, and culture, and in assisting this process, this small institution did play a very significant role.

Translated from the Hebrew by Roger Kaplan

Associations and Institutions, Certificates and Documents

Envelope addressed in Spanish to Mr. J. Spievak, 830 Corrientes,
Buenos Aires, Argentina. Działoszyce postmark.

Receipt: Hatchyo [Revival] Jewish Public Library, Działoszyce
Received from Lejbuś Rolnicki, active member, 5.00 Marks. December 9, 1925

Hanoar Hatzioni and Its Activities (pp. 126–28)

Ze'ev Szternfinkiel

When I recall the period of my youth, the vision of the Zionist youth organizations flash before my eyes—Hanoar Hatzioni, Herzliya, Betar, Gordonia, Hashomer Hatzair. And, as one who headed one of these organizations, there will always be a place in my heart for them.

The Hanoar Hatzioni [Zionist Youth] chapter in Działoszyce was the largest of all the youth organizations in town. As time went on, our chapter founded additional chapters in neighboring towns, such as in Kazimierza Wielka, which were led by Herszel Doński, Lejbuś Zalcman, and Lejbl Miller. Fiszel London and Szydłowska headed a chapter in Wiślica; in Koszyce, it was led by J. M. Lewensztajn. Even in Nowy Korczyn (Neustadt) and Pińczów, there were chapters founded by us. And as time went on, the Działoszyce chapter became the regional headquarters for the Hanoar Hatzioni chapters in the area.

As to organizational preparedness and mutual closeness among the chapters from both far and near, our region united with the Miechów area. This was at the end of 1933, when during a celebratory parade, the Miechów, Miechów-Charsznica, Słomniki, Wolbrom, Żarnowiec, Książ Wielki, Wodzisław, Jędrzejów, and Sędziszów chapters united into one unit under the name Miechów-Działoszyce. Mejlech Frydrych, Moszek Pińczowski, and the author of this account were part of this [regional] chapter's leadership.

When we dreamt of emigrating to the Land [of Israel], all of our desires got caught up in the idea of making this come true, but when would the stage of really getting ready to emigrate begin?

In 1934, the work of the Miechów-Działoszyce region chapters resulted in the establishment of three *hakhshara* [pioneer training] camps in the towns of Wodzisław, Sędziszów, and Szczekociny. The group worked mainly on paving roads and in the sawmills.

During the first period, when the Działoszyce chapter was founded, they operated out of the Zionist Union room in the Jewish community building in the town market square.

When the chapter grew, it moved to a new clubhouse, to the house of Nusyn Rolnicki (Nusyn, the American), where they also had a large yard at their disposal for holding processions. The yard buzzed with activity on summer nights. There were dozens and dozens of boys and girls in their uniforms with songs of Zion in their mouths echoing into the distance.

Over time, due to various reasons, the chapter moved to new clubhouses—on Chmielowska Street (in the Palarz family home), on Kościelna Street (in the Karmioł family home), and on Skalbmierska Street (at a non-Jew's by the name of Laskowski).

Every move from clubhouse to clubhouse, from place to place, symbolized a different stage in the history of the chapter, its existence and its work, its troubles, the arguments and the conflicts that were then our lot. There were arguments and attempts to find a solution to ideological and organizational problems that plagued our movement. Of course, there was no lack of arguments with other Zionist youth movements, and certainly with opponents of Zionism.

I must point out, with great satisfaction and pride, that the chapter in Działoszyce consisted of the best of those in Hanoar Halomed Vehaoved in the town.[1] It was also the largest in number of all the youth movements in the area, and in terms of quality, it ranked right up there with all the other movements.

This chapter was alive and exciting, full of active members; it organized a meeting of the regional directors in Działoszyce in cooperation with the leaders of the Zagłębie area, in which members from all of the regions participated. Representing the head leadership chapter, Noach Chirik, an intellectual man, facilitated the directors' meeting. It was a prize moment in all of his existence, and all of us fell in love with his melodic voice when he took charge of the processions or explained to us the details of setting up tents or organizing camps; everything was done according to the scouting rules. Zoszka Orbach represented the leadership of the Zagłębie region, and Mejlech Frydrych and I represented our region.

At the end of the meeting, I was asked by Noach Chirik to arrange an evening procession celebrating the end of the directors' meeting. I stood before the lines of the procession, reading the proclamation. The atmosphere was electric; the summer sky with the stars shining was above our heads, yet all of us in our hearts thought only of nights in the Land of Israel and promised to continue the work even there. We'd be defenders of our own Land, we'd work by day in the orchards, and at night, we'd stand guard, protecting the lives of our kibbutz members in Kfar Saba or other places.

The melodic voice of Noach Chirik made your heart stop. He asked us, Mejlech Frydrych and me, to make a sworn oath in honor of the ceremony in which we were granted the "Defenders of the Movement" insignia. Shaking with great excitement, I declared the oath. Moments of uplifting glory and excitement from this high status were the rewards for the two of us who had achieved this title and symbol "Defenders of the Movement." These moments will remain unforgettable in every stage of the fortunate and the unfortunate life of a young Jew, guard, and member of the movement in our generation.

The extensive work included organizing summer and winter gatherings. In the summer of 1934, we organized a summer gathering near Sędziszów, in which both men and women from all of the chapters participated. Mejlech Frydrych, Dawid Stern (now David Kohav, a member of Kibbutz Usha), and I directed the gathering.

In the winter of 1935, we organized a winter gathering in Miechów-Charsznica with the same directors, and representing the main leadership were Munia Langer and Ze'ev Frydrych.

In the middle of the 30s, the Działoszyce chapter had about 150 members, men and women. And as was said, this chapter was the biggest of all the youth movements in the town. The cultural organizational activity was very intense. Every week we posted a newspaper wall on which we provided the activists an opportunity to express themselves in writing about all of the problems that concerned the chapter, in general, and our

---

[1] Hanoar Halomed Vehaoved was a combined organization of Hanoar Halomed and Hanoar Haoved, both Zionist youth organizations.

movement, in particular. We created a permanent Jewish National Fund corner. We organized a drama club with Jankiel Leszman as director. We presented plays by Goldfaden, with musical accompaniment by the Lokaj family orchestra, which was a highly regarded group in our town and the area.

Over the years, we managed to also establish a library.

The chapter's Lag B'Omer trips and processions through the town streets were an impressive event.[1]

Contact between the area's chapters was very close. Every week, we published, by mimeograph, written reports and reviews of current events, and every month, the regional leadership met.

Members of the leadership group were Josek Szulimowicz, z"l, Dov Bejski, Wolf Hercberg, Zalman Ryba, Judka Nożycer, and Lejzor Pińczowski.

The Działoszyce chapter secured a number of immigration visas [to the Land of Israel] and a few of our members did emigrate: David Shlomi [Szulimowicz], Bajla Bursztyn, Josek Brandys, z"l, and Necha Brener. We'll never forget the period of their emigration; we held going away parties for them, we took lots of pictures, and we wished them well on their new journey, the road to fulfillment as defenders of Zion. Meanwhile, all those who remained dreamt of their turn to emigrate. We accompanied them to the train station, sang songs, and dreamt. In our minds, we saw ourselves together with them, a group of Działoszyce residents in the Land of Israel.

Not only was our life full of emigrations, celebrations, and emotions of satisfaction and happiness; there were also days of arguments, anger, and sorrow. We had stormy and emotional arguments that bordered on civil war. (Remember, among other things, that there was a split in the movement between Warsaw and Lwów.) Today, with the passage of time, everything seems so gray, so innocent, and so unique. But every fighting group meant what they said with absolute seriousness. "We took everything seriously," as the old-timers like to point out today during their friendly conversations in Israel when remembering those days. If there is such a things as "a disagreement for heaven's sake," then the aforementioned argument was one. But, as I said, we believed in our destiny, and "we took everything seriously."

World War II was the war of the Holocaust, in which the great Polish Jewry was exterminated, including the many, many Zionist youth of our movement and the rest of the movements. As is well known, Ashmodai [the king of demons] and all of his murderous messengers did not differentiate among the Jews. Everyone was sentenced to the extermination camps.

Not all of those in our chapter, the many activists in Działoszyce, its members, and associates succeeded in coming to live with us in the Land of Israel and to see the fulfillment of their youthful dreams. This fact will always be engraved on the tablets of our heart.

---

[1] Lag Ba'Omer is the 33rd day of the Omer, the days following Pesakh and before Shavuos. The first part of the Omer is a period of mourning for the plague that occured at the time of the Bar Kokhba Revolt in the first century. Jews traditionally do not have weddings or anniversary celebrations during that time. Lag Ba'Omer is celebrated to mark the end of the mourning period.

Let us remember our friends who traveled the distance with us, over many years, nurturing the Zionist goal. We left in the hearts of the youth faith in the national rebirth of the Jewish nation in our historic land and the fulfillment of building the land. But to our anguish, many did not live to be among those of us who fulfilled this dream. This is the Zionist goal, but only a few of us actually managed to fulfill it in our own independent country.

Translated from the Hebrew by Roger Kaplan

Hanoar Hatzioni (pp. 129–30)

Izrael Brandys

Thirty years ago, when I was busy with my final preparations to emigrate to Israel, I sat one day in my house, whose windows faced the town market square, and thought much about the new path upon which I was embarking—which wasn't familiar to me yet—and about my past, which I was about to leave behind and abandon.

The small town of Działoszyce, where I was born, is well known to those who lived in it, and it is not my intent here to describe its rich and poor inhabitants, its homes and hovels, its daily life and holiday celebrations.

In this account I only want to describe, briefly, the youth groups of the town; this was specifically what my thoughts were about during that time, approximately thirty years ago. I belonged to this group of young people; it was an inseparable part of me, and just as it was for me, so, too, it was for many others of my generation.

Most of the young people belonged to the Zionist pioneer movement, and the lions among them to Hanoar Hatzioni [Zionist Youth]. And this, I think, is because of the insignificant number of leaders of stature who belonged to and were active in the other movements, the non-Zionist ones in our town.

I will enumerate here some of the young people who stood at the helm of the Zionist activities in the town. My deceased brother, Josek Brandys, *z"l*, Josek Szulimowicz, *z"l*, and, may they be selected for long life, David Shlomi and Dov Bejski.

The activities and meetings of the youth in the town concentrated solely along several paths. And the meeting of the youth in the nests of their movement on Shabes evenings was just one of the activities that left this experience entrenched so deeply in my heart.

After the Shabes meal, the youth would leave their homes and flock to their nest. Our nest existed for many years in two adjoining rented rooms outside the town. Around these rooms was a big yard with an orchard of apples and pears, and in these quarters, by the light of a petroleum lamp, we would gather around our advisor who would lecture us about the Zionist movement, its personalities, about the Land of Israel, and on the work of the pioneers there. We would sit there and swallow every word the advisor or the leader of the nest spoke, and we would sit as though in a trance. Many times the leader of the group would request that one of us give a talk about the prominent leaders of this Zionist movement in front of the members or also prepare a topic to be debated with the other members. Many of my friends would certainly remember the talks we had about Achad Haam [pseudonym of Aszer Ginsberg], Tshlenov, Ussishkin, Weizmann, and others. We were young then and experts on these topics, since we read a lot, and the philosophy of Zionism was the breath and blood of our lives.

After such talk, we would launch into pioneer dances, without a harmonica and without an accordion. We would sing and dance, dance and sing, until we couldn't catch our breath. In the late hours of the night, on our way home, each one of us saw it as his duty to walk along the length of the well-known highway until the night watchman with the white beard, who was a familiar figure to all of us, would approach us and ask that we go home and give the neighbors some rest and peace. Many others would go walking outside the town (not by car, but on foot) to enjoy nature with a few companions.

The nights of *moytse-shabes* [close of Shabes] resembled those of Shabes evenings; however, during those evenings, there was a livelier atmosphere, without lectures. We would spend our time dancing and playing sports, especially the game of ping pong.

Most of this youth were studying and acquiring knowledge of Torah; very few individuals went around doing or studying nothing.

Education caused many to move from our place to other larger towns where there were high schools or post secondary higher education. Only for the Pesakh holidays or during summertime would these students who had wandered afar come back home. During the annual vacations, there was a greater reawakening among the youth. Those who had returned from far away, from the larger towns, were an attractive source of information for us, and we all heard from them what was happening and going on in the world at large and especially in the Zionist movement. New ideas were heard, arguments and debates took place regarding emigration to Israel, protecting our homeland, and regarding the battles of Jews in Poland, this same country that had received so much from its Jewish citizens and had given back so little in return.

With the conclusion of these summer vacations, life would return to its old course, and the days would become gray and boring. The library of the Jewish community would again regain more of its readers, and life in the youth movements would return to being quiet.

Many from our town went on to receive pioneering training to prepare for emigration to Israel. They wandered to cities and far away places and for many years worked under very difficult conditions in order to prepare themselves to go to Israel. Only very few were fortunate enough to receive permission to go, and in spite of all this, the ones who remained behind continued to work in places that would prepare them for this event.

The departure of one of our youth members to go to Israel became a major event and cause for celebration in the town. All of us from the town, without exception, saw it as our duty to go to the train station and say farewell to the person who had the good fortune of emigrating to Israel. The good-byes were very difficult.

Our yearnings and willingness to go to our homeland was so strong, intense, and ingrained in all of this youth, that it was like a burning desire. Many shed tears at this small railway station when the train pulled out from the station.

Translated from the Hebrew by Rochel Semp

A group of Hanoar Hatzioni

A farewell to Dawid Szulimowicz and Bajla Bursztyn as they depart for Eretz Yisroel

A farewell party. Two pioneers leave for Eretz Yisroel

Hanoar Hatzioni
summer camp

Participants at camp

A younger group in
Hanoar Hatzioni

Group of girls of Hanoar Hatzioni with their group leader

A Gordonia training group in Dziekanowice
together with members of Hanoar Hatzioni

Hashomer Hatzair (pp. 135–37)

Moshe Pułka

The dynamic youth of the town of Działoszyce, yearning for something, was seeking a place to spend their limited free time. This was still during the time that an organization by the name of Hashomer Haleumi [The National Guard] existed, and in it were concentrated the Jewish youth of Poland, especially youth whose parents had financial means.

In the years 1927 to 1928, a group that consisted partially of the youth who were members of the organization Hashomer Haleumi established an additional group by the name of Hashomer Hatzair [The Young Guard]. Its first members in our town were Josek Rozenfrucht, Ezryel Drobiarz, Moszek Smolarczyk, Fajgla Szajnfeld, Moshe Pułka, and Henoch Cudzynowski, along with some other friends whose names I can no longer recall.

The initial group, at whose helm stood Jakób Hupert, began attracting to their vision a great number of youth—children of laborers and the working classes. Since Hashomer Hatzair was, from its beginning, a leftist youth organization in our town of Działoszyce, Mr. Hupert was forced to acquire for himself an apartment on the outskirts of town, specifically owned by Christians, to serve as a club house. Near the Catholic church, in the home of the Adamczyks, was where the organizational club came into being, and that is where the second Zionist youth organization, by the name of Hashomer Hatzair, started to develop. This youth organization, whose origin was of a socialist character, grew more and more. A great number of youth joined its ranks, the majority being girls, such as Małka Śpiewak, Chana Szulimowicz, Bajla Goldwaser, and Bajla Osnat. A constant feud and battle raged between the children and their parents, who would not allow, in the beginning, under any circumstances, for their children to join this Hashomer Hatzair. However, in spite of everything, young people who came from all strata of the population joined its ranks in great numbers. In the course of time, Hashomer Hatzair grew and developed and was one of the most active organizations in town. It supported many activities within the Zionist movement, including appeals for Keren Kayemet [Jewish National Fund] and Keren Hayesod [United Israel Appeal] and was involved in many other activities and campaigns that took place for the cause of Eretz Yisroel. With our vision toward Zion, the trips and campaigns we conducted on Lag B'Omer, as we marched for the first time through the streets of Działoszyce, were received by the entire Jewish population with much enthusiasm and applause.

It is noteworthy to mention the devotion of the "guards" Chaim Pułka and Lejb Frajman, who summoned, with a trumpet, the members of Hashomer Hatzair to organize and to march. The first trip was to the village of Sancygniów, and on horseback, at the head of the march, rode the head of our chapter in those days, Josek Rozenfrucht, who was the manager of Szental's laundry. This inspired the youth so much. Also the parents of the members in the Hashomer Hatzair very slowly became accustomed to the fact of the movement's existence. Therefore, we moved the club from the outskirts of town to its center, and its activities grew and developed. A sports center by the name of "Shomria" was also established, and there, we witnessed the great athletic skill of Jakób Wolf

Hupert, Szymon Pilc, Tuwia Ptasznik, Szyja Krycer, Moshe Pułka, Jakób Gryner, Michał and Jakób Łatacz, Michał Majtek, Lejb Fink, and others, whose names have become erased from my memory. This drew more and more youth to Hashomer Hatzair. Many remember the happiness and joy that would envelop the town each week when Sunday arrived. When the sports team from Shomria confronted a Polish team, there was a true battle between the two teams. And when the Jewish side won the match, it is hard to describe the ecstasy, joy, and happiness of the Jews.

With the strengthening of the chapter's activities locally, the idea of a summer camp developed. This involved great difficulties. A double problem arose. One could not expect parents to provide any financial assistance to their children for the expenses involved in the running of a camp. And also, one could not imagine that the parents would allow their sons and daughters to simply go to a summer camp, far from their homes, where boys and girls would spend time together. With the passage of time, we overcame these difficulties as well.

In order to enable our friends, the members of this movement, to be able to attend the summer camps, we initiated and conducted various fundraising campaigns that brought in a substantial amount of money. We collected money at weddings, and we also promoted various entertainment events, just to prove that our town wasn't inferior to the others in the area.

The first to go to the summer camp of Hashomer Hatzair were the boys and girls who were members of Hashomer Hatzair. The campsite was established in the area of Kielce, and I can even remember the names of the people who attended the camp.

The first person from our chapter of Hashomer Hatzair in Działoszyce who left for pioneer training was Ezryel Drobiarz. After him, Lejzor Czosnek traveled to Wołyń, and Henoch Cudzynowski and Moshe Pułka went for training in the south. A number of active members left the chapter; some went for training, and others moved to the big cities in order to find work.

After a while, some very active members of Hashomer Hatzair left and established a new youth group by the name of Gordonia.[1] The names of these members were Nusyn Krelman, Icze Rubin, Chaskiel Frajman, and others, whose names I no longer recall. They continued their energetic activities in this new movement in Działoszyce.

The activities of Hashomer Hatzair became newly reorganized. Jakób Hupert was elected head of the chapter. The group for which he served as leader included the most active "guards" in the chapter. Their names were Tuwia Ptasznik, Wolf Arkusz, *z"l*, Motel Arkusz, Jakób Pułka, Zalman Frydman, and the Krycer brothers. The activities of the chapter did not decrease at all after they moved from their old headquarters to the new. Many of Hashomer Hatzair members were forced to leave the town and settle in Kraków, due to their difficult economic situation, and a small number even went to Upper Silesia. Even though they were far away, they did not break off their ties with the youth of Działoszyce and their organization, Hashomer Hatzair. They also supported the chapter as much as they could, so that its existence would continue.

---

[1] Gordonia was a Zionist pioneering youth movement named for Aaron David Gordon, a philosopher of Labor Zionism.

In the chapter itself, the basic work to provide an education continued. So, for instance, they brought in a Hebrew teacher from Wołyń for the special purpose of teaching the Hebrew language to its members. The chapter continued sending its senior members for pioneering training. Among these were Szlama Glajt and Zalman Frydman. Z. Frydman was one of the last to leave for training from this chapter of Hashomer Hatzair.

The years passed. The economic situation worsened, and anti-Semitism reared its ugly head and increased from day to day. The young people who were employed in small workshops were being exploited. They labored without just compensation from the early morning hours until very late at night. The lack of a professional organization to unite the laborers was keenly felt.

Through the initiatives of Hashomer Hatzair and some of its friends—Tuwia Ptasznik, Szymon Pilc, Icze Rubin, Lejb Fink, Josel Lorja, and others—a union of leather workers was created that proclaimed a strike. After several weeks, the strike ended with the workers coming out the winners. They settled for a nine-hour workday, a fact that was a big success for the working youth of Działoszyce.

After that, they organized other trade unions as well, e.g., for the needle and baking industry. A strong labor union arose. During World War II, the German murderers and their assistants annihilated the majority of this vibrant youth. During the occupation years, the members of Hashomer Hatzair conducted a fierce war against the German and Polish murderers. Josek Ptasznik and others joined the partisans. Szymon Pilc and Tuwia Ptasznik were murdered while in the underground movement.

May the name of Hashomer Hatzair and its many areas of activities in our town endure for a long time.

Translated from the Hebrew by Rochel Semp

The Gordonia Movement (pp. 138–40)

Natan Krelman

When we come now, after many years, to write about the young Zionist movements in our town, we feel as though these things happened only yesterday. However, these memories are plagued by a void. Missing are not only the years that have passed from then until now, but we also feel the loss of all those beautiful, dear and good people who sacrificed such a large part of their lives. And missing, above all, are all those young people who did whatever they did and produced whatever they produced in spite of life's difficult circumstances. They could not rest and be still, since a strong desire burned in them to be the sons of an independent nation, possessing an independent country, all their own, just like all the other nations.

We felt very strongly our inferior status as young Jews whenever and wherever we went. In the towns, there were acts of violence and terror against us. Jewish stores were robbed; Jewish crowds got attacked. In the market square and elsewhere, everywhere, we saw ourselves as superfluous. We slowly learned from this situation that the place where we were was becoming more and more dangerous for us. We decided that we had to become a nation that was worthy of its name and that on each one of us lay the task of being a Zionist and a pioneer at the same time. We felt we had to do something to make a difference.

In our town there already existed several Zionist youth organizations, such as Hashomer Haleumi [National Guard], Hanoar Hatzioni [Zionist Youth], Hashomer Hatzair [Young Guard], and Hechalutz Klal-Tzioni [General Zionist Pioneers]. The youth were deeply conscious of having to change their nature and character. They traveled to training sites and got ready to emigrate to Israel. None of this was simple. Many obstacles were placed in our paths, mainly, by our parents who did not believe in a national revival, in the creation of a nation worthy of its name. They would say sarcastically, "So you want to be pioneers!" Similar words of mockery and scorn were heard from all sides.

In 1931, a group affiliating with Gordonia was formed. Eventually, there occurred a change among the parents. Within this training organization, our friends, both boys and girls, did whatever job or work came their way. They did not object to any hard labor— tilling the fields, chopping trees, etc. The youth prepared and readied themselves to become helpful in their land. Also the face of Działoszyce started to see changes. The Gordonia chapter began with feverish activity. Lectures were given, courses established for Hebrew, and whoever wished came to study and learn. In my town, I was friendly with other members of this chapter and with many other groups of youth that had already been organized. We were successful in establishing an independent branch of Gordonia in Działoszyce as well.

All levels of youth were represented within our branch. The young people who agreed to join us found their own proper place. Our education encompassed the level of *nizanim* [budding beginners] as well as other levels, until the level that was called *magshimim* [achievers]. The members of this division learned quite a bit of Hebrew, much about the history of Israel, about pioneering, the nature of Zionism, etc. We sent our members to summer colonies, to *hakhshara* [pioneer] training sites, or for activities for Keren Kayemet [Jewish National Fund]. The parents were very thankful and appreciative that we invested so much work and effort in educating their children and teaching them to follow the right path. I recall that many of our male and female friends expressed their opinion that Gordonia was educating the young in the spirit of A. D. Gordon. His photograph, appearing with his face covered by a long beard, made an impression. He also captured the imagination because he was a simple man, a man of the people. The students of Gordonia tried to be loyal and devoted to the idealism of A. D. Gordon and the movement. And suddenly, in the midst of all this work and activity came along the barbarian Hitler and his war and destroyed everything without leaving a trace. Only a small group of us made our way to Eretz Yisroel. The rest suffered the same fate that befell all the other Jews of our town and the country. At the beginning, they tried to continue under the new circumstances—performing work, collecting money from various sources—so they could give support to our friends who found themselves in extremely dire economic circumstances. Some were deported to labor and death camps. Small groups escaped to America and never returned.

A special gratefulness and appreciation is due to our friends for their superhuman efforts and sacrifice put forth during the Holocaust. Chaskiel Frydman, *z"l*, spent two years in pioneer training and afterward was imprisoned in a camp. He was extremely devoted to all the other inmates with him in the camp and shared his last piece of bread with them. He died a few months before liberation. And here are the words he spoke before his soul departed, "Nusyn [the author of this account], when we overcome everything, and it comes to an end, we will not wait but immediately make *aliye* [immigration to Israel]." You could tell on his face that he had reached the end of his strength, which had already left him, but the teachings of Gordonia continued to live within him.

They tell the same thing about his younger brother, Kalman Frydman. They were sons of a poor working family of tailors. Their father's name was Josek, and his nickname was "Pupek." I bow my head in recognition of the head of this family who raised such sons with such ambition and dedication.

They were not the only ones. This tragedy befell many of our friends, both boys and girls, whom Hitler murdered. We had a friend by the name of Icek Rubin, *z"l*. He was full of energy and willingness to work. All the Jews in Działoszyce knew him. He was actively involved in all aspects of fundraising for Keren Kayemet. He was a pioneer in the full meaning of the word. He trained together with other friends and got permission to immigrate to Israel. He did not have the good fortune to achieve this goal but was murdered by the Germans.

In the kibbutz of Mishmar-Hasharon, there are many friends who spent their pioneer training in Działoszyce and helped with many of our activities in the town. On the whole, their participation was visible in the cultural life, in the communal meetings, and in the evening question and answer sessions discussing Zionism and pioneering, as well as many other topics. These activities awakened an interest among the youth, and this led to many being able to broaden their educational scope both generally and with regard to Zionism.

I recall the elections to the eighteenth [Zionist] Congress that were held in our town. There were lectures and election speeches. Various spokespersons and party representatives arrived from many different towns. Działoszyce evoked interest among all the different Zionist parties, because it was a very vibrant town, especially its youth. One cannot forget the Zionist activities of our friends; our anguish over their irreplaceable loss is overwhelming, and we can never forget them.

All those who remained from the ruins, whether here in Israel or in other lands, will never forget them. Their memories will never fade from us.

Translated from the Hebrew by Rochel Semp

The Agudas Yisroel (pp. 141–45)

Aryeh Shahar (Lejbl Jutrzenka)

Polish Jewry began to organize itself into political groups after World War I. This new development affected observant Jews no less than others, and led to the emergence of the Agudas Yisroel [non-Zionist Orthodox party]. This had started in 1912 in Germany and came largely from the ultra-observant Frankfort Jews who had set up their own communal institutions, etc., even earlier, as a countermeasure against the widespread Jewish assimilation within Germany in the early twentieth century and before. A similar process had taken place in Hungary, where the observant Jews had broken away from the "Neologists." But in Poland and Lithuania, the overwhelming majority of Jewry was still observant, the study of Torah was the essence of Jewish life, Hasidism was continuing to spread, and the steps taken further west were felt to be unnecessary.

By the end of World War I, the situation had changed, and the Gerer *rebbe*, the beloved moralist Reb Izrael Meir Cohen (known after his major work as "Hefetz Hayyim"),[1] the saintly and learned Reb Chaim Ozer Grodziński, and others summoned a Knessia Gedola, or Great Assembly, and called upon Polish Jewry to organize as the Agudas Yisroel for the purposes of strengthening the study of the Torah and the education of children, while maintaining the fully observant ritual structure of the Jewish communities, and act against alien influences. Agudas Yisroel was prepared to accept all who lived according to the Torah and its *mitzvot* (commandments).

And so it came about in Działoszyce as elsewhere that all the Hasidim and fully observant Jews joined the Aguda [Agudas Yisroel], which, among other activities, maintained the *yeshivot* and Talmud Torahs [Jewish elementary schools]. The first Agudas Yisroel committee was headed by Reb Szmul Jutrzenka, Reb Icek Majer Frydberg, the *shoykhet* (slaughterer), Reb Chaim Josek Dziewięcki, Reb Moszek Wajnsztajn, and Reb Izrael Josek Mandelbaum. At the first Działoszyce Vaad Hakehila (community council) elections in independent Poland, the Aguda received a majority. Reb Icek Rubin was elected first chairman and won general approval for his dedication to the public welfare, in Polish eyes as well. When the first municipal elections were held, he was appointed deputy mayor. He actually received a majority of the votes, but the Polish government could not stomach having a Jewish mayor. From the beginning, he worked for the good of all Jews without exception and was appreciated accordingly. Naturally, things became lively at election times, but they calmed down once the elections were over.

At the international Agudas Yisroel conference in 1933, Działoszyce sent Rabbi Yehuda Halevi Frankel and Reb Icek Majer Frydberg as its delegates. They called on the conference to take all steps, both spiritual and practical, to secure the opening of the gates of Eretz Yisroel to the tens of thousands of young Agudas Yisroel members and others who wished to proceed there. That appeal was met with general acclamation.

This chapter is reprinted from pp. 17–19 of the English section of the original Działoszyce Yizkor Book, with minor changes.

[1] Izrael Meir Cohen, author of *Hefetz Hayyim*, was a rabbi in Raduń, Poland (now in Belarus).

After this conference, the Aguda underwent a revival in Działoszyce, and more than one hundred new members joined the youth organization. They were given premises by Mrs. Bluma Rafałowicz (Bluma Hindla's) and commenced working intensively for Eretz Yisroel. When Rabbi Szabtai Rapaport, the rabbi of Pińczów came to speak to the young men, the latter, led by Lejbl Jutrzenka, brought him to town by a special coach. The rabbi delivered a fiery address, and within a short time 15,000 *złoty* were collected towards the Million Złoty Eretz Yisroel Campaign.

Reb Chaim Klajner, chairman of the youth organization, together with the secretary Szmul Formalski, extended activities on behalf of the Keren Hayishuv [Fund for Palestine] of the Aguda. This secretary dedicated himself heart and soul to the development of the local Tseirei Agudas Yisroel [youth group] and established a junior section of Pirchei Agudas Yisroel, a *Yeshiva Ketana* [small yeshiva] of about 120 members thirteen to sixteen years of age, who studied their daily Talmud portion after work. The lessons were given by Lejbl Jutrzenka, Berl Ptasznik, Abram Waga, Jankiel Kaźmierski, etc. A library was established containing the works of all the Orthodox writers, and Yisrolke Kamelgarten was librarian. Courses in modern Hebrew were given by Lejzor Kac. Reb Icek Majer Frydberg conducted a course in Torah for all and sundry every Sunday, which included the Book of Psalms. His course proved increasingly popular.

Later the Tseirei Agudas Yisroel helped to establish the Poalei Agudas Yisroel [workers group] headed by Hercke Einhorn, Josek Przędza, etc., which prepared for life in Eretz Yisroel and found work for members. About five hundred children attended the Talmud Torah, whose chairman was Reb Szmul Jutrzenka. He was also responsible for Beit Yaakov [school for girls], with two hundred children, and the yeshiva with its seventy to eighty senior students, many of them from the neighboring small towns.

Indeed, the Aguda's activities encompassed all aspects of Jewish life—economic, religious, and political—until the outbreak of the bestial Hitler War, during which our town was destroyed with all its institutions. The Poles even destroyed the cemetery, leaving no trace at all of the long-flourishing Jewish community of Działoszyce.

Trends of the Zionist Movement (Pages 146–48)

Naftali Szydłowski

My memories about the Zionist movement in Działoszyce go to the time when I was studying in the *talmed-toyre* [Jewish elementary school]. This was in the first years after the Balfour Declaration.[1]

Almost all the youth of the town were under the influence of Zionism, except for a small number of yeshiva young men, who were under the influence of Agudas Yisroel [non-Zionist Orthodox party], and another smaller number of young people whose orientation was to the extreme left.

In our small town, we had a very nice large library called Hatchyo [Ha-t-khih-yo],[2] which was run by young adults, the majority of whom were Zionists.

This library has a history of its own. The library was situated in a building that belonged to the Działoszyce Jewish community. One family, whose name I do not recall, left the building as an estate for the community to use for its own purposes and needs. In the beginning, so I think, there existed in this building all types of community offices. Afterward, when I was about nine years old, in 1917 to 1919, they established in our town a school called *talmed-toyre*. The community paid the salaries for all the religious teachers as well as for the secular teachers for the Polish and Hebrew languages, so that the children of the poor could study and learn Torah, just the same as the children of the rich. The school had five classes, which were held in this community building. In one of these rooms was also the library. We studied until eight o'clock in the evening, and the library also opened at eight o'clock in the evening, so, sometimes, there was a conflict between the studying of Torah and the secular library.

These small conflicts, and perhaps other factors as well, brought about a fight between the Zionist youth and the older generation, the keepers of the faith, until it became a court case that had to be adjudicated by the authorities, the *starosta* [district administrator]. And at times, it even erupted into the raising of fists or the burning of library books. In the end, the Zionists won, and the library remained in the same place. With the passing of years, the library expanded and was located in two rooms that also served as a club for the Zionist movement, in general, and its different activities, such as showing films, etc.

There was a custom in our town that when a lecturer or even an ordinary speaker would come to town, he would speak from the *bime* [raised platform] in the *bes hamedresh* [house of study]. Once there came a lecturer from the Histadrut [Zionist Federation] or from one of the seed organizations, Keren Kayemet [JNF] or Keren Hayesod [United Israel Appeal], and he went up to the stage in the *bes hamedresh* to deliver his speech. A big commotion ensued. The older generation, whose members were in the majority, disrupted the speaker and prevented him from delivering his speech,

---

[1] On November 2, 1917, British Foreign Secretary Lord Balfour issued a declaration favoring the establishment of a national homeland for the Jewish people in Palestine.
[2] Named after the Zionist youth group התחיה [Revival] that established the library.

while the young Zionists stood by defiantly. It reached a point where fists were raised, and one could witness and also hear the sound of cheeks being slapped when parents "honored" their children in this way.

All this was during the first years after the Balfour Declaration, in the early 1930s. In the forthcoming years, the situation changed at a rapid pace. The Zionist philosophy became entrenched in all levels of the town's citizenry except for the Aguda [Agudas Yisroel], the small Left, the Communists, and the Bund [Socialist Labor Party].

The older people generally belonged mostly to the Mizrachi [Orthodox Zionists]. During this same time, different groups were established that sent their representatives to Eretz Yisroel to acquire real estate in partnerships and, maybe, to prepare for immigration to Israel. At approximately the same time, if I'm not mistaken, the immigration started that was called the "Aliye Grabski."[1] However, to our great dismay, a great depression erupted in the Land [of Israel], and almost all of the people who had gone there returned.

The Zionist movement became well established in Działoszyce. There arose different streams from various Zionist organizations. The majority of people in our town belonged to the General Zionists; however, there were also the followers of the Revisionists. I imagine that most of the Mizrachi people followed the Revisionist movement. Apart from this, there also arose a branch of Hatzair [Hashomer Hatzair] and Betar [Revisionist Zionist youth]. This started conflicts between one brother and another, fathers and sons, friend and friend. The ideological conflicts took on the form of personal animosities. Each side, of course, was convinced of its righteousness. In the Land [of Israel] the idea of restraint was heard, but the Revisionists were against restraint. They argued that we needed to fight against the Arabs and the British and to get ready for a real struggle, etc.

Betar, which became established in our midst, was very active. Its members wore uniforms, and they trained and practiced the use of weaponry and following military commands.

Across from the Betar club was a branch of the Hashomer Hatzair [Young Guards]. In both of these organizations, the boys and girls came from good homes. They knew what they wanted, participated in various Zionist activities, and learned Hebrew and spoke it among themselves. Although everything was done on a small scale, nonetheless, the main thing was that the necessary motivation was both here and there. Other Zionist channels were also established, for instance, Hashomer Haleumi [The National Guard], which later changed its name and called itself Hanoar Hatzioni [The Zionist Youth], the right wing of the Zionists, whose membership was quite minimal, and also a movement that was called by the name of Hitachdut. Boys and girls who did not restrict themselves to a particular [political] party joined the latter. They, however, participated in the various Zionist activities in the campaigns from different groups, such as the selling of *shekels*,[2] etc., but they were not an organized group. During the same time, there was another group that was called, if my memory is correct, by the name of Herzliya [based on name

---

[1] Named for Władysław Grabski, Polish prime minister and minister of finance, who had imposed harsh economic measures on Jews, causing them to make *aliye* in increasing numbers.

[2] A *shekel*, now an Israeli coin, was then a personal membership certificate in the World Zionist Organization and was proof of payment of membership fees. Paying of the *shekel* was a condition for the right to vote and eligibility for election to the Zionist Congress.

of founder of Zionism, Theodore Herzl]. Its members also came from the young people who were not organized.

Stormy arguments occurred between the members of these two groups. The members of Hitachdut were followers of the General Zionist movement during those times, with connections to the labor movement, while the members in Herzliya were more aligned with the Revisionists. During that time, there almost wasn't a person in our town who wasn't involved in Zionist activities or, at the very least, considered himself a Zionist—of course, with the exception of a few Communists and Bundists. As for myself, personally, I was not acquainted with anyone from the Bundists and with very few of the Communists. The Zionist life was extremely turbulent during this period. Great fierce and fiery discussions and arguments took place between the members of the various groups, and each one thought, of course, that he was right.

At a later time, an additional branch of the Hechalutz Haklal-Tzioni [General Zionist Pioneers] was created. I was then serving in the Polish army. As far as I know, this branch was established by the oldest youth group, with the encouragement of the elder members of the branch of the General Zionists. The purpose of this branch was to enable the younger members, who came from the organizations of Hitachdut and Herzliya, and those who were not part of any organization who wanted to make *aliye* to Israel, to go for training and receive a certificate for *aliye*.

During this time, the members of various movements were involved in different *hakhshara* [pioneer training] kibbutzim.

I cannot write any more regarding Hechalutz Haklal-Tzioni, since during that time I served in the army, and right after my discharge, I left to go to a *hakhshara* kibbutz. Most of the members who went for training with Hechalutz Haklal-Tzioni left before me.

From the day I got discharged from the army until I left for training, a few weeks passed by during which I was not actively involved in the work of the organization. In spite of this, I was active in the Hitachdut, to which I had belonged already for several years. We were a group of sixteen to nineteen year olds; we felt it was our responsibility to do something. We used to meet, raise money, each one of us donating as much as he could. We rented a room, requested informational material and received it, in quantity, from the organizational center in Łódź. We publicized the establishment of our branch in town advertisements. In the beginning, we were a small group, but during a short time, we grew, and increased, I think, to seventy or eighty members.

Also active in our town—I don't recall when—was an organization by the name of Gedud Keren Kayemet L'Yisroel [Keren Kayemet Brigade]. Its function was to increase the fundraising to the Keren Kayemet [JNF]. However, this wasn't the only activity in which it engaged. A very vibrant social life existed, and many cultural functions and activities were provided. In the realm of the Keren Kayemet L'Yisroel, there were also members who were not Zionists, to the extent that there still remained in Działoszyce anyone who was not a member of some Zionist movement.

Translated from the Hebrew by Rochel Semp

Keren Kayemet L'Yisroel Committee (1929)

Members of Hechalutz HaKlal-Tzioni

Members of Keren Kayemet L'Yisroel

Associations and Institutions, Certificates and Documents

Membership card for Histradut Hatzioni
issued to Rajzla Zonenfeld, 1933

Membership card for Zionist Organization in Poland,
issued to Arje Rolnicki, 1928.

Drama Groups and Entertainment Activities (pp. 152–55)

Shoshana Rolnicka

During the initial years following World War I, after Poland regained its independence, groups of actors from Warsaw and Kielce used to come to Działoszyce. They used to perform various plays, the majority being dramas and comedies, but sometimes they would also put on satiric-realistic-political performances that reflected current events.

Reflecting on Current Times

As the years went by, these groups were also joined by local residents, such as Dawid Skóra and his sister, Moszek Chilewicz, Szlama Kołatacz, Moszek Kołatacz, the deaf Hersz, Jakób Leszman, Balcia Sternberg, Mendel Wdowiński, and others.

As far as I can remember, they performed the following plays: *Bar Kokhba, Shulamit, Motke the Thief, Kiddush Hashem* [Sanctification of God's name], and *Gott, Mensch und Teufel* [God, Man, and the Devil]—which achieved great success throughout the entire public spectrum. In 1924, Dawid Skóra discontinued his appearances on the stage, since he had to move to Warsaw because of his work.

A few years passed and they created a broad drama circle that included a large number of youngsters, the cream of the crop of the youth, who came from the best families in town. That circle acted intermittently under the direction of three stage managers who developed and became accomplished on their own. With constant practice and with years of experience, they gave endearing performances. Their names were Dawid Skóra, Szmul Wdowiński, and Jakób Leszman. Each one of them directed this circle at a different period of time, but all of them succeeded in gathering around them boys and girls with great talent in acting and singing. Jakób Leszman, who excelled in comedy, had completed a school of drama; he could have achieved a great career on the stage.

Among the plays that were performed by the outside groups was a play with a clear Zionist theme. In it, much was spoken regarding Eretz Yisroel, and they sang many national songs. In this play, the central topic was the longing and yearning for our homeland and also our anticipation of the redemption of the nation and the land.

The songs that were heard in this play were sung by the citizens of the town for a very long time. This helped to ingrain the idea of Zionism into the minds of the Jewish population. This particular nationalistic play that was performed left a very great and profound impression on its viewers, and almost all the young people came to see it.

Moreover, thanks to this play, the youth became strongly motivated to escape their sheltered, isolated lives, in which they had existed until then, and to strive for enlightenment and culture and to spread them among the various sectors of the population.

From 1927 on, the Zionist committee took this drama circle under its auspices. The group grew wings and expanded greatly. The young ones from all the movements found their niche in it and participated in the many rehearsals that were necessary before each play.

During this period, the person directing this drama circle was Jakób Leszman. He was a teacher, and in spite of the fact that he had a large family with many children, he devoted himself to the theatre and to this group with all his heart and soul.

In those years, they performed on stage the following plays: *The Golden Chain* by Peretz, *Der Zapasne Soldat* [*The Reserve Soldier*], under the direction of Szmul Wdowiński and others, *Shir Hashirim* [*Song of Songs*], and *Kol Nidre* [*All Vows*],[1] under the direction of Jakób Leszman. The parents of the players would come to these plays and performances, in which the finest youth participated, to see how their sons and daughters were succeeding in their various roles. Much of the time they did not even recognize them, since they were in costume and made up to portray the role they were playing.

Many preparations were needed before each new performance. First of all, one had to choose the topic, and debates about this continued at times for weeks and weeks. They wanted the play to attract as large an audience as possible, and also it was necessary to choose scenes the actors would be able to perform. However, this wasn't the main issue! The challenge in every play was to choose the actors and actresses and to cast them in the roles they needed to portray. There was no lack of applicants. However, not everyone was a proper fit for their allotted role.

In addition, it was very important that some of the actors have a good singing voice, since the plays consisted mainly of operettas and musical scenarios. It is also worthwhile to note here that because of the central fund into which all of the profits of the plays were collected, the directors of this drama group didn't rule out any applicants belonging to any specific movement; rather, they tried to encourage members from all the groups to join. Jakób Leszman saw to it that every player got the part that fit him or her best. That was the reason they generally enjoyed such great successes in the production of these plays that won the hearts and minds of the viewing audiences.

Most of the time, the initial opening play would take place the night following a holiday or on a Saturday night, the night following Shabes. This caused the Jews from the entire area to come flocking in throngs to view the play. An atmosphere of mutual reciprocity and unity between the actors on the stage and the viewing audience permeated the hall. It is worth noting another very important aspect. Since the viewing public knew the players personally, and in the majority of the cases were also related, they were curious to see how their relatives and friends would perform the roles they had taken upon themselves or that were given to them by the producer. Of very special importance was the performance of the main actor's role in the play or of the supporting actress to the main actor, the "prima donna."

Taking part in the play *A Mensch Zol Men Zein* [*A Person You Shall Be*] that took place in the month of April 1927 were: M. Ungier, Róża Chęcińska, Róża Zonenfeld, J. Wdowiński, F. Baum, Jakób Leszman, Fajgla Wdowińska, and Herszel Szenkier. The director was Leszman.

In the play *Kol Nidre* that took place in the month of October 1927, participants were: Chaim Meryn, Herszel Szenkier, Icek Kołatacz, H. Smolarczyk, Mordka Ungier,

---

[1] Kol Nidre is the opening prayer of Yom Kippur, which includes a plea that all vows a person was unable to fulfill that year be annulled.

Róża Zonenfeld, Jakób Leszman, T. Piekarski, and Josek Garfinkiel. The director was Wdowiński.

In the play *The Reserve Soldier* that took place in September 1928, the following people participated: Motel Ungier, Róża Zonenfeld, Mindla Wdowińska, H. Meryn, M. Kołatacz, and Jakób Leszman. The director was Leszman.

In most of these performances, a choir also participated, which involved those youth who knew and prepared especially for this part. And it is interesting to note that during half a year following the initial performance, the entire town would be singing and repeating the songs and tunes that were heard during the performance of the play.

In the play *Shulamit*, the second time around, which was performed during the years 1935 to 1937, those participating were: Lejbl Pomeranc, Drobiarz, Manela Miller, Zysia Ptasznik, Frajdla Rolnicka, Hadassa Bursztyn, and others.

Moszek Hersz Rozenfrucht, the master technician of Wdowiński's power plant in the town, constructed and organized the lighting and illuminations. The orchestra that accompanied almost all of the plays was put together by the well-known Lokaj family, who played on different instruments under the direction of Abram Lokaj, who was also the leading violinist. In addition, two sons of Jakób Leszman, Dov and Dawid Leszman, played in the orchestra.

Aside from the performances of the theatre, there also took place in the town different "academic" events that were organized by the Zionist committee in Działoszyce. Generally, their topics were about the lives of the pioneers in Israel, the vast challenges that the settling of Jews in Eretz Yisroel created, the great struggles and wars that the Jews had to fight in order for them to immigrate to Israel, and so forth…

So that the "academics" would make the best impression, they usually invited a speaker from outside the area, from the [Zionist] headquarters, and he was asked to speak about a subject that was relevant to that evening's topic. There were also events where an artist was invited from out of town, a lecturer or actor, and his presence served as the climax, the high point of the evening. Local issues supplemented the main topic. In addition, in order to put together the fitting decorations for the play, the director would first prepare a list for each actor and actress, describing the costumes that they would need to wear for their respective roles. It was the actors' responsibilities to make sure that they got all that was necessary for them. Often an actress would sew for herself the dress that she needed for the role she was performing in the play. And this is how all the costumes were prepared, as well as all the other necessary props and decorations for the stage. All the plays took place in Firemen's Hall, and the stage was permanent, so everything was prepared in advance behind the curtain—a scenery of a forest and so forth; and it could be said, that they used this "forest" in almost all the scenes. Usually the scenery would be drawn by a gentile named Woźniakowski, whose occupation was inflating tires and repairing bicycles. The drawings served him as a hobby, and he was especially fond of painting scenery for the purpose of the theater.

It is noteworthy to relate another fact. Generally, the electric plant would stop lighting the town at twelve o'clock midnight. But since these plays would continue sometimes until two or three in the morning, the organizers would approach Mr. Wdowiński, the owner of the electric plant, and ask that he continue the lighting on these nights until the conclusion of the performance.

In conclusion, it is worth noting that the drama groups and their activities served as a true beacon of light, especially for the young, but also for the general Jewish population. Their appearances breathed new life into the town and enthused everyone without exception; it was as though a window had been opened onto what was happening in the world. The horizons and perspectives of all those who participated in them were broadened, including the majority of the viewing audiences who had a passive role as listeners and viewers.

Entertainment

There were days, sometimes the days between the first and last days of a holiday, when an idea would originate with one of the active youths to organize an evening of entertainment. And then we would approach the leader of the orchestra, Abram Lokaj, and we would organize an evening of plays, comedy, and dance. We would plan a spontaneous program that would be carried out with the active participation of the drama circles. Abram Lokaj organized the family orchestra, and the youth spent a pleasant evening with singing and dancing until the morning hours. In the intermissions between singing and dancing, we would raffle off items that were collected from the citizens of the town.

There was a time when the youth became passionate about the current faddish dances, and this mania took hold of almost the entire youth of the town. They brought in a dance teacher by the name of Kohl, from Kielce, and he was the one who began giving dance lessons to many of the boys and girls.

This fact encouraged the arrangement of all types of balls, mostly dancing balls. And these balls attracted a very large concentration of diversified youth belonging to the many different youth movements. The first ones who learned how to dance were Gitma Richter, Josek Tauman, Blumcia Zylber, Ester Zylber, and others.

During a later period, the "dance master" Awramcze appeared, and through his lessons, many boys and girls learned how to dance the modern dances. Perec Dutkiewicz also continued the teaching of dancing. A gentile player by the name of Filipowski accompanied these lessons by playing on the violin, and he was the one who set the rhythms that were necessary for the dance steps. The names of the dances that they learned were: the Charleston, the Shimmy, the Step Dance, the Quadrille, the English Waltz, the Ladies Waltz, and others.

The director of the comedies and dance balls was the barber Izrael Świczarczyk.

The young dancers were looking to express their feelings while having a good time. And this is how the entertainment started developing. Very quickly new programs were created that demanded to be implemented. The Firemen's Hall was rented, along with the musical orchestra of the Lokaj family. Big posters with drawings on them, advertising the date and time of these dancing balls, were posted along the length and width of the town by Pincia Alter. These took place mostly on a *moytse-shabes* or *moytse-yomtov* [the night when Shabes or the holiday was over]. And it was most interesting to observe the youth of all levels of society streaming to this type of a ball. Of course, the admission to the hall cost money in order to cover the expenses. The extra revenue was put aside for a specific purpose, mostly for Keren Kayemet [Jewish National Fund]. Such a dance ball attracted most of the youth. Admission to this event was by invitation; otherwise, they could not accommodate all the young people who came knocking on the doors of the hall. Not a few mishaps happened on such an evening, especially from those who complained about why they were not invited to the dance and thus were deprived of an evening of good times and other experiences. The organizers saw to it that male guards stood at the entrance to the hall to prevent break-ins through the door by force. Usually, these balls lasted until the wee hours of the morning.

It is also worth mentioning that the organizers, in order to maximize their revenues, established a canteen whose supplies had been donated earlier by the active members in the town. In addition, they had raffle prizes, and during the intermission between one dance and another, they would sell raffle tickets. In reality, the value of the winning prizes was minimal. However, the experience and hustle and bustle generated by these drawings created great happiness and excitement among the celebrating participants.

Such were the entertainments and recreations during an entire generation of the youth in Działoszyce. This was all in order to celebrate, as it is written in Megiles Esther [the scroll/book of Esther]: "And the Jews had light, happiness, joy, and honor."

Translated from the Hebrew by Rochel Semp

138

The Drama Circle performs *Kol Nidre* (1927)

Programs of Performances by the Drama Circle

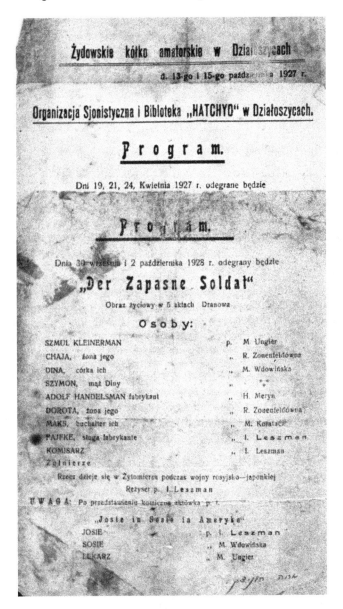

Der Zapasne Soldat [The Reserve Soldier]
Josie and Sosie in America

The Flood (pp. 158–60)

Natan Krelman

It happened in May 1936, on a Saturday afternoon, when the whole town was taking a rest after the Shabes meal. There was a meeting of the committee of Keren Kayemeth scheduled, coincidentally, at that time, at the headquarters of the Zionist organization Hatchyo [Ha-t-khih-yo] [Revival].

A very light rain started suddenly, which immediately became a downpour, then a cloudburst.

From the hills around the town, rivers of water began to pour down, and a great panic developed.

I started out for the other end of town, where the young people were. I understood that one had to be on the alert to rescue the town from the flood. When I got to the courtyard, the water had already reached twenty-five centimeters [ten inches]. Before the young people noticed the true downpour, everything was already covered by water. The water divided the town into two parts. When I wanted to communicate with my parents on the other side, it became, indeed, impossible.

Suddenly, there was a large bang heard near the bridge at Moszek Beker's. It turned out that the bridge had been destroyed by the rushing waters, and, at the same time, the two-story house had also been dragged down and collapsed. Many other small houses in the flooded area had collapsed.

I decided to go back to the youth organization; I attempted to calm them somewhat, and, at the same time, I organized them to climb out through the windows and go toward the hills where the cemetery was. There were approximately sixty to eighty young people there. After I was able to get the remaining young people to the hills and position them there, I remembered that the tailors' association of the Poale Zion [Labor Zionists] were meeting in a two-story wooden house that served as a retreat. Every Saturday afternoon, the place was full of young people. Without thinking too long, we rushed over there, and using ladders, we were able to rescue dozens of friends who were gathered there.

It is truly impossible to describe the scene, the terror and panic that gripped the whole town as they watched the great destruction that the flood was causing. The hysterical screaming of the people accentuated their powerlessness—not being able to fight against nature turned savage.

We had at that time no communication with the other side of town. It had become dark all around, the lights had gone out. There was nothing to see but small houses floating in the water, with great impetus, until they were destroyed by the waves.

We only saw light in one of the houses as it happened to flow past.

Later, when we were able to work our way across Skalbmierz Street, I and a few friends—Icze Rubin, *z"l*, Chaskiel Frajman, *z"l*, and some others—crossed over the hills on the property of the Dziekanowice landowner Spiro to look for a way to connect through to that side of the town, but to no avail. Like all the other fields, the Szczotkowice meadows were immersed in water. The reason for that was that these were the low lying areas, and the floating small houses, cattle, and a lot of Jewish goods and property had drifted there. The books from the *bes hamedresh* [house of study] were there, among them the prayer book that the *khazn* [cantor] had received as a gift from my grandfather, Reb Moszek Krelman, *z"l,* of Warsaw, when he officiated at the wedding of his daughter to Sender Ryba.

I remember well the day when the flood struck. It is indeed impossible to describe. This natural disaster caused a major portion of the population to lose the roofs over their heads. Many families abandoned the town. A few simply walked around the neighboring towns asking for charity to cover the necessities for their families.

Some of the [Zionist] movement's young men immediately set themselves the task of distributing help to the victims. They started a communal kitchen where those who had no means could come for their midday meal. We appealed to other communities and immediately received quantities of clothing, shoes, provisions, and other articles for daily use.

I feel a sacred duty to recognize the warm generosity at that time of the brothers Kaczka, brothers Kamelgericht [Kamelgart?], Josek Szulimowicz, *z"l,* and others. Alter Frydman and I, with a few other companions, gave up days and nights to alleviate the disasters caused by the flood.

Within a short period of time, the town slowly recovered. The organizations again took up their activities. The professional societies also renewed their work, and the economic and social life in the town returned to its normal appearance with its usual worries and events.

Translated from the Yiddish by Zulema Seligson

The synagogue after the flood

Destroyed wooden houses

The train station – boxcars overturned by the flood

After the flood

144

The Cudzynowski house –
half destroyed in the flood

One of the victims of the flood

Grandfather's House (pp. 164–66)

Chaim Cycowski

In the village of Trzonów, a distance of ten kilometers from the town of Działoszyce, lived but one Jew, my grandfather, Reb Symcha Lautersztajn. He was a lone Jew in a sea of thousands of gentiles. He was in a village among dozens of other villages and farms dispersed within an area of dozens of kilometers.

He was God fearing and generous of heart, and his entire goal and mission in life was to provide hot food and lodging to the passersby and to merchants who got stuck in their business travels from town to town. His house was also a lodging along the way for the poor who went begging from door to door—a Jewish house that provided hospitality to guests. His was a warm house in the cold wintertime and a shelter and shield from the steamy heat of summer.

Even in his old age, when his children got married and left the house and everyone left the village, Grandfather did not abandon his home and place. He remained in the village, not because of his livelihood, but only to observe, as before, the *mitsve* [commandment/good deed] of *hakhnoses orkhim* [hospitality to guests] in its fullest sense. It is necessary to note that this Jew did not take a step in all the days of his life, whether small or large, without consulting his *rebbe*. Formerly, he was one of the close Hasidim of the *rebbe* Reb Chaim Majer Zalc of Pińczów, and after the *rebbe*'s passing, Grandfather continued traveling to his son, Reb Eliezer, the *Admor* [Hasidic religious leader] from Pińczów, and after that also to his grandson, Reb Pinkus, *zts"l* [of blessed righteous memory], who perished during the terrible Holocaust. My grandfather wouldn't take a small or large step without the counsel of this chain of generations of the *Admorim* of Pińczów.

He used to wake up on a Friday morning, take his prayer shawl under his arm, and say to Grandmother, "I am going to the *rebbe*." Grandmother didn't ask or make any inquiries, because she knew that her husband wanted to spend Shabes near his *rebbe*, *zts"l*. Grandfather didn't look for any means of transportation; he left with his prayer shawl and cane and walked on foot with the goal of sanctifying the Shabes and taking joy in the holy heavenly spirit in the court of the *rebbe*.

I especially remember a miraculous episode that Grandfather would tell to the entire family at every opportunity and which became engraved in my memory forever. The incident took place as follows:

In his young years, Grandfather leased from a wealthy landowner all of the milk production of his farm. A contract was written up and signed according to all the necessary regulations. Grandfather received from this landowner also a house in which to live, and all of his other needs were to be provided for, as well. This was a customary thing among the landowners. The payments were made on a monthly or annual basis.

According to the contract, the landowner could at any given time cancel the agreement if he found it necessary. In spite of this provision, many Jews knew how to manage; they raised children and educated them in the old Jewish traditions that had been passed along from generation to generation.

Grandfather was a talented man who knew how to get along with people, and that's why he was able to get along not only with Jews but with gentiles as well. In spite of the fact that the landowners were generally mean people with peculiar demands, Grandfather would stay on the best of terms with them.

One time, Grandfather was requested to come immediately to the landowner. He arrived hastily and worried. The landowner demanded, without any explanation, that at the end of a week's time he should leave the farm. In other words, he had until Wednesday of the following week. This sudden news had the effect of putting Grandfather in great shock. This sudden expulsion meant not only that he would lose his livelihood but also that he must leave his home. What was he to do with his family of many children without a roof over their heads? His mind kept on ceaselessly reverberating with questions. What to do? Where to go?

Grandfather, of course, immediately found the answer. He would go to his *rebbe* and ask him what to do. He came to his *rebbe* and told him the story and, while doing so, gazed at him beseechingly. The *rebbe* asked, "What is the final date that this landowner gave you?" And Grandfather answered, "Until Wednesday." The *rebbe* answered him with a question, "Until Wednesday?" and told him to go back home. Meanwhile, nothing had changed at home. The time drew closer, and Grandfather stood to lose his house and his livelihood. Sunday passed, Monday went by, and nothing changed. The verdict was pending and was intact. Grandfather, with a bitter heart again ran to his *rebbe* and repeated his request, and the *rebbe* again responded with a question, "Until Wednesday?" Grandfather burst into tears. "Today is Monday and altogether there are only two days until the date of my expulsion. What should I do? Where can I turn with small children? And the *rebbe* stood his ground, "Until Wednesday?"...

With no other choice Grandfather went back home, with hope and trust that finally, finally, salvation would come from the merit of his *rebbe*, *zts"l*.

On Monday, very late in the evening, a messenger arrived from the landowner and informed my Grandfather that he was to appear immediately. The landowner received him in his reception room with a pleasant countenance and related to him all that had transpired during that fateful week. It became clear that another Jew had come to him and offered him more money for the right of acquiring the lease of the milk production on his farmstead. The landowner agreed to the Jew's offer. However, his peace of mind was taken away from him. The entire week, he had experienced sleeplessness. The end result was that he left Grandfather in his house. And not only this; he didn't add a penny, and the contract between them remained without change. The rationale was that Grandfather was a good and devoted Jew.

Grandfather merited very good children, God fearing, lofty, noble, of distinguished character, who continued following his ways with devotion and dedication. They excelled in giving charity and caring for their fellow beings. His daughters especially excelled in their virtuous good deeds and served as role models to others. It is worthwhile to note that the girls did not receive an education in a Jewish school, for example at a "Bes Yaakov" [school for girls]. Instead, their Jewish spirit was acquired through the books that were in their parents' home. They remembered by heart the *Tzena Urena* [book for women explaining weekly Torah portions] and many of the chapters of the Book of Psalms as well. Grandfather said that his daughters also helped to bring in income to the household. One of them was a seamstress who sewed nightgowns and coats for the farmers in the area. They paid very handsomely for her work, which was very much in demand. The second daughter, by the name of Frymeta (it is my honor to be her son), used to work the entire day and, in the evening, would sit near the big stove (in the farms there used to be wide and tall stoves that could hold heat in them for a long time) until the wee hours of the night and study the Torah portion of the week along with chapters of Psalms. When his daughters reached marriageable age and it was necessary to marry them off, Grandfather suffered greatly, since he wanted them to marry men who were *talmide-khakhomim* [Torah scholars]. The girls, of their own will, were willing to forego money and external appearances, since they only wanted to marry yeshiva boys. Their desire was granted them. My father, *z"l*, Judka Lejbuś, was a Hasidic young man, a great Torah scholar and God fearing. Also my uncle Chaskiel, *z"l*, was blessed with these virtuous characteristics. Both belonged to the sect of the Ger [Góra Kalwaria] Hasidim in Działoszyce.

Every year, when the days of *slikhes* [penitent prayers before Yom Kippur] would come, Grandfather would make preparations to travel to Działoszyce for the *slikhes* prayers. As I have already mentioned, in his village there was no minyan [group of ten men needed for prayer]. It was not a small sacrifice to get up in the middle of the night so as to arrive before the morning for *slikhes*. In the dark of the night, the citizenry of Działoszyce would suddenly hear the noise of wheels traveling on the paved road. They immediately guessed that this was the carriage of Reb Symcha Lautersztajn, a sign to all the Jews in the town to get up and go to *slikhes*.

Translated from the Hebrew by Rochel Semp

My Memories (pp. 167–70)

Menachem Laskier (New York)

Szental's Garden

Not far from the market square, just after going through the wide gate of Laskier's and Meryn's house, you already found yourself in Szental's garden. It is interesting that there wasn't actually a garden there, only the name remained. Here and there a tree remained from the good old days, a witness that there had once been a garden here. And if one can believe the old people of Działoszyce, there was once a very lovely garden here with many trees and flowers. The garden was tended for many years. The residents of Działoszyce really enjoyed the garden in those days. Jews used to take walks there on Shabes after their naps, as befits respectable *balebatim* [houseowners/men of stature]. More than once a Jew dozed off under a tree and snored, to boot. Even later, the solitary trees served the same purpose—in the hot summer days, people still dozed there. Naturally, they also snored respectably. Nobody knew why the garden became neglected. It has stayed in my memory for a totally different reason.

My grandfather, Moszek Laskier, *z"l*, lived in Działoszyce. When my mother was still alive, we used to come from Łódź to Działoszyce to spend the summer vacations. However, in 1934, my mother, *z"l*, died, and after that I was raised in Działoszyce at my grandfather's, *z"l*. Only then did I find out what kind of a place Działoszyce was. I used to study my immediate surroundings—and that meant Szental's garden and the two streams.

The Streams

There were two streams in the garden, right next to each other. Only a small path divided them. Szental's garden barely had more than a few trees, and in the streams, there were no fish. It is possible that there had once been fish there. In my day, we only caught small prickly fish (*kalkes*) and frogs. The streams did not dry out because a spring, which came from a nearby hill, always filled them.

Can there be anything better for children than water creatures—*kalkes* and frogs? I spent my youth in this area. Together with my friends, summer and winter, we played near the water and passed the time away. Summers we splashed around in the water, caught tadpoles, or just simply sat and talked with friends. This was no small thing, as there are, after all, enough problems in the world that need to be solved. So we discussed, we argued, and then made up. Not infrequently a friend would suddenly go flying into the stream while clowning around; somebody had pushed him in. He emerged not just wet, but like a black person—black from mud. The stream was not deep, but the bottom was muddy. There was no reason to envy such a dupe. For weeks we talked about it. In the daytime, life revolved around the streams, but at night, the streams themselves came to life. As soon as it was dark, a real frog symphony began, or, better said, a frog cacophony. The croaking of the frogs was so great that throughout the market square only "kva-kva-kva" could be heard—from millions of frogs. We always wondered where the frogs were all day long. There were many of them in the streams, the croaking was so resounding, but we did not see them during the day. Frogs come to life at night.

In the winter the streams had a different appearance. The Polish winter is not easy. As soon as the freezing weather set in, the streams were covered over with ice. In the beginning, when the ice was thin, it was dangerous to slide on it, but later, when the freezing temperatures became greater, the ice became thick enough to support us, and a new life began on the streams. If someone owned skates, he was really a big shot and went gliding on the ice—if only he could. If he couldn't, he rode more on his bottom than on the skates. But those who didn't have skates also had the time of their lives, gliding on iron horseshoes. And everybody was lively on the streams.

Our enjoyment was often disturbed. Suddenly, on a beautiful bright day, when it was particularly cold, workers with axes and saws chopped up the ice cover and dragged great pieces of ice out of the stream, putting them together not far from the stream until quite a fine ice mountain rose up. The gentiles poured water on the ice. In the evening, when the freezing temperatures increased, the ice and water froze together. After that, they would cover the ice with sawdust, and the pile of ice was ready for the summer. This is how the Jews of Działoszyce enjoyed a bit of cold weather in the wintertime and also saved the ice to use on hot summer days. With the removal of the ice from the streams, our skating would also come to an end, but our sleds were long active on other slippery paths and roads.

Hardware stores in Działoszyce

Being young, I did not understand business, but day in and day out, I hung around the business that my grandfather, Moszek Laskier, z"l, ran in partnership with Tuwia Meryn, z"l, and so gradually, I caught on to the business. Działoszyce was the commercial center for the surrounding villages. Here the peasants bought everything that they needed, from a nail to threshing machines. A business had to have everything in stock. What didn't they have in the store? Chains and bars of iron of various thicknesses and forms, screws, nails, locks, iron for blacksmiths, materials for barrel-makers, parts for machinery, etc. In fact, it was a small supermarket; everything made of iron was there. In town there were, however, two more hardware stores. What I liked most of all was that although they actually competed with each other, yet they helped each other and lent each other different kinds of iron that the other didn't have. I liked to spend time in the store listening to the stories that were told there.

Why my father, Nuchim Chaskiel Laskier, z"l, did not remain in the hardware business and left Działoszyce as early as 1921, went to Łódź, and went into another line of work—spinning—is not clear to me to this very day. But in time of trouble, he came home, together with my brother, Abram Benjamin, who was married to Rajzla Lorja and had a little girl, Surele.

Troubles

In Działoszyce it was possible to live peacefully. Unfortunately, the war broke out and there was no shortage of *tsores* [troubles]. Nonetheless, we managed to live, some a little better, some a little worse.

The worst and most tragic began with the deportations. The Germans, with the help of the Poles, cleansed the city of its Jews. My grandfather, *z"l*, still had the privilege to die a normal death in bed. Thirty-two days before the deportation, he returned his soul to his Creator, being eighty-four years of age. We followed the funeral procession, but in our hearts, there was apprehension, pain. What was still to come? Terrible rumors abounded. To believe them or not? Fear ate at our hearts. Unfortunately, they were true. Ten days before the deportation, I was sent to Kostrze [labor camp near Kraków], to the Strauch factory. I was still a child, but I carried the yoke and suffered. I heard about the first and second deportations from Działoszyce. Silently, I suffered equally with all the others, not knowing what happened to my family. Two weeks after the second deportation, my father and brother, *z"l*, came to Kostrze. In the interim, they had been hiding in the attic of Moszek Wajnsztajn's home and had come to me through Wolbrom. All the [surviving] Działoszycers were together working for Strauch. When they liquidated the Strauch camp, we were all transferred to Płaszów. From there, we went to Kielce, Birkenau, and Buna [Auschwitz subcamp]. However, a great selection occurred in Buna in 1944. At that time I lost my loved ones forever. My father, Nuchim Laskier, *z"l*, together with Zale Wajnbaum and Icek Kruk, *z"l*, died.

The measure of affliction was not yet complete. I was sent further, hungry and cold, naked and barefoot, until I arrived in Gliwice. From there, I was sent with other surviving Działoszycers to Buchenwald, skeletons in the form of human beings, chased by wild animals. Further marching, together with Jechiel Krycer, until Ehring. The troubles never ceased. Who can possibly endure such pain and affliction? Three thousand of us Jews were marched from Buchenwald. In the course of the march, almost all died from exhaustion or were shot.

Extremely exhausted, I survived until the end of the war. Unfortunately, I was unable to rejoice. The destruction for me had been too great, as it was for all Jews who had lived until the moment of liberation. Only 128 Jews [from Działoszyce] had the privilege of being freed.

Translated from the Yiddish by Zulema Seligson

Memories (pp. 171–74)

Bracha Pozner (Zając)

After my thirty-four years of living in Israel, I am trying to recall from memory the varied spices and flavors that characterized the existence of the Jews in our small town outside the Land [of Israel].

Many and varied are the memories about these things that colored our lives and caused them to be full of interest, aspiration, and strong faith.

The Jews in the town constituted a substantially high proportion of the residents of the town, about ninety per cent. There was only a small stratum of Jews whose livelihoods were secure and who lived a comfortable life. As a matter of fact, on the contrary, the majority of the Jews barely earned a living; their working conditions were poor and their circumstances quite miserable. Their dwellings were primitive, and their livelihoods very meager.

I don't want to dwell on descriptions of the material situation in our town. This I will leave to those more capable than myself. However, I do want to focus on the other side of the coin and describe the spiritual aspects, the Jewish heart and soul that beat in our town.

Everyone was busy with pressing daily problems, some with earning a living for their household, some with dealing with the disabled, such as retarded children, or with marrying off a daughter. There came into being organizations whose goal and mission was to give support and help to the needy. A public assistance fund and a Women's Histadrut [Zionist Labor Federation] were started, organizations that supported the needy, gave aid to the less fortunate, and prevented those without families from feeling totally alone and isolated. Women used to collect money and supplies and distribute them to the needy. Individual sick people were fortunate that members of the organizations supported them in their illness, and things reached such a state that the problem of the individual became everyone's problem. Anyone who was able tried to help and became involved to lighten the suffering. I am certain that these actions lifted the spirit of the needy and raised their hope and faith that tomorrow would be better and their faith would be strengthened.

I recall an incident when I went in the evening hours to Ajzyk, the shoemaker in the town—he lived in a dark cramped cellar and a small stool served as his workbench—to pick up my shoes that he had promised he would repair in the afternoon. He replied that he didn't have a chance to get them ready yet. I complained to him, "You promised me to fix them this afternoon." Ajzyk started laughing and said, "You are right. However, it is not yet afternoon here, since I haven't even eaten lunch." And he immediately turned to his wife with the promise that when they became the winners of the lottery for such and such amount of *zlotys*, then they would have a hearty, sumptuous meal. When I asked him if he had a lottery ticket, he replied in the negative. Thus, you see that even though he didn't have any ticket in his hands, he trusted that he would win those valuable *zlotys*.

Another source of pride was the youth of the city, young people who gave their elders much joy and *nakhes* [pleasure], since they were active and accomplished young people. The young who got involved in youth organizations would come together, and during the course of long hours, they would listen to stories told by Israeli emissaries. They would dance stormy *hora*s [Israeli national dances] and sing our nation's songs. There were also several parents who, because of their religious beliefs and their reliance upon the coming of the Messiah for salvation, opposed this Zionist movement. One of the organizations was the Revisionist movement Betar, where differences of opinion would be raised that at times turned into bitter fights. Sometimes, these differences became magnified. One day, my uncle arrived from Canada—he was a representative in the Zionist Congress and was invited to speak in our town. He did not bother to get a permit, and he started talking about his representation in the Congress in front of a hall fully packed with Jews who had streamed in from all parts of the town and filled the hall from corner to corner. He ignited the anger of these Revisionists, who didn't look upon his lecture with a favorable eye. In the beginning, they tried to disrupt it, but when they couldn't accomplish this, they turned to the police, who hastened to arrive at the place to disperse those assembled and to arrest my uncle. He was only freed the next day thanks to my grandfather's connections.

Another source of light in the town was the drama circle that had been established by young people. The creation of this circle met with many problems. Some of them were technical, caused by inappropriate equipment that was vital to the establishment of such a group. Another was the opposition of some parents who didn't view with favor the fact that their children would appear on stage. In spite of this, and in spite of all those other obstacles, the group did become established and succeeded during its existence to produce many, many plays and performances. My grandfather was among those heads of household who opposed this circle. Once, there erupted a controversy between the musicians and a stage manager who wanted his sons to perform in the play. They turned to my grandfather and tried to put pressure on him to intervene, although he was troubled by the fact that his granddaughter was appearing on the stage. But, as I mentioned, in spite of all this, I continued to perform, and the other youths did as well. This drama group continued to exist and produce serious plays that were met with very great success.

Even though thirty-four years have passed since then, one cannot forget the holidays in the town. Well ahead of the official holiday, they would be sensed in the atmosphere of the town. Each holiday with its special colors, each with its special atmosphere, permeated the town. The activity that ran like a red thread throughout the town regarding all the different holidays was the aid and assistance that was extended to all those who needed it. They saw to it that their tables were set as they were supposed to be according to *halakha* [Jewish religious law] and that nothing should be missing from their tables for that particular holiday.

Despite my wishes not to relay too many stories about my immediate family, I must say that I cannot remember even one holiday where a guest who was without the means of celebrating the holiday on his own was not sitting at our table. My grandfather would go to the *bes hamedresh* and look for homeless people who would hang around after prayers were finished, and he would invite them to eat at his table and celebrate with us. All of this, in spite of the fact that my grandfather was not considered one of the prosperous people in the town and had more than a few worries about earning a livelihood.

Even today, it is difficult for me to comprehend the link between the many daily worries, hardships, and obstacles and the warmth and deep caring for others, along with the readiness and willingness to help and support the needy.

As I have already said, the coming of the holidays cast a special atmosphere that united our town. I want to pause here for two of them—the High Holy Days and the holiday of Pesakh and all that was connected with them. The atmosphere between the night of *slikhes* [penitent prayers] until after the holiday of Sukes [Feast of Tabernacles] lent an air of repentance and the asking of forgiveness for the sins and transgressions that were committed between men and heaven and men and mankind, whether intentionally or unintentionally.

During those days, all the people in the town would stream into the synagogue. Among them would also appear those who during the other days of the year were not in the habit of attending the synagogue.

On Rosh Hashanah, we girls were instructed to be present in the synagogue only during the blowing of the shofar and the ceremony following it. After that, we would go back home where a hearty meal awaited us, and afterward, we went to the river for the prayer of *tashlikh* [casting off one's sins]. Along the embankment of the river, the people praying would stand and empty out their pockets into the water, as though they were emptying and throwing into the ocean all their sins and transgressions. Along the banks of the river an atmosphere of pleasantness and calm prevailed, and from each and every corner, the laughter of children was carried in the air. The eve of Yom Kippur turned into the height of anticipation and holiness that I felt everywhere. This intensified with the arrival of dusk. My excitement and nervousness grew to such an extent that I worried whether or not I could stand it. As a matter of fact, the High Holy Days would start to be felt in our home yet an entire month before their arrival. All of this was because my grandfather was the *shaliakh tzibur* [prayer leader] who stood before the reader's stand for the Kol Nidre [plaintive prayer on Yom Kippur eve] and Neilah [closing of the gates], etc. He used to train groups of young lads to sing in the choir and accompany him with the prayer melodies. These boys used to be in rehearsals for many hours. We girls were restricted in our movements because of this, since we were totally forbidden to draw their attention to ourselves. When the eve of Yom Kippur arrived, the preparations became more intense and the pace quickened in order to be prepared with everything for the concluding mealtime and the arrival of the holy day. Throughout the day, dozens of friends and acquaintances would come to visit us in order to bless us with a good and happy New Year. These visits would always be accompanied with tears and the pouring forth of the soul. The scenario would reach its peak when our mother would take us children into her arms, raise her eyes toward heaven, and with intense pleading, ask God for well being, health, and happiness for her children.

Until this very day, a shiver runs through me and a very strong nostalgia is awakened in me when I remember all of those moments that have gone by never to return. The entire population streamed to the prayer of Kol Nidre without any distinction in their level of observance. Hundreds of Jews wrapped in their *talesim* [prayer shawls] appeared to the light of hundreds of candelabras and candles, like a very strong force. The prayers, along with the boys' singing, reached toward heaven and penetrated deep into each and every Jew's heart and awakened in all of them hope, faith, and courage for the morrow.

The scene in the synagogue and its praying congregants during the prayer of Kol Nidre is one that cannot be forgotten.

The next day passed by with prayers and fasting that caused more than one of the people who were fasting to faint. At the end of the day, the men used to go outside, dressed in white and holding candles in their hands in order to bless the new moon, while the women would hurry to go home and prepare the meal that was to be eaten after the lengthy fast. After the meal, the Jews used to hammer in the first beam for the building of the *suke* [booth], and with this, they actually began the preparations for the holiday of Sukes. For this holiday, several neighboring families used to prepare a *suke* together. They would bring trees, poles, wood, and roof coverings to erect the *suke*. Right afterward, when the *suke* was already built, the boys would start with the decorations and interior arrangements. During the holiday itself, as already said, the neighboring families would celebrate together, with the men folk eating together in the *suke*.

From the holiday of Sukes, let us pass with one jump to the holiday of Pesakh.

The preparations were deeply felt. A long time before the holiday itself arrived, massive preparations would be conducted in the homes, which were turned inside out. In the doorway of the homes, dozens of objects would be seen that were put outside for scrubbing and cleaning. The house would be emptied of many dishes, and inside the house, the essential cleaning work would begin. This included a special whitewashing and intense detailed inspection of all the corners in the house. All of the dishes that were used during the entire year would be hidden away, and a new array of shining ones would adorn the apartment—everything would be new, shiny, and festive. The preparations did not skimp on the food being prepared for the holiday. Emphasis would be placed on the preparations of the special Pesakh holiday dishes. And the preparations of the *matse* [unleavened bread] especially turned into a very impressive event. In our home, they used to bake the *matse* on *moytse-shabes* [close of Shabes] after the ovens had rested during the course of twenty-four hours. Some of the bakeries would kosher their ovens for the upcoming holiday and burn out all of the leaven so the ovens would be kosher for even the most stringent. On *moytse-shabes*, the entire family, without exception, would go out to the bakery and bake the *matse*. The workers in the bakery were not allowed to interfere; we did the entire job ourselves. Everyone would work with gusto and zeal in the job of baking, while my grandfather would oversee and direct the operation with great strictness and adherence to the laws. The work was done with enthusiasm and extended until the morning. Then we would wrap the *matse* in white bags and store them in prepared places with great strictness.

Translated from the Hebrew by Rochel Semp

Memories from the Old Days (pp. 175–77)

Klara Waks (Kajla Akerman)

Alas, my Działoszyce, my dear little town!

Many years have gone by since I left you, but as in the old days, you have remained deep in my heart. Often I wish to see the little town in my dreams as it looked thirty-five years ago with its special way of life as a typical small Jewish town.

I remember Kraków Street and my small one-story house on whose other side the little river flowed.

Not far from there, there was a well at which the water carriers gathered every morning. There, they argued and wrangled; they each wanted to be the first to draw water from the well. Through the windows I saw the people who were going to the train station. With all this, I did not need an alarm clock.

The childhood years passed like a dream. The hours free from lessons were spent in the fields, between flowers and fields of corn. In the spring, we wove fragrant flowers into garlands and sang all the way home.

In the summertime, we greatly enjoyed bathing in Łysowiec. How wonderful everything was then. I didn't yet understand what anti-Semitism meant or the difficulties of earning a living. Our livelihood was connected to many Christians in the surrounding area. When I grew older, I was often required to call on them, and that is when I felt how false they were to us, how they sought various ways to bring us down.

When I was twelve years old, I joined a Zionist youth organization. We got together in the evening and passed many enjoyable hours dancing and singing. We also spent time in cultural pursuits. We joined with other towns around us and made excursions to summer camps. A few also went on to *hakhshara* [pioneer training] as *chalutzim* [pioneers].

When one of us was able to actually make *aliye* [immigration] to Eretz Yisroel, the whole town was proud. We were very envious of the happy *oylim* [immigrants], and each one of us dreamt and thought, "Oh, if only it were our turn."

In 1934, I left Działoszyce. We moved to Nowy Targ, a larger, more modern city in Galicia. But I did not forget my little town of Działoszyce. I used to go back and visit from time to time to see my friends, boys and girls, and would leave with tears in my eyes.

The last time I saw the town was a month after the war began. That time I had a whole different sense of it. Everything looked different already, as if from a distance, not the way I remembered it from my childhood. I walked almost fifty kilometers, hungry and thirsty. I went through several villages and saw how the farmers were working their blossoming fields, as if there were no war going on.

When I approached a house and asked for some water, they laughed at me. "Jewesses can drink blood, not water. Look at all the Jews lying around on the roads, and she wants water." I choked down my sobs and walked on.

But I became totally disillusioned when I arrived in Działoszyce... the lines for bread, the fears of the Jews. They feared saying a word out loud. People were walking around as if they had been poisoned, helpless. Every one just wanted to make it through that day. The situation was dire. I could not bear it. Many of those close to me were no longer among the living.

I was chased away further. I joined a group of friends from my youth in order to smuggle ourselves across the Russian border. About the several years I spent in Russia, there is much to tell. They were years of hunger, hard work, fear for the future, etc.

Finally, there were rumors afoot that our Jews, Polish citizens, would be returned to Poland. At first we were happy, we thought that we would at last begin to live like human beings, but unfortunately, as soon as we came to the Polish border, the gentiles threw rocks at us, shouting, "You're still alive? We thought there was no one left of you. *Żydzi do Palestyny* [Jews to Palestine] !!!"

With great difficulty, we arrived in Szczecin.[1] I immediately joined a Zionist organization, where I worked as a teacher with orphaned children who had lost their parents. We tried to give them everything they needed—education, knowledge, and, above all, love.

After three months, I was sent to Berlin with a group of the children I was in charge of. Later on we went to Rosenheim, where I lived with the children for almost two years. My hope and longing was to journey as soon as possible to Israel, the land of my dreams.

I decided to find a way for it to become a reality. I joined a group of older people. We went through a *hakhshara*, a preparatory camp. After a very long journey, we were able to get to Israel in 1948. Here I have built my home anew.

The little town of my birth has remained etched in my heart and mind as the place of the beautiful dreams of my childhood.

But my enmity toward Poles has become ever stronger. I am amazed at the Jews who can live there and walk those streets that are paved with the gravestones of our near and dear ones.

When a wind blows there, I think it must be their souls asking that their bones and their ashes be freed from that blood-soaked earth.

Translated from the Yiddish by Zulema Seligson

---

[1] Szczecin, formerly Stettin, Germany, was annexed to Poland to compensate for the eastern territories that Poland was forced to cede to the USSR. When displaced persons from the former Polish territories were repatriated to Poland, they were generally resettled in the newly annexed western territories acquired after the war from Germany.

From My Memories (pp. 178–79)

Benjamin Włoski

I was born in Poland in 1901, in the District of Pińczów. Until the thirteenth year of my life, I was raised in a courtyard in a village called Pierocice. My father's name was Jojne Włoski, and my mother's, Taube. My mother bore him eleven children, seven of whom lived until the time of Hitler, may his name and memory be erased. My father perished at the hands of the Nazis in Działoszyce during the first "resettlement" [deportation].

We, Benjamin and Izrael, two brothers, miraculously survived. Both of us are now in Israel.

*

In 1919, I was drafted into the Polish army and sent to the front. I went on foot to just beyond Kiev and back. I was wounded suddenly and took sick and was sent to the hospital in Kraków. After that, I was sent to Warsaw, where I remained until 1924, when I was discharged.

In 1928, I married Chaja, the oldest daughter of Aron Sołoducha. I had five children with her.

From the Kraków ghetto, I was sent to the camp in Płaszów. There, Commander Pilarzik seriously wounded me in the stomach and in the leg. I then fled back to the ghetto until it was completely "resettled" on March 13, 1943.

My wife and five children were sent to Auschwitz, where they perished.

After that, I was sent to Mauthausen, where I worked even though I was sick. From there, I was sent to a work camp at Melk [subcamp of Mauthausen].

For thirteen months I worked in the camp at Melk under very difficult conditions. Then, finally, I was sent to Ebensee [subcamp of Mauthausen], where I was liberated; at the time I weighed all of twenty-eight kilograms [sixty-two pounds].

After the liberation, the Jewish Brigade sent me to Salzburg and from there to Italy where I was reunited with my brother Izrael.

*

My mother was called, "Taubele Jojne's."[1] She was very pious and would share her butter and milk with poor but respectable people and gave generously to charity.

I recall an episode about the rabbi of Działoszyce, *z"l*. When my son was born, I went to the rabbi for a note that I needed to take to town hall in order to register him. At the rabbi's place, I met another Jew who had also come for the same reason. You had to give fifty *groszen* [small currency] for the note, and the man complained that he didn't have the money. He also complained about the poor behavior of people at Nusyn the American's. The rabbi chided the man, saying, "Awramcze, one shouldn't speak ill of

---

[1] It was common for people to be known by the names of persons to whom they were related. Taubele Jojne's meant "Taubele who belonged to Jojne," i.e., wife of Jojne. This practice was in part due to the fact that Jews did not use surnames in Poland for many years, so this was a means of distinguishing one Taube from another.

other Jews, because one never knows who will bring the redemption, whether it will be those who are completely virtuous or those who are completely sinful." This story, I recall, happened in 1934.

In 1947, I left Italy and went illegally to Palestine. The English government exiled us to Cypress where I stayed for eighteen months. I arrived in Israel only after the state was established in 1948. I was sent to work at the salt plant in Atlit.

Translated from the Yiddish by Sheva Zucker

Memories (pp. 180–81)

Majer Cudzynowski

I, Majer Cudzynowski, am reporting on what I remember of the flood:

Hercke Topoler had wanted to beat up Alter Cudzynowski, because he had cheated him in connection with buying a calf from Skalbmierz. So we were standing on the Skalbmierz bridge and waiting for the attackers. It was a Shabes in the month of May. And while waiting for the tough guys, we got, instead of them, a powerful wave of water. First, the bridge was ripped off. Later, Chaja Chaba's house was lifted up, turned over four times, went up and sideways, fell apart, and floated toward Grandfather Moszek Beker's house, which itself had lost a section torn off by the powerful stream.

Aunt Ester, holding a small child, was hanging from a half-open window shouting, "Help!" But she could not be reached because of the very dangerous situation. Afterward, Szmul Szpitz's house was also seen carried off by the water. In the house were Szmul Szpitz and his wife. I, with a few other firemen were able to extricate him and his wife with the help of ropes. Afterward, when the water had somewhat subsided, I noticed a telegraph pole floating by. I dragged it out, got it to the half-open window where Aunt Ester was and brought her and the child out. This was my first rescue.

The second rescue happened with Moszek Targownik. He had a coal storehouse at the Cukiermans, and the turbulent waters flattened the storehouse and carried off a flock of sheep that belonged to Menasze.

Menasze's son tried to run after the sheep. It was lucky that I caught up with him and saved his life. Sadly, he later perished under Hitler's gangs, *ym"sh* [may their name be erased].

The third event was the rescue of the police chief, who lived on the second floor of Szental's house in the center of the market square. The house began to shake like a tree in the strong wind. The police chief began to shout and call for help. So, using various clever tactics, we reached his balcony and carried him out of there and brought him to the firemen's coach house. From there, we took long poles and saved a lot of people with them.

Sunday morning, after everything was over, the emergency services arrived from Warsaw, sent by the Interior Ministry, but they did not have much to do.

For many years, the inhabitants of Działoszyce spoke of the miracles that occurred during the flood.

Translated from the Yiddish by Zulema Seligson

Stories from the Past (pp. 182–83)

Chaim Jakób Kac

A Pogrom Averted

About eighty-five years ago, on a market day in the little town of Działoszyce, the peasants in the market square assaulted the Jews and simultaneously began to rob Jewish shops. Suddenly, an extraordinary thing occurred. Two young men, one, Izrael Kac, *z"l* [of blessed memory], a grandson of the rabbi of Stopnica, Reb Izrael Kohn, *ztsk"l* [the holy righteous of blessed memory], and the second young man, Josek Mardyks, whom they called Long Josel, grabbed pieces of lumber from the wagons and threw themselves on the gentiles, hitting them right and left. In a short time there were fifty or sixty wounded peasants lying on the ground. The rest ran off. The police came and arrested the two young men. The gentiles surrounded the police building and demanded that the police chief release the young people to them. When questioned by the police, they said that if two Jews could beat them up the way they did, they wanted to drink a true toast to them. The young men were freed, and at Maszka's tavern, they all drank barrels of schnapps. A market day like this had never before been seen in Działoszyce.

Social Assistance

About sixty or seventy years ago, there was a family living in Działoszyce by the name of Rożenek. The father of the family, Reb Abram Rożenek, *z"l*, who was known as "Awram the Redhead," was the owner of the mill in Nieszków. His wife Fajgele, *e"h* [may she rest in peace], the sister of Reb Izrael Kac, was, personally, the social assistance in Działoszyce. There was cooking at her home twenty-four hours a day. If anyone was ill in town and needed some fresh soup, they would come to Aunt Fajgele. If there was an impoverished woman who had given birth, Aunt Fajgele made sure she had what was required, and when poor people got married, Aunt Fajgele made sure that the wedding would not be skimpy. She would prepare a meal fit for a king, and the joy of the parents and in-laws was without measure. The whole town rejoiced at the wedding. This is how Aunt Fajgele always lived her life. The main thing was that everything she gave had to be given secretly. No one knew who gave all these things. The father of Reb Izrael Kac, *z"l*, was Reb Michał Rachmiel Kac, *z"l*, and the mother was Zelda.

*

Fajwel Rożenek, the son of Reb Abram and Fajgele, had seven children: Mejlech, Izrael, Hinda, Michał, Marjem, Jojne, and Golda. In the year 1905, Fajwel had a grocery business in Działoszyce. Thanks to his connection with Count Maszkowski, he became the representative of the chicory manufacturer in Łabędź for the whole province.

As the representative of such an important firm, he was the first one to have a telephone in Działoszyce. In 1915, during World War I, he was accused of espionage because of his telephone. After strong intervention by the heads of the community, he was freed.

In 1918, the whole family moved to Łódź. There, they opened a wool and silk manufacturing plant, which was known for the quality of its products.

Hitler, may his name and memory be erased, annihilated Fajwel and his wife, Rywka, and their children Mejlech, Marjem, and Golda. The other children survived the Hell. Izrael settled in Israel. Michał, Jojne, and Hinda left for Argentina.

Various Characters

Chenandel, the watchmaker, when they gave him a watch to repair and he found he had a tiny screw or wheel left over, he returned it immediately to its owner.

Reb Moszek, the Hasid, was a great God-fearing man and a decidedly strange one; in the summer, when it was warm, he would wear his winter coat and warm clothes underneath. He would say that if God sends heat, one should attempt to be warm... In the winter, when it was cold outside, he would put on summer clothes and a thin smock, with the same reason given: When God gives cold, it should be cold...

Translated from the Yiddish by Zulema Seligson

Part III:

Customs and Tradition

What the Beit Hamidrash Was (pp. 187–89)

Hayyim Balitzki

Our Beit Hamidrash [house of prayer] was a large grey brick building that served most of the Jewish community as a second home. Almost every Jew visited it at least once a day or more. *Minyanim* (prayer quorums of ten or more) were praying there from dawn till late in the afternoon. The Khevre Tehilim (Psalms-reciting society) completed the reading of the Book of Psalms there once every day, starting early in the morning before going about their daily work.

The young students and older scholars engaged in the study of the Talmud from dawn till after midnight. Among them was the martyred Reb Abramcze Zylber, who would be found in the Beit Hamidrash every morning by four o'clock. An outstanding scholar, he was always ready to help others in their difficulties with the text. Beside him sat his companion in study, the martyred Reb Kalman Blady. Yet another such was the martyred Reb Abram Icek Zając, a sweet-voiced leader of prayer, who dedicated himself to Bible study no less than Talmud. The gentle-eyed and martyred Reb Abram Dayan, a qualified rabbi, would be found amid his group of young students, to whom he dedicated all his free time. Reb Abram Moszek Szenkier would be seated elsewhere with his group of "Little Yeshiva" students, clarifying all difficulties in knotty Talmudic texts. The perpetual student, the martyred Reb Jakób Skop, would be seated at the last table near the bookcases, to have easy access to all the works of reference he might require as he guided the youngsters through their studies.

A special committee saw to the purchase, binding, and good condition of the large selection of books in constant use. The late Reb Chaim Jechiel and Rabbi Herszel Lida gave lessons for exceptionally gifted students. There were many many more, but I do not remember their names. At the time of the afternoon prayers, the streets leading to the Beit Hamidrash were crowded with those going there, and it was crammed full until the evening prayers were over. Most Zionist and similar addresses were delivered there, as well as the sermons of *maggidim* (preachers), to which women also came in large numbers. Money was raised for hospital treatment, for "secret gifts" to those who had come down in the world, and for help to wayfarers and needy travelers, some of whom lodged there at night. Even the town fools found refuge from the children here. And sometimes, women in distress, or praying for the sick or those in difficult labor, would dash in, fling open the Holy Ark, and utter their imploring prayer before the Torah Scrolls. Ten Psalms daily were recited between the afternoon and evening prayers. On the Sabbath, the tables were covered with clean white cloths, and Jews who had no time all the week round came and joined their own groups for the study of what was closest to their hearts. May these lines be a memorial to the Jewish spiritual center and those who made it the center.

This chapter is reprinted from pp. 19–20 of the English section of the original Działoszyce Yizkor Book, with minor changes.

Torah and Worship (pp. 190–94)

Dov Ptasznik

Until it became mandatory for all children to attend public school, every Jewish child born in Działoszyce before and after World War I had more than one option on how to receive an education. Naturally, there was only one way that was closest to my heart. Therefore, I will attempt to briefly describe some of the names that became institutions, and, in my opinion, the life and flavor of the city cannot be described without them.

I am using the word "city," because I never felt as though I were living in a "little town," and that is because "whatever is on the earth also exists in the sea." Everything that existed in the big city was also present in our town, and not only on a small scale—merchants from all the branches, craftsmen of all the professions, people from all levels of intelligence, both secular and Orthodox, Hasidim from all the various *rebbes'* courts, and youth movements of all types.

I remember the celebration at the conclusion of the writing of the *seyfer-toyre* [Torah scroll] that was commissioned by Reb Zvi Drobiarz, *z"l* [of blessed memory],[1] for the *shtibl* [Hasidic house of prayer] of the Gerer Hasidim [followers of the *rebbe* from Ger (Góra Kalwaria)], where he prayed. Over the years he had assumed responsibility for paying the rent for the *shtibl,* and, in the end, he even built a special building and dedicated it as a place of prayer and Torah study for the Gerer Hasidim. During the dedication of the Torah scroll, major festivities took place. There were riders with multicolored banners on festively bedecked horses who galloped throughout the city in order to add to the feeling of enjoyment.

Many honors were given out to everyone in the home of Reb Zvi, *z"l*. From there, they transferred the Torah scroll to its permanent dwelling place. Thousands of people gathered around the house, located in the vicinity of the bridge near the post office, which was the home of Reb Abram Majerczyk, *z"l*, and waited for the procession to begin. Leaning on the railings of the bridge were two beggars from out of town, full of enthusiasm at this magnificent sight and the masses of people before their eyes. Then one of them turned to his friend and said, "Indeed, it is true what they say, that Działoszyce is a small Warsaw."

A. Reb Heszele Melamed, *z"l*.[2] Thousands of Jews lived in the city, and perhaps there were some who knew one another only from an occasional encounter in the *bes hamedresh* [house of prayer/study]. However, Reb Heszele, *z"l*, the teacher of beginners, was someone everyone knew up close. He was the very first teacher of several generations of Jewish children who took the first steps of their education in the *kheyder* [Jewish elementary school] with him. In comparison to those many other *melamdim* [teachers] who taught at a higher grade level, this teacher, so far as I can remember, was

---

[1] Zvi is the Hebrew equivalent of Hersz [stag]. This same man is referred to as Herszel Drobiarz in other chapters.

[2] Occupations such as *melamed* [teacher] and *dayan* [judge]) are often used as if they were surnames. "Reb Heszele Melamed" means "Reb Heszele the teacher."

the only one for beginners, and every child had to go through this initial stage of study. And that's why Reb Heszele, *z"l*, was not only the name of a *melamed* but of a "concept."

He was of short stature, thin, and with a hoarse voice. He sat every day with a *taytl-tsel* [wooden pointer] in his hand, teaching the Torah *aleph-bes* [ABC's].[1] As is usual, the children learned the Torah *aleph-bes* and the beginnings of reading in two to three semesters, called *zmanim* (a *zman* is a period of half a year that is between Pesakh and Sukes or between Sukes and Pesakh). However, when a student was quiet and diligent, and Reb Heszele had *nakhes* [pleasure] and satisfaction from him, and also the tuition was paid regularly, he would come during the holidays to the student's home and cajole his parents into leaving the student with him for an additional semester. Sometimes, he actually succeeded in doing so.

He lived in an apartment consisting of two rooms. One of them served as the *kheyder* and also housed a washing machine for the laundry run by his wife, Hinka, *z"l*. In the evenings Jewish women would come, and even some gentiles, to bring their laundry for a spin. While doing it, they would gossip with each other about the latest news and current events.

Near the *kheyder* flowed a small river, and the windows of the *kheyder* were reflected in its stream. During breaks, the children would go out and play in the yard or on the small bridge that spanned this stream. In the event that one of the children fell into this water while playing, Rebetsn [rabbi's wife] Hinka, *z"l*, would sit him on the window sill to dry out in the sun, and in order to calm him down, she would give him a few of the *pulim* [broad beans] that she would boil and sell to the students. This was their third source of income—after teaching and laundering—the cooking of beans.

By the way, this stream supplied energy for the flour mills that belonged to Reb Abram Kac, *z"l*, on the upper banks of this river, while the Wdowiński family owned land lower downstream. And every summer, they would gather the chaff that had gathered there during the year in order to ease the flow. The flour mill of the Wdowiński family was located near the center of the community (just as in the song "Here in the *shul*, and here in the mill") that is, near the *beysakneses* [synagogue], the *bes hamedresh*, the bathhouse, and the community building. In the back entrance of the *bes hamedresh*, on the left side, lived the *shames* [sexton] of the *bes hamedresh*, Reb Hersz Mendel, *z"l*. The *shames* of the synagogue, Reb Wolf Federman, *z"l*, used to live on the top floor of the bathhouse. On the same floor also lived the cantor of the synagogue, Reb Szyja [Śpiewak], *z"l*, and afterward, also his son, Reb Moszek [Śpiewak], *z"l*—who served after him as the cantor, following his marriage to the daughter of Reb Henoch Szental, *z"l*. Also Reb Wolf Habalan [ritual bath attendant], *z"l*, used to live on the same floor. The bathhouse itself was a most important establishment and consisted of a large steam room that got steam through the pouring of water on very hot stones, and at the bottom were two pools (*mikves*) [ritual baths]. One was for very hot water, almost at the boiling

---

[1] The letters of the Hebrew alphabet are written in a stylized manner in the Torah and without vowels. Presumably, the children were learning not only the letters but how they were written in the Torah.

point, and the second, for cold water. In addition, there were dressing rooms and also several baths covered with ceramic tiles.

B. After a child finished his education in the *kheyder* of Reb Heszele, *z"l*, he had a few choices as to which of the *melamdim* he would go. In accordance with his parent's decision, the boy was sent to continue his studies with one of the following *melamdim*: Reb Abram Aba Goldwaser, *z"l*, Reb Mendel Krzykacz, *z"l*, or Reb Pejsach'l. And as for myself, I went to Reb Jakób Goldwaser, *z"l*, son of Reb Abram Aba, *z"l*, who was also a *melamed*, as mentioned above.

Reb Jakób Goldwaser wasn't only a *melamed* but a *morah* as well.[1] Perhaps because he didn't only teach fluent reading and Khumash [Torah] but also writing and math. He was a very good-looking man, and with his well-groomed beard and gold-framed eyeglasses, he commanded great respect. He was very well liked by his students. The man was the same on the inside as he was on the outside, very organized both in his manner and his instruction. He was very emphatic about being precise and orderly, and his entire temperament was slow and patient. In those days, when the stick and the ruler were an inseparable part of the *kheyder* trappings, he was an exception to the rule. I don't remember even one incident in which he hit or insulted any of his students. Every time, prior to our going home, each one of us would have to read a paragraph from the Tanakh [Holy Scriptures], one part written and one part oral, with translation, to emphasize reading correctly.

He used to live with his family on Dziekanowska Street in an apartment consisting of one room that was divided by a partition. In the section that was designated as the *kheyder* stood benches, just like in the public schools, and not tables, as in the usual *kheyder*. The circumstances and the crowdedness were extremely difficult to tolerate, but in spite of it all, we loved the place and hated to leave and go to a different *melamed*.

C. At the third stage of the education ladder was the *melamed* Reb Kopel Brandys, *z"l*, who was also called *bal alukos* [owner of leeches] since he sold leeches for medical healing purposes. In my time, Reb Kopel was already an old man. He lived under very trying conditions as well. He didn't smoke, but he would inhale a very large amount of snuff, and when he breathed, a constant raspy sound could be heard coming from his lungs.

During this time an additional *kheyder*, the *talmed-toyre*, was established, which incorporated almost all the other *kheyders*, and at its helm was a very nice young man whose first name I forget, H. Landau, *z"l*. The *yo"r* [*yoshev rosh*—chairman] of the *talmed-toyre* committee was Reb Josek Judka Mandelbaum, *z"l*. Now, the selection of the *melamdim* by the students or their parents was discontinued. Classes became established according to level of instruction. Examinations were administered at the end of every six months, and report cards were given out. This way the students would pass from grade to grade with the administration making the decision.

D. The fourth level was the highest level in the *talmed-toyre*. The *melamed* was Reb Chaim Jechiel, *z"l* (I forgot his family name). One of his hands was disabled. I think that he was a very great *talmed-khokhem* [Talmudic scholar]. At that time, the entire *talmed-*

---

[1] Both words mean teacher, but it seems that the author considered a *melamed* as a teacher of religious studies and a *morah* as a teacher of secular studies.

toyre kheyder was concentrated in the building of the Jewish community, which was across from the home of Reb Abram Majerczyk, *z"l*. Also located there was the public library. However, after the collapse of the home of Reb Wolf Bachmajer, *z"l*, across from the *bes hamedresh*, the school was moved to the community offices. The family of Reb Moszek Dayan, *zts"l* [of blessed righteous memory], and the community offices moved to the top floor of the *talmed-toyre*, and the upper classes were compelled to wander and moved to the *bes hamedresh* of Reb Abele, *z"l*, (the name of the *melamed* was Reb Kopel Ungier, *z"l*), to the hallway of the synagogue (the name of the *melamed* was Reb Chaim-Jakób—I forgot his last name), and to the women's section in the *bes hamedresh* (where Reb Abram Moszek Szenkier, *z"l*, was teaching). The personalities of these *melamdim* should have been described separately, but that would have been too much for this article. May their memory be blessed.

The studies and the organization in the *talmed-toyre* were very good, thanks to the talented and energetic headmaster, H. Landau, *z"l*. Secular studies were also conducted in the *talmed-toyre* three times a week. The teachers were Reb Szlama Rozenfrucht, *z"l*, for Hebrew and Yiddish, and the brothers Mojszele and Abramele, the sons of Reb Szymon Kołatacz, *z"l*. The first one taught Polish, and the second, mathematics.

And so, when a boy was approximately twelve years of age, *kheyder* was completed, and the paths of the students diverged.

Some went on for further studies, some for vocations, and some for business, to help in their parents' shops.

E. Other youths joined the graduates of the *talmed-toyre* and, with time, they congregated into a cohesive group under the tutelage of Reb Abram, *z"l*, who served as a *dayan* after the demise of his father, Harav [Rabbi] Reb Moszek Dayan, *zts"l*. This group spent most of their daily hours as well as nights in the *bes hamedresh* or near it, learning Torah, reciting prayers, going on excursions, and playing *shakhmat* [chess] during their leisure.

And these were the names in the group: Chaimele Koźma, *z"l*, the brother of Reb Abram and the son of Rabbi Reb Moszek Dayan, *zts"l*; Abramele Waga, *z"l*, son of Reb Moszek, *z"l*; Alter Zalcberg, *z"l*, who was better known as the grandson of Reb Chaim Szaja Kac, *z"l*; Herszele Nagelblat, *z"l*, who later moved to Kraków; Jekiel Kaźmierski, *z"l*; and, may they have long life, Lejbl Jutrzenka (Aryeh Shahar); Motel Jagoda, who is now in Germany; and myself, the one writing these lines. All these came to the *bes hamedresh* in addition to the older generation that spent the entire day at the *bes hamedresh* or at least part of it.

F. The voices of people chanting Torah almost never ceased within the gates of the town, voices of both those studying late into the night and of those getting up very early. During the Thursdays of the Shovavim-TAT, the learners would stay up the entire night busy with studying Torah.[1]

The learning of the Torah was inseparable from all other aspects of Jewish life in the town. It encompassed all ages—those who looked into *Hok Yaakov* [a rabbinic

---

[1] Shovavim is an acronym for the first six Torah portions found in the book of Exodus. During a leap year, two more portions are added for which the acronym is TAT. Thus, during a leap year, Torah study was even longer than usual.

manuscript], the study of Mishnayos [segments of the Mishne], or the Talmud and *poskim* [post-Talmudic commentators]. Women would read *Tzena Urena*.[1] The singsong voice of Reb Pejsach Sternberg, *z"l* [of blessed memory], in his studying of the Gemore [part of the Talmud]—which could be heard during the warm summer months through the open windows that looked out on the central market square—remains an unforgettable impression. As is well known, Reb Pejsach, *z"l,* served for many years as chairman of the community council and of the Mizrachi Party.

The situation with the young during this particular period, i.e. the fifteen years prior to the outbreak of the war, was different. However, even among the youth, there was a recognizable sector that studied Torah, those who studied the entire day and others only partially.

And here I want to take special note of two large groups of young people, one in the community *bes hamedresh* and the other in the *bes hamedresh* of the Admor [Hasidic religious leader], *ztsk"l* [the holy righteous of blessed memory]. At the helm of the first group stood Harav [Rabbi] Abram Koźma, *z"l*, who I have previously mentioned, the son of Harav Reb Moszek Dayan, *zts"l* [the righteous of blessed memory].[2]

Rabbi Reb Moszek Dayan was from the Trisk Hasidim;[3] however, his son, Rabbi Abram, was one of the enthusiastic Gerer Hasidim. His prominent personality in Torah and *musar* [ethical teachings] had a strong influence upon all his students, and most, like the others, became Gerer Hasidim. They were well known for their Hasidic zealousness and cohesiveness and valued the study of Torah above all. This group was busy learning Torah day and night and excelled in delving very deeply into Talmudic studies. There were also questions brought by Rabbi Abram in writing to be presented to the Rabbi Hagaon from Dvinsk, *ztsk"l,* who wrote the *Tzafnat Paneach* and was well known as the genius of Rogachev.[4] During this period, the young men yearned to receive *smikhe* [rabbinic ordination] and for this purpose would go to various yeshivas, mainly to the Mesivta [yeshiva of a higher level] in Warsaw. Rabbi Abram was opposed to his students studying Torah for the purpose of rabbinic ordination, and he didn't seek it for himself until he was compelled to take on the position of *dayan* after his father passed away. Only then was he ordained by the giants of Torah in his day, such as Rabbi [Jehuda Majer] Szapiro of Lublin, *zts"l,* and Rabbi [Dov Ber] Wajdenfeld of Tschebin [Trzebinia], *zts"l*, etc.

These above mentioned students themselves taught and spread the learning of Torah to younger students, both on an individual basis and through the organization of lectures

---

[1] *Tzena Urena* was a book with Torah and Haftorah weekly portions written in Yiddish, so that women, who usually did not know Hebrew, could understand them.

[2] Different terms were used to honor deceased persons, depending on their standing in the religious community. The abreviation *z"l* [of blessed memory] could be used for any person, *zts"l* [the righteous of blessed memory] for a scholar or rabbi, and *ztsk"l* [the holy righteous of blessed memory] usually for a religious leader.

[3] Turisk, Poland, now Turijs'k, Ukraine.

[4] Tzafnat Paneach was the pseudonym of Joseph when he served as governor of Egypt. The author of the book *Tzafnat Paneach* [Discloser of Secrets—a compilation of Responsa on the Talmud and Jewish law] was Rabbi Hagaon [eminent scholar] Josef Rozen from Dvinsk [Daugavpils, Latvia], who was originally from Rogachev [Belarus].

in Talmud for the Pirchei Agudas Yisroel [Agudas Yisroel Youth] groups. There was also a period when the above group moved their teaching headquarters from the *bes hamedresh* to the *shtibl* of the Gerer Hasidim. However, after pressure was applied, with the complaint that this had caused the *bes hamedresh* to become deserted, they were forced to return to the large *bes hamedresh*, which again reverberated with life. All the Shabosim [Sabbath days] were kept fully holy according to the Torah and its commandments, and an atmosphere of holiness engulfed all the learners from which they were nourished spiritually the entire week. The sessions with Rabbi Abram, which lasted many hours in the passageway between the *bes hamedresh* and the *beysakneses* [synagogue] during the warm summer months, as well as the discussions relating to religious philosophy and other pertinent subject matters of the day, left a deep-rooted lasting impression in the hearts of all the participants.

For a period of many years we also had a yeshiva, under the direction of graduates from the yeshiva of Slabodka [Lithuania]. This yeshiva was very sought after by young men from the entire area, and they were offered meals by the local citizens. Their goal, together with the studying of Torah, was to deepen Jewish Orthodox values in the hearts of the young and to improve their character.

Regarding the other center, well, this concentrated group used to gather in the *bes hamedresh* of the *rebbe, ztsk"l.* I will leave some room for his son-in-law, Rabbi Frankel, and his brothers-in-law, who currently live with us here, to write about this topic.

Sometimes, it seems to us that all that I have described above is still in existence and that we all left it only temporarily. This is because in our subconscious mind we cannot make peace with the thought that all of this has perished and not a trace remains.

Translated from the Hebrew by Rochel Semp

Hasidic Shtiblekh (pp. 195–96)

Aryeh Shahar (Lejbl Jutrzenka)

The town of Działoszyce was known in the entire area as a center for Hasids and Hasidism. It was especially known as a center of Chernobyl Hasidism. Even prior to the war [World War I], Rebbe Motele of Chernobyl would come to Działoszyce from time to time. The first time he visited the town was in 1917, and he was a guest in the home of Reb Symcha Rafałowicz. This house became the center of Hasidism after Reb Motele's influence on the population-at-large increased. He was well known for his love of each and every Jew. People from all walks of life would come to him to ask for his good advice and counsel—some on the issue of *shiduchim* [marriages] and others with problems of ill health, God forbid. Rebbe Reb Motele, *zts"l* [the righteous of blessed memory], dispensed amulets widely, and the common folk were especially fervent followers of the *rebbe*. All of them believed with complete faith that the *rebbe's* blessings helped them with their troubles, and they especially guarded his amulets faithfully.

After the passing of the Rebbe Reb Motele, *zts"l*, the Chernobyl Hasidim divided their loyalty among the grandchildren of the old *rebbe*. Thus, there existed in town a *shtibl* [small Hasidic house of prayer] of the followers of Reb Moszele, who lived permanently in Lublin. The *shtibl* of his followers was in the home of Bluma Rafałowicz. To this *shtibl* used to come the true Hasidim such as Reb Chaim Szaja Kac, *z"l*, Abram Majerczyk, and others. Among those who came were also the youth.

There was also the *rebbe* from Żarki who lived in Częstochowa and had very many followers. They prayed together with the Lublin Hasidim.

Reb Lejbniu, who lived in Kielce, also had Hasidim in Działoszyce.

And there was Reb Nachumcze, who lived in Warsaw. There was a special *shtibl* just for his followers, where a concentration of prominent and honored Jews such as Reb Becalel Biter and others attended. Reb Chaim Josek Dziewięcki was a loyal disciple of the *rebbes* from the House of Trisk. He used to pour whiskey from a small bottle for a few hundred men.

In the second rank of Hasidism stood the Ger Hasidim. Ger had two *shtiblekh*, one of them was at Reb Szyja Fiszer's, and the second one was established by Reb Herszel Drobiarz with his own personal funds. The Ger Hasidim *shtibl* also served as a center for Torah scholars. To it came Reb Icek Majer Szu"b, Reb Fiszel (Malekh) Szulimowicz, Jechiel Englander, and Reb Abram Dayan, *zts"l*.[1] In the Ger *shtibl* there was also a concentration of young men who were scholars, and at their head stood Reb Abram Dayan. Here they sat and worked at studying Torah with the greatest diligence from four o'clock in the morning until twelve o'clock midnight. I remember that usually we had two lessons with Reb Abram Dayan, one that started at five o'clock in the morning and continued until eleven o'clock. In this lecture we would learn the Talmudic Tractate

---

[1] Szu"b, an abbreviation of the Hebrew term for *shoykhet* [ritual slaughterer], and Dayan [religious judge] are used here as titles rather than true surnames.

Chulin with all the interpretations and commentaries. The second lecture began at five o'clock in the afternoon and continued until eleven o'clock at night. During this time, we would study Tractate Zevachim.

During the day, we would learn Tanakh and the Daf Hayomi [page of the day] that had been initiated by Reb Abram Dayan, *zts"l*, may God avenge his blood.

There were also in Działoszyce Hasidic *shtibl*s in which common householders prayed. For instance, the *shtibl* that was in the house of Pinkus Banach. Jews who were ordinary workers used to pray there. The *gaboim* [trustees] of this *shtibl* were Moszek Dawid Zelcer (Pomeranc), Majer Harchav [Big Majer], who taught preschoolers, and Abele Grandapel. To this type also belonged the *shtibl* of the Chęciny Hasidim. In Reb Abele's *bes hamedresh*, Reb Awigdor and Reb Moszek Waga, *z"l*, served as *gaboim*, and Reb Moszek Fiszel Ostrowski was the communal prayer leader during the High Holy Days. The home of Heszel Melamed housed the *shtibl* of the Hasidim of Pińczów. The peddlers who traveled to the villages, ordinary workmen, shoemakers, and tailors, etc., used to pray there.

In our town dwelt the *rebbe* Reb Lejzor Halevi Epsztajn. He was the son of the *rebbe* Kalman Epsztajn from Neustadt [Nowy Korczyn] and the grandson of the "Hamaor Veshemesh."[1] His home was also a center for home owners and also for many of the young people. The home of the rabbi served as a meeting place for *talmed-khokhem* [Talmudic scholars]. Poor people who studied the Torah were especially attracted there. Whoever went in there hungry came out full and satiated.

Prayer services designated for Jews who were of means and possessed great wealth were held in the home of Tuwia Meryn and Moszek Laskier. Anszel Horowicz was the main leader of the communal prayers. On every Shabes and *yom tov* [holiday], a *kidesh* [collation] would be served that would be sponsored by Reb Moszek Laskier and his brother-in-law, Tuwia Meryn. Moszele Laskier used to recite a Hasidic Torah teaching during the *kidesh*. A beautiful *suke* [booth used during the Feast of Tabernacles] stood there that was open to all. Whoever wished would come into the *suke* in order to observe the *mitsve* [commandment] "Dwell in the *suke*" and also to observe the *mitsve* of *arba minim* [the waving of four species].

In addition to the *shtiblekh,* there was in the town a large *bes hamedresh* where the sound of prayer did not cease. In it were to be found quorums of men praying from dawn until sunset. Even as late as one o'clock in the afternoon, one could find in this *bes hamedresh* a minyan praying; and immediately after that, they would start Mincha [the afternoon prayer]. And so it would continue until dark, and then they would start Maariv [the evening prayer]. This *bes hamedresh* was always buzzing with Jewish men. It served as a second home to the Jewish men of the city.

In addition to the *bes hamedresh*, there was also the great synagogue of the town in which the morning, afternoon, and evening prayers were recited only once a day.

Alongside of this, there was in the town the *bes hamedresh* of Reb Abele, *zts"l.* They tell a story about Reb Abele that during the great fire that engulfed the city, his house initially did not catch fire. He poured his heart out before the Holy One, blessed be He,

---

[1] Rabbi Kalonymus Kalman Halevi Epsztajn [*rebbe* in Kraków] was known as the Maor Vashemesh (The Light and the Sun) from the title of his work.

"Am I, God forbid, not one of your sons?" His beseeching was heard, and the fire spread and took hold of his home as well, and it burned down. When he saw this, he raised his hands to heaven and said, "May the name of God be blessed! Now I know that I, too, am one of the children of Abram, Isaac, and Jacob!"

In the *bes hamedresh* of Reb Abele used to sit the Melamed Reb Abram Aba who imparted Torah to his students. Also there was Reb Kopel Ungier with his group of students. This *bes hamedresh* was situated in the home of Reb Gerszon Szental, and there was also the *shtibl* of the Grodzisk Hasidim in which Jews of great wealth used to pray.

Translated from the Hebrew by Rochel Semp

Dedication of Torah Scrolls to the Synagogue (p. 197)

Josef Kac

This happened in the years when the Russians still ruled the Kingdom of Poland.

I remember how one day Torah scrolls were dedicated in the synagogue in Działoszyce. I was a young boy of about six or seven years old, a pupil in the *kheyder*, God fearing with my whole being. The joy and happiness that prevailed during the dedication of the Torah scrolls to the synagogue was communal but also involved each and every individual. For three days the town celebrated; all of the businesses were closed. The festivities were apparent in the streets and in the homes. In front of every other house its inhabitants put out a stand, and on it, they served baked goods, sweets, and also various drinks. Horses were brought to the town, and riders with effigies rode on them. It was like a big carnival. The riders rode through the streets of the town and were treated everywhere with food and drink. In my eyes, it seemed like a very impressive procession the likes of which I had never seen before. We children were happy and exuberant. We accompanied the carnival, and we, too, partook of the refreshments.

For three days, happiness prevailed in our midst. On the third day, a formal parade was organized and included all the citizenry of the town. Heading this procession marched the rabbi with the musicians, the Torah scrolls were put under the *khupe* [canopy], and with music, song, and dancing, and with honor befitting kings, the Torah scrolls were placed into the Aron Kodesh [holy ark] in the synagogue.

Prior to the Invasion of the Town by the Austrians

During World War I, when the Russians abandoned the town and before the Austrians occupied it, the Jews, together with the Poles, planned to establish a joint militia. Right from the outset the Poles showed their true faces. They agreed, as if to cooperate with us. However, immediately, on the first day of this joint venture, a bullet escaped from someone's rifle, and one of the Jewish boys was killed. Due to this incident and because of the influence of some of the community leaders, the young Jews left this militia. The first experience of this youth organization had ended in failure.

After some time, the plague of typhus erupted in the town, and again the Jewish youth got organized into a group that was called Lines Hatsedek [Sheltering the Righteous]. The purpose of the organization was to assist the sick with money and medication and treat the poor who became ill. The money was collected on a "Flower Day" [day when flowers were sold to raise money]. We would stick a flower into the lapel of people's clothing, and they would donate whatever amount of money they wished. On holidays, we would help the poor with food supplies. Slowly, slowly, the organization started to change its image. A Zionist spirit seeped into the town. People started learning Hebrew, and with the passage of time, this group evolved to become the organization Hapoel Hamizrachi [Mizrachi Labor Federation].

Translated from the Hebrew by Rochel Semp

The Arrival of Shabes In Our Town (pp. 198–200)

Tova Avni (Szydłowska)

There was a special character to Shabes, which had been kept sacred throughout all the generations as a day of holiness, rest, and joy in which man followed in the footsteps of God, who had Himself rested from all His work.

An atmosphere of holiness and peace descended as though from heaven and brought with it an extra soul that is implanted into a Jew on the eve of Shabes, and this influences his experience of life on Shabes. This festiveness puts its distinctive imprint on this special day and causes a change from the weekday behavior of Jews. Not everything is permitted. One is not allowed to think about mundane affairs. This day was created for rest, and this is the reason that change is noticeable in all one's actions. People are involved in praying, in delving into holy books, and especially in reading the Torah portion of the week. They repeat the reading in order to remember and to again reflect in their thoughts on the holiness and special character of Shabes. And afterward, they involve themselves in actions for the sake of the Creator. This day was designated by the Creator of the World for prayer and rest, and this is how Jews maintained this day in all their years of exile. They fought with all their being those who wanted to desecrate the holiness and peace of the Sabbath day. Preparations for Shabes actually started at noon on Friday. The preparations to celebrate Shabes involved no small effort—everything needed to be made ready already on Friday. A Jew had to be careful not to stumble, God forbid. One had to avoid the forbidden and use caution to stay away from any sin.

Six days they toiled and worked very hard in order to earn a livelihood. But when Friday arrived, all those Jews whose work took them away from their homes returned. They came back laden down with bundles associated with their trade. In their pockets were a few golden coins for the upkeep of the household that was filled with small children. The truth was that everyone awaited the arrival of Shabes. Most of the town's inhabitants were in dire need of rest, since many of them barely eked out a living in their wanderings during the week from village to village in their quest—by the sweat of their brow—for a livelihood. After they brushed off the dust of their wanderings from themselves, they prepared to welcome the holy Shabes queen.

Darkness descended on the town, and the *bes hamedresh* [house of study] and the *shtiblekh* [small Hasidic houses of prayer], each according to their type, filled up with congregants, and the voices of singing and praying were heard from all sides. And in the homes, the table was covered with a white tablecloth, fully set, with wine ready for *kidesh* [benediction over wine], and near it, the *kidesh* cup made of silver—a wedding present. Freshly baked *challah*s, covered with a cloth embroidered with the words "*Lichvod Shabbat,*" in honor of Shabes. The Shabes candles in their candelabras glowed with a light that not only lit up the darkness but also penetrated one's heart with a new adorned light. A light of hope that life would yet be good. And so, together with their family, they celebrated Shabes. They partook wholeheartedly with pleasure from a fulfilling meal, sang verses of *zmires* [Shabes songs], and concluded by reciting the Birkat Hamazon, the grace after a meal, in a quiet tone due to their fatigue, which had accumulated from the pressures and responsibilities of the week gone by. Slowly, slowly, the streets of the town became quiet. Peace and tranquility descended, and the town became enveloped in the holy spirit of Shabes.

The Study of Hebrew in our Town

In my youth, it was customary for each Jewish household to send their children to study, to learn to read a *sidur* [daily prayer book] while they were still small.

My first teacher who taught me the Hebrew letters was Rebetsn Pesla. She herself had few credentials in this respect. However, her husband, Reb Akiba, was the *rov* [official town rabbi] and *dayan* [religious judge] and altogether a most pleasant man. He was the one who "lent" her some of his authority.

Both were poor and destitute. The house they lived in was poor and dark, and a tall person had to bend down in order to enter it. In their entire lives neither of them had ever voiced a complaint against the Creator.

He, for his good counsel, and she, for her reading lessons given to girls, refused compensation. I remember that on more than one occasion when I came there to study, I left a small bundle of money in a corner without anyone noticing.

An open *sidur* always lay on her table, and on it, the small pointer to help in the reading. When a girl came to study, Rebetsn Pesla would drop her work and immediately proceed to teach the holy letters. She was happiest when her efforts were rewarded with good results.

When I grew older, I entered a public school where we did not have any religious studies. That is why in the evenings I studied Hebrew with Rabbi Reb Heszele. He was a well-known rabbi in the city; he had a designated *kheyder* where he taught Torah to the children in the town. He also took us on for a monthly fee, even though he really didn't have any time available.

I remember how a few of us girls came together in order to study with him. The rabbi drove all the children outside, took the pointer in his hand, and read with us page after page. He felt very proud that he was also teaching girls. He was a very good person and a devoted rabbi. These small students were his pride and joy. Who knows what the fate of our teachers was? Who died peacefully and who perished as a holy martyr at the hands of the German animals?

May the memories of all those holy individuals that dispensed Torah publicly be blessed.

The Donation of Money to KKL [Keren Kayemeth l'Yisroel] on Tu B'Shvat

Tu B'Shvat [holiday on which trees are planted] occurs, as is known, in the wintertime. Also, in our country, the children await its arrival and hope for a nice day so they can celebrate this occasion with great joy.

In our town, cloudiness and very cold temperatures marked this day. In the evening of this day, I was asked by Josek Brandys, *z"l*, who was then responsible for the activities of Keren Kayemeth l'Yisroel [Jewish National Fund], to find myself a partner and go collect money for this fund.

Everyone took on this job with great willingness. Brandys gave me a bag with unshelled peanuts (we called them then peanuts of Eretz Yisroel), a bag with figs, and many more small bags. He asked that I distribute the fruits and collect thirty-five kopeks for each fruit bag. My partner was Mancia Brojgies, *z"l*.

This job was a great honor for us. We started this work in the afternoon, but since this was the wintertime, by four o'clock, it was already dark outside.

But who paid attention to the darkness? We went from house to house, collecting donations, and we felt that a great responsibility rested on us—as though with this money, we could redeem all of the Land of Israel.

I remember entering one home. This Jew, the head of the household, didn't have enough money to donate the entire amount of thirty-five kopeks and only gave us ten kopeks. We, on our part couldn't give him the full bag with fruits for this amount. He was very sad. What did we do? We took money from another, larger donation, added this to his amount, and gave him the bag with fruit. He was very glad that he got something, and we were again happy that the amount of ten kopeks was added to the fund.

It was already seven o'clock. The box became filled with coins and our hearts with joy and pleasure. All of a sudden, I remembered that we hadn't as yet visited the Dziekanowice area. Three brothers lived there; two of them were Zionists and would donate very willingly to the blue box. But what would happen if, when we got there, to spite us, only the third brother would be home? We asked and decided to go, but just as I had suspected, we were out of luck this time. The third brother (whose name I don't recall) refused to donate even one coin to the cause.

We were greatly disappointed and wanted to go home. Suddenly, it seems as though a spark had ignited his heart. He made us come back inside the house, gave us refreshments, and even donated a nice amount. He told us, "Wait for Majerek (the name of the loyal Zionist brother). He will give more, so that your coming should be worthwhile."

And this is how it was; Majerek came in, greeted us warmly, complimented us profusely, filled our boxes, and sent us home.

I remember that it seemed to us that in the whole entire world, there wasn't another person happier than we.

Translated from the Hebrew by Rochel Semp

Teachers in Działoszyce (pp. 201–3)

Aryeh Shahar (Lejbl Jutrzenka)

Before the outbreak of World War I, and after the war as well, there weren't any organized schools in Działoszyce. The education of Jewish children was left entirely in the hands of private teachers, and each of these would take students into his private home and teach them Torah there. The teachers were divided into five groups: 1) Teachers of *dardeke* [the youngest children], 2) Teachers of Khumesh und Rashi [Torah and Rashi commentaries], 3) Teachers of Mishnayos [passages from the Mishne (code of oral law)], 4) Teachers of Gemore [commentaries on the Mishne], and 5) Teachers who belonged to a special group who taught Torah to grown young men and "geniuses."

The custom in Działoszyce was that when a boy reached the age of three, he would immediately have his hair shaved off, leaving him with nice long *peos* [sidelocks] alongside his face, and he would be brought to *kheyder* [Jewish religious school]. Those who belonged to the group that taught *dardeke* were: Heszele Melamed, Josek Lejb Melamed, and Henoch (Heniek) Szental.[1] It was customary that the *melamed* [teacher] would be invited to come to the home of the child and, together with the parents as a group, would escort the child to the *kheyder*. And there the child would start learning the *alef-bes* [ABC's—alphabet].

Each teacher had his own method of motivating the children to learn Torah. For example, Heszele would combine his teaching with the awarding of peas. When he was teaching the little tots the *alef-bes* and wanted the toddler to repeat after him, "*Alef*," he would put a pea on the letter "*alef.*" Of course, the tot would want the pea, but he would not get it until he first said, "Alef." Josek Lejb used to pass out candies when the child read the Krias Shema [recitation of the Shema] well.[2] Henoch Szental would put fear into the children, since he was handicapped and limped from the waist. Each of these *dardeke* teachers had a pointer that was used to point out each letter. In addition, each of these teachers had an assistant. The job of the assistant was to bring the children to the *kheyder* and take them back home after their studies.

After a year or two of learning to read the *alef-bes*, the little fellow would be transferred to a teacher of Khumesh [Torah]. The teachers of Khumesh were: Josek Pejsach'l, Lejb Wolf, and Abram Aba. Their custom was to make a big festive Khumesh celebration at the beginning of the "season." During it, the children would proclaim and affirm that they, thank God, were already big and mature, and now the time had arrived for them to learn Khumesh. It was no longer necessary to bring them to the *kheyder*; they already knew their way and could get there on their own. With the Khumesh teacher, the children would study for two to three years, and this was because they would also begin

---

[1] Melamed [teacher] is used here as a title rather than as a true surname.
[2] The Shema is the Jewish declaration of faith: "Hear O Israel, The Lord our God, The Lord is One."

learning Rashi.[1] Learning Rashi was for them a totally new phenomenon, since the letters used by Rashi were completely different from the usual lettering, and also, there was no punctuation.

At this Khumesh celebration, the teacher would ask the child, "My child, my dear one, what are you learning?" "Khumesh." "What is the meaning of Khumesh?" "Five." "Five? What does five mean?" "Five, these are the five books of the Torah, and they are Breyshes, Shmoys, Vayikro, Bamidbor, and Dvorim [Genesis, Exodus, Leviticus, Numbers, and Deuteronomy]." "Which Khumesh are you learning?" "Vayikro." "What is the meaning of the word 'Vayikro'?" "To call. God called to Moses and taught him the order of sacrificial offerings… and just as the sacrifices are holy, so too, the children of Israel are holy (a holy flock)."

When the children had finished their studying with a Khumesh teacher, they immediately transferred to continue their studies with a Mishnayos teacher. Those who belonged to the group of Mishnayos instructors were: Szymon Ungier (son of Kopel Szymon Ruchel's [son of Kopel who was the son of Szymon and Ruchel]), Kopel Brandys (Pipczuk) and Mendel Krzykacz. The instructors of the Mishnayos had a much tighter regimen. During the winter they would sit and study at night. Each child would make a lamp constructed from paper. He would put a candle inside it that would light the way to the *kheyder* and the way back home. They would conclude their studies at night. Toward the end of the winter, they would make a big festive celebration for all the children. A large number of children stayed to study at the Mishnayos instructor two to three years, and then, with this festive celebration, they would conclude their studies in the *kheyder*.

The main reason for this was the large expense incurred by the tuition. Not everyone could afford to pay for the continuation of studies. Only those students whose parents could afford it economically, or the children who were really gifted and showed promise, continued to study with the Gemore instructors. The group of Gemore teachers were: Kopel Ungier (Kopel Szymon Ruchel's), Jakób Melamed, and Akiba Dayan (Bock). Those who continued to study with these teachers had to apply themselves very intently to their studies. Here, in the Gemore *kheyder*, the students reached the age of *bar mitsve* [coming-of-age ceremony at age thirteen].

It was customary with these teachers that on Shabes, after the noon meal, the pupils would visit the prominent scholars in the city in order for the students to be tested on the extent of their knowledge of the Gemore. The examiners were: Reb Icek Majer Szu"b (Frydberg), Fiszel Szulimowicz (Malekh), Chaim Szaja Kac, and others. When a student did well on his test, the examiners would reward him with a portion of Shabes fruit.

After the pupils completed studying with the Gemore teachers for two semesters, those boys who really excelled in their studies transferred to study with the teachers for adults. Actually, only a very small number of young men reached this level, since the teachers for adults would lecture on the Torah before only eight to ten students. Among the adult educators were: Chaim Jechiel, Jakób Melamed, Abram Moszek Szenkier, and Benjamin Rotsztajn. They would study Gemore with *toysfes* [supplementary

---

[1] Rashi is a Hebrew acronym for Rabbi Shlomo Yitzhaqi (1040–1105), a rabbi in France who was the author of the first comprehensive commentaries on the Talmud and the Tanakh [Scriptures].

commentaries on the Talmud] and all the other commentators and their interpretations with them. Whoever was worthy and succeeded to study with these instructors for a year or two didn't leave them until he became a true Torah scholar.

A portion of these students continued afterward in the large yeshivas of the Mesivta type [yeshiva of a higher level] in Warsaw, Beit Meir in Kraków, and other yeshivas, or they would elect to study in the *bes hamedresh* in our town that was under the direction of Abram Dayan, *zts"l.*

Among those who studied in the big yeshivas were: Jakób Kaźmierski, Alter Kac, Herszel Nagelblat, and others. All of them perished in the great Holocaust that engulfed Polish Jewry.

Among the rest of the educators there was also a modern one. They nicknamed him Yekl Hamorah [teacher, in Hebrew] (Jakób Goldwaser).[1] He educated the sons of modern families with higher economic standings. He had a special room that was like a classroom, equipped with a blackboard, rulers, and benches that were suitable for young children in which were ink holders and a place to put pens. He accepted students from the age of five until Gemore level.

In Działoszyce, there was also a woman who was active, Rebetsn Pesla, the wife of Reb Akiba Dayan, *zts"l* [may the memory of a righteous person be blessed]. She would go to private homes and teach girls how to read and pray from a *sidur.*

This was the Orthodox and traditional way of teaching in Działoszyce before the axe descended on the holy congregation.

Translated from the Hebrew by Rochel Semp

---

[1] Yekl was the nickname for a German Jew.

The Rebbe Reb Joskele (pp. 204–5)

Naftali Szydłowski

Reb Joskele's full name was Josek Dawid Frydman. His father's name was Szulim. He descended from a family of *kohanim* [priests], and this illustrious lineage was handwritten in a genealogical document. My mother told me that the father of the *rebbe* traveled in his youth to a far away place and took along with him this scroll of noble ancestry. The father was a God-fearing man, a Hasid, and a businessman who would travel to the big market fairs that were taking place during that time. His home was in our town of Działoszyce.

His son, Josek Dawid, learned much Torah in the yeshivas and was quite outstanding in his studies, actions, and behavior. He was very modest, with a good temperament, loved people, and was a Hasid. It seems that he developed a very good reputation, because after the rabbi of our town passed away, the Orthodox community of Działoszyce asked that he become the *rov* [official town rabbi].[1] He was then still a young man, married, and living with his wife in a different town. It seems that he probably was part of the *tish* [table] of his father-in-law, which was the custom in those days.[2] In any event, one thing is for sure, he did not own a large estate or rich farmland. As we have already mentioned, his lineage was not of a rabbinic family, but he had earned the reputation of a prodigy whose expertise in Torah and *poskim* [post-Talmudic commentators] was of a very high level, as was his personal conduct and behavior.

From the stories that my mother, *z"l*, told me, I recall two:

1) One time a man from Działoszyce traveled to a rabbi in a different town to ask that he pray for his sick wife. This rabbi told him: "In your town there is Reb Joskele, so why are you coming to me? Go back to your town and turn to him to pray for your wife." And this is what happened; he returned, came to the *rebbe* Reb Joskele, the *rebbe* prayed, God helped, and the woman returned to good health.

2) Reb Joskele's first wife passed away at a young age, and he married a second time. His [second] wife bore him a daughter (by the way, I remember this daughter who used to come to Działoszyce to her ancestors' gravesites; my mother, *z"l*, introduced her to me with these words: "This is Aunt Pifa, the daughter of [my] grandfather, Reb Joskele."

The *rebbe* detested gifts and refused to accept them. One time a Jew came to seek counsel from the *rebbe*, and since he knew that the *rebbe* refused to accept money, this Jew gave a large monetary gift to the *rebbe*'s wife in order for her to marry off their daughter who was already an older single girl. When the *rebbe* heard of this, he became very angry and demanded that the money be returned. But this Jew had already gone away and disappeared. My mother told this story during one of Aunt Pifa's visits to us.

---

[1] There were sometimes disagreements between the Orthodox and the Hasidic community as to who should become the official town rabbi, who was paid by the state. The fact that Reb Joskele, a Hasid, was chosen by the Orthodox, shows that he must have been very well respected.

[2] The disciples or followers who had the honor of sitting at a *rebbe*'s table were known as the *rebbe*'s *tish*.

I also know that the *rebbe* did not want his son, Naftali, who was my grandfather, to become the next *rebbe* after him. He stood his ground on this, insisting that his son become a merchant instead.

I have no knowledge when he was born or died; however, according to my calculations, he was born in the beginning of the last century and passed away during the 70s or 80s of the nineteenth century. As I mentioned above, he left after him a son by the name of Naftali and a daughter from his second wife by the name of Pifa—who married, if I am not mistaken, someone from her town, Chmielnik. This is all that I know, and perhaps there were other offspring, but I myself have no knowledge.

After he passed away, the Jews of Działoszyce erected an *oyel* [structure over a grave] at his gravesite. This is probably because of his exalted and widespread reputation. People used to come to his grave to pray and ask for God's mercy.

Translated from the Hebrew by Rochel Semp

Reb Kalman Dayan, *z"l* (p. 206)

Alter Horowicz

My grandfather, Reb Kalman Dayan, *z"l*, was the head judge in the town and also a wise Jew. Because of this, he appeared on many occasions as a representative on behalf of the [Jewish] community before governmental administrative offices in Kielce.

They tell of an interesting episode that happened during one of his travels. Reb Kalman went to Kielce once on a horse-drawn wagon, which was the customary means of travel in those days. The wagon passed by a Catholic church that stood along the road, and the gentile driver continued to travel without removing his hat or crossing himself. So Grandfather demanded that the driver return him to his home. When he refused, my grandfather disembarked from the wagon and spoke to him these words: "I refuse to go on my way with a person who does not respect his own religion."

The gentile was very surprised to hear such an observation, and all his pleadings with Grandfather to continue traveling with him were to no avail.

Reb Kalman Dayan was one of the founders of the Chęciny *shtibl* in Działoszyce and was beloved and revered by the entire large Hasidic community.

Translated from the Hebrew by Rochel Semp

Ignacy Mann—The Rabbi and his Pupil (pp. 207–9)

Chaim Schwimer

In Działoszyce there lived a beloved Jew, Szyja the *khazn*, who came from a very well known family of cantors. Their last name was Śpiewak, a literal translation of the word *khazn* or "singer," and as his name, so was he—his whole being was permeated with song.

If Szyja the *khazn* had lived in a big city where there was a possibility of studying music, he would surely have attained the status of conductor or composer or even beyond. But since he was born and raised in a small town, he was limited by his fate. Still, he performed his position as cantor in the *shul* in the best way he could and conducted a choir that would not have embarrassed towns far larger than Działoszyce.

In Cantor Szyja's choir, there was a boy by the name of Ajzyk Bułówka, who was blessed with a glorious voice. People from the area would come to listen to him in awe.

Ajzyk Bułówka, or Ajzyk Bułka, was an orphan, with no father, no mother, hungry, unclothed, and barefoot, as if he had fallen from a strange planet.[1]

As the month of Elul approaches, the days become shorter. Leaves drop from the trees, and there is a cool wind blowing. The town wraps itself in sanctity. The fish in the sea begin to tremble and, certainly, also the Jews. They are seized by the fear of the Day of Judgment, the Days of Awe [High Holy Days].

The Jews test the *shofar*s [rams' horns], and the prayer leaders walk around with their necks wrapped in shawls to avoid catching cold, God forbid, which would prevent them from being able to carry out their mission. They gargle all day long. The sextons polish the windows and the copper candelabra in the *shul* and the *bes hamedresh*. The women dig out old *makhzoyrim* [holiday prayer books] yellowed by time and tears. The cemetery comes alive with the whole town coming to visit their deceased relatives to ask them to intercede for a good year for their near and dear ones who are still alive.

Ajzyk Bułówka used to spend the whole month of Elul at the cemetery, singing "El Mole Rakhamim" [memorial prayer for the dead] for everyone, and his heavenly voice rolled over hill and dale around the cemetery. Some gave him money for his efforts, some just gave him thanks, but this is how he earned his living, and it had to suffice him for the whole year.

When he turned eighteen, they married him off to Mizer, the grain-merchant's daughter. A young man who was involved in holiness, a chorister for the *khazn* who sang "El Mole Rakhamim" [God of Compassion—memorial prayer for the dead] at the cemetery and perhaps might even achieve the post of *khazn* himself in a neighboring *shul*—it just didn't seem right that he be by himself. There is, after all, an explicit verse: "At eighteen to the *khupe* [marriage canopy]," so some kind people intervened and put together the *shidekh* [match].

---

[1] Bułówka and Bułka appear to be nicknames, as there is a birth record for Ajzyk Man in Działoszyce in 1889.

Despite his father-in-law not being in the least bit wealthy, Ajzyk's situation became infinitely better. He left his loneliness behind him and joined a family that reanimated him to some extent. Ajzyk did not at that time have great ambitions, but Szyja the *khazn* fretted about how such a treasure, such a dear voice, might be lost. He begged and cajoled the Jews who were well-off to provide the possibility of his being able to study, until they acceded to his demands.

Ajzyk began to study music in the big city, and his teachers foresaw a great career for him. His voice developed a richer tone, and he gave concerts throughout Poland. Later, he was accepted at the Lemberg [now Lviv] opera, where out of Ajzyk Bułówka, the great opera singer Ignacy Mann came into being. He was especially known for his performance in Halevy's opera *La Juive* [the Jewess]. After the premiere of *La Juive*, the applause and wonder were so great that when he left the theater, people raised him aloft and carried him on their shoulders out of great enthusiasm. This was during the years when his artistry was at its greatest.

In 1923, when I was in Szczawnica, I saw posters advertising a concert by Ignacy Mann. I walked over to the hall, and in the ticket office sat a red-haired woman. I did not know that she was Mann's wife. As I was standing there, I remembered Szyja the *khazn*'s story. I said then that I wished to speak with the singer. And suddenly, he came out. As soon as he saw me, he recalled his childhood in Działoszyce. He had kept a strong feeling for the little town and the memory of his experiences in Działoszyce even until he attained his present status.

He later came to Israel and took a position as the cantor of the Great Synagogue in Haifa, where he enjoyed the fruits of his mentor, Reb Szyja Śpiewak, *z"l*.

He also became an instructor in the development of the voices of the younger generation in Israel. He died in Haifa a few years ago.

May his memory be blessed.

Translated from the Yiddish by Zeva Shapiro

The Town Cantor (pp. 210–12)

Moshe Salomon

One of the most interesting and special individuals in Działoszyce was the town cantor, Reb Szyja Śpiewak, *z"l*. He was the *shaliakh tzibur* [prayer leader] with a very pleasant voice and was a great expert in the interpretation of passages. He served the community of Działoszyce for the duration of two generations.

Reb Szyja was born in the 60s of the past century [19th]. He studied in the *kheyders* and absorbed the fear of heaven and love of people. During his youth, the congregants, while sitting on the benches of the *bes hamedresh*, would listen to his pleasant voice when he chanted Torah. The learned elders of the town predicted for him a glowing future as a cantor. His voice was a legacy that he had inherited, since he came from a family of cantors going back several generations.

Until the day of his marriage, he perfected himself in the various styles of prayer, deepened his knowledge in the ways of singing, enhanced and enriched his voice, and was privileged to be offered the position of chief cantor in the town synagogue right after his wedding.

However, Reb Szyja wasn't content to merely do this one job but followed in the path of other famous cantors. He organized a choir that at the beginning was small and inadequate, but, ever so slowly, it attracted more youth as well as adults with pleasant voices. The beautifully harmonized singing of this choir on Shabes and holidays could be heard from afar, and the gentiles in the area would listen to it sometimes as well.

The apartment of Reb Szyja was located in the building that contained the public bathhouse and wasn't far from the synagogue. This apartment was spacious, and in it resided the branches of the cantor's family, which included his many sons and daughters. The apartment also served as a conservatory for the choir, which would meet there on a regular basis during the weekdays in order to study and perfect the different styles and melodies for the holidays that occurred.

Reb Szyja succeeded in raising and bringing up his offspring in the ways of the Torah and their Jewish heritage. Even before his sons matured, they left the town one by one, and also Poland, and dispersed to the wide world. Among different destinations, they went to the United States, Argentina, Holland, and so forth. They found their niches, some in business and some in other enterprises, and their economic situation was secure.

His two daughters and one of his sons (who first emigrated to Holland and then returned) stayed in Poland and greatly helped their father to maintain the legacy that had been bequeathed him by his father.

Reb Szyja Śpiewak was a Jew of average height, broad shouldered, with a long beard that adorned his smiling warmhearted face. His eyes reflected softness and goodness, and in them a constant spark was glowing.

His large home was open to any visitor, and all who stepped across his threshold immediately felt the warmth that emanated from the personality of their host. It was a customary tradition in the cantor's family to run an open house, and the acceptance of guests into their home was looked upon as emulating the values and qualities of our forefather Abraham. In addition to this, Reb Szyja distinguished himself with his open heartedness and selfless willingness to help each and every needy Jew.

It is worth mentioning that the daughter of the cantor, Taubele, was blessed with great talent in the art of music as well, and it was she who conducted the choir when it was first formed. She was also knowledgeable in the reading of musical notes and talented as a conductor. Because of this, she was able to imbue in the choir's members a love and enthusiasm for their singing, so that their attitude created an aura of worship adorned with a halo of heavenly holiness. In the years when this choir was at its peak, it had thirty-four singers, who were divided by Taubele, the conductor, into four separate groups of voices. They brought immense pleasure to the ears of their listeners with their harmonious melodic singing. The members of the synagogue greatly appreciated their choir.

It is worth noting here that the members of the choir worked devotedly for a relatively long time without compensation. Their singing was more than just a simple hobby. They viewed it as a holy work perhaps similar to the task of the Levites in the holy Temple.

One of Reb Szyja's sons, Moszek, followed in the footsteps of his father. He learned from him the most important aspects of being a cantor and later continued this holy work on a high level.

For forty years Reb Szyja served as the cantor for the community of Działoszyce and as its prayer leader—with his pleasurable melodies during the holidays and festivals and on those Sabbaths where they blessed the new month, as well as each day of the year. The congregants of the synagogue viewed him as their defender-protector-mediator, who, with the help of the accompanying choir, offered his prayers to our Creator, blessed be He, and their singing was like hearing the conversations of the heavenly angels.

The cantor, Reb Szyja, was particularly moving during the High Holy Day services. Covered with a *talis* [prayer shawl] and a white *kitl* [robe], he would stand in front of the *bime* [platform], spilling out his heart before the Creator, asking that the forthcoming new year be a healthy, prosperous, and peaceful one. The entire large congregation listened with awe and trepidation to his pleas. While all of these prayers were being recited, the Holy Ark was opened and the holy *seyfer-toyres* [Torah scrolls], with their ornaments and decorations, looked as if they were gazing at the congregants. It seemed as though they were silent witnesses to the struggle and conversation that was taking place between the cantor, Reb Szyja, and the Creator of the World.

It was very pleasant indeed to observe how people would shake the hands of the cantor at the conclusion of the prayers and say with great devotion, "Thank you so much Reb Szyja. May it be so, that your prayers emanating from the depth of your heart be recorded and received by the Creator of the World."

The lofty virtues of Reb Szyja strengthened the choir members' faith and their love of the Creator and also their love of their fellow men, as it is written: "Love thy neighbor as thyself."

The daughter of the cantor, who conducted the choir for many years, discovered among her friends a poor orphaned boy by the name of Icek Man. He had a strong voice and was very musically talented. She persuaded her father to take upon himself another superhuman effort, to collect funds from the wealthy and prominent people in town to send this youth to the big city so he could complete his studies at the music conservatory.

It came to pass. This lad studied and excelled and with the passage of years became an opera singer [as Ignacy Mann] in Lwów [now Lviv, Ukraine] and in other places. In the late 30s, he arrived in Eretz Yisroel and assumed the position of chief cantor in Haifa. He was also an instructor for voice training, and many well-known prominent singers and cantors graduated from his school. A few years ago, he passed away in Haifa, where he was greatly respected and held in high esteem by all.

When the cantor Reb Szyja reached the age of fifty and beyond, he became sick with all sorts of illnesses and ailments. His strength left him, and he was unable to continue his cantorial duties. Left with no other choice and unwilling to break the continuous chain of his forefathers' legacy, he appointed his son Moszek to serve as cantor and holy envoy in his stead. He also put forth a tremendous amount of effort, in spite of many difficulties, to continue the existence of the choir. This was the final effort of Reb Szyja on this earth. As though mimicking the work of ants without weariness, and with the help of Taubele, as the conductor, his son Moszek continued to serve as the cantor of the synagogue together with the choir, the pride and glory of the entire city of Działoszyce.

Thus the cantor Reb Szyja Śpiewak and his son Moszek performed their holy work, and the choir along with them, until the arrival of the great destruction. Suddenly, the horrible Shoah descended upon our people and destroyed everything, the Jews of the city, the community, and along with them their prayer leaders forever.

Translated from the Hebrew by Rochel Semp

My Father, the Community Activist (pp. 213–15)

Moshe Drobiarz

My grandfather, Abram Icek Drobiarz, may he rest in peace, was a Działoszyce Jew with a majestic face, a beautiful long beard, and a penchant for doing good deeds. His whole life was spent in philanthropy. He loved to do good deeds for people with his whole heart, as Jews did in the old days. Among other things, he gave up a room in his house for a house of prayer, where forty or fifty men would come together on Shabes and Holy Days. He himself was a Hasid [Hasidic follower] of the old Pińczów *rebbe*, *z"l*, who fasted many entire days. I stood at his bedside when he died at the age of eighty-seven.

My father, Herszel Drobiarz, had someone from whom he learned good character and to do good deeds—his father.

As I remember from my earliest days, he carried a list of Hasidic rabbis, other rabbis, rabbis' associates, sextons, sages, and educated Jews who, as was customary, did not have great wealth. Father sent gifts of money to them with an open hand to make sure that no Jewish household, God forbid, suffered any need on Shabes and the Holy Days.

When I had grown up a bit and began to understand the essence of the world, he sent me more than once to carry out this sacred duty.

When winter arrived, Father bought whole wagonfuls of potatoes, coal, and wood, which he distributed to the needy families, according to his own understanding. Some called on Father themselves to collect their portion, and to others, he sent the winter aid with coachmen and carriers to their homes.

In addition, he founded an interest-free loan institution. At the beginning, he gave loans without interest to ten people. Later, he systematically broadened the credit to about fifty families. Every Sunday, the fund gave out loans, and on Fridays, the people who owed money paid back a portion of their debt. But he did not think this institution was enough, so he created something else.

We were seven children in a two-room house, so it is obvious he could not do what his father, *z"l*, had done and offer a room for prayer. So he decided to rent a dwelling from a woman, Grusi Alter, which was located near the kosher butcher shops. He paid the rent and turned it over to a group of Gerer Hasidim to use as their *shtibl*. For this, and for his many other good deeds, my father, *z"l*, was held in great honor and esteem.

In the meanwhile, he ordered a new Torah for the prayer house from the scribe. It took two years to write the scroll. The procession and the glorious ceremony of carrying the Torah to the *shul* became the most joyful event for the Jews of Działoszyce. I believe there may be sons of the town among us who remember that jubilation.

With time, the congregation grew, and the *shtibl* became too crowded. Then, my pious father bought a piece of land to build a larger prayer house on it, so that it would attract more and more worshippers. His plan included the building of an extra room, with a number of beds, in front of the building, for hospitality for respectable Jews.

As this was happening, my father, *z"l*, suddenly became ill, and before he was taken to Kraków, left a will in which he ordained that everything be built as he had envisioned, with his own money.

To our sorrow, he was brought back on the third day no longer alive. All the Hasidim came to offer their last respects to the true Hasid; they read paragraphs from the Mishne, recited Psalms, and accompanied him on his final journey. He left a great sadness, not just in his own family, but in the whole town.

*

Within the year, the hospitality house was built according to my father's plan under the supervision of my eldest brother-in-law, Mejlech Kulimek, *z"l*. My sister Rywka, *z"l*, the mother of eight children, took upon herself the difficult task of keeping track of all matters relating to the building of the hospitality center.

I would like to describe the house where my brother-in-law Mejlech came from. His parents had a food store next to the post office, and he used to sit all the time in the *bes hamedresh* studying day and night. My father, may his soul rest in paradise, took him as a son-in-law for my oldest sister. For a while, he boarded with us. He was a follower of the Działoszyce *rebbe*, Reb Lejzor Epsztajn, *zts"l*. During the Days of Awe, he served there as the cantor, officiating at the morning service. He also willingly joined the Khevre Kedishe [Burial Society]. Since the Khevre Kedishe members in Działoszyce never took any money, it is evident that he was always one of the first volunteers to do good deeds.

During World War II, the Polish police knew no one else to go to when someone died or someone was killed. They came to let him know so that he would have them buried.

During the first deportation, he was hidden in his house. He was discovered there. His family was sent to an unknown place, and he was sent to Stalowa Wola.

My brother Szmul and my oldest brother, Mordka Drobiarz, and his son Abram Icek were also there. Szmul and my brother-in-law Mejlech were able to escape. The Germans in Stalowa Wola shot Mordka and his son Abram Icek.

I later met my brother-in-law Mejlech Kulimek in the camp in Płaszów. There was a decree there that if anyone escaped from the camp, ten others would be shot in his place. The wicked man, the murderer [Amon] Goeth, ordered that if anyone escaped, the Jews from a whole barracks would be shot. There were six hundred Jews there.

I don't exactly recall the date when the following happened. On a Shabes, two people escaped, one from Block 28 and the other from Block 29. Goeth, the camp leader, demanded that the Jewish commander, Chilowicz, sign the order to shoot 1200 people, according to the decree. No one went to work that day. At two o'clock in the afternoon, there came an order that everyone in the camp should assemble in the inspection area. The elders in the camp divided the people into groups and allotted various jobs to each group.

Afterward, a death committee of the SS people looked over each group. I was in a small group from which they took out three persons to be shot, among them a young boy, Motele Rozenblum, who broke away from the Jewish guards who were leading the people to the area where they would be shot. In one place, my brother-in-law Mejlech worked without a shirt on, and he was emaciated. They noticed that and led him to the assembly point where they shot seventy-six Jews.

From our family—Mejlech Kulimek, my sister Rywka, their eight children, and one grandchild—no trace remains. They all perished through Hitler's beasts.

May the Lord avenge their blood.

Translated from the Yiddish by Zeva Shapiro

From Działoszyce Folklore (pp. 216–18)

Dov Bejski

The Jewish folklore in Eastern Europe was rich. Over the course of generations, a national literature was established that enriched and took its creativity from the way of life of our forefathers and their traditions and heritage. It was expressed in prose and songs, legends and stories, proverbs and riddles, and comedy and jokes that were created over time. Name calling and even curses were transmitted by word of mouth from generation to generation. Our town of Działoszyce, in spite of its being a Jewish center in a forsaken area, particularly excelled in its own folklore. Its population was mostly comprised of ordinary Jews who had been in this town starting in the 1400s. The town was a social and cultural center according to the standard that was applicable during those days. Along with the traditional connection to the study of the Torah and the unlimited belief in a God that was in heaven above, there also developed, during generations, a folklore of the secular segment of Działoszyce. And we have been successful in compiling only a little bit of it. There was some folk literature, rich and unique to our town of Działoszyce, and it used to reveal to us, in a folkloristic manner, the lifestyle of our fathers—their intelligence, biting wit, ingenuity, and sense of humor, which accompanied them through all the generations.

To our anguish, everything has been destroyed. The Nazi enemy destroyed all traces. Nothing survived. And from the stories that we heard during our youth from our grandmothers and grandfathers, only vague memories remain with us. And this is too little. In spite of this, I want to relate, as much as possible, not the stories but at least the other things that remain in my memory. Perhaps I'll remember a specific Działoszyce proverb or saying that was part of our colloquial speech, the human image or the story that was hidden behind the specific saying or quote.

The Jesters

The comedians and jesters comprised a special group. Their job, as is well known, was to bring joy to people during wedding celebrations. Still in my youth, I was privileged to hear them and to derive pleasure from their presence. These popular rhymesters, in spite of having been poverty stricken, knew how to cheer up a human heart with lively song, to blend the needs of the hour with pleasant prose that drew the gathered guests close together. I was always surprised when I heard them how they succeeded, without a moment's hesitation, to continue singing the praises of so and so or to invent a new song that we had never heard in the town before. But, on each occasion, they managed to compose new words and songs that fitted that particular occasion.

Their images stand before my eyes as I viewed them at weddings. Of course, a prominent jester was invited only to the wedding of a wealthy person. The poor folks could not afford one. It was sufficient for them to supply the dowry and expenses of the wedding. A comedian by the name of Frydman, not from Działoszyce, was the most famous one in the area. And even though he lived in Kraków, he was invited to our town on many occasions and became very well liked by our residents. He was a Jew of

Icekl the Victim

Ancestors' graves

Zvi Ptasznik and Lejb Ajnbinder reading newspapers

Two unfortunate souls taking a rest

Rebetsn Epsztajn in her youth

Cantor Moszek Śpiewak chanting
"El Mole Rachamim" [memorial prayer for the dead]

Szyja Śpiewak, town cantor

A Wagoner

A bagel vendor at the fair

Szymele, the *Meshugene*
[crazy one]

A family in town

A family in town

A mother and her children who died in the Holocaust
Chawa Arkusz and her children Estera and Dawid

Three friends: Dawid Targownik, *z"l*, Jakób Jabl'a, Icek Kołatacz, *z"l*

Moszek Hersz Rozenfrucht, *z"l*
returning from
Russian imprisonment

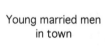

Young married men
in town

The *shoykhet*, Icze Majer Frydberg, and his daughter

The west side of the synagogue

The *rebbe* Reb Lejzor Epsztajn, his son Jonatan, and one of his Hasidim

The rabbi and the *shames* – the elderly rabbi Reb Icek Halevi
Staszewski, *z"l*, and the *shames,* Hersz Mendel, *z"l.*

The Goldkorn family wedding

Part IV:

Shoah and Destruction

Days of the Shoah (pp. 233–60)

Dr. Moshe Bejski

Foreword

When friends and acquaintances who had launched the project to honor the memory of our holy community of Działoszyce, which has been destroyed, asked me to write a few chapters about the town and its history during the Holocaust,[1] in order to include them in the upcoming Yizkor book, I initially turned them down. For this refusal I must apologize to those undertaking this holy task and explain myself.

As someone who was raised and educated in this town and who absorbed from it the entrenched Jewish values within the unique and extraordinary environment with which this town was blessed, memories from it are very dear to me also, and, like others, it is of great interest to me that at the very least, the history and account of this holy community be preserved for the future. I do not make light of the obligation that the former residents of the town, Holocaust survivors, have to lend a hand, to the degree to which they are able, to establish a memorial for this Jewish town.

My refusal stemmed from fears and doubts as to my ability to bear the heavy weight of this responsibility. Anyone who undertakes to record accounts of the history of the Działoszyce community, which is no more, faces a very difficult task. There never was a more cruel and efficient annihilation effort! The remains of its holy martyrs were never brought to a Jewish burial. Other than the near certain knowledge that most of its Jews were murdered in the Bełżec death camp, where they arrived in a transport after the first mass deportation on September 2, 1942,[2] no trace remains of the rest of the town's Jews who perished in various death and labor camps to which they were deported. The thousands who died in the town, during the deportations or before them, were also not interred in a Jewish cemetery. The local Polish population bears responsibility for this, for it made sure that even the cemetery vanished both from above and below ground.

The same situation holds true for the documentary material that spanned the hundreds of years of the community's life and included the Holocaust period. The community's records, its documents and its archives—nothing remains of them! What German efficiency did not manage to eradicate, the local Polish residents destroyed. For this reason, not only is there no documentary basis on which to conduct research about the community, but there is also no method to validate memories in cases of doubt. There is no greater challenge than recording the memory of a community that has been destroyed without the assistance of any archival material.

---

[1] Throughout the rest of this chapter, the word *Shoah*, which means disaster or catastrophe, is translated as Holocaust, as that is the term Bejski used when writing a parallel chapter in English.
[2] While the *Aktion* began on September 2, the deportations occurred on September 3, 1942.

There were also further doubts. The community of Działoszyce was under the hell of Nazi rule for about three years until its final annihilation. Every year had 365 days, each of which was an ocean of ever increasing hardships and calamities. Who could ever count and record the suffering of the Jewish population in general and of each family in particular? Even if all the leaders of the community who took care of the population's daily needs had survived, it is doubtful whether they would have been able to describe the history of the community during those dreadful years. How much more so is this true for me, as I understand these matters so much less.

Approximately thirty years have passed since the destruction of the Jews in Poland. This period is much too short for any of us to forget the atrocities and horrors that we experienced and to gloss over the open festering wounds that have remained and that will never heal. Perhaps, due to the fact that each daily verdict became more vicious and horrible than the one before it, this creates a difficulty to relate all that occurred in a chronological order. There is no doubt that tens and hundreds of incidents that happened then are still reappearing, floating in front of the eyes, tearing out the hair and congealing the blood in their viciousness—just in the order in which they had happened. Certainly there are many important events relating to the birth of the community that perhaps didn't come to my knowledge, or they became faded with the time that has passed. Please understand my hesitation to deal with such difficult, painful matters. And in addition, I greatly suspect that I will not be able to relate the events in sufficient detail, due to my lack of knowledge or inability to remember, especially regarding matters that will be recalled and brought forth in this book by others, and I will find myself committing a double sin. These were the reasons for my initial refusal.

However, after additional thought, I became convinced that in spite of my hesitation, the initiators of this project were correct in their goal. The truth is that my reservations have not diminished at all. However, there is yet another bitter and vicious reality to this. We who are the survivors of the Holocaust are the last generation to leave Działoszyce. Except for us, there will be no one able to talk about the glory and magnificence of the community, to describe its scholars and wise men, its righteous and pious inhabitants, to recall the joy of youth that long existed in that place and to remember the days filled with happiness. In those days, we had the vision and dreams of returning to Zion while being active in the Zionist youth movements. When our generation will cease to exist, no one will know about the *bes hamedresh* that hummed with students and scholars, about the young yeshiva men who passed their nights like days in the study of Torah, about Rov [Rabbi] Icek Halevi Staszewski, *ztsk"l* [the holy righteous of blessed memory], and Rebbe Epsztajn, *ztsk"l*, whose words inspired the entire community. Our children, who were born here in Israel, even though they have heard that their parents were born in a town called Działoszyce, have difficulty pronouncing the name correctly.

The earth in Działoszyce has become barren; it will never again produce another Jewish generation. Can we permit an entire Jewish community, with almost all of its residents, to be totally erased and wiped off the face of the earth and nothing remembered of it? After all, for hundreds of years, Jewish life bustled there in all of its magnificence and glory, steeped in tradition and full of character and faith. There our parents grew up and warm Jewish hearts beat, Torah and Hebrew institutions were created, and we, their children, absorbed from teachers and wise Torah scholars the values and mores of

Orthodox Judaism. And we few survivors, who drank from the poisoned cup until the end and due to sheer miracles remained alive, suffered the hellish bitterness of the Nazi era— along with those who were and are now gone. Our parents, brothers, and children were separated from us and sent to a place from which no one returned. We were partners in the efforts and superhuman attempts to survive this hellish period. Woe be to us, the few remnants who managed to remain alive. The others did not succeed.

For the memory of our dear ones and the holy congregation that was annihilated, it is a *mitsve* [good deed] to tell their story, even though it may not be a complete account and only the main aspect of their general existence will be recorded in this book.

The Beginning

On the day the war broke out, I was in Kraków, the city where I had lived for several years. Already the next day, the troubling news arrived that the German armies were closing in quickly and it was necessary to leave the city immediately. Where to escape? The only escape route led to Działoszyce, to my parents' home. Please note: From the very first day, there was no means of transportation. Just like tens and hundreds of other people, we, too, embarked on the trip by foot. My eldest brother, Dov, accompanied me. For three days and nights we made progress with strenuous walking, while the roads and ways were congested with people trying to escape. The trip was frightening and disorganized. Every so often, German airplanes would bomb the slowly moving throngs, and countless victims died then and there. The worst thing was that not one person out of all those leaving had any idea exactly as to where he was fleeing. Along the same road, heading toward the northeast, trekked tens of thousands of people with their children, food supplies, and meager belongings. At the same time, from the opposite direction, the same sight was seen. Masses of human beings dragging their feet, lost and bewildered. Each of them had the same news to tell, that the Germans were approaching the very place from which they were fleeing. To us it was clear that, first of all, we had to reunite with our families. And indeed, we succeeded in arriving in Działoszyce at the end of the third day of our flight.

The situation in the town wasn't much different than in the other places that we had passed while running away. Thousands of refugees congregated and were arriving here. From a logical point of view, they rationalized that a small town not on the main highway and away from the main traffic might not become one of the German casualties, especially not in the initial stages of the war. However, this proved to be a futile hope. On the evening of that very same day when we arrived in Działoszyce, an order was issued by the Polish government that all reserves, as well as men up to fifty years old, were to leave town and direct themselves toward Pińczów and Kielce. Masses of frightened people started fleeing. All of this was accompanied by the knowledge and clear signs that the Germans were following directly behind our footsteps the entire time. And, in fact, none of us arrived at the right destination or enlistment center, since the German army had already preceded us to each place. We found ourselves in a constant state of fright and flight, while machinegun fire was directed at us the entire time. Poland became engulfed in a sea of steel, lead, and burned dust. When we finally arrived breathless and totally exhausted at the banks of the River San, we became aware that on the night of Rosh Hashanah [Jewish New Year], the Germans had captured it from one side, while the opposite bank was under the control of the Russians.[1] That's when the torturous way back began, but this time, under the rule of the Germans. While on the way, it became clear to us how justified our fear of the Nazis was.

When we came back to Działoszyce, we found a totally different town than the one we had left. Even though it had not suffered any victims as yet and had not been bombed, the composition of the population had changed. From among the residents of the town who had escaped, whether because they were ordered to or on their own initiative, many did not return. After months and years, it became evident that there were those who managed to reach the River San before it became a dividing line between the Germans and the Russians. They suddenly found themselves in the territories occupied by the Russians and were totally separated from their homes and families. The great effort that these refugees made in order to reunite with their families on both sides of the river is a chapter in itself. Many sacrificed their own lives while doing so. Others started on their own wanderings and ended up in the Donbas region [Donetsk], in the Ural Mountains, or in Siberia. For instance, it became clear that Mr. Szlama Gertler and his son Poldek [Leopold] were under the Russian regime in Lwów, while the rest of their family stayed in Działoszyce. At the end of 1940, or maybe 1941, Poldek succeeded in crossing the border and arrived back home, while his father stayed and was sent into the depths of Russia.[2] Very many of our brethren from Działoszyce ended up with the same fate.

In contrast to the families—still intact or divided—that were unable to return back to their homes from their first flight at the beginning of the war, a large number of refugees were added whose fate drew them here and who now remained in the town and could go no further.

The Population and Living Arrangements

When the initial upheaval passed and the fighting ceased, the first edicts against the Jews began. One decree followed another, and each day brought new restrictions against the Jews. Some were national decrees that involved all the Jews in the country, and some were local decrees that applied only to local Jews. It is beyond my ability to remember and recall all the limitations that were imposed during that period even before the end of 1939. Our money, gold, and jewelry were stolen. It was forbidden for Jews to leave their homes when it was dark, it was forbidden to go beyond the outskirts of the town, and it was mandatory to wear an armband identifying oneself as a Jew (a white band, ten centimeters wide and on it a blue Star of David, eight centimeters in size). It was

---

[1] Through the secret Ribbentrop-Molotov Non-Aggression Pact, Germany and the Soviet Union had agreed to divide Poland between them. On September 17, 1939, the army of the Soviet Union invaded the eastern half of Poland, occupying territories east of the River San (and further north, on the eastern side of the River Bug), while Germany occupied the western half of the country. When western Poland was overrun by the Germans, the Polish military, not expecting the Soviet invasion, ordered all able-bodied men to proceed east and regroup to push back the Germans. Unable to form an effective fighting unit, most men either escaped to other countries (many to fight in Allied armies) or returned home to be with their families.

[2] Under the Russian occupation of eastern Poland (1939–41), one and a half million Poles, considered by the Soviets to be bourgeois enemies of the people, were deported to Siberia or other remote places, including many Jews.

forbidden for Jews to travel on trains or deal in business, their properties were confiscated, etc., etc. Dozens of different and varied decrees were enacted and passed that limited the living conditions of Jews already during the first months of the war.

In order to make things easier on myself, I decided to return to Kraków and try to get reemployed in my former workplace. However, I was only able to stay there for a few months. When they started to establish the [Kraków] ghetto in the beginning of 1940 and the Jews were forced to move into it, it seemed more reasonable for me to return to my parents' home in Działoszyce and not be confined inside the ghetto. The truth is that, in the end, Działoszyce itself became a ghetto as well. Here, too, the strict decree not to leave the town was in effect, and whoever attempted to do so did it at the risk of his life. However, to all outside appearances, at least, the feeling here was more comfortable. Barbed wire was not erected around the town, and guards were not posted at the gates. Of course, it was prohibited to leave the town to go to the adjoining towns. But because we were not confronted by the sight of barbed wire around the town, this seemed to be a somewhat more peaceful existence. However, there was an additional reason that I chose to remain in Działoszyce and not in the ghetto in Kraków. During that time, and we're talking about 1940, there did not yet exist a German police station in Działoszyce. Actually, one had been established at the beginning of the war in the town, but later on, it was transferred to Kazimierza Wielka. For the time being, this was a very big plus for the Jews, since the town was not under constant German control. The local German authorities were situated in Miechów, and the gendarmerie made its permanent location in Kazimierza Wielka. Nonetheless, their representatives visited often and sometimes even on a daily basis. Although none of the decrees skipped our town, there still was an advantage, in that the Stormtroopers were not sitting inside the town. Each visit by the authorities became quickly known from the moment that they arrived in town. However, it seemed that our situation was better than that in the neighboring communities, where the Germans were permanently ensconced, both the Gestapo and the SS, along with the German police and administrators.[1]

This was probably also the reason that from the beginning of the first half of 1940, Jews from the larger cities started streaming into Działoszyce. The first to return were the former residents of Działoszyce who had left the town in order to seek better livelihoods. Because these people had family ties and affiliations with the local residents, they now returned without anything, in order to get far away from other locations that were more central. In those places, the situation of the Jews was much more horrible than in Działoszyce. Many from our town had moved during the twenty or so years before the war to Silesia and Zagłębie. In 1940, a great majority of them found their way back to their birthplace. Moreover, many Jews were forced to flee their dwelling places from many different areas when these became part of the Third Reich,[2] and it was self-evident

---

[1] Gestapo is an abbreviation for *Geheime Staatspolizei*, the German secret police, known for its brutality. SS is the abbreviation for *Schutzstaffel*, the elite military unit of the Nazi Party that served as a special police force.

[2] In 1939, the westernmost parts of Poland were incorporated into the Third Reich, while the middle section, though occupied by the Germans, was made into a separate province called the General Government. The eastern half of Poland was occupied by the Soviet Union until June 1941, when Germany attacked the Soviet Union and drove the Soviet forces out of Poland.

what the fate of these Jews would be. Also, there were many who arrived in Działoszyce closer to 1941 or in the ensuing period when the ghettos in the big cities were completely sealed off and the conditions reached unbearable levels. All who could sought to escape to an area that appeared to be somewhat better in order to endure these difficult times.

As a result, from the beginning of the war and approximately until the end of 1941, the population of Działoszyce grew at a steady rate to enormous proportions. It wasn't easy to escape. However, some Jews took the risk and, posing as native-born gentiles, boarded trains without any possessions at all after escaping the ghettos and other areas that had been declared free of Jews. The lucky ones among them succeeded in arriving somewhere that appeared to be a better place for them to live through this hellish period, until it passed, than the place from which they had fled.

Statistics and numbers of our town's population during the war are not available, but it is clear that it amounted to more than 10,000 souls. This means that approximately two-thirds were refugees who had settled in our town, the majority without even proper clothing to cover their bodies.

Our town was never well known for its spacious living quarters. The families grew steadily—but not so the housing. Many of the permanent residents dwelt in difficult and substandard conditions. And now during this short period of time were added thousands of refugees without a roof over their heads. Almost every family, regardless of how poor or cramped, was forced to absorb relatives who had escaped from hell and share their homes. Despite the poverty and overcrowding, the local citizenry could not find dwellings for all those looking for a place to live. Each hole, nook, and cranny was used. The town resembled a refugee town. Hundreds of people were placed in public buildings under conditions that cannot even be described. In the *bes hamedresh* and the synagogue alone, close to a thousand persons were housed. Each family was entitled to a certain number of square meters in accordance with its size. Sleeping arrangements were made that enabled them to find a place for their heads during the night.

A depression that one cannot even imagine overcame anyone who entered these public places that had been turned into refugee centers. The few meager possessions that each family had placed near them only heightened the feelings of terrible poverty. If someone got hold of a piece of fabric or cloth, they put up a partition to indicate their private area. Dozens of babies and toddlers grew up under these circumstances without basic sanitary facilities. In order to drink, it was necessary to bring water in pails from afar. One of the most difficult problems was the preparation of cooked food. (During this stage we're not talking about earning a livelihood but just having a physical spot in which to dwell). The spaces for the refugees kept shrinking along with the growing numbers of people seeking them, until the area that was assigned to each family could not even be passed through, and certainly, there was not a corner in which to cook. Some measure of assistance was provided to these dwellers through the communal kitchen (we will talk about it later), through which people received at least one hot meal a day, but that did not solve the general appalling situation.

Another great difficulty of life was the issue of heat. This problem was common to the general population and especially to those who now lived in the public quarters. Among other provisions whose shortage was already felt from the beginning of the war were heating materials. Coal was very scarce, and wood was totally unattainable. In addition to the great troubles caused by the enemy, sufferings from heaven also befell them. The winter of 1940 was especially harsh. While in private homes, some means of heating the stove still existed, in public places like the synagogue and the *bes hamedresh*, this was non-existent. One of my responsibilities as a member of the sanitation committee was to visit these places almost daily, and I was witness to scenes that really tore my heart. I saw babies and children lying on wooden planks for days at a time, covered by some blankets or rags that had been collected from the residents in order to protect these little ones from the fierce cold.

The situation worsened even more toward the winter of 1941. The Jewish population was squeezed and crowded into the meager dwellings until it was unbearable. And under these circumstances, it was now necessary to absorb even more hundreds of families. A decree went out from the enemy authorities that Jews could congregate only in certain areas and that it was totally forbidden to be in small villages or farms. As is well known, there almost wasn't a village in the area that didn't have a few individual Jewish families living in them. Within a number of days, it was mandated for them to leave their homes and go to Działoszyce. I remember the fights and arguments between the *Judenrat* [Jewish council appointed by the Germans] and the homeowners and refugees, when it became necessary to squeeze in some more beds and mattresses into places where one couldn't even fit a pin. And even though this part of the suffering was minute in contrast to what the Jewish population of the town experienced during all the years of the occupation until its physical annihilation, this only served to make an already bitter enough life even more difficult and prolonged the day-to-day sufferings.

Hygiene and Epidemics

The horrible crowding and living conditions presented yet another most dangerous time bomb—the outbreak of epidemics so prevalent in times of war. The community leaders were very much aware of this from the very beginning, and much work and effort were invested to try to prevent it from happening. This was not an easy feat to accomplish because of the lack of sanitary facilities and the malnutrition suffered by most of the population. An outbreak of an epidemic would mean a double annihilation problem: First of all, its quick contagiousness, which would cause it to spread without any ability to control it, and second, the extreme measures the enemy authorities might take in such an event. In the beginning of the war, there was only one doctor in the town, Dr. Grębowski. At the beginning of 1940, Dr. Dwojra Lazar arrived from Kraków and settled in our place. (We are talking about the daughter of Reb Szymon Menachem Lazar, the editor of the Hebrew newspaper *Hamitzpah* [The Watchtower] and the sister of Dr. Dawid Lazar, the editor of *Maariv* [Evening]). She was the only Jewish doctor in town. Aside from her normal medical treatment of the population that now numbered above the 10,000 range, she also had to prevent the outbreak of epidemics, which under these very trying health hazards and impossible living conditions were most susceptible to occur and spread. The job was an impossible one, what with the contagious diseases and epidemics that were rampant in the area and with no vaccines, medical supplies, or other vital necessities with which to fight them.

Under the direction of Dr. Lazar, a sanitation committee was established. Its main function was to implement ways and means to take emergency action, to assure that sanitary conditions existed in both private homes and especially in public places, and to provide means and centers for decontamination purposes. The local committee members paid vigilant daily visits throughout the entire town and inspected every nook and cranny. They disinfected with sulfur and by other means. A center for decontamination was established using steam at very high temperatures, and those dwelling in public places had to disinfect their meager belongings during appointed times. And sure enough, for a relatively long period of time, the town was spared an epidemic, in spite of all the detrimental dire situations that existed.

However, all the frantic efforts and investments could not prevent the infiltration of epidemics that were already swirling in the nearby vicinity.

In 1941, all at once, there erupted epidemics of dysentery, typhoid fever, and typhus. A grave danger descended on our town, since according to the law, it was imperative to inform the authorities of any outbreak of a contagious disease. And the results were not long in coming. The epidemic became widespread and caused many casualties. To the credit of Dr. Dwojra Lazar, *z"l* [of blessed memory], the fact is that information about the epidemic did not reach the ears of the authorities. Thanks to her outstanding efforts, dedication, and devotion, the typhus epidemic quieted down after several months. The hands of the doctor and the sanitation committee were overloaded with work. Aside from the crowding and malnourishment, which nothing could be done to improve, other harsh difficulties existed. It was essential to conduct a fundamental disinfectant procedure throughout the entire population and, as much as possible, to do so all at once. But the accommodations that were available for this procedure were too few and totally insufficient.

The other great hardship that existed was that there was no local hospital or even suitable quarantine facilities to house all the sick people and treat them. The conditions in this respect were so very difficult that the ones suffering from typhus with the most critical symptoms were housed in a building called the *hekdesh* [shelter for the poor], located near the cemetery. As a result of this awful situation, people refrained from seeking medical intervention and only did so for a member of their family when the symptoms of the disease were already very apparent. They were most afraid that the sick one would be removed to one of these places. But the bitter truth was that in the entire town, one could not find any other suitable space that was still not occupied by the refugees.

Toward the winter of 1942, the epidemics quieted down. Afterward, only individual cases of typhus would surface.

Livelihoods and Occupations

Even in normal times prior to the war, Działoszyce was not known for having many rich and prosperous citizens. The poverty level was very great. And it is not an exaggeration to say that the large majority of the population lived from hand to mouth in great poverty, and so during the entire year, there was no lack of extremely poor people in the town. The main livelihood of the largest group of workers came from trading with the farmers in the surrounding areas. The storeowners were considered among the rich in the town. Many others found their livelihood in small businesses, spending the majority of the week making rounds among the farmers in the surrounding areas, acquiring their products in order to sell them during market days or to wholesalers whose distribution reached distant places. Adding to this all the other typical Jewish trades, including the ones involving community affairs and religious holy trades, we have in front of us a clear and wide-ranging array of different occupations existing in Działoszyce.

With the outbreak of the war, the sources of livelihood for most of the residents in the town became closed off. Already in the first weeks of the war, the Nazi regime appointed commissioners called *Treuhändlers* [trustees] for the larger businesses. The fact was that the owners stopped being in control of their possessions. Other businesses and stores liquidated themselves due to the fact that they could not obtain the merchandise that they were used to selling. To mention some of them: fabrics, textiles, manufactured goods, leather, shoes, and a very long list of products and necessities. Truthfully, most products were under surveillance. Still, many of the merchants managed to hide some of their merchandise in different hiding places, to take it out at one time or another, and do business with it in order to survive. However, during the three years of occupation and until the extermination of the population, innumerable troubles were brought upon them as well. Every Monday and Thursday, thorough searches were conducted for merchandise that was restricted, and the fact was that the gendarmerie would sooner or later find each and every hiding place and take out everything of value and confiscate it. So they found many goods belonging to various merchants, among them Icek Majer Waga, Alter Spokojny, Dula, Gałązka, Szulimowicz, Płatkiewicz, and others. Most of the time these discoveries were accompanied by jail time, fines, and, in some instances, even by a worse fate.

The prohibition not to leave the boundaries of the town suddenly prevented all those who were accustomed to doing business with the surrounding farmers from making a living. But the pangs of hunger were worse to suffer than the danger, and more than a few risked their lives out of sheer necessity. They went back to the farms secretly to buy food products and stealthily brought them into town. There were instances where they got caught and were jailed. Sometimes, they were even shot to death when they were found to have violated the prohibition not to leave the boundaries of the town.

The situation of the workers in town wasn't any better; the visits of farmers to the town lessened, simply because there was no longer any reason to enter it. In the wake of this impossible situation, they couldn't obtain any merchandise. Raw materials also could not be found, and the selling of produce was also prohibited. In addition to this, it was decreed that the majority of the farmers had to supply the main bulk of their produce to the authorities. Trading between communities totally stopped. The worry about obtaining a piece of bread for the children eliminated thought of any other purchase. Most of the refugees were bereft of any means of earning a livelihood, and only very few of them had any means of survival. Generally speaking, with every passing month of the war, the destitution, overcrowding, and poverty grew. In the beginning, householders sold anything possible for food or money. Later, there was nothing more to sell.

On top of all this, more decrees were added. Due to constant new rulings, the Jews were forced to surrender all their possessions of value to the Germans. In the beginning, they had to give all foreign currency; later on, gold, silver, radio equipment, and furs, etc. were added. Casualties accompanied every confiscation in order to instill fear and terror. Likewise, many times, people were fined large sums of money. These contributions had to be paid exactly on time; otherwise, there was murder. In this way, many of the prominent inhabitants of the town perished. In addition to this, there was the *Judenrat,* which, on a constant basis, needed huge sums of money in order to bribe the authorities to nullify the verdicts or at least to postpone them for some time.

The majority of the inhabitants existed in a terrible state of dire poverty. Many didn't even possess the few coins needed to purchase the small amount of flour and sugar allotted according to a "point" rationing system. Under these circumstances, there blossomed various unusual occupations, such as ways and means of taking food to the big cities by posing as a gentile, etc. These people put their lives in very grave danger, where each of their steps was subject to death. What other choices did the Jews have when they couldn't earn a livelihood?

In the beginning, the Jews were forced to carry out different types of jobs within the town's borders and, occasionally, other work as well. Those working still did not include the entire population, and from time to time, groups would be rounded up in order to accomplish certain tasks. But even during the first winter, the *Judenrat* [Jewish community council] had to supply a specific number of people in order to clean up the snow, etc. In the ensuing periods, they started to carry out the plan of drying up swamps, paving roads, building new railroad tracks, and other such types of work. A German labor director by the name of Mucha arrived in town. Every day he would send out many hundreds of Jews to the central labor areas such as Cudzynowice, Rosiejów, Słaboszów, and Kazimierza Wielka. There they would work on development projects according to the German plans. In this area there was great cooperation with the *Judenrat.*

In order for the continuity of certain groups to keep on working, they established a labor division under the direction of Mr. Hofman. According to the rules, all able-bodied men had to perform forced labor. There was a rotation system of all able-bodied men, where every few weeks the groups would change in accordance with the decisions of this labor division to meet the changing demands of the authorities with regard to the number of workers who were needed each time. Of course, certain considerations were given to the heads of large households and also in certain social cases. This was the cause of much complaining and unhappiness regarding favoritism. As much as it is strange to say, this forced labor supplied a large number of families with some measure of a livelihood. This was carried out as follows: As long as there were able-bodied people in town who still had some money, they preferred, of course, not to go out to do this back-breaking labor that lasted from sunrise to sunset under the ruling hand of vicious supervisors. They looked for substitutes when their turn came. They were willing to pay a daily fee of five to twelve *zloty*, depending on the working place and the time frame. As far as the purchasing power was concerned, these amounts were abysmal sums. However, there were always those who were ready to take on this labor even for this pittance of a wage as long as they could earn a little money in order to buy bread. The labor division of the *Judenrat* allowed these substitutions and even supported them.

During the period that followed, this forced labor took on another form. On several occasions, German police officers appeared in town and rounded up dozens of young people and took them away with them. In the beginning, no one knew their fate, but after a while, it became clear that they were taken to labor camps near Kraków in the town of

Kostrze or Podgórze (Kobierzyńska Street) to the German company Richard Strauch.[1] In the beginning, measures were taken to send packages of clothing and food as much as possible in an organized fashion to those in the camps. The *Judenrat* was successful in obtaining a permit to send a truck to these camps and take along a small quantity of food, clothing, and blankets. The news that arrived from these camps was very troubling, both because of the unbearable living conditions and lack of food and also because of the harsh labor. After several months, the *Judenrat* made an effort to replace these people with others. And indeed, they organized a system where those who had been caught during the first roundup would be exchanged, on the condition that they supply replacements to Kostrze and to the camp on Kobierzyńska Street in Podgórze.

So the question arose, of course, as to who would be the ones to be sent. This problem led to bitter fights and arguments among the population with the *Judenrat,* and I want to point out that there wasn't a person in the town who was willing to go to these camps of his own free will. At other times, the *Ordnungsdienst* (the order service—the Jewish police affiliated with the *Judenrat*) got involved with these issues, and this resulted in great clashes and led to animosity between brothers. And again, this will appear as strange today, but in a few unique cases, there existed exchanges as follows: Among those who were sent to the labor camps in the first transports were those whose families still had some means. Such a family was interested, of course, in having their son freed and was willing to pay for another person to be exchanged for him. They provided a certain amount of money as compensation for the substitute to go out to the labor camp for several months. When the arrangements were completed for this exchange, several people would be found who offered to go to the labor camps for a sum of money. Also, they were assured by the *Judenrat* that they would be sent packages on a consistent basis. And indeed, these exchanges took place several times, but each time this came about with great hardship, controversy, and bitter fighting. The *Judenrat* used the money they collected from this to send additional shipments of food to the camps.

The last groups placed in Kostrze and on Kobierzyńska Street [in Podgórze] were saved from the hell of the first deportation to Bełżec, since they were far from the town and were already situated in a camp. Fate decreed that those who had been sent to the labor camps were among those who avoided the selection and segregation on the day of deportation and were thus not sent to their deaths. Several hundred had been sent to the camp in Prokocim [suburb of Kraków] to strengthen the two labor camps that already housed former people from Działoszyce. From this aspect, it proved to be a salvation from annihilation, since it is a well-known fact that no one returned alive from Bełżec.

Relief and Welfare (The Communal Kitchen)

Endless daily worries beset each family starting from the first day of the war. Family separation, the lack of the means of survival, imprisonment, searches, forced labor, monetary fines, murder, and communal punishments. These decrees and others brought along with them grave troubles and awakened heavy and burdensome problems. In addition to the multiple problems that worried each and every individual, it was also necessary during that time to also worry about the larger community as a whole,

---

[1] Podgórze is the section of Kraków where many Jews lived and where the ghetto was created.

especially the great number of refugees, which was constantly growing. The problems in regard to dwelling space has already been mentioned, and this was just one of many, many other various problems. If the local townspeople were made to suffer with each day that the war continued, the refugees were without a roof over their heads from the very start. In the beginning, all were convinced that the war wouldn't last a very long time. However, as the weeks and months passed by, the situation grew worse and worse. As far as the organizations offering relief to the refugees, this also didn't come easily, since the number of people with means dwindled, while the number of needy people multiplied and mounted. To the flow of refugees that didn't cease were steadily added many of the local residents who had now also arrived at the brink, having no bread to eat.

The relief workers were joined by the younger generation, especially the active ones from the Zionist youth organizations. All of them saw the need of the hour. At first, everything was done on an individual basis. They collected clothing, blankets, and basic primitive furnishings and, in this manner, lightened the burden of the initial arrangements of the refugees. However, the main problem was how to feed and supply a hot meal on a consistent and steady basis. Not only was there the problem that many had no means to do this, but due to the overcrowding and the fact that all available space had been turned into living quarters, it was impossible to find any space to accomplish this. At the time all this took place, in the beginning of 1940, the floor above the *bes hamedresh* still remained vacant, or better said, in one section of this floor, there was still space, while in the other section, there were already refugees.

In this vacant wing, they established a communal kitchen and a dining room under the initiative of an active group from the youth organization. At the helm stood Mrs. Salomea Gertler, *z"l* (the wife of Szlama Gertler). The beginning was relatively modest, and in the first few months, only a few hundred refugees ate there on a daily basis. However, as time went on, the number of people eating there grew tremendously, so that this institution very rapidly turned into the most important one in town. Without it, thousands of people in the town wouldn't have been able to survive.

It is impossible for me to even begin to describe the superhuman work and effort that this group of active volunteers put forth. All of them dedicated themselves to the continual existence of this kitchen. I am hopeful that one of my surviving friends who was among those who carried out this virtuous action, and who turned nights into days for the duration of three innocent years, will give more of an account about this. In spite of the dire lack of provisions existing in the town, they provided nourishing food, cooking dishes, and heating supplies to anyone who needed them. The kitchen never rested and provided each and every day, in addition to a portion of bread, thousands of hot tasty meals. I would not do ample justice if I did not mention here at least some of the names of those people, who, among others, devoted and dedicated all of their energies and time to this holy project. The first and foremost of them and the one who organized the kitchen was the noble woman, Mrs. Salomea Gertler, *z"l*, and by her side worked the brothers Kaczka, Josek and Szlama Szulimowicz, Moszek Kamelgart, and Motel Rożenek, who have all perished, *hi"d* [may God avenge their blood], and may they be blessed with long life: Dov Bejski, Moshe Rożenek, Alter Frydman, and others.

Today, I am convinced beyond any doubt that under the circumstances existing during those times, this group of activists earned anew each and every day their shares in the world to come.

One cannot forget how very difficult it was during the war years to acquire food products for a single family and so much more so to collect food to prepare thousands of meals on a daily basis. As time went on, a part of these supplies was provided by the *Judenrat* from the rations of food made available by the authorities. But all this provided only a minimal amount of what was necessary. The main food supplies and products had to be acquired by the people dealing with this and was carried out both by honest and dishonest ways and means. All of this was in addition to the collection of funds in order to enable the operation of this huge project.

To all those who needed the provisions of this communal kitchen, the meal that was provided was the only hot meal for the entire day. For many among them, this meal and the portion of bread given was the only food they received for themselves and their family. As the war continued and was prolonged, the numbers of those in need of the communal kitchen continued to grow. In the beginning, only the refugees partook, and the local residents tried as much as possible to refrain from using it. There was a certain degree of embarrassment for one to need this public kitchen. However, the times and circumstances played their part, and eventually, even honorable citizens couldn't withstand the hardship and dire need. And so the number of people registered for this kitchen grew day by day.

With regard to these people, what they did was unusual. The refugees who had come to the town used to eat their meals in the general dining room (that meanwhile had spread and now encompassed the entire floor), whereas the local citizens would take their own and their family's portion of food to their homes. So it would not be an exaggeration for me to say that this action of volunteerism and heroism was the most important and significant one that lightened the bitter circumstances of thousands who lived in the town as well as those who came in from the outside to find refuge. Not possessing adequate and sufficient words, I cannot begin to express the true appreciation to all those valiant people who dealt with and were active in the foundation and steady organized existence of this kitchen in spite of all the many difficulties, obstacles, and hardships.

The Judenrat [Jewish Council]

Much has been written about the organizations that existed in the Jewish quarter during the Holocaust—and especially about the *Judenrat*. Whether it is just or unjust, the word *Judenrat* brings forth nowadays a derogatory sense and image. The institution itself has become a negative symbol, especially with its stumbling leadership that didn't have the know-how to deal properly with the community during difficult and fateful times. Many also identify the people in the *Judenrat* as collaborators with the German enemy. This is not the place to pass judgment on this painful topic and certainly not in a general way. In the context of my bringing forth memories of my town during the Holocaust years, I will try to describe along general lines the activities of the *Judenrat* that existed in Działoszyce. This is from the viewpoint of one of its residents, and this is also without my attempting to analyze its activities or to evaluate them. I only wish to make one remark here in view of the reality that existed—it is not fair, just, or realistic to treat the

Judenrat as a uniform phenomenon. And it is also unfair to lend a general image to the entire institution. I also know of instances in which the negative actions of *Judenrat*s overshadowed their positive ones. These were mainly those *Judenrat*s that were appointed by the occupation authorities after the Germans first liquidated, with great viciousness, the *Judenrat*s that had previously held the job, due to the fact that they [the Germans] were displeased with them. Such a newly appointed *Judenrat* was generally very obedient—since the authorities saw to it from the beginning that their orders were to be followed. However, I am also aware of other *Judenrat*s, and they were not few in number, whose main concern and worry standing in front of their eyes during their entire time in office (on the whole, until they themselves perished) was to lighten the load and offer help on an individual and general basis.

I do not exactly remember when the *Judenrat* became established in Działoszyce. When I traveled to Kraków at the end of 1939, the *kehile* [Jewish community council] was still in operation.[1] It had been elected, during its time (a long time before the outbreak of the war), and at its head presided Mr. Moszek Josek Kruk. I would like to emphasize the fact that this council was formed from honorable residents of the town, even though today I would find it difficult to enumerate all of their names. Immediately after the casualties in Poland began, this council was besieged with new and varied responsibilities with which they had never dealt in their entire lives and had never dreamed they would ever have to shoulder. No longer were the most important aspects of their jobs the overseeing of ritual slaughter, the inspections of the *bes hamedresh,* or not even the salary payments for the *rov* [rabbi] of the town and the existence of the *talmed-toyre* [Jewish elementary school] and the Hebrew school.

This community council now became the central destination for all those many many refugees who were searching for a temporary roof over their heads in their escape or wanted to settle down in this place until the hostile period passed. And these people were bereft of any possessions, torn and bedraggled, without proper coverings for their bodies. And the problems only grew worse and became more intensified with the arrival of fall and the approach of winter. The community council itself was without means and in the midst of a pandemonium even when a portion of the town hadn't yet returned from its wanderings, and they couldn't stand up to the circumstances. Nonetheless, it is important to shed a positive and supportive stance for all the great efforts that were exerted during that first period to absorb the steady flow of the refugees or those passing through the town and especially for the provisions of food and a roof over their heads.

When I returned after a few months from Kraków, the *Judenrat* was already in existence. Although the name the Germans gave it was new, its make up hadn't changed. At the head of the *Judenrat*, same as in the *kehile* during its former years, stood Mr. Moszek Josek Kruk. If I remember correctly, also included were all of the members from the former council. It is clear that the number of members in the *Judenrat* was greater than the number in the former community council, but I cannot recall if this was the case immediately from the beginning or only during the time when other members were added.

---

[1] Although both the *kehile* and the *Judenrat* were Jewish community councils, members of the prewar *kehile* had been elected by the community, while members of the wartime *Judenrat* were appointed by the Germans to interface with them and carry out their orders.

With the passage of time, changes took place in the mission of the *Judenrat*. In addition to the necessity of taking care of the community's affairs that grew from day to day, the *Judenrat* served as a contact point for the Germans. They were to carry out the anti-Jewish orders and verdicts that were established each morning anew and also to meet the varied needs of the occupation authorities in the area. When the decree was established for Jews to wear identifying armbands with the Star of David, carrying this out became the responsibility of the *Judenrat*. All residents were forced to surrender their valuable possessions, gold and silver, to the Germans. The *Judenrat* had to oversee this collection. Any time a contribution was levied on the Jews, all of the members in the *Judenrat* were responsible that this money would be handed over in cash to the local authorities on such and such a date and by a specific hour. In most cases, this was accompanied with a warning that if this decree was not carried out by the appointed time, the members of the *Judenrat* would pay with their lives. It was a well-known fact from occurrences in other communities that these were not empty threats.

In addition to the general decrees of the central or local authorities, the *Judenrat* served as a sponge to be squeezed by each and every authoritative Nazi in the district. A Gestapo man needed so many pairs of boots, and a gendarme asked that he and his friend be supplied with so many yards of material for suits. These demands were mostly turned over to the *Judenrat*, whose members knew that if the requests were not granted, bitter troubles and misfortunes would befall the community. And these often came again even after their demands were fulfilled. Those making such demands were very many; among them were high-level officers from Miechów such as Schmidt, Beyerlein, Vogt, Becker, and Redinger, along with the most vicious gendarmes such as Kozak, Dachauer-Kornhäuser, Schubert, and many many others who were active in the area and became steady visitors to the town.

The opinion of the *Judenrat* was, and in this they did not differ from the opinion of the rest of the population, that by fulfilling the Nazis' demands and supplying their needs, they would succeed in lessening the evil decrees and sometimes in eliminating them altogether. The truth is that on a small scale, this did get accomplished when the beast got satisfied for the moment. We're talking now mainly about individual instances of destruction. And an additional bitter truth is that the *Judenrat* didn't have any other choice when it came to fulfilling the various material demands that were passed on to them along with threats of initiating bitter sanctions on the entire population or against the members of the *Judenrat* itself.

However, it is a self-evident fact that these situations brought the *Judenrat* into conflict with the population. First, it was the *Judenrat* that was responsible to pass and enact the bitter decrees levied by the authorities. In addition, the implementations themselves were beset with confrontations. For instance, when a head of a household was requested to give his part of the contribution that was required and the amount was large, he viewed this as being the fault of the members of the *Judenrat*. Whether this was because of the constant pressures, fear, and dread, or due to living under the ceaseless threats of the Germans or the great burdens that they found themselves confronting, all of these factors gave rise to the situation. But the truth is that at certain times, the behavior of the members indeed underwent a change. When I see in front of my eyes the image of the head of the *Judenrat*, Moszek Josek Kruk, going from door to door to complete the collection of the money to pay for the third contribution, while the zero hour was nearing and the amount of money collected was very far from that demanded, of course, his behavior and attitude to the head of the household was far different than would be expected from the head of a community leader under normal circumstances. This wasn't the same honored Jew who used to dance at the head of the congregation on Simkhes Toyre. But, God forbid, we should turn to judging the people of the *Judenrat* about this episode or any similar one.

We should never forget that not a single person among them (and we are only talking about those in Działoszyce) brought this responsibility upon themselves during the war. They all continued in their former positions under new circumstances that were created and over which no one from the town had any control. Also, all that happened and the way it developed was in such a manner that no one could have foreseen or even imagined it. The *Judenrat* was confronted with problems that were impossible for them to solve, and heavy burdens were placed upon it that the members could not withstand. Basically, the members of the *Judenrat* were the same honorable citizens. Their goal was to lighten the burden as much as they possibly could. They tried valiantly with the wit and traditional intelligence of the Jews to outsmart the Nazi beast, while rationalizing that with time and without any extra mishaps and casualties in the Jewish population, there was increasing hope that they would witness the downfall of the enemy.

I refrain from voicing any opinions regarding the general questioning of the *Judenrat* from the way things look from a historical viewpoint and the passage of time. These questions are open to heavy controversies even today. However, it is next to impossible not to mention the causes that on a daily basis brought about differences of opinion between the population and the *Judenrat*, and as a result, there developed a mutual distrust, even in our town. It seems to me that I can freely say, with total conviction, that during the entire period that the *Judenrat* existed in Działoszyce, there was never an incident when any action taken by it had any other motive than to lighten the sufferings and to find an organized approach to the difficult issues that the times brought about. All that was done took into consideration the various options that existed under the prevailing circumstances and that seemed to be the best and most logical.

In contrast, the occupying authorities saw the job of the *Judenrat* not as one that lent assistance and support to the Jewish population but as an institution through which their different and varied demands could be levied against the Jews. To this end, the *Judenrat* was given some power. They were not free to ignore the Germans instructions—just the opposite. In very many instances, they had to issue edicts on their own so that the instructions could be carried out—for example, the payment of dues, the supply of forced laborers, etc. And even though in the beginning the *Judenrat* tried to collect the money from the townspeople who had the means, with the intention of not overburdening those who had nothing, this nevertheless evoked anger and wrath among a part of the population that felt they were being taken advantage of. The same thing pertained to the exchange of workers being sent for forced labor. In actuality, the effort of the *Judenrat* to exchange from time to time those who had been rounded up for forced labor was justified. Moreover, many of them were the single providers for their families. However, this was dependent upon sending other laborers in exchange, both in the local area as well as to the more distant camps. And this was also a good enough reason to provoke the fury of those who had to go out as replacements.

And there were times when, without realizing it, the *Judenrat* found itself involved in horrible incidents. As an example, I will mention the episode of the family Rafałowicz. One day, the Gestapo or the gendarmerie (or both of these together) appeared at the offices of the *Judenrat* and instructed them to assemble all the males in town by the name of Rafałowicz. Since exact records of the entire population in the town existed, it was no use and even impossible to hide anything from the authorities. All those whose name was Rafałowicz were gathered, and after inquiries that indicated suspicion that one of them belonged to the Communist Party, they were all taken outside of the town by the Germans, and the people of the *Ordnungsdienst* (the Jewish police) were commanded to go along with them. When they were out in the field, the one who supposedly belonged to the Communist Party was ordered to come forth, and when no one admitted to any guilt, one of the Germans murdered four or five members of the Rafałowicz family without distinction. (As was later reported, the one who shot them was the gendarme Kozak, who is still alive and living peacefully today in Germany.)

Many people had many reasons, whether justified or unjustified, for their anger and severe criticism of the *Judenrat*. From an objective point of view, it is very doubtful that they could have acted otherwise. One could not count the very many refugees and local inhabitants who knocked on the office doors and complained, for instance, about rain penetrating and streaming into their wretched allotted dwelling place or something else of that nature. Clearly, there was no use explaining that even the last of the last available spots had already been occupied. All of these complaints and many more were submitted to the *Judenrat,* which served as the institution to which the public turned in spite of the fact that its possibilities were minimal in the face of unceasing demands.

And this is what I started to say in the beginning. The problems with which the *Judenrat* was confronted by the Nazis went beyond any Jewish institution's ability to withstand and cope. And even from a current prospective, it is essential to say that as one tries to view the activities of the *Judenrat*s from the vantage point of the dire constant demand for help and the efforts to lighten the daily sufferings of the Jewish population's extreme distress, at least here, in our town of Działoszyce, the *Judenrat* fulfilled all its obligations to the local Jews. And this is not the place to discuss the attitude adopted in general by Jewish leaders toward all rebellious and resistance activities.

Faith and Hope

Even though I am unable to say any more and describe in greater detail life's conditions and all that the Działoszyce Jewish population lived through during the Holocaust years, the little that has been said until now should be sufficient to enable the reader to obtain a good understanding of how terrible and miserable life was during all of the three innocent years until the total annihilation of the entire community—day in and day out with its decrees, week in and week out with its sufferings. Dire poverty and overcrowding like one cannot imagine, hunger, murder, imprisonment, and all the other catastrophes that the Nazi enemy invented to oppress its victims slowly and to prepare them through a slow weakening of opposition for the final solution. The satanic Nazi brain knew mentally how to prepare its steps toward the final solution, and in this, its success was complete.

However, in spite of the terrible oppressions and horrors that the Jews endured, the enemy could not affect two of their Jewish characteristics in the many towns and villages in Poland—their faith and their hope! The more I think about those days, the more astounded I am at these two magic qualities without which it would have been impossible to live through the hell of the Nazis. This subject is worthy of very careful study and deep research, but here I just want to point out the presence of these traits in our small town. The subject seems to me to be of great importance, given the people's abilities to live through the great sufferings of this era.

It is difficult to point out instances when the Jews actually lost their hope and faith. Not only during the period of the ghettos, during which time they hadn't even started toward the final solution, but even at a later period, when the suffering and pain continued in the concentration and extermination camps.

Allow me to mention that even during the first days of the war, public prayers were forbidden, and synagogues and houses of prayer were closed. In our town, as already mentioned, there existed a *bes hamedresh* [house of prayer/study] and a *beysakneses* [synagogue] along with many *shtiblekh* [small Hasidic houses of prayer], which now housed the refugees. In spite of the strict prohibition not to assemble in groups, Jews used to pray in any place where they could squeeze a *minyan* [quorum of ten men needed for prayer], in spite of the great danger that this imposed. And this took place not only on Shabes and the festivals but also during the week. The town didn't lose a bit of its exemplary Orthodoxy, even though efforts were made that this not be visible. Jewish ritual slaughtering and the sale of kosher meat were also totally prohibited, under the severest restrictions. Despite the dangers facing the ritual slaughterers and butchers, if ever there was meat for sale, it was always kosher.

Of the many decrees that came forth from the authorities was one that hit the population in Działoszyce very hard. Growing a beard was prohibited. I cannot recall the exact time this edict was issued (I believe it was at the end of 1941) nor the specified time when a mass shaving was instituted. However, I do remember very well how great the upheaval was among the men in our town. There were the jokers in our midst who pointed their fingers at this one and that one who couldn't wait for such a decree to get rid of their beards. But the truth was that this decree caused great spiritual anguish, not only to those who wore beards but also to those who had always shaved.

Indeed, it was very strange to meet Jews who, since my early childhood, I was used to seeing with beards. Their beards evoked a degree of respectability, and suddenly, now with their shaven faces, they seemed to be in disguise. Nonetheless, there were many who disobeyed this order, including my own father, *z"l*, who preferred to stay at home for many months and not remove his beard. When necessity required him to go out into the street, he would wrap his face in a scarf as though he had a toothache, and this is how he would go through the street with great caution. God forbid he should meet up with a German. But finally, he was caught and punished. I want to also note that my father, *z"l*, was not the only one who kept his beard; many others did likewise. And when the bitter day arrived, the day of deportation never to return, as they marched into the gas chambers, Jews who were successful in not shaving off their beards had their pure Jewish faith unblemished, both in a spiritual sense as well as in their outer physical appearance. Indeed, these holy martyrs perished *al Kiddush Hashem*, the sanctification of God's name fulfilled in all its glory.

The never-ending hope was a miracle. It did not drain away from the heart of the Jewish population even during the days of the Nazis' resounding victories in the first few years of the war. The Germans, so it seemed, marched from triumph to triumph, with countries falling before them, and soon all of Europe was mowed down by their troops. The Jews, however, saw every small sign as an indicator of the Germans' imminent defeat with salvation in its wake. There was no end to the rumors that cropped up from unknown sources and, for the moment at least, raised morale. The most important news source was the YVA, an abbreviation for *"Yidn Viln Azoi"* (Jews Want Thus).[1] Even when a rumor proved baseless, the Jews did not despair. Another rumor would take its place and raise the spirits. Everyone said: *"Mir vellen sei iberleben"* (We will outlive them). How cruel is fate! Most of these wonderful Jews did not manage to fulfill this wish.

The First Deportation

By the end of the third year of the war, it was possible to hope that we would see the defeat of the Nazis. The hope was no longer based on rumor but on actual facts. Although the Germans continued to proclaim loudly their ongoing glorified victories, one could read between the lines that not everything was going well on the Russian front. The Jews could read between the lines of official statements, and the YVA intensified its activities.

However, along with this encouraging news, there also filtered worrisome bad news as well. Although our town was entirely cut off from the outer world, rumors and information began to spread in the summer of 1942 about *Aktion*s [roundups and deportations] in different parts of Poland during which Jews were deported to unknown destinations. No one knew for sure the truth of this and where these deported people were being sent or what their fate had become. Today, with subsequent information, it is clear that there were Jewish settlements and ghettos that had heard of the existence of the death camps even during the summer of 1942. I can say in full truth that this news did not reach our town. Not one person suspected, even in his or her worst thoughts, that this type of thing was happening. It was clear to all that the deportation in and of itself was a terrible, horrible phenomenon. According to the rumors, Jews were being transferred to nearby areas of the Russian front in order to perform different types of labor, etc. I cannot say exactly as to when such news was heard, but in my estimation, this was approximately during the months of June or July 1942.

Even after the bitter experiences during the three years under the rule of the occupying Nazis, and even after the Jews had already gone through seven degrees of hell due to the decrees and horrors, not one person could fathom that the sole goal of the enemy was to totally and thoroughly destroy the entire Jewish people and to eradicate its name from the face of the earth. The Germans were also clever at concealing their actions and directing the rumors in ways that suited them in order to avoid any terrible

---

[1] YVA was a clandestine journalistic group that was present in other camps and ghettos as well. In Polish, it was called *"Agencja JWA"* [*Jidn Wiln Azoj*].

suspicions. Among all kinds of news flooding the ghettos, the people were able to tell with reassurance and calmness about news they had received regarding their deported brethren on the other side of the River San, a fact that in and of itself was probably true. And the fact is that at a later time, when I was already in a concentration camp, it happened that letters were received from people who had been sent to Auschwitz. Despite this, it did not prevent the Germans from exterminating the writers of these letters in the gas chambers immediately after the letters were written. This was also one of the ways and means the Nazis employed to fool and shrewdly hide their horrid inhumane activities and actions.

In spite of all this, the news intensified during the last week of August 1942. There were suspicions, and in the atmosphere hovered the hidden fearful feeling that something was about to happen, but no one knew exactly what. During this same week, one heard that *Aktion*s had already taken place in Zagłębie and that most of the Jews were transported to an unknown place. It seemed as though something was happening in our area as well. The *Judenrat* members (who had special permit papers) traveled on a daily basis to Miechów, the site of the German administration, but were unable to gather any information whatsoever. And even if they caught some sort of news, there was nothing they could do about it. There were individuals who had good connections with the farmers in the area, and they tried to make contact with them to secure a hiding place for themselves. However, only a few rare individuals were successful in doing this. And this, of course, is no surprise, since the Polish population was anti-Semitic toward the Jews, not only today. In the best of circumstances, they viewed the current ordeals with total equanimity and peace, and in the majority of cases, with complete satisfaction. Indeed, we have a very long reckoning with the Poles, filled with a bloody trail.

Rosh Hashanah drew closer; this time the suspicions mounted before the "Days of Awe." Yom Kippur appeared in the distance indeed like the Day of Judgment in its full terror. But the thing that we feared the most arrived even before Rosh Hashanah. This terrible thing became a reality on September 2, 1942. By evening, before fear and nervousness reached its peak, one knew that an *Aktion* had started in our immediate area—in Słomniki, Wiślica, Żarnowiec, and the closest vicinities. A feeling of helplessness and fear of the unknown overcame us. There remained only one option—to escape.

However, any attempt at escape wasn't realistic for the majority of the population. And this is not even mentioning the difficulties involved in starting to wander the treacherous routes together with children and the elderly. The main question was: Where should we run? The Poles not only refused to give us shelter, but, in most instances, they themselves would denounce and turn over to the Germans any Jew who was found wandering around. Even prior to this, when a Jew was found wandering outside the borders of the town, his fate was certain death. This was much more so during an *Aktion*. Only those rare individuals who had arranged for a secret refuge—after prior negotiations and accompanied by hefty sums—tried to escape that night to their hiding place in the adjoining farm areas. But merely wandering around served no purpose whatever. In addition, in our area, forests didn't even exist. Even to those with the utmost courage, who had thought of this, it was very clear that within a few days they would be caught. Greater than any fear was the fear that night, and it was no less the following day.

During the afternoon hours, the word spread like lightning that the angels of destruction had already arrived in the village. Even on normal days the streets would become deserted when it became known that the Germans had arrived. But this time, a deathly silence descended at once on the town. Not one person looked through their windows or even peeked through their door. We were terrified and petrified when we got the warning that the town in its entirety was surrounded by heavy guards.

I tried to go out to Kościuszko Street, which was generally bustling with people all the way from the train tracks to the center of town, but here, too, an eerie heavy silence prevailed. I noted that the Catholic Poles who lived on that street had put crosses on their doors and in their windows to show that Jews did not live there. I didn't dare walk the length of the deserted street. What's more, I was totally alone and the only person on it. In spite of it all, I was very curious to know what was happening in the center of town where, according to my understanding, the Germans were probably gathering. I sneaked along the riverbed and behind the houses, and in this manner, I succeeded in arriving at the back yard of the Targownik home where the Sternberg pharmacy was also located.

I peeked through a crack, and the following scenario unfolded before my eyes. At a distance of about twenty to twenty-five meters from where I stood were a number of armed Germans, and in the center of the market square, near the statue of Kościuszko, they forced four to five Jews to stand in a row with several meters between them. The Germans barked to the Jews to perform various exercises: "Fall to the ground! Stand up! Hands up! Hands down!" And this was repeated all over again. Because of the distance from where I stood, I could not recognize the exact identity of the people being tormented. Suddenly, when all the Jews standing had their hands raised upward, the guns were drawn and single shots were heard. With these shots, the live targets fell to the ground. Thoroughly shocked and frightened from what I had just witnessed, I slipped back to my house the same way I had come.

Meanwhile, night fell, and with it deep depression, fearfulness, and anxiety. First, I went to my neighbors, but from them I could only learn about their own fears and hopelessness. At a later hour, I summoned up more courage, and through the house of Wdowiński, near the synagogue and the butcher shops, I made my way to the offices of the *Judenrat,* somewhat in the hope that I could gather some information. Here in the yard stood a number of people saying that the heads of the local authorities and other officials were in the offices together with the members of the *Judenrat*. It was clear to all that indeed the *Aktion* had already begun. There was even someone who said that what was going on was the deportation of the entire Jewish population from the town, including the *Judenrat,* as well as the members of the *Ordnungsdienst* [Jewish police]. I also heard that in the last minute, before the Germans succeeded in encircling the entire town on all sides, very many people succeeded in escaping ahead of the enclosing chain of Germans. Someone else claimed that even then there probably weren't very many guards in the area of the soccer field near the Stawisko.

Although I had no clue as to where I was supposed to escape with my family, I myself decided to test whether this was a possibility at all. The fact that in the yard of the *Judenrat* I met people gave me additional courage. I started proceeding toward the Stawisko, but all I did was progress maybe one hundred to one hundred fifty meters when I saw in front of me a shadow escaping—and immediately afterward a shot. Someone who had tried to escape before me was shot and fell. After a second, another shot was heard, and then a third. I stopped a bit in the yard of one of the houses and, after another few minutes, frightened, I returned the way I had come. On the way, I encountered the body of a person lying on the sidewalk. I arrived home in one piece. This was for me and everyone else a night of terror. I don't recall what we did until the morning. I think we sat without uttering a sound. This silence was strange and filled with terror. Every so often, someone else from our family would look out of the window to see whether we could see anything in the darkness. Every so often, we would hear gunshots from different directions, and only this disturbed the deep depressing silence.

With the arrival of morning, individuals with courage could be seen on the streets. The daylight lessened the fear somewhat. Much movement was felt in the center of town. There were very many Germans, and among them all the "important" ones from Miechów. Their cars were parked along the sidewalk near the stores of Formalski and Rolnicki. It was very clear to us that we were now surrounded on all sides and this would be our last day in Działoszyce.

In the hours before noon, the order was already given that all residents were to appear at specified times according to their street in the center of the market square. Everyone was allowed to take along a small bundle including work clothes, since we were all traveling to a working place. Those living on my family's street were told to assemble at two o'clock. Silently, each one of us gathered some possessions and put a knapsack on his back. My father, z"l, gave each one of us possessions of value that still remained from the family valuables and also evenly divided the small amount of cash that was being held in reserve. Who could justifiably imagine and comprehend the acute pain of leaving the house that contained so much and never to return to it anymore? My father, may he rest in paradise, kissed the *mezuze* and set out with faltering steps, looking backward every so often.[1] It wasn't difficult for me to guess what his thoughts were during those moments. I knew how hard he had toiled to build this house and how many years he had worked on it. Now all this was at an end, and, as to the future, who could fathom?

The picture that met one's eyes on the streets evoked a feeling of pity and mercy, even in the hearts of the most vicious and unfeeling. Here were human beings who were created in the image of God, with faltering steps, old men and women, women with children. On the back of each one rested a backpack or sack and therein a few meager possessions. Where were they going? To the unknown. Even without knowing where, it was certainly a horrible place! As I was passing by with the others, I saw every once in a while a familiar face looking out of the apartments, one of the Polish Christian neighbors. The face was watching and not uttering even a word of goodbye. Were they so callous? Or were they waiting impatiently for the last Jew to leave town? Their real celebration would start after all the German authorities had left—the division of abandoned property. More than once during the war they had their eyes on so and so and on his furnishings, and, in the end, they succeeded in confiscating the booty.

---

[1] A *mezuze* is a small tube attached to the doorpost of a Jewish home that contains a piece of parchment inscribed with verses from the Torah, fulfilling the commandment: "And you shall inscribe these words upon the doorposts of your house."

Many people had already assembled in the area of the market square. Others kept flocking there from all sides. Armed guards were seen all around, and they made sure that all those who were there could not leave anymore. We were standing when an armed officer suddenly approached our rows and took out four youths, including myself, and ordered us to follow him. He brought us into the yard where Gertler lived. Here lay the bodies of several women. We were ordered to pile them into one area. From utter fright and terror, I could not identify the bodies. During the time that we were busy dealing with the women who had been murdered, a person appeared on the porch of the first floor. The officer yelled in his direction, "Come, come!" He started descending the stairs, and while he was walking, a shot rang out. The man buckled under and fell, releasing his soul there and then. We were forced to deal with this corpse as well. When we went out of the yard and the officer turned to go to the adjoining house, that of Richter, I seized the opportunity to escape as fast as I could and mingled with the people in the market square. I found myself again near my family, which hid me in case this same officer came looking for me.

After some time, many carts harnessed to horses, with farmers serving as the drivers, started arriving in the area. The Germans and men of the *Ordnungsdienst* walked through the rows of standing people and announced that all those for whom walking to the train station some distance away would be difficult should climb onto the carts and be transported there. Very many women and elderly were persuaded to climb on. They did this in the hope that they would save themselves the effort of walking while their meager possessions were on their backs. The row of carts started on its way—but we immediately observed that something was not as it should be; instead of leaving the market square in the direction of Kościuszko Street that led to the train station, the carts continued going straight down Skalbmierska Street, the street that led to the cemetery.

In the meantime, the market square had become full of people. We were ordered to march in the direction of the train station while the SS armed officers escorted us. While we were underway, we heard machinegun fire shooting non-stop. Our thoughts were with all those people who had traveled on the carts. This machinegun shooting was probably aimed at them. After some time, when I returned to the town after having escaped from a camp, it became clear that this was indeed the truth. Three huge mass graves were visible in the cemetery in which were buried all those who had been shot and murdered—which, to my anguish, included all the elderly and the women who had traveled on those carts. We will never ever know the exact numbers of the murdered victims. The estimates are between 1,200–2,000 holy martyrs.

At the station, they loaded us onto open train wagons. All the Jews of the town were taken to Miechów. We arrived before nightfall and made our way by foot from the train station to a large open field at the edge of town. Here we found other Jews from other places and vicinities who had arrived before us. Among other things, we learned that despite the promises that were given to the *Judenrat* and the *Ordnungsdienst* that they would remain in Działoszyce and not be deported with the others, they, too, found themselves here with us. The explanation was that indeed they were given this promise, and it was even sealed with a proper seal. However, after the Germans discovered that in spite of everything there were quite a few who had succeeded in escaping from the town, they included the *Judenrat* and the Jewish police at the last minute.

That night we spent under the sky while armed German officers kept watch. The next day, before noon, Jews from Miechów, and I think also from Kazimierza Wielka and Skalbmierz, started arriving. (It is possible that they had already arrived the day before from the latter two places). According to my estimation, there must have been a concentration of about 20,000 Jews from the entire nearby vicinity.

I don't remember how long we stood there. I estimate that it was until noon or close to it. All of a sudden, we were ordered to organize in groups of five. Each family tried to stay together. We realized that they meant only the men. A great commotion began. Everything was done with lightning speed, making it impossible for us to pay attention to what was happening. While the guards were still busy forming groups of five, in another section of the field the selections had already begun. From the long lines they quickly separated out almost a fifth of the people and had them continue on to the leader in the front. All five people walked together with their hands raised upward, and the guard, without any hesitation, pointed with his finger—right, left, right, left. While he was still at it, another five people stood in front of him awaiting his verdict.

It became immediately apparent that the young were being sent to the left side and all the others to the right. The armed guards immediately separated those who were sent to the left, without allowing them a second to hesitate. Even before I could realize what was happening, I found myself with my two brothers, Uri, z"l, and Dov, may he live a long life, standing on the left side of the field, while the rest of my family, together with the others, were being led in the opposite direction. I didn't have any way to signal my parents or my sister, and there was absolutely no way I could go over from my group to the one on the other side. Everything was carried out with the utmost speed. A mere few seconds had passed, and my family members had disappeared and become swallowed among the throng of people directed to the right. These events took place unexpectedly and with the speed of lightning. Only the mutual turning of heads and silent looks of deepest pain signaled these silent partings, the partings forever. All this took place without a single word of blessing, without any hugs or kisses, without saying our goodbyes.

Approximately 2,000 young people remained after this selection, standing on the other side, while at some distance stood our closest loved ones, and not a person knew what their fate would be. All these activities, which involved about 20,000 people, had only lasted approximately two hours altogether. Under strict surveillance, we were immediately brought to the train station and this time loaded into cattle cars.

Suddenly, we were ignited with a spark of hope when the 2,000 of us inside the cars saw the other family members also arriving at the train station. We became aware that some of them were also traveling on this same train but in different wagons. We thought this meant that we would be traveling together. However, this hope was quickly shattered. The train stopped after a while at the station in Prokocim. Some of the wagons, those carrying us young ones, stayed put, while the others, which contained the [other] Jews from our vicinity, continued on. Their last station was the extermination camp at Bełżec! In that camp all the Jews of Działoszyce, Miechów, Słomniki, Wolbrom, Skalbmierz, Kazimierza Wielka, Pińczów, Proszowice, Charsznica, and all the other dwelling places met their deaths. From all of these places, only approximately 2,000 people were left alive, temporarily. For them a horrid and torturous life was about to begin, first, in the labor camps, and afterward, in the concentration and death camps.

My friends have done me a favor, since they released me from the need to tell in detail this torturous episode. In my opinion, it is difficult to find a person with enough descriptive powers who can portray even in the driest manner our lives from that day on, when we were put into the camp in Prokocim, until our liberation on May 8, 1945. If it has been determined that hell has seven levels, I myself wish to revoke this theory, since we ourselves passed through not seven, but seventy-seven layers of it. We went from level to level and stayed there again and again. However, this distracts from my story about the entire community of Działoszyce during the Holocaust and only concerns a few hundred of its sons that only blind fate and the flick of the finger of a Nazi general directed to the left side of the field during the selection.

I don't know the exact numbers of Działoszycers who were sent on a separate transport to the Prokocim camp. My estimate is about 600 to 700 people from among the 2,000. However, I may be mistaken, since there are no figures available for this. However, it is clear that the majority, together with the others who were already in the concentration camps before the deportation, as well as those who managed to hide for a while in various places, perished in the different camps in Poland and Germany. These souls were tortured before their deaths with indescribable horrors that could be thought of only by the satanic brains of the Nazis.

No exact statistical reports are available on the people of Działoszyce who survived and succeeded in seeing the downfall of the enemy and the end of the war. What we know is that there are now about 330 survivors in Israel and another few hundred dispersed throughout the world. That is all who survived the Nazi beast out of a large community that consisted of over 10,000 Jews (during the war) and that had existed for hundreds of years. This is how the Jewish community of Działoszyce was annihilated, only one community among many, many others in Poland. It became erased from the face of the earth except for another very short period. More about this will be told further on.

The Final Liquidation

I will skip the stories of what happened to us in the camp at Prokocim except for one episode that I find fitting to bring forth on paper. Immediately upon our arrival, a thorough search was conducted of each one of us for our "valuables." We stood in long lines, and Ukrainian guards conducted these searches. They did an even better job than the Germans. The first two people who tried to conceal some of their valuables such as a watch were instructed to get out of line and were shot on the spot. This was enough of a warning to us that we shouldn't leave anything behind not even worth a penny. This is how we started our lives in the camps, naked, without any possessions. The only thing that existed in abundance was the backbreaking labor that began on the first day. As time went on, groups and groups were sent out from this camp to other camps. It was my fate to be sent to a camp that was in Podgórze [a section of Kraków] on Kobierzyńska Street, with which I was already familiar. This was the same camp to which many Jews from Działoszyce had been sent months before. And indeed this was where I found many more from our town; they were in the majority, and only a few had come from Proszowice and

Miechów. This camp, even though the labor was very hard, had the distinctive advantage that there were no German guards in it.

Two weeks went by, and an escapee from Działoszyce came and told us that Jews had gathered again in Działoszyce, namely those who had escaped before the deportation. It became clear that after the deportation, they were hiding in fields and other hiding places and that the night before the roundup, they had succeeded in escaping the Germans. But the bottom line was that they didn't have any place to put down their heads nor any source of sustenance. In addition, their fear of the Polish farmers grew. And also the autumn rains began. Lacking any other options, and since they heard that the Germans had left the town, individuals started drifting back into the town like thieves. Slowly, slowly, they could be counted by tens, and after several weeks, the returnees amounted to a few hundred. Another episode had taken place. While we were in Prokocim, the Germans rounded up all the members of the *Ordnungsdienst* who had been expelled together with us to this camp and returned them to Działoszyce and their other hometowns. The motive behind this was probably that the members of the *Ordnungsdienst* could be used to collect and liquidate the properties and assets that were left behind by Jews, since Christian Poles had already started doing so. Of course the Germans couldn't tolerate this.

When news of this arrived, several of the camp inmates escaped back to Działoszyce. After a few days, some of the escapees returned to the camp bringing a few belongings with them, while the rest remained in the town. In order to make things easier for my brother and myself, I also decided to do this. I said to myself that I would return home on a temporary basis and would take everything I could carry from the house. The bartering and exchange business had grown and was flourishing in the camp. A shirt could be traded for bread that we hungered for so much. The food supply in the camp was already poor and limited. Among my working friends was a Polish fellow by the name of Marian Włodarczyk, who also decided to go to Działoszyce. I turned over to him mainly the articles of clothing that one could exchange for food.

Upon my return to the town, I found there several hundred Jews who had arrived before me. The town itself lacked any life. No one thought that anyone could remain. The misfortune was that there was nowhere else to go except back to the labor camps. Whoever had already experienced camp life knew what this entailed, and those who had wandered from place to place in the hope of finding some type of hiding place knew that one could not expect any assistance or help whatsoever from the Poles, not even a stay of one night. This was at the end of October 1942. The ghetto in Kraków still existed, but this wouldn't solve the rescue issue at all. Earlier, I had been in touch with members of the Zionist youth movement both in Kraków and Częstochowa and suggested that they take steps to make contact with the partisans. The trouble was that in our part of Poland, this, too, was impossible for Jews.

I stayed a few days in the town and tried to find some solution to my situation. Suddenly, one night, they awakened me with fright, and I was told that the town was surrounded again and probably they were about to carry out another deportation. A few days earlier, the brothers Lewit of Miechów, who had moved to our town during the war, told me they had prepared a hiding place for an emergency situation, and being that I was very good friends with them, they said that I could join them. The place was in an attic in what had formerly been the home of the Moszenberg family. I went there at once, and within a few moments, twelve persons had assembled: the brothers Lewit, their brother-in-law, Salek Kacengold, Szaniecki, and Jechiel Rajsfeld. The bunker was well hidden. When we were all inside, the Polish policeman Kamerdyniak appeared and put a padlock on the outer door, taking the key with him. To the naked eye, it appeared as though not a living soul was inside. I personally did not trust him, since I didn't think of him as a Jew lover. But Jechiel Rajsfeld, *z"l*, reassured me and told me the policeman was trustworthy and would keep us informed of what was going on. The advantage was that since Kamerdyniak was a policeman, he had free-ranging privileges without himself being suspect.

For twenty-four hours we were totally disconnected from any contact with the outside and had no idea of what was happening. We were imprisoned in the dark without the ability to make any physical move due to the lack of space. Our apprehensions grew with the oncoming darkness, and one thought bothered us all: Would Kamerdyniak keep his promise and come, or would he reveal our hiding place to the Germans and seal our fate? Close to midnight, we heard sounds in the lock, and Kamerdyniak appeared. Even though it was clear to us that he would not bring our salvation, at least we had some communication with the outside. And so we had some hope that he might direct and lead us in some way. He told us that all the Jews in town had been rounded up during the day and taken away under heavy guard. The town was still surrounded, and there was no chance of escaping. When he turned to leave, he again locked us in from the outside, promising to return the following night.

A day of fear and waiting followed while each of us was thinking aloud as to where we could make our way once we had escaped alive from the town. Hiding places with farmers who had been paid large sums of money in advance were waiting for the Lewit and Rajsfeld brothers. The question that stood before them was only how to get to the farm. Also Szaniecki possessed some kind of an address. For the others, myself included, no address awaited, and I also possessed no money. The only idea that I could think of was to try to reach Kraków. First, my two brothers were in the camp and expected some news of me. Second, in the Kraków ghetto were my friends from the movement with whom I had kept in touch during the war in the hope that we could plan something. My friend Zelig Bajuk lived on the Polish side, armed with Aryan papers,[1] and, together with my friends from the movement from Sosnowiec, was searching for a way to get to Slovakia. This seemed to me to be the only solution at that moment. However, the question remained how to get there.

On the second night, we waited in vain for the arrival of Kamerdyniak, but he didn't show his face. Terrible thoughts crowded our minds. We started to debate how to proceed and what to do. In the end, without information about the guards surrounding the town, we couldn't see any possibility of going out of our hiding place. The situation and our apprehensions grew worse during the third day when we heard shots close by. It was clear that the Germans were searching for those in hiding, and we could imagine what these shots meant. Our forebodings were confirmed when relatively early in the evening, Kamerdyniak appeared. He told us that for two days the Germans had been conducting

---

[1] False papers stating that he was a Christian Pole.

thorough searches in each nook and cranny for anyone in hiding. Those caught were shot, murdered on the spot. His opinion was that the house in which we were hidden would be searched tomorrow. Based on their method of searching, he was concerned they would locate us in spite of the successful camouflage. We also heard from him that the majority of the Germans were still staying in the town, but they were satisfied with putting just a few guards in the outlying area. His opinion was that there was a good chance of escaping the town by way of the Christian cemetery, where there seemed to be no guards.

After the policeman left, there wasn't much time to think. We agreed that we would leave our hideout in pairs, at intervals of half an hour. I left with my friend Salek Kacengold. Our first surprise was the snow everywhere. The snow kept on falling, and everything became white. The snow made things more difficult, since our coats were dark. However even this wasn't enough to stop us. We crossed the church courtyard and cemetery and, without meeting up with any guards, found ourselves outside the town. The big question now was where to go. Of course, it would have been simple and easy to go the seven kilometers from the town to the train station in Słaboszów and to go from there through Miechów to Kraków, posing as Poles. However, this seemed to be most dangerous; we assumed that at each train station the Germans were searching for Jews and we had no papers. I now remembered a farmer who had sat together with me in school for an entire seven years and that he lived in Jakubowice—this was the closest farm to us. We decided to try our luck and turned our steps toward this place. We made the distance without meeting up with anyone. However, we were soon disappointed. I begged my former classmate to allow us to stay for one night only and immediately afterward we would be gone. My friend and his father didn't even bother opening the door. This was the "assistance" that the "good" Poles were willing to extend to their persecuted Jews!

Meanwhile, the hour was already very late (or maybe early), and it was clear to us that we could not go anywhere since the morning was upon us. In the yard of this same farmer was a barn, and the door was unlocked. Without hesitation, we snuck in and dove deep into the piles of hay. For three nights and days, we stayed there hidden among the straw without the owner even being aware of our existence. Except that the only loaf of bread in our possession had already been consumed by the second day. On the third night, we decided to leave our temporary bunker. We managed to get to the train station in Janowice and succeeded in arriving in Kraków.

From then on started for me a chapter full of pain and tribulations that is not the place here to elaborate upon, since we are talking about the fate of our town—Działoszyce.

Działoszyce was cleansed of its Jews. This time the annihilation was final and total.

The Final Word

At the end of 1942, several hundred Jews from Działoszyce found themselves together in the Płaszów camp.[1] We were transferred there from various labor camps that surrounded Kraków. We still endured another two and a half years of inhuman sufferings and torture that one cannot even imagine. Very many lost their lives there after very harsh torture, while others perished in other camps dispersed throughout Poland,

---

[1] The Płaszów camp, on the outskirts of Kraków, was the site of the film *Schindler's List*.

Germany, Czechoslovakia, and Austria. Who can relay all the hell that each one of us went through at the hands of the Nazis? Even the handful that survived to see the day of May 8, 1945, with life still in them were totally broken in body and spirit. The survivors were one from a family and a few from an entire town. While the whole world rejoiced at the end of the hostilities, we suddenly became fully aware of our situation. We became orphaned from our parents, relatives, or anyone to help us, broken in body and spirit, without a roof over our heads. Under these circumstances, we had to take the first steps toward freedom. And again the question stood before us—where should we go?

While hundreds of thousands of refugees roamed Europe immediately after the war, the Poles and Frenchmen could turn to go to Poland or France. They now only had to confront transportation difficulties. But what about us? What were we to do now? Where were we to go? Where were our homes, our parents, our wives, children, and relatives?

There were those who saw it as their duty to make the effort and return to their hometowns to see what had happened to the home in which they had spent their lives before the Holocaust. Others hoped they might find surviving kinfolk, and it was only natural to suppose that they would make their way home as well. So two or three dozen Jews arrived in Działoszyce, naked and barefoot, and lacking everything. But the Poles were not prepared to accept even this miserable remnant. The Poles had made up their minds that once the town was without Jews, it should remain so. This was said and done! One day the bloodthirsty anti-Semites murdered Szmul Piekarz, Bencion Czarnocha, and Jurysta. Those murders served as a warning to the others who fled that same night.

Since then, no Jewish foot has trodden the streets of Działoszyce.

Translated from the Hebrew by Rochel Semp
(The first five paragraphs were translated by Tamar Duke-Cohen)

The Outbreak of World War II (pp. 261–66)

Moshe Rożenek

The rising international tension was felt in town by the middle of August, and the Yiddish newspapers from Warsaw were anxiously awaited every afternoon, while the few radios were listened to carefully. We first learned that war had begun on September 1, 1939, when my father returned from his business trip to neighbouring villages, because German planes had machine-gunned the road. The complete unpreparedness of the Polish army for this kind of war was evident by September 2. The German Luftwaffe was in complete control of the skies. On September 3, Działoszyce was bombed, a number of Jews digging trenches were wounded, and Reb Moszek Jurysta was killed. Refugees began to arrive from Zagłębie [industrial region in southwestern Poland], Kraków, etc., far more than the population. There was an immediate shortage of bread.

The Meeting with the Germans

The mayor, police, and all official Polish representatives were the first to vanish. German motorcyclists arrived on Thursday, September 7, rode through the crowded streets several times and disappeared. On Friday morning, mechanized German forces, tanks and artillery, entered the town, which was occupied without bloodshed. During the first few days, there were no active anti-Jewish measures. However, when they bombed the trains, both Poles and Jews were wounded, and the Poles attended to their own people only. Wounded Jews were found in the streets on September 5 in the midst of the general confusion. They were taken to the community library, given beds and food, and a refugee doctor treated them and said they must be taken to a hospital. The nearest was in Kraków fifty kilometers away, and there was no transportation. On Saturday, I stopped a German military ambulance and asked the driver to transport the wounded. He asked, "Who are they, people or Jews?" He had no room for Jews. A week later, I hired a Polish wagon and had them transferred to the Kraków Jewish hospital. They recovered and managed to reach the Russian-occupied territory.

In Pińczów, the district center, a young Pole fired a few shots as the Germans entered the town, which was put on fire as a consequence. The surviving Jews came to us. The Germans appropriated the larger and better apartments, and the Pińczów and other refugees were housed in the *bes hamedresh*, the synagogue, and the *shtiblekh* [small houses of prayer] without any amenities whatsoever. It was the end of autumn; all ordinary livelihoods had come to a standstill, the community council did not function, there was no Polish government, the German government had not yet taken over, and masses of refugees began to arrive from Łódź. Representatives of the youth movements met, in spite of German prohibitions of public assembly, to find ways and means of helping the helpless newcomers. Special units were appointed to collect warm clothes,

---

This chapter is reprinted from pp. 23–25 of the English section of the original Działoszyce Yizkor Book, with minor changes.

blankets, pillows, etc. They went from house to house and met with a very generous response. This in spite of the poverty of most of the Jews in town. Money was also collected. When we bypassed some poverty-stricken homes, we were called back so that they could give their share.

That was the start of a Jewish mutual aid service, which functioned until the liquidation of the community and expulsion of the Jews in Autumn 1942. We set up a communal kitchen providing about 1500 meals twice a day, either free or at a nominal charge. It operated for two and one half years. The members of this committee were the brothers Szlama and Chaim Kaczka, Josek Szulimowicz and his wife, née Wajntraub, Mrs. Salomea Gertler, Eli Zylber, Moszek Kamelgarten, Fajgele Dula, Mira Rolnicka, and Jakób Groswald, all of them martyred. The survivors are Dov Bejski and his brother Moshe Bejski, Alter Frydman, Moshe Rożenek, and Izrael Ber Skóra. Special mention should be made of Mrs. Gertler who managed the kitchen as a volunteer from dawn till late at night in spite of her own very difficult economic position. Josek Szulimowicz was the treasurer, and Szlama Kaczka handled supplies. The committee secured not only material but spiritual resources as well, under the inconceivably difficult conditions of the times. At Hanukkah 1941, a special children's party was arranged, and a play on the heroism of the Maccabees was presented, with sweets, etc. Moszek Kaczka spoke and openly compared those times to our own. Next day, he was severely rebuked by Moszek Josel Kruk, head of the communal council and the Judenrat, who threatened to close down all activities. Nor can he be blamed in the circumstances.

The situation grew steadily worse. All males over fourteen were taken for forced labor such as digging drainage and sewage canals, without pay or food. The kitchen began to supply food to the workers. During the first years, money was supplied by the Joint Distribution Committee, until the United States entered the war. Thus we received *matse* for Passover but had to go get it ourselves from Częstochowa, at a time when Jews were forbidden to travel. Still Moszek Kamelgarten and I obtained travel permits, hired a truck, made the journey, obtained the *matse*, and after all kinds of adventures, brought it back. In addition, each family contributed whatever it could every month. The *kehila* [Jewish community council] also provided food and sold it cheap.

But the situation became worse and worse. Most of the young men were sent to labor camps, and the old people, women, and children moved about as though awaiting execution. The entire community spent the last three days before the expulsion in the cemetery, praying at the graves of their fathers and ancestors. On Thursday, 24 Elul,[1] the Jews were assembled and classified in the market square. The old folk, more than 1500 in number, were taken to the cemetery and murdered. Rabbi Staszewski, who was ill, was shot and killed in his bed. The rest were taken to Miechów and left for a day and a night in the open. Then those young folk who looked healthy were taken in open railway trucks to a labor camp at Prokocim near Kraków, and all the others were sent to the Bełżec extermination camp. Not one of them survived.

---

[1] The date 24 Elul corresponds to September 6, 1942. In actuality, the deportations occurred on September 3, 1942.

Social Assistance During the Nazi Occupation (pp. 267–70)

Dov Bejski

As is well known, war brings pain and suffering to civilians, who become innocent victims. It uproots people from their homes and sometimes even scatters them great distances. The main reason for this mass movement is that people wish to escape from the front lines where the greatest danger lies. Whenever a war is fought between two nations, the civilian populations of these warring countries are affected. This war, however, in addition to being a war involving many nations, was also a war between the civilized world and Nazism. And for the Jews, there was an additional war, the war between Nazism and Judaism. This war was carried out without any mercy. The plan of the Nazis, may their memory and name be erased forever, was a cruel and vicious plan, the total annihilation of all Jews.

When the war broke out, no one could have fathomed that this would be a war directed especially against the Jews. However, even on the first day of the war, because of the immense hatred of the Germans towards Jews, there were already suspicions of a policy of exterminating Jews. Masses of Jews started running away from the front line areas, which couldn't be held [by the Polish army]. They ran away from the big cities and wandered to the smaller cities, towns, and farms. But the murderous German bombs were aimed to kill these refugees who were traveling on the roads at that time. One could see an endless mass of people trying to run away—men, women, and children. There was a large percentage of Jews among the refugees. The naive among them thought that maybe, in spite of everything, the Polish army would manage to hold back the German advance. They thought that in the meantime they would be able to go on with their lives, even if they did not go back home. The most important thing was to avoid living under the German occupation.

However, after a while, it became apparent that their attempt to escape was futile, because the murderous Germans managed to go in and take control everywhere before any refugees even arrived. When the refugees arrived at their destination, they would find that the German army had already invaded that place. The only change experienced by the people running away was that from now on they were refugees—without any possessions, without a home or a livelihood—and they were tired, exhausted, and broken from their arduous journeys. Many of the Jewish refugees who arrived in Działoszyce had at one time or another lived here but had left in search of a better livelihood. But now, in these troubled times, they returned to their town to be with their families. Some of them had an aunt, an uncle, or some other distant relative here. And some of them didn't know anyone in this town, but when they realized the futility of their continuous wandering, they also remained here.

In the beginning, the situation didn't look so bleak. All of the refugees had brought some cash along with them, and, very slowly, they started to establish themselves in the town. Some of them lived in attics, some in rented rooms, and some with a relative or acquaintance. It was well known that even in normal times, Działoszyce was not a wealthy town. The poverty here had always been felt but was even more so now in time of war. If we were able to help the local poor during normal times, there was now the added burden of thousands upon thousands of refugees who had arrived in the town. Most of them were extremely poor, and we could not close our eyes to this major dilemma. It was apparent that we were not talking about the level of assistance that was customary in Działoszyce. Most of the impoverished Jews in Działoszyce used to be embarrassed by their poverty. When neighbors would become aware that so and so needed support, two prominent ladies would go out and collect funds for this purpose. Or else some influential persons would make an announcement to the members in the synagogue between the Mincha and Ma'ariv [morning and evening] prayers that contributions were needed for a poor person. Money was collected—fifty or one hundred *złoty*, and this assistance would be given as an anonymous gift.

It was clear to all involved that we cared for one another and that it was now necessary to give aid from a community fund for the needy. In the present situation, however, we were not concerned about embarrassment or anonymous gifts. Now, it was a question of life. It simply became an absolute obligation to give aid to the needy who were starving for bread. The usual one-time aid in the form of collections for money, food, or clothing was not sufficient. The type of aid that used to be provided could only help for the moment, but what about tomorrow? What are we to do with children crying from hunger when there is no bread? Could we remain bystanders and not do anything in the face of this situation? The *Judenrat* [Jewish council] and the leaders of the community were busy enough with their own matters, with pondering over decisions in the face of very serious and difficult problems for the Jews of Działoszyce. One decree followed another decree; payments and contributions were levied for the benefit of the Germans. The community representatives were busy trying to see what could be done, either with the SS or the Gestapo, to ease or cancel them. In light of the foregoing, the leaders had no time to deal with the poverty issue. This responsibility was thus taken over by the activists of the Zionist youth movement, and the writer of these lines was among them.

The Communal Kitchen

The general economic situation was very bad. They closed off the town; no one could go in or out. Business was mainly conducted "under the table," and prices skyrocketed. One can forego an item of clothing or shoes, but one must eat. One has to fill the stomach with something. Under these circumstances, the organizers, leaders, and activists of the youth movement got together. In its leadership was Szlama Kaczka and his brother, Chaim Kaczka, *z"l*, Mrs. Salomea Gertler, *z"l*, Josek Szulimowicz, *z"l*, and his brother, Szlama Szulimowicz, *z"l*, Motel Rożenek, *z"l*, Moszek Kamelgart, *z"l*, and, may they have a long life: Alter Frydman, Moshe Rożenek, Szmul Wdowiński, the one writing these lines, and others. They were the ones who decided to take some action, to help out the starving population. It was decided to establish a kitchen whose function would be to serve the needy with cooked meals.

In the women's section of the synagogue, which was still free of refugees, we established this communal kitchen. From money that was collected in the town, we bought a 150 liter [40 gallon] kettle. Under the supervision of Mrs. Gertler, who had volunteered to accept the position of kitchen manager, we started cooking and distributing free meals to the needy. The meals we provided were hot and nutritious and included two slices of bread. A small part of the hall of the women's section was combined with the kitchen, and in the rest of the section, we placed tables and benches to enable the people to eat.

It seems that we ourselves didn't even begin to comprehend the great amount of starvation that existed in the town. Our purchased kettle, which indeed had a very large capacity, was in a very short time insufficient to fill all of our needs. We were very quickly forced to purchase a second one, and, after a while, even a third. From the two to three hundred meals that we first thought would be enough for the needy, we had to increase to preparing more than one thousand hot meals daily. Prominent and honored heads of households, who at one time were known for their wealth, would gather a few hours prior to the opening of the kitchen in order to be among the first to receive the food. In many instances, this was the one and only meal they had for the day. The people were left bereft of anything and everything and starving for a piece of bread.

This work was not easy at all; our expenses grew, and the contributions that we were able to collect from the local residents were only enough to cover a very small part of our expenditures. We were compelled to turn to the *Judenrat* and seek their help. I would like to emphasize that in spite of the many troubles that befell this unfortunate group, the person who headed it, Mr. Moszek Josek Kruk, *z"l*, tried very hard to help us. The argument always revolved around the extent of the assistance. In view of our escalating needs, we always requested much more funding than was granted for our kitchen. Interfacing with the authorities fell upon Szlama Kaczka and Josek Szulimowicz, *z"l*, and this wasn't very easy to accomplish. Day after day and week after week, we were compelled to request a lot of money from an administrative authority that had to deal with very difficult problems and was in constant conflict with the German decrees and extortions. In spite of everything, we still succeeded in maintaining this kitchen and even expanded our activities.

With effort, we even established a children's aid center. About fifty children, orphaned by both mother and father, roamed the town without any care or supervision, and we decided to meet their needs as much as possible. We organized a group of girls, headed by Lola Brandys, Rajzfeld, G. Gertler, and others, who took upon themselves the responsibility to care for these poor orphaned children. In the very same hall of the women's section, near the synagogue, these children would gather every morning where they received food and even some food for the soul, in spite of this being forbidden and the dangers that were involved. How much sacrifice and toil this involved! And how much additional work did these girls invest in order to entertain these orphans and produce a smile on their sad faces. All of the volunteers, without exception, sacrificed a great deal in order for this establishment called the "communal kitchen" to succeed. With the help of the community, we received a legitimate budget of food products from the local authorities. In the end, it wasn't a small kitchen any longer. In view of the great pressures caused by the poverty and starvation in the town, we established an enterprise that during those times of war and hunger was the only one of its kind in the town that really helped save people from starving to death. And, if in Działoszyce during 1940–41, until the time of the deportations, Jews didn't perish from starvation, it was only thanks to the sacrifices of those few people mentioned, who had given up their days and nights and worked tirelessly and endlessly while endangering their lives just so that they could obtain another few sacks of oats and potatoes. They wandered at night on forbidden roads and paths and worried where to get food so there would be something to put on the stoves the next day.

It is very difficult to write this when I remember that from all of that selfless group, the only ones remaining alive—and may they be blessed with long life—are Alter Frydman, Moshe Rożenek, Szmul Wdowiński, and the writer of these lines. And the rest are gone. Where are you, Mrs. Salomea Gertler, *z"l*? A noble woman with a refined soul, the mother of this group. It was not as if she herself didn't have plenty of worries on her mind. You put all of your worries aside and, first and foremost, you worried about others. Day in and day out, you prepared the menu, you created something from nothing, and in addition to this, you helped Mrs. Hupert with the cooking itself. The main thing in your eyes was that there shouldn't be any starving people in Działoszyce.

Where are you, my companion and childhood friend, Josek Szulimowicz, *z"l*? You always liked quiet work, you were the treasurer of this enterprise, you worked with dedication that is difficult to describe, you worked very much for the common purpose. You were full of resourceful ideas, imagination, and creativity, and all this with the goal to amass more funds for this purpose. You did all of this without anger or frustration. You said, "All that was resolved must be acted upon!" And this indeed happened. Your theme was: "As long as we ourselves have something to eat, we cannot allow anybody else to walk around hungry among us."

Where are you all? You, Szlama and Chaim Kaczka, *z"l*? Szlama, the manager of the kitchen, the life of the party in the group, the one who worried about every detail, and the one who knew all the starving souls in town. And his brother, Chaim, *z"l*, the quiet one, the loyal and devoted worker, the one who spoke slowly and weighed every word. However, when it came to do work, you were always the first one.

Where are you, Moszek Kamelgart, *z"l*? My beautiful friend with the sunny disposition who got excited with every new venture and the one who found ways to implement them. In great danger you traveled to Częstochowa together with Alter Frydman, mainly to bring a loaded truck with *matse* for Pesakh, in 1941, for the poor of the town.

Where are you, Motel Rożenek, *z"l*? You always looked for the most difficult jobs and completed them. You ran a race to see who would finish first, and you won the race.

Where are you all, the youth of Działoszyce? The golden youth, the educated youth of the Zionist movements, the future of the nation? You drank the cups of grief, sadness, and sorrow of our nation till the end.

May their memories be blessed forever.

Translated from the Hebrew by Rochel Semp

My First Fear of Death (pp. 271–72)

Avraham Chobeh (Chaba)

Within the first few days of the war, during the "Days of Awe" [between Rosh Hashanah and Yom Kippur], several German soldiers came into town after the midday meal on a certain day. They demanded a place to spend the night. The Hebrew teacher Landau went immediately to Nuchim Laskier, the treasurer of the newly formed committee to help the needy. He and Szulim Majerczyk took the Germans to Chaiml Chaba's restaurant. They ordered food for them, and, to humor them even more, they ordered some strong liquor for them as well. And then they showed them where they could spend the night—in the new, not yet finished school.

During the night, one of the soldiers went out into the street carrying a firearm. This was after it had rained, and it was quite dark. Since he had drunk a lot, he slipped, and as he fell, his gun went off and hit him under the arm. But not wanting his commander to know what had happened, he said that he had been shot at from a distance of twelve meters and, of course, he was believed. The soldiers left at dawn. A few hours later, hundreds of vehicles came and surrounded the town on all sides. No one realized that this was related to what had happened the night before.

As I stood in my store, a messenger from the town hall came in holding a list in his hand on which the names of all the previous members of the town council had been recorded, mine among them. We were all ordered to come immediately to the town hall. I tried to explain to the messenger that I believed an error had been made and that instead of the names of the present council, he had a list of previous members who had left office when the war broke out. He insisted, however, and said that everyone but three persons was already there. On the way there, he picked up two additional Christian members [of the council]. Arriving at the town hall, they led us under a strong guard to the school where the event involving the soldier had taken place the day before.

At the school, a German officer asked our guard, "*Was für Leute sind diese?*" [What kind of people are these?] He answered, "*Sie sind Geiseln*" [They are hostages]. Then he asked, "*Sind auch Juden dabei* " [Are there Jews here also]? To the answer "*Ja*" [Yes], he asked where the Jewish cemetery was and added, "*Sofort die alle niederlegen*" [They should all lie down immediately]. At that point another officer arrived, and he led us into the school. We were just two Jews, the writer of these lines and Szmul Lewkowicz, along with seven Christians. The officer admonished us for having done such a thing, saying that because of it we were being arrested as "hostages" and that at this time there would be a search in the whole town for weapons. If they found weapons, we would all be shot and they would set the town on fire.

The current mayor of the town, Książek, stood up then and declared in Polish that he was the current mayor and that he also happened to be mayor during the occupation in the year 1914 and that the conduct of all the inhabitants of the town, and his own especially, had been one of loyalty toward the occupiers. And he assured them that all the inhabitants of our town were clear of any suspicion.

It can be understood that his words did not particularly impress the German officers. We sat there the whole day between life and death. The military then got into their automobiles and left without saying a word. When we saw that we had been left alone, we all went home. I never imagined that this was just the beginning of our troubles. The real sorrow and pain came later.

Translated from the Yiddish by Zulema Seligson

Jews Repent (pp. 273–74)

Chaim Icek Wohlgelernter

A chapter from "The Book of Tears" as retold by his brother David[1]

Tuesday, Elul 19, 5702 [September 1, 1942]. The town of Działoszyce is greatly distressed. The tragic happenings in Proszowice, Brzesko, Skała, and Słomniki, which occurred on Friday and Shabes, have shaken everyone. It is true that the entire community was assembled in Słomniki. We are waiting for a miracle. Different opinions are being voiced. Some say that there has been foreign intervention and they will not be sent away. Meanwhile, they are being guarded with tighter security. Everyone is thinking how to save themselves from the danger that is so close, almost upon them. Many take the risk and escape.

Already for the second time, some wagons with bread are being sent to Słomniki. Clothing is also being gathered. Monies are being collected for their redemption. We go to the cemetery for the third time. It is already the third day of a public fast. Today we will sound the ram's horn at the cemetery, and, it is being said, a wedding canopy will be set up for poor orphans. The *oyel* [structure over a grave] of Reb Joskele is full of *kvitlekh* [notes of supplication]. All the graves are besieged. We pour out our bitter hearts. Women, children, the elderly, and even the sick have come. The paralyzed rabbi [Staszewski?] was brought by his two grandchildren. He speaks words that tear at the heart. They glow like hot coals. He prays at the grave of his father.

> Tata [Papa], for this you left me to fill your place for over forty years so that in my old age I should see this dark tragedy that has befallen my congregation? Tata, I beg you, go to Grandfather Reb Mordchele Stersziwer [Strzyżower?] so that he and his holy brother, Reb Majerl Apter, should bang on the gates of mercy that have been hammered shut. My only father, for what are you waiting? Don't say that Jews have sinned. Repentance can always help.

Turning to the townspeople: "Will you all say that you will repent?"
A thousand-headed crowd answers, "Yes, Rabbi! We will repent."

> I won't leave you, Tata. I have a place next to you, a grave that was prepared right after you passed away.

> What pleasure have I had in my life? Berko, my fine son, who lies next to you, departed this world in his youth and in his best years. That was during World War I. That was a punishment for me and my family. And now in my old age why should I see my congregation being destroyed? How a community of Jews is slaughtered. And my second son, the Skalbmierzer rabbi who died recently, is he a minor sacrifice? What additional sacrifice is still being demanded of me?"

---

[1] The "Book of Lamentations," which mourns the destroyed city of Jerusalem, is also known as "The Book of Tears."

Jews, I will be the sacrifice, to expiate the sins of the entire town of Działoszyce. I will be the sacrificial sin offering for you. I will…also…

The rabbi fell in a faint.

When the rabbi revived, he sounded the ram's horn, and the crowd gradually left the cemetery.

It felt lighter, as if a stone had been removed from my heart.

On the way, however, we heard the bitter news that in Słomniki, it was all over. The Jews were loaded onto wagons and sent away.

A black cloud descended upon the town of Działoszyce.

Translated from the Yiddish by Menachem Daum

The Horror Has Begun (pp. 275–77)

David Wohlgelernter

The wheel of history has been turned back; before one's eyes an original picture is revealed, an Exodus in a new edition. They walk in haste, carrying walking sticks in their hands and bundles on their backs. Sadly, they walk in the wrong direction. Their fortunes, which they acquired through generations of hard work, both physically and with their hearts, they leave to their neighbors, our neighbors, the new Egypt, taking only the scars with them…

One by one, even before the appointed deadline, the people, in a rush, faces frightened, in long rows, crowd into the Działoszyce market square. One's mind works quickly, many different thoughts fly into it, hopes flare every second. God will help, no doubt.

Here and there, a child starts crying, demanding food. Somewhere on the ground, an old woman murmurs a prayer: "Merciful Creator, make a miracle happen, take pity on the innocent babies." The town *rebbe* [Lejzor Halevi Epsztajn] leans on the market lamppost. He is the grandson of Rabbi Reb Kalmus [Epsztajn] of Neustadt [Nowy Korczyn], fourth generation of the holy luminary, a son-in-law of the most renowned Komarner [*rebbe* from Komarno], the great saint who sat for so many years in his little *bes hamedresh,* devoting himself to prayer with great simplicity, and who without magic kept weaving the chain of his saintly genealogy. The murderers tore him away from his open Psalter. Thus he stands, finishing in a sea of tears the Psalms he left unsaid in the Psalter. The only baggage he brought was his *tfilen* and his *talis* [phylacteries and prayer shawl]. The *tfilen*, which he inherited from his famous grandfather, the pious Jew, he had to have them with him. He believed that by tradition they would keep all evil away. He was sorry he could not take with him the five books of the Torah, each one of which had a noble pedigree.

How can it be allowed that such holiness should fall into such impure hands? Perhaps "God be praised" will help, and the merits of my ancestors will protect us. It can't be helped. We shall return, pray, give thanks to the Creator of the World for the favors He will have bestowed on us. Do we then have merits of our own? Is it at all possible that in this, our hour of need, when the mind is not in any condition to welcome such large concepts and arrive at the status of the passionate divine service of my great ancestors? Of course, I am not in the category of "the righteous one commands, and God obeys," so therefore we must wait for pure kindness as in the times when we stood by the sea. But where can one find a Moshe Rabeinu [Moses Our Teacher], someone who can be a leader? All the great holy men of our day, it is said, are no longer here. However, it is said that "the righteous are even greater in their death then in their lifetimes." Let them therefore arouse mercy for us up above.

On one side stands the *rebetsn* [rabbi's wife]. Her charities and good deeds have no limits. She ran her whole house with a very generous hand, which she had inherited from the regal house that was kept by her great father, the Komarner *rebbe*. She accepted everything as her duty, whether a meal had to be sent—and what is the name of that poor porter who can no longer stand on his feet in his old age? He is lying there and cannot move. Who will remember him? He could starve to death. So she remembered, every day, sending hot meals to him—at the same time being very careful that no one should find out. Because proclaiming one's charity, as she learned from her grandfather, Reb Ajzykl Komarner, removes the spirit from the good deed. And then the solicitor of funds for the yeshiva has surely not had any breakfast, and it is nine o'clock already." Not waiting for anyone, she prepared food for him. And "I just saw an acquaintance today; go, Jancze, call him." The Jew, a simple guest, has no idea what this means. The *rebetsn* herself—and not in the kitchen, God forbid, but inside the house—serves him, and what a festive meal! As he leaves, she puts a certain amount of money and a package in his bag. Outside, he sees that it is a shirt. With a quick eye she had noticed that he wore a torn shirt.

She, a weak and overworked woman, takes the time to collect money in town for an ailing person or just the plain needy. She thinks nothing of spending the night with a sick woman or of cleansing and preparing the body of a dead woman which no one wants to go near. At home things are very difficult. There is no income. She sells, without her husband's knowledge, the valuable possessions, the clothes that she had brought with her from her wealthy childhood home. One must not skimp on charity. At marriage celebrations, she is the leader in the rabbinical court.

The eldest son, Josek, son-in-law of the Przecławer [rabbi in Przecław], grandson of the Ropczycer [from Ropczyce], is himself already a rabbi. Her son-in-law, Dinale's husband, Lejbuś, a scholar, is considered a blessing by everyone. The greetings she received from the land of Israel about what a Jewish and rabbinical home they have and their two wonderful children fill her heart with joy. Izraelke, the son-in-law of the Kinsker [from Końskie], is himself a rabbi; Ajzyk, the son-in-law of the Pokrzywnicer [from Pokrzywnica] is in Łódź. During the brief time he has lived there, he has become very popular; he is a *mohel* [performs circumcisions] in a clinic and a community activist. The rest of the children, unmarried yet, God keep us from complaining, are good-hearted and delicate souls...

Alas, the bitter war that suddenly broke out, and because of the need to earn a living, the children had to slowly move away. It's a small matter, and with God's help, it will end. There will be marriages, and again there will be holy children.

She, the *rebetsn*, stands now but is not idle. She approaches the weak, gives them something, a few tidbits for other people. And the pills she has with her for her bad heart. Now she picks up the crying children, now she comforts the people.

Her sister, the widow of the Radzymin rabbi—who, wanting to escape the hell in Warsaw, came here with her eldest son and daughter—stands wringing her hands, thinking did she have to come all the way from Warsaw? Wouldn't it have been better to have stayed there in the cemetery lying on her husband's and her son Mendel's graves—Mendel, the son-in-law of the Alexander [from Alexandrów] rabbi, who was taken away by typhus?

Altela [the elderly one] has lost the children of Izraelke as well as Ajzyk's youngest daughter, whose mother was deported from Tarnów together with her father, the rabbi of Pokrzywnica.

Translated from the Yiddish by Zulema Seligson

The Evil Decrees (pp. 278–79)

Shalom Szlamowicz

The Destruction of the *Oyel* of my Grandfather, the Revered Rabbi Josef Frydman, *zts"l*

In September 1942, all sorts of rumors filtered into our town about "actions" [roundups and deportations] that were taking place in the vicinity. A week before the "action" in our town, all the Jews gathered in front of the *oyel* [structure over a tomb] that was in the Jewish cemetery in Działoszyce. For the entire week the Jews prayed, cried, and beseeched the Creator of the World if only He would cancel these terrible decrees. Nothing else mattered to them that entire week. They were ready to hand over everything to God, if only this awful decree of the "actions" would not take place. They hoped to escape this decree through fasting, prayer, and many tears.

But nothing helped. They could not escape the evil decree.

In 1945, when I was liberated from the concentration camps, I returned to my town of Działoszyce. My first stop was at the *oyel* of my holy grandfather, Rabbi Josef Frydman, *zts"l* [of blessed righteous memory]. With a broken heart, I realized that the tomb had been destroyed. The vicious and merciless Germans had no mercy even on the cemetery and had desecrated the resting places of the holy deceased.

My Farewell to the Revered, Elderly Rabbi Staszewski on the day of the "Action"

In September 1942, like thunder before a storm, our town was invaded by many, many SS men, *Sonderkommando*s, who surrounded our town from all sides.[1] There was total silence in the town as though before an impending storm. An awful fear permeated the town, one that could practically be felt through the windows of the homes.

My father, *z"l*, took me along with him to bid our farewells to the rabbi of our town, Rabbi Staszewski. When we arrived, Rabbi Staszewski interrupted his prayers and told us, "You ought to do everything to save your lives. As far as I am concerned, I have already put on my *kitl*, *talis*, and *tfilen* [robe, prayer shawl, and phylacteries];[2] I am already too old to escape my fate. I will return my soul here, in this place, to my Creator."

Pogrom in Działoszyce in 1945

I returned to my town as soon as I was liberated from the concentration camp. All of us few survivors who had returned to Działoszyce got together in order to reorganize ourselves and start our lives anew. We wanted to get back to a normal way of life. We all lived in one area. The Poles could not believe that any Jews had survived. Their intense hatred of the Jews now stemmed from another reason as well. We had left our worldly

---

[1] The *Sonderkommando* was a special task force.
[2] To be ready for a proper Jewish burial, i.e., wrapped in *kitl*, *talis*, and *tfilen*.

possessions (for safekeeping) with many of them, and sometimes, this was an enormous amount. They feared we would bring up this matter about all that we had left with them but that was now gone. They therefore determined in their hearts that they would destroy the remaining few Jews as well.

One night in 1945, they attacked our dwelling place, turned off the electricity, and very cruelly murdered some of us. Among the murdered were Chaim Jurysta, Szmul Piekarz, z"l, and others. That same night, we were again forced to escape our town. This time I left my hometown of Działoszyce forever. In the hands of the gentiles was left all that we possessed, and in my heart, the memories.

My Revenge on the Commander of Płaszów (Jerozolimska)[1]

After the pogrom in Działoszyce, I escaped to Germany. I was informed that the commander of Płaszów, the vicious Amon Goeth, was imprisoned in Dachau, which was now under American occupation. A few surviving Jews from Działoszyce, I among them, wrote an urgent letter to the American authorities in which we requested to see the cursed perpetrator and serve as witnesses against him. To our delight and happiness, we were invited to appear a week later at the prison in Dachau in order to identify him and serve as witnesses.

When we arrived, we were ushered into a large hall, and there we saw him. There immediately appeared in my mind's eye the scenario of this monumental vicious criminal, Amon Goeth. He would hold a bottle of cognac in one hand, and in the other, a gun, and this was how he would shoot totally innocent people. This is how this Nazi murderer conducted himself. His breakfast consisted not only of food but also of murdered people. How many innocent martyred Jews had he shot in this manner from his window?

Now he looked taller and thinner. My cousin, Chaim Szlamowicz, couldn't contain himself, pushed away his guards, and beat him. We requested a death sentence on the spot, but we were given to understand that the Polish authorities had requested his extradition in order to sentence him in Poland for the crimes he had committed. He was extradited to Poland in conjunction with our having served as witnesses.

The Revenge on the Commander of Brynica—Leopold

After the war, my brother Nusyn and I found ourselves in Deggendorf, Germany. In the train station in Deggendorf, we encountered a very familiar-looking person. He was dressed in civilian cloths, wearing an elegant suit, and accompanied by a young woman. I said to my brother that I believed this was Leopold, the commander of Brynica.[2]

My brother went over to him and said, "Leopold, do you recognize me? Weren't you the commander of Brynica?" Upon hearing this, he tried to escape. We grabbed him and prevented his escaping into a train car.

At that moment, he started screaming, "The Jews are attacking me!" A group of Germans rushed to his aid. To our good fortune, there was a representative of the American police force present who evidently was a Jew. Leopold was arrested on the

---

[1] The main entrance of the Płaszów camp was located on Jerozolimska Street.
[2] Brynica [Brynitz] was a camp in Sudetenland (western Czechoslovakia).

spot. They found a tattoo of a cross on his underarm.[1] They jailed him, and we served as witnesses. Aba Balicki, *z"l,* also served as a witness against him.

Again, the Polish authorities requested that he be delivered into their hands.

We got word that he was hanged—another criminal who got the punishment he deserved.

Translated from the Hebrew by Rochel Semp

---

[1] Most SS men had such a tattoo under their left arm.

Chapters from the Past (pp. 280–97)

Aryeh Shahar (Lejbl Jutrzenka)

1.

My grandfather and great-grandfather were both born in Działoszyce. My great-grandfather's father, Icek Josek Jutrzenka, was one of those who built the town's first synagogue in 1864. His son, Ezriel, was a prominent member of the community, a synagogue official, and a scholar. He built many houses in the town. Great-grandfather Ezriel had three sons. Grandfather Mendel, the oldest and most observant, had a dry goods store as well as a seltzer factory, which was managed by his wife, Witla, who also ran a school with thirty students. They had seven children who lived up to the phrase "good with God and good with people." Their eldest son, Chaim Chaskiel, was a *shoykhet* [ritual slaughterer], devoted to study and prayer. Their second son was my father, Szmul, who was dedicated to community needs, Torah study, fulfilling the commandments, and doing good deeds. My father was one of the founders of the *talmed-toyre* [Jewish elementary school] and Beit Yaakov school [for girls] and organized yeshivas for young men who wanted to pursue advanced studies of the Talmud, etc. Typically, there were many guests at his table every day of the week and especially on Shabes and holidays. His wife, my mother, Fajga, *hi"d* [may God avenge her soul], would serve the guests first, then the children; she would eat whatever was left, never complaining, making do with little. The third son, Icze [Icek], was a very special young man, who gave charity in secret and set aside ten percent of his monthly earnings for the poor. Gitel, the only daughter, was an enlightened young woman who knew languages, among them French, which she taught. Jankiel, the next son, was an ardent Zionist who argued endlessly about Zionist ideology but wasn't able to fulfill his ideal and live in Eretz Yisroel. To his great sorrow, he was childless. Young Abram was observant, good-natured and sensitive, accepted everything with love and was uncomplaining. Dawid emigrated to the United States in 1905 and lives in Philadelphia.

2.

Only I remain from this entire extended family. I married a woman named Chaja, daughter of Reb Alter Frajnd, the ritual slaughterer from Skalbmierz, who bore me a daughter. The week the talk about deportations began, my wife, Chaja, and I decided to flee, rather than be led like cattle to the slaughter, as was the intent of the Germans. We had to deal with the problem of our young daughter, who was almost one year old. It was impossible to take her with us, as we were not escaping to any specific place. We had, in fact, decided to try to survive in the countryside, in the woods. There was no way we could take the child along. We negotiated with the Christian midwife in Skalbmierz, promising her a considerable sum if she would take the child and care for her until the crisis was over. She agreed.

3.

The day before the deportation, on a Tuesday, I was uneasy because I had left my mother and sister at home in Działoszyce without discussing with them what they should do. So on that very day, I went to Działoszyce to bid them farewell. When I approached the town, I heard cries and screams. As I moved closer, I realized that the sounds were coming from the cemetery. I ran right home. At 20 Rynek [Market Square], actually the home of Szmul Szental, I found my younger sister, Witla. I asked where I could find my mother, my older sister, Ester, and her husband, Moszek. Witla said, "They're all at the cemetery, at the ancestral graves, praying for the bitter decree to be canceled. They all now believe that the end is near."

I ran to the cemetery, where I found my mother and sister. My mother was standing near the fresh grave of my father, who had died so recently that there was no stone to mark the spot. When I arrived, I pointed out my father's grave to her. She prostrated herself and cried out, "Szmul! You are lucky, your son knows where you are buried and can find the spot. No one will know where to look for my grave."

4.

Standing there in the cemetery, I saw a mass of men, women, and children in the hundreds, maybe thousands. I saw and heard a man I had known for years crying and declaring:

> Holy Jews! We must all turn our thoughts to penitence! It's not enough to repent in our hearts; everyone must declare his sins out loud, and the Lord above will forgive and cancel the evil decree. Let every person confess his sins, and they will be forgiven. Our sages have said that God on Yom Kippur does not forgive the sins of one person against another. We must ask each other for forgiveness. We may have caused harm by our actions or thoughts. Let us repent, and God will forgive us and find us worthy.

The general confession of sins began. The *dayan* [religious judge] led the prayers, calling out the verses, and the crowd responded: "*Al het shehatanu lefanecha* [For the sins we have committed]."[1] All hearts, all souls were as one, no longer praying for mere personal salvation, as though their physical being was suspended for the moment. Their souls, purged and sanctified, clung to God in heaven.

At the conclusion of the prayer, the *dayan* spoke:

> Hear me, my sons and daughters! Our sages, of blessed memory, taught us that even when a sword is at your throat, one must not despair of mercy! God's mercy is abundant. If the decree cannot be reversed, let us ask mercy for our souls, that we be privileged to sanctify His Blessed Name and fulfill the verse: " In their life and in their death they were not parted."

At that moment I remembered that I had to go back to my wife and child. I took leave of my mother and sister and headed toward Skalbmierz. I met two German policemen on the road. They asked, "Why all the shouts and cries from the cemetery?" I told them, "The Jews are praying to God." One of the Germans retorted: "Yes! Let them pray to God today, but tomorrow we'll be the ones to 'help' them."

---

[1] Excerpt from a prayer recited on Yom Kippur.

5.

When I arrived at Skalbmierz, it was dark. I went right home and told my wife, Chaja, that it was time to take our one-year-old daughter, Golda, to the midwife. By the time she agreed, it was too late, as Jews were not permitted to leave the house at night.

In the morning I got up early and went to the midwife. I repeated my offer, promising her a considerable sum if she would care for the child. She agreed. Then, at eight o'clock in the morning, I went back home and said to my wife, "Take Golda'le and bring her to the midwife." My mother-in-law, Cylka, intervened and absolutely refused to leave the child with the aforementioned midwife. Meanwhile, time was passing. We knew that at eleven o'clock in the morning the Gestapo would come and close off the town, that Jews would not be allowed to come or go. Having no alternative, at the last moment, I went to my landlord, Witek Niewiadomski, and said to him, "Listen, my wife and I have decided to flee before the Gestapo arrives. I'll leave everything I own with you if you will keep our child until the storm passes. I am sure you will do whatever you can to care for her." He accepted my proposal. We shook hands.

I went back to my room, took my wife's coat, put it on her, and said, "Let's go; we can leave the child with Niewiadomski." My wife agreed immediately, but my mother-in-law began to cry because the child was being left behind. I said to Cylka, "Come with us." Because we had to leave quickly, the three of us set out together to take the child to Niewiadomski. Once again, my mother-in-law refused to let us leave the child. As it was late, we hurried out of town and walked toward Działoszyce. We came to a crossroads and arrived at the first town, Skalbmierz. It was dangerous to be in the fields with the child, so I said to my mother-in-law, "You know all the local farmers. Go to the nearest one and leave the child with him." The first farmer she approached agreed to keep the child along with her mother. My wife, Chaja, having no alternative, stayed with the farmer. My mother-in-law and I continued to flee.

Suddenly, in the distance, I saw a car approaching. We ran faster, over the top of the hill, with the thought that even if the car came our way, we would not be noticed. When we were on the other side, we lay down on the ground, exhausted by our frantic run. We saw that the vehicle had stopped at the spot where we had been when we ran up the hill. We were unaware, at that point, that our friends, members of my wife's family, Moszek Płatkiewicz and his wife, Rywka, were running behind us. They had not yet reached the top of the hill. The Germans got out of the car, ordered them to strip, took their money, and shot them on the spot. We stood by, witnesses to this cold-blooded murder by the Gestapo, may their name be erased.

After a few minutes, the Gestapo men climbed back into the car and drove to town. When my mother-in-law saw the Germans murdering her good friends, she said, "I don't want them to kill me like that." She turned around and ran back toward home. My wife, Chaja, looking out the window of the farmer's house, saw her mother headed for home, so she left the farmer's house with the baby. They went back to Skalbmierz.

Alone in the field, I hid among the potato plants. Lying there, I watched as the Germans led the Jews of Skalbmierz, my wife, child, and mother-in-law among them, to Działoszyce. From there they were taken to Miechów and then to the death camp, Bełzec, which was the end of their life on earth.

6.

I remained in the field for a week. On Friday, around noon, after I had been there two days, a man appeared who seemed to own the property. He promised that his wife would bring me food, that I need not be afraid. And, in fact, after half an hour, his wife brought me cooked potatoes. When I finished eating, she asked for the watch that was in my pocket. I had no choice but to give it to her.

I was, for some reason, afraid to stay there, and, in the middle of the night, I moved to a spot about a kilometer away where there was a haystack in which I could dig a hole and hide. The next day I could hear the local gentiles searching the fields for Jews. Somehow, they didn't notice me.

This was my routine: At night I ventured out to look for something to eat, and I spent the day in hiding. I would find carrots, tomatoes, and potatoes and was able to hold out for a week. Because of this diet, to which I was unaccustomed, I had diarrhea and couldn't remain in the fields. I got up in the morning and went to Działoszyce. At the outskirts of the town, I met a farmer who told me that a few Jews had gathered in Szmul Szental's courtyard. I made my way there and joined them.

7.

My parents had lived in the house that belonged to Szental. This is where I had grown up, so I knew it well. From the window of our apartment, I could see what was going on in the street. Our store was also in that building. In short, this is where we gathered, a few hundred Jews, on that Eve of Rosh Hashanah. Mendel Szental had constructed some large, solid storage sheds in this yard, which the Germans had used to keep Jewish prisoners.

We set up one of these storage sheds for prayer. On Rosh Hashanah we entered the "synagogue" to pray. I led the prayer services. In normal times it was not my role to lead the prayers. But we had neither a *sidur* [regular prayer book] nor a *makhzor* [holiday prayer book], and I was the only one who knew the prayers by heart. I called out each verse, and the congregation responded. We spent several days in the courtyard. The gendarmes appeared regularly and announced that we were about to be led away—to the places to which our parents had already been taken.

We were not allowed to leave the yard except to clean the streets, and we remained there until the eve of Yom Kippur, at which point those who were in charge informed us that we would be able to return home the next day. This information was at once heartening and disheartening, as ninety percent of our families were already gone. We nonetheless returned to our homes. I returned to Skalbmierz, where I went to the *Judenrat* to ask for the keys to my house. I met two of my brothers-in-law, Mordka and Jankiel Frajnd, who had returned from Kazimierz, and we opened the house together. But my wife, child, and mother-in-law were no longer there. The house was completely empty. The brothers-in-law said, "Let's go to Lejzor Kac's. All those who returned are gathered there." So, with our dwindling strength, we went there. From the distance, we heard sounds of singing and laughter. We didn't understand what this meant. We went in and were shocked. The entire *Judenrat*, along with the *Ordnungsdienst* [Jewish police], were eating, drinking, carrying on, men and women together, like at a wedding celebration. I couldn't stand this shameful scene and left immediately, returning to my home in Działoszyce. In Działoszyce, I got the keys to my [parents'] house, but the commissar in charge of our store was there. Without receiving permission from the authorities, he left the house as soon as he saw me. Meanwhile, I saw that my mother and sister had not returned. After several days in the house, I was joined by my brother-in-law, Moszek Jutrzenka. I was glad to have his company, and we spent a few more days in the house. Then, suddenly, we got the news that the Germans were planning to deport all the remaining Jews.

We decided, Moszek Jutrzenka and I, to flee once again. This time we went toward Pińczów. On the way, we asked a farmer for refuge. He offered to hide us in his barn. We spent a few days there. One day we heard that all those who had remained in Działoszyce were already on the way to extermination. It was the beginning of November 1942. The farmer we were staying with was poor and had no way to feed us, though we paid him good money.

At this point, my brother-in-law, Moszek, heard that the Pińczów rabbi was now in Wodzisław. Being one of his admirers, without giving the matter much thought, he left and headed for Wodzisław. A few days later, I learned that the Germans had seized the rabbi, along with hundreds of his followers, and murdered all of them.

I left the farmer, crushed and dejected, hoping to find a better hiding place. I went to another farmer, Nowak, and asked if he would give me shelter in return for ample payment. He agreed instantly, providing me with half a room in his house. He set two conditions: 1) I must eat whatever he had to offer, and 2) I must not let it be known that I was Jewish. I accepted the two conditions and was with him for a week. I had good food and a place to sleep, also not bad. Once, on Sunday morning, the farmer appeared, unexpectedly, and saw me wrapped in a *talis* and *tfilen*. He was very angry and said he was reneging on his offer and was unwilling to keep me any longer. I told him that I had left a large sum of money in a secret place in Skalbmierz and would give it all to him if he would let me stay in his house. He agreed to go to Skalbmierz with me to get the money.

8.

On a snowy wintry night, Nowak brought two horses and told me to mount one of them. He would take the other horse and we would ride to Skalbmierz. I was thrown right off the horse, as I had never been on horseback before. But Nowak persisted and forced me to try until I was comfortable enough to set out. I was carrying two bundles, one with clothes, the other with a *talis* and *tfilen*. What did Nowak do? He took the *talis* and *tfilen* and threw them into the field, saying, "What if, God, forbid, the Germans stop us. I'll say that I don't know who you are, and they won't be able to tell whether or not you are Jewish. But if they catch you with your *talis* and *tfilen* in hand, we'll both be buried deep in the ground." We rode together through side roads and woods. I was in the lead with Nowak following at a slight distance. When we approached Skalbmierz, it was about two o'clock in the morning. Nowak stopped his horse and told me to do the same. We dismounted. After a sharp exchange between the two of us, Nowak took both horses and rode home, leaving me in the dark field. I saw Skalbmierz in the distance.

9.

I entered the town and went to the apartment I had lived in earlier. I knocked on the door of Niewiadomski's house, gave my name, and asked to be let in. Mrs. Niewiadomska arranged a place for me to sleep in the attic and gave me some food. I went up to the attic, and, after Mrs. Niewiadomska returned to her quarters, I went to the hiding place where I had left gold coins worth hundreds of dollars. I searched and searched but didn't find the money. Having no choice, I went back to the attic and fell asleep, deeply distressed. Mr. Niewiadomski appeared on the following day. I told him I had searched for my money and found nothing. He said, "Your brothers-in-law were here, and they must have taken the money with them." Niewiadomski advised me to go to Wodzisław, where there were still Jews, and from there on to Kraków.

That evening I left Niewiadomski's house and went to Karasiński's store. He was the mayor at the time. Before leaving town I had left four thousand *złoty* with him, which I asked him to return. He received me graciously and returned the money. I headed toward Wodzisław. The journey was difficult. All sorts of people attached themselves to me, girls and boys, who threatened to turn me over to the German police unless I gave them money. I claimed I had none, and they tried to take the clothing that was in my bag. I fought them off, shouting: "I have nothing to lose; if the Germans come, you will be hung, too," since Poles were also not allowed to rob and steal. They finally left me alone, and I managed to reach Wodzisław. There were many Jews there. Among those I knew were Mania Skrzypek and her nephew, who had no place to go. They had been hidden by a local gentile who threw them out. The boy, a six- to seven-year-old, was the main problem. No one wanted to take him in.

Meanwhile, I learned that on a certain day the Germans were going to liquidate the remaining Jews who had gathered in the town. I decided to leave and head for Kraków. On the way I met three other Jews from Działoszyce: Motel Rożenek, Abram Polak's son, and Zalman Frajfeld, who was in Działoszyce during the war. We agreed to travel together. The trip was one of endless pain and suffering. Wherever we went, the Poles robbed us. We moved through fields, avoiding the main road. When we were about twenty to thirty kilometers from Kraków, a horse and cart came down the road carrying a Polish police official from Kazimierz. He saw us, fired a shot into the air, and ordered us to approach. Having no choice, we did as we were told. He asked where we were going. We told him we were going to Kraków. He said, "Do you know that Jews are not allowed on the roads, under penalty of death?" We answered, "What do you mean to do with us? We know all the decrees." His driver got down from the cart and told us that the commandant wanted money. We balked at the size of the sum he was demanding, declaring that we didn't have that much money. We finally reached an agreement and paid him five hundred *złoty*. After receiving the money, the commandant said to us, "If you take this road to Kraków, you'll run into German gendarmes. Stay on the road to Kazimierz." And so we continued to make our way to the Kraków ghetto. The ghetto entrance was guarded by an *Ordnungsdienst* [Jewish police] patrol; we were allowed to enter. It was November 1942.

10.

A few minutes later, another member of the *Ordnungsdienst* stopped and arrested us as illegals and took us to the place where non-residents were being detained. We were questioned—where were we from, why did we choose to come here? A few hundred people were being held. After a day in a *Judenrat* prison, we were taken to a building at 17 Krakowska Street in the ghetto. We received orders to go to Płaszów, where we would be working on the construction of a camp.

The next day, we were each given a slice of bread and taken to Płaszów. Our first task was to tear down the fence surrounding the cemetery. We were also ordered to uproot the gravestones so they could be used to pave roads. I remember one typical event. Hercyk, Jurysta, Jakubowicz, and I were dismantling a barbed wire fence. Suddenly, we heard a shot that hit Hercyk's hand. We turned and saw Pilarzik, an SS man, a few meters away. We knew he had fired the shot but we didn't react. Otherwise, this Pilarzik would have killed us. We continued to work, even Hercyk, despite his injury, and returned home in the evening.

Before leaving Płaszów to go back to the ghetto, there was a head count; there were ninety-nine of us. This number was reported to Pilarzik, who was in charge.

At the entrance to the cemetery stood a small structure. We were on the way back to the ghetto when a few people, who had been inside this structure, came out and fell into line with us. Pilarzik rode by on his motorcycle and took note of this. He ordered another count. There were now 106 of us. He then ordered those who had arrived after the first count to step out of line. Needless to say, no one stepped out, since the latecomers had been buying bread from the gentiles to take back to the ghetto. Pilarzik ordered everyone back to Płaszów, where we were lined up against the wall of the building used for ritual purification of the dead. He returned ten minutes later with a machinegun in his hand. Seeing this, we understood that we were all lost. I took out a knife I had hidden in my pack, intending to attack Pilarzik, but the people around me prevented me from carrying out my plan. I saw that I was lost, so I tried to lie down, as close as possible to the ground with all the others piled on top of me. After a few seconds, Pilarzik began to shoot, killing fourteen. Then he took twenty more people out of the line to bury the dead. These twenty were handed over to the Ukrainians, who killed them, one by one. Those who survived this ghastly slaughter returned to the ghetto.

Back at the ghetto, the situation was miserable. There was no food, there were no warm clothes. After a day like this, we didn't want to go back to Płaszów. I made a plan. The next day I left the *Arbeitsblock* [workers' quarters] and went from house to house asking for food and clothing. The room I lived in accommodated forty people. I collected half a sack of potatoes, shoes, jackets, and pants. I offered everyone cooked potatoes along with the other food I had acquired and distributed the clothing to the most needy. The following morning, I cooked soup, which I served to everyone. At 6:00 AM we were ready to go back to work in Płaszów. One person was expected to stay behind and clean our quarters. The men I lived with chose Jutrzenka (me) to stay "since he provides for us." And so it was. This continued throughout November and December 1942.

At the beginning of January 1943, we were all transferred to Płaszów. I didn't want to continue to clean rooms and decided to work as a glazier. I made an effort to get a diamond with which to cut glass and was the only glazier in Płaszów. I remember that there was once a roll call of all the *Barackenbau* residents in Płaszów.[1] The Jewish police force requested that in the daily roll call of the *Barackenbau* residents, each person respond to a previously agreed upon invented name. At the appointed time, the *Schutzhauptlagerführer* [SS chief camp commander] Müller, the SS man, began to call out the names of those present, but of course they did not exist. He was very angry at the Jewish police, pulled them out of the yard, removed their police hats, and shot them on the spot, because they had given him fictitious names of people who had received "work permits" and were idly roaming the streets of the ghetto. It was clear that the Jewish policemen had been paid for manipulating the names of these permit holders.

After a while, on March 13, 1943, the Germans liquidated the Kraków ghetto and transferred its inhabitants to Płaszów. In Płaszów, *Arbeitsgemeinschaften* [workers' groups] of tailors, shoemakers, glaziers, etc. were set up. I was one of the glaziers, but not on the master level. I remember that once, the Gestapo in Kraków called for various tradesmen to be sent to them. Three glaziers were sent, myself among them. When we arrived at the Gestapo building, they gave us couches and armchairs to repair. We said that we were glaziers, not upholsterers. They answered, "We were told you know all the trades, so we expect you to do the repairs." We were frightened and did what was required.

One day some Jewish policemen entered our workshop and asked, "Which of you have relatives in Płaszów?" Everyone was afraid to respond. Only I dared to say that I had no family there. My name was recorded. About two weeks later, I was called in by the police and told to collect my belongings and report to the *Emailwarenfabrik* (the enamel goods factory) on Zabłocie Street in Kraków that was managed by Mr. [Oskar] Schindler.[2] I was, of course, happy to be leaving Płaszów, which was a virtual slaughterhouse. Every day people were killed, and severe punishment was meted out for every minor transgression. People were tortured, beaten, hung. So I was envied because I was leaving.

11.

That same day, eighty people left Płaszów for Zabłocie, where we were welcomed. Most of those who came from Płaszów had relatives at Zabłocie Street. We felt as though we were moving from darkness to great light, from slavery to freedom. The person in charge of us there was named Rajch, and Mr. Schindler welcomed us warmly, too. I was given a special room in which to work and was comfortable there.

In June 1943, I went to Mr. Schindler and said to him, "I have two brothers-in-law in Płaszów, skilled tradesmen. I would like to ask that you have them transferred to you." I told him their names: "the brothers Motel Frajnd and Jankiel Frajnd." He made a note of this, and two weeks later, about a hundred men arrived from Płaszów, and they were in the group. I welcomed them with bread and potatoes. We remained together for about a year. One of them worked with me as a glazier, and the other was employed in a different workshop. I remember one event. As Passover approached, those who were observant

---

[1] The *Barackenbau* group was composed of Jews engaged in building barracks and other buildings for the camp.

[2] The factory was actually located on Lipowa Street in the Zabłocie district of Kraków.

made an effort to obtain *matse*. My work gave me access to a large oven, and I was able to buy flour from gentiles who worked in the pots and pans factory. My brother-in-law Motel and I baked several hundred *matse*, which we distributed to all of the Jews. There was a fellow with us in Zabłocie, Abram Bankier, who once owned a factory—he took on all the expenses involved in baking the *matse*. Just before Shavuos, Schindler made a big party for his Gestapo men to mark the production of a million grenades in the factory he was overseeing. He chose ten people to arrange the event.

On the night of the celebration, his men were in high spirits and somewhat drunk. Two of them got up from their places at the table and declared, "Let's have some fun!" They took out their pistols, intending to kill some "little Yids." Schindler, with his sharp eye, took note of this, turned to them and said, "*Meine Herren*! (Gentlemen), I won't have such vile behavior here." They were taken aback and muttered, "We only meant to amuse ourselves with some Jewish blood." Schindler called out in a louder voice, "No way! I have a letter from Himmler!" Hearing the name Himmler, they returned the pistols to their holsters. These words from Schindler prevented the spilling of Jewish blood.

In June 1944, there was a rumor that the Germans were about to liquidate our camp. We immediately organized to plan an escape. However, for various reasons, this was not what happened. At the end of June, we received an order that 1200 people were to leave for Mauthausen immediately. My two brothers-in-law and I were in this group.

12.

The trip to Mauthausen was horrendous. We left Płaszów and made our way to the train on foot with the Gestapo beating us mercilessly. When we reached the train, forty of us were crowded into a wagon meant for horses that could hold thirty people in an upright position. After herding us into this wagon, two Gestapo men arrived with whips and beat us brutally until we fell on top of one another. Then they shoved an additional forty people onto the train. They continued to beat us and managed to push in more bodies until, finally, there were 140 of us. Then they closed the doors. It is hard to imagine what went on inside. Those who were lying down were unable to get up. It was impossible to even move a limb. We were in this train wagon for three days without food or water, without a breath of air, and without the possibility of relieving ourselves. There were those who lost their minds; others died standing up. At last, the train arrived at a station in Austria. Those who were still alive and able to breathe began to scream. We asked to be killed rather than be left to die a slow death. Those in charge of the train were apparently overcome by shame, and one of the Gestapo men asked what was going on. We told him that there were many dead on the train and others who were barely alive, that in those crowded conditions it was as if the flesh of the living was in a cooking pot on a high flame. They deigned to open the doors and ordered everyone out. Those who could, got out of the car. The dead were left inside. Then we were told that anyone who went back into the car would get food. I, and a few others, went back in. They did, in fact, give us bread and water. We counted the occupants of the train. Out of the 140, there were only thirty left who were alive and breathing. We continued on our way until we reached Mauthausen.

In Mauthausen, we were led off the train. The dead were buried, and the rest of us were taken to the showers. After we washed up, they took our clothes, leaving us naked.

They checked our entire bodies, including our mouths, to be sure no one was hiding money or gold. Then they gave us camp uniforms and led us to empty bunks where we were given hot soup. Several hundred people were crowded into one space. We had to sleep in this condition, too. By day we were forced to stand naked in the sun. Scores of people fainted every day; there were incidents of sunstroke. No medical help was offered. I remember one particular incident. At night we were forbidden to leave the bunk. One night I woke up, not knowing the hour, and needed to relieve myself. I decided to go outside. I knew this was a dangerous move, because people were sleeping on top of each other and there was simply no way to get out without stepping on someone. It was dark. When I began to move, there were shouts all around: "Why are you stepping on me?" After a difficult struggle, I managed to extricate myself from the mass of bodies and made my way to the outhouse. Before I had a chance to lower my pants, I was approached by the guard, a Spaniard with a heavy cane, who hit me in the head so hard that I bled. When I left the outhouse, I was covered with blood from head to toe and had no way of cleaning up. In addition, I was not totally conscious and couldn't find my way back. I roamed around for a while in this state. Luckily, one of the workers found me, cleaned up the blood, and led me back to my place.

13.

In Mauthausen clothes were distributed only to those who were going out to work. On the first day about 200 people were sent to the quarry, which was situated in a deep valley in the bowels of the earth. We had to go down 180 steps. A *Kapo*,[1] who was stationed at the bottom, ordered each one of us to take a stone weighing about twenty kilograms and carry it up. As soon as the first person, stone in hand, reached the top step, another *Kapo* kicked him. He fell on the man behind him, who fell on the next in line—and so on, so that we all rolled downward, our stones in hand. After such a day's work, at least twenty percent of us were killed. This is what it was like in Mauthausen. After two weeks, some people were selected and sent to work in factories. At this point, I was separated from my brother-in-law. I was sent to Sankt Valentin, and he was sent to Melk, both in Austria [subcamps of Mauthausen].

I arrived in Sankt Valentin in July 1944. We were given clothes and taken to huts in which the beds were arranged one on top of the other in four levels. We were each given our own spot. The next day we went to work in a large factory five kilometers from the camp that produced "Tiger" tanks. This factory, known as Nibelungenwerke, consisted of eleven huge buildings, each with 1,000 to 1,200 workers. The workers were a varied mixture, from many different nations: Yugoslavs, Germans, Italians, Poles, Czechs, and others. Those in charge were all German. Every one of us was assigned a particular task. I, for example, worked with a whetting machine. I had five such machines and was in charge of sharpening blades and other equipment. My superior was an older man, a German from Austria. The factory work was done in two shifts: the first one from 6:00 AM until 6:00 PM, and the second, from 6:00 PM until 6:00 AM. A total of about 25,000 workers were employed in this factory, which produced eleven Tiger tanks a day. There

---

[1] A *Kapo* was a prisoner who received special privileges for supervising (often cruelly) other prisoners.

were 2,000 inmates in our camp, about 500 of them Jewish. The Jews lived in one area, non-Jews in another. The food was more or less adequate, but discipline within the camp was very strict. For any minor infraction, there were beatings. The *Blockältester* [block elder] was a German called Fritz, and the *Stubenältester* [room elder] was a *Volksdeutscher* called Paweł.[1]

At one point, a man from Kraków approached me. He said he had one hundred dollars and wanted me to offer the German, Fritz, the dollars in exchange for food. I took this up with Fritz, who agreed to accept the money and, in return, he promised to provide the fellow from Kraków with an entire loaf of bread and a bowl of soup every day, and, on alternate days, some sausage. I, as the intermediary, would also receive a daily bowl of soup. This arrangement was to last for a month. When the month was up, I asked the fellow to give the hundred dollars to the German, but he refused. The *Blockältester* demanded to know the name of the Jew with the dollars. I was, of course, afraid to disclose his name, as Fritz was likely to kill him because he had refused to hand over the money. Those in charge decided to take me out to the courtyard where they beat me harshly, demanding that I reveal the name. I remained silent and didn't disclose anything, though they continued to beat me until my body was swollen from their blows. When they saw that it was no use, they decided to hang me in the bathtub. I realized I was likely to lose my life and told them that the man lived in Block 5. They went right to Block 5, but, fortunately for him, the fellow was at work and, for the time being, they merely searched his possessions. They checked his mattress and, to their delight, found the treasure. After this, they released me.

The work in Sankt Valentin continued from July 1944 to February 1945. There was a unit of the *Bombenkommando* [bomb squad] in the camp whose task it was to dismantle the bombs directed at us—by day by the American forces, and by night by the Russians. Only Germans and *Volksdeutsche* belonged to this unit. They received all sorts of privileges—permission to leave the camp, cigarettes, and better rations. One bright day, they went out, as usual, to deal with unexploded bombs. There was a sudden explosion, and the entire group was killed. The German authorities had to organize a new unit on the spot. This time, they were ordered by the Gestapo to recruit only Jews. They began to look for healthy, sturdy Jews. I had returned from a night's work and was asleep when the search began. They came to my block, woke me up, and announced that I was now a member of the *Bombenkommando*. I was to begin work immediately. Having no alternative, I set out with fifteen Jews, escorted by a Wehrmacht guard,[2] who instructed us in the work.

When I was in Sankt Valentin, there were usually two raids a day. At about twelve noon, American planes bombed the camp, and at twelve midnight, it was the turn of the Russian aircraft. In a whole year of bombardment, neither the factory nor the camp was hit. All of the bombs fell in the fields. It was our task to dismantle them. We walked

---

[1] The *Blockältester* [block elder] and *Stubenältester* [room elder] were prisoners chosen by the Germans to supervise other prisoners.
A *Volksdeutscher/Volksdeutsche*, though a citizen of Poland, was an ethnic German, who usually received better treatment than other Poles (often having signed a statement of loyalty to Germany).
[2] The Wehrmacht was the regular German army. Its members were usually considered to be less cruel than the SS or Gestapo.

around, and when we spotted a small mound of earth, we had to clear away the dirt carefully and dig until the bomb was uncovered. First, we cleared the surrounding area. Then, one of the Wehrmacht teams arrived and removed the detonator, at which point there was no longer any danger. I must note that on several occasions the Wehrmacht soldier explained to us why the bomb had not exploded. He said that a piece of cotton had been placed alongside the fuse to prevent an explosion. He pointed out that this was no doubt an act of sabotage by the factory workers. We continued in this job for about a month.

14.

One day, we returned from work at about six o'clock in the evening, expecting to get supper, as usual. But there was no one in the kitchen to provide the meal. It turned out that the chief cook had fled. The *Schutzhauptlagerführer* [SS chief camp commander], an SS man, who was informed immediately, ordered the assistant to be brought in—but he, too, had disappeared. Returning to his office, he found the door open; his pistol was missing, as were several packs of cigarettes. He ordered a lineup of all the inmates. When we were all assembled, he discovered that the *Lagerältester* [camp elder] was also gone, along with one of the Russians. The camp commander was enraged and began to shout and threaten that he would kill us all if they didn't return. The camp clerk, a racially pure Aryan, a prisoner who was a member of royalty, turned to him and said, "I warned you many times not to put too much trust in the filthy Poles." This clerk killed someone every day if he was displeased with that person's attire.

After a few days, the *Lagerältester* and the Russian were both found. The commandant gave the *Lagerältester* several sound slaps and said to the Russian, "Take a rope and hang yourself in the bathtub!" The next day, two *Volksdeutsche* led him to the tub, where they hung him from a rope.

For a reason I no longer remember, I was sent back to work in the factory. The managers claimed that they were unable to find anyone to do my job. A few days later, in March 1945, at exactly twelve noon, an alarm sounded in the camp. All the workers ran to the shelter. A few minutes later, the alarm was canceled, and we left the shelter. We were given lunch, all the while watching an aircraft that circled around the factory, leaving purple signs in the sky above every industrial building—five wheels were printed in each corner and a single wheel in the center. When we finished eating, the aircraft vanished, and we returned to work. A quarter of an hour later, there was another prolonged alert, and we returned to the shelter. We stayed there about three quarters of an hour until the "all clear" signal was given. When we emerged, we were shocked by what we saw. The entire factory was in ruins. Not a single building remained intact. Fires raged everywhere. We returned to the camp only to be greeted by the same scene— everything was bombed out, not a single structure was spared. We learned that this was the work of the American Air Force, which was determined to destroy both the factory and the camp.

Here I would like to mention those inmates of this camp who were from Działoszyce. If my memory is not deceiving me, the following individuals were there: Icek Rodał, Poldek Gertler, Moszek Klingberg, Szlama Dąbrowski, Abram Kac, Zalman Grześ, Chaim Klajner, who now lives in the United States, and I, the writer of these lines.

As I had always engaged in trading, this was an occupation I pursued in the camp as well. Thus, for example, I exchanged, among other things, bread for sausage. Icek Rodał once approached me and asked me to exchange some sausage for bread. Though he was very weak, he didn't want to eat unkosher food. I told him that he very much needed the sausage, that it would strengthen him. But he persisted. He would not agree to eat the sausage, though I tried hard to convince him. A few days after the conversation, he was beaten by the *Blockältester*. He stumbled, fell, and never got up again. We buried him in the camp.

Zalman Grześ met a similar fate. He was beaten brutally by his superiors. Too weak to withstand this treatment, he died in Sankt Valentin and was buried there. Poldek Gertler was transferred to Mauthausen, where he died. Chaim Klajner took sick and was sent to Mauthausen. He was liberated by the Americans and went on to the United States.

Now, back to our factory. After the Americans destroyed the entire operation, along with the camp we had lived in since July 1944, we had no place to sleep. Work was also interrupted as everything had been destroyed. We wandered around the camp, idle for several days. One day, the SS ordered us to empty all the storehouses and distribute food and blankets to everyone. We each received several loaves of bread, clothing, and blankets. Then there was a roll call, and we were informed that we had to leave the place and go to Ebensee [Mauthausen subcamp].

15.

The trip to Ebensee was not particularly difficult. At the end of March 1945, we were put in freight cars, and, in a civilized manner, taken to the village of Ebensee. This was not a work place but a giant camp accommodating 20,000 people. At Ebensee everyone was given forty grams of bread a day and, at lunch, half a liter of foul water known as "soup." Of course, with such nourishment, many died of starvation. Ebensee is located in Austria. The camp was situated in a wooded grove and surrounded by an electric fence. Its crematorium operated night and day but wasn't able to burn all the bodies. Bodies and body parts from other regions were sent to the ovens in this camp. A shipment of 4,000 people arrived every week, and as the population of the camp remained steady, at about 20,000, the number of weekly dead must have been 4,000.

I met Chaim Skrzypek, a brother-in-law of my Uncle Jankiel, in Ebensee. He was naked as on the day he was born. I offered him bread, and he rejected it; he no longer needed anything. I also found my-brother-in law, Motel Frajnd, and asked him about his brother, Jankiel. He told me that Jankiel had fallen into a pit at Melk from which he never came out alive.

At Ebensee, 2,000 people went to work every day as slave labor. We assembled at 4:00 AM, and at 6:00 AM, we headed toward Attnang-Puchheim [Mauthausen subcamp]. There was a large train station there that had been blown up along with the village. People from our camp were engaged in cleaning up the ruins and in repairing the train tracks. Since almost no food was provided in Ebensee, I decided to join that work force. I got up at 4:00 AM and went to the assembly point. At exactly 6:00 AM, we set out on foot to Attnang-Puchheim. I was to work on track repair. The work was arduous. Our supervisor, an Austrian, circulated among the workers and beat them with his whip to get them to work faster. We were hungry and looked in every corner and hole for a morsel of food.

One day, when our shift was over, as we were getting ready to go back to the camp at Ebensee, a Polish fellow from Warsaw by the name of Dąbrowski, whom I had met at Sankt Valentin, came over to me and told me to lick his hand, which had some grains of sugar on it. I did this gladly because sugar is a source of energy and strength. I understood from this that he was working in a place that had a supply of sugar. We got back to the camp at midnight, and I decided to work at Attnang-Puchheim again and to stay close to this Polish fellow Dąbrowski, who knew where there was sugar. Before leaving for work, I put on two long-sleeved shirts and a coat with many pockets. When I arrived at the assembly point, I stood next to Dąbrowski. About 2,000 of us set out. When we were assigned to the various workstations, I was included in the *Zuckerkommando* [sugar commando], along with Dąbrowski. We arrived at the spot and found a bombed-out train, each car filled with sacks of sugar. We were ordered to collect the sacks and bring them to a particular place. The SS men were guarding us. We were ordered not to allow anyone to touch the sugar. We, however, were allowed to eat as much as we could. All day long we gorged ourselves on sugar. We finished our shift and, in the evening, returned to Ebensee. All the people who had worked the previous day, as well, had brought along packs, which they filled with sugar. I, myself, filled my pockets, as well as the sleeves of the shirts I was wearing. At the gate, all the members of the *Zuckerkommando* were ordered to step out of the line. They were inspected, and their packs of sugar were confiscated. Only I, who had no pack, was allowed through without being inspected. I was the happiest person. I gave the friend who slept next to me a plate full of sugar. Then I also gave my brother-in-law, Motel, the sugar that was in one sleeve. In addition, I bartered some sugar for cigarettes. When I went to sleep, I put my treasure under my head. My friend who slept beside me couldn't control himself and stole my pants while I was asleep. He ate the sugar that was in the pockets and threw the pants in the latrine. In the morning, I woke up and discovered that I had no pants to wear. Then I learned that my closest friend had stolen them. I had already given him a plate full of sugar, but still he could not restrain himself and did what he did. Since I had more sugar, I was able to trade it for a pair of pants. From that day on, I no longer went to work, as everyone felt that the day of liberation was near.

On Thursday, May 3, 1945, there was a rumor that in the afternoon there would be a roll call of the entire camp and that the *Lagerführer* [camp commander] would order us to go into a vast underground shelter where we would stay until Sunday. The move to the shelter was undertaken to protect us, as the Americans were planning to bomb the entire camp. One of the SS men secretly informed the *Lagerführer* that the SS had placed explosives in the shelter, which they planned to detonate as soon as we were inside. After some deliberation, those in charge of the work force decided that as soon as we received the order to go down to the shelter, we would all rise up as one and declare that we did not want to be killed, come what may.

And this is what happened. That afternoon, there was a roll call of the entire camp. The *Schutzhauptlagerführer* made a speech and explained that as the war was about to end, the Americans were planning to bomb the camp, and he was, therefore, proposing that we all go to the underground shelter and wait there for the danger to pass. Then the strangest thing happened—for the first time in the history of the camps—we didn't comply. We all cried out, "We won't do it!" Immediately thereafter, the *Lagerführer* and his Ukrainian assistant left the camp. It was as if they were fleeing. The camp guards, who were SS men, disappeared somewhat later and were replaced by armed civilians.

On Shabes, at 10:00 AM, the first American tank arrived at Ebensee. As it crashed through the gate, all the guards vanished. Those inmates who still had some strength welcomed the tank and the soldiers with great elation, kissing the tank in their excitement. It is hard to describe the great joy that prevailed at that moment in Block 4, where I lived. The *Blockältester* and the *Stubenältester* were playing cards. It was almost lunchtime. All of a sudden, an inmate appeared, a fellow from Yugoslavia, and asked the *Stubenältester*, Paweł—who, earlier, in Sankt Valentin had hung the Russian officer—to come outside with him, He, of course, refused. We all got up and pushed him out. The Yugoslav beat him on the head, and he fell in a pool of blood. Thus began the punishment of those still in the camp whose record was not clean.

16.

I and several other Jews went to the American soldiers stationed in the camp and informed them that the underground shelter was mined and that it was essential that it be checked out carefully lest it explode and cause unnecessary deaths. They brought in an expert who checked out the shelter with appropriate caution. He found a quantity of explosives near the entrance that, if it had been set off, could have destroyed an entire city. And, indeed, this was the intention of the SS, even in their final moment, as they were retreating. The mine expert dismissed his crew and gradually neutralized the danger. The soldiers tied the *Lagerführer* to a tank and led him through the camp as a spectacle "to make them listen, take note, and perpetrate no further evil." We were also granted permission to beat him. Still, despite the joy that prevailed, I didn't forget that many people were lying in the bunks too exhausted to celebrate. As I still had some strength, I decided to leave camp and find food for these unfortunates. I headed for the closest village, seized a chicken from one of the farmyards, slaughtered it, and cooked soup, adding some potatoes to the dish. I served this to the sick and infirm, and they revived. Among them was Benjamin Goldberg from Miechów, who now lives in Haifa, and Szlama Dąbrowski, who died shortly thereafter in Ebensee, as well as several other friends whose names I don't remember. They all ate the soup, thanked me, and said I had restored their soul with this deed. The next day, the Americans brought a supply of food, mostly in cans. The starving crowd "snatched" the food and ingested such large quantities that many of them were sick. It is worth noting that, as a result, in the first week after liberation, about 3,000 people died at Ebensee. They were buried in the camp without being identified, their deaths unrecorded.

After a few days, I left the camp and went to Linz, Austria, with my brother-in-law, Motel. In Linz we learned about the *Bricha*, headed by a woman named Pesia Szereszewska who was arranging for transportation to Italy.[1] We joined this group. The trip to Italy was long and difficult as there were no trains. Thousands of people crowded the railway stations. But, thanks to the [Jewish] Brigade from Eretz Yisroel [Palestine],

---

[1] *Bricha* [escape] was a movement that aided survivors to illegally make their way to Palestine.

which was in charge, trains were arranged to transport us. Actually, in the eyes of the British, the entire operation was illegal. At the time, the British were not allowing Jewish immigration to Palestine, especially from among survivors of the camps. When we were finally en route, two Italians entered our car. We were afraid they would report to the British that the entire train was occupied by Jews heading for Palestine. When the train reached the station, soldiers from the Brigade came aboard and announced, in Italian, that the passengers on this train were tuberculosis patients being transported to a sanitarium in Italy, that this disease was highly contagious, and it was therefore dangerous to remain in that car. Hearing this, the Italians left immediately.

17.

We arrived in Modena, where the Brigade soldiers had arranged for us to stay until our date of departure. In the meanwhile, the British officer who governed the area learned our true destination. He met with Pesia Szereszewska, who was in charge of the camp, and tried to convince her to send us all back to our countries of origin. She, of course, would not agree. Then he turned directly to us and argued that it would be better if we would return to our homes. When he realized he would not succeed in persuading us, he announced that he would not hesitate to use force. At this point, Mrs. Szereszewska turned to him, weeping and tearful, addressing herself to his heart and conscience— which seemed to move him.

As a result, the British provided us with a train and permission to travel to Rome. We arrived in Rome and were assigned to Cinecittà—a camp for refugees and displaced persons.[1] From Rome we were transferred to Santa Maria di Bagni, where UNRRA [United Nations Relief and Rehabilitation Administration] provided us with food and clothing.

Here we were organized into several sections—one group was going to Israel, another would join family in the United States, and a third group was going back to Poland to search for surviving family members. My brother-in-law, Motel, was among the latter group. I set out for Norway, where I had an Uncle Benjamin, my mother's brother. I met my present wife, Miriam, there—like me an ember plucked from the fire. She, too, is a survivor—from Piotrków. We were married in Oslo.

After our marriage, we decided to go to Israel. In June 1949, we left Norway. At first, we settled in Givat Shaul, near Jerusalem. But, after awhile, the Jewish Agency disbanded the settlement. When I began to work at the Ministry of Welfare in Jerusalem, we became city dwellers. We now live in Ramat Gan. We have, thank God, a son and a daughter. The boy is named Shmuel for my father, of blessed memory; the girl is named for my mother, of blessed memory, Feige-Zipporah.

Thus do we carry on the tradition of our family, whose origins are in Działoszyce, in a new life here in our holy and ideal land.

Translated from the Hebrew by Roger Kaplan

---

[1] Cinecittà, a film studio built by Mussolini, was turned into a DP camp after the war.

In the Polish Underground (pp. 298–303)

Szlama Leszman (ben Jakób)

The lives of people on this earth are generally difficult; however, the lives of the Jews in Poland were incomparably more difficult even in normal times. And when World War II broke out, waves of hatred engulfed Europe, and the seeds of anti-Semitism found fertile soil in Poland, although the main thrust came from Nazi Germany. A very strong anti-Semitic movement blossomed in Poland. Polish workers, who officially opposed anti-Semitism, were not excluded. Jews, especially the progressive youth, were active in certain of the labor parties, the PPS [*Polska Partia Socjalistyczna*—Polish Socialist Party] and the PPR [*Polska Partia Robotnicza*—Polish Workers' Party] [Communist]. With the outbreak of World War II and the defeat of Poland, these same Jews began fleeing to the territories occupied by Russia. The idea of living under the Communist regime fascinated them, and they also saw this as an opportunity of making their dreams become a reality. I did not belong to those parties. Their thinking was strange to me, and I did not cross over the border from Poland to Russia. I remained in Poland and in Działoszyce, and here events began to unfold.

Influenced by my cousin, Szlama Leszman, who was a member of the Polish Socialist Party, PPS, I drew closer to this party, since the idea of engaging in underground activities against the occupying Nazis attracted me. This was in 1940, when the cruel and depressing decrees of the Germans were escalating from day to day. Jews were put into ghettos and marked with yellow patches. Dire poverty and widespread epidemics befell the Jews in the ghettos, who dwelt in dense, overcrowded, and abhorrent circumstances.

Equipped with Polish identification papers under the name of Władek Dobia, I began my underground activities around the area of Kraków. I worked together with my cousin, whose first and last name were exactly like mine. We were both blond, and in our appearance, we looked more like Aryans than Jews. We kept our distance from Działoszyce, since the locals knew me well, and I was accepted into the Socialist Party as a pure Polish Aryan. In this party we went through certain training that emphasized the use of light arms and materials of destruction. As I already mentioned, our activities were carried out around Kraków. I don't want to prolong and describe all our activities, as this is not my purpose at this time. I just want to describe the lives of the Jewish partisans in the Polish underground and the three times that I was saved from certain death. Only one for whom life is decreed and signed in heaven above will live. And I, myself, as I already mentioned, was saved from certain death three times.

Once in a while, when I got permission from the underground, I would visit my home. My entire family remained in the town—my parents, sisters, and brother. All who were dear to me were there—my extended family, uncles, aunts, and cousins. Most of them were young people, bubbling over with the joy of life. The town itself appeared to me like a beehive, noisy and abnormally overcrowded. People were living in every attic and basement. The refugees dwelt in each available corner, and people were placed in every hole. The emigration from the big cities, and especially from the territories annexed to the Third Reich,[1] was great, and everyone looked for a relative he could count on.

This is how all of those who had relatives there returned to Działoszyce. In the beginning, they thought it would be easier for them to find some sort of livelihood there. However, after being unable to make a living, they started selling off their possessions. For starters, ornaments and jewelry, then clothing, etc. The poverty was dire and was accompanied by malnutrition, and this brought about an escalation of illnesses. The town was transformed into a huge Jewish ghetto. No one could go in or out, and, as a result, worries of how to earn a living mounted. All of these conditions forced people to risk their lives and travel secretly to the nearby villages and farms to attempt some type of trading that would enable them to bring home some means of sustenance. People lost their lives on the roads to the villages when they encountered a German official or Polish police, whose primary activity was to capture such Jews.

I visited the town in the summer of 1942. I did not fathom that this would be the last time I would see my loved ones. Many rumors were widespread throughout the city. The worries gnawed at me, and who could predict the future? I still planned to save my family and to disperse them among the cells of the underground. To my misfortune, I didn't manage to do it. What I feared the most suddenly came to pass. On September 2,[2] at dawn, the Jews of Działoszyce were deported, and among them were my mother, father, and brother, of blessed memory. There remained in the city only about 2,000 dead, half of whom were buried alive in the ravine behind the cemetery. And this was the end of the Jewish town that had existed who knows how many generations. It passed away from life. I didn't have anyone to visit any more, no parents, no brothers or sisters. All of them I lost at once and forever. With a heavy heart, permeated with grief and sadness and feelings of revenge, I continued my activities in the Polish underground. A Jew posing as a Pole (in the underground they weren't aware of my Jewish origins) by the name of Władek Dobia.

In the first months after the deportations, my soul could not find peace, and once in a while, I would return to the Działoszyce area, and I even passed by there when it became dark. I searched for my loved ones. I thought that in spite of everything maybe someone had managed to escape. And when the Jews again started to reassemble in the town, I thought maybe, maybe, I would discover my relatives and take them with me. To my deep anguish, no one from my entire family remained alive in the town.

When we entered Działoszyce, we would pose as farmers, and sometimes, we would arrive on wagons so as not to draw attention to ourselves. And so it happened that on one of these visits, right after the second deportation, we passed by Działoszyce. No Jews were left there anymore. Every one of the few Jews who had regrouped in the town after surviving the first deportation had been killed by the Germans.

---

[1] Territories closest to Germany (The Third Reich) were incorporated into Germany proper, into a new province called Warthegau. Poles living in these territories (Jews among them) were forced out of their homes to make room for German families. Most of those expelled sought refuge in the German occupied area of Poland newly named the "General Government."

[2] While the *Aktion* began on September 2, the deportations occurred on September 3, 1942.

Not far from this large mass grave in the ravine behind the cemetery, an additional holy tomb was added by us two "Poles," Władek and Stefek. We left Działoszyce with sadness and sorrow in a wagon going up along the road that leads to Drożejowice. The road was filled with dirt, and due to the mud and the steepness of the hill, the horses were going slowly. We only managed to go a little further from the valley when we noticed, on the side of the road, a woman walking, wrapped in a sweater, walking and stumbling. After a fall, she would get up, continue walking, and again fall, and this would repeat itself. I got down from the wagon, went over to the woman, and in Polish, with a farmer's accent, asked her, "What's with you? Are you not feeling well?" I couldn't recognize her face at first, but the fright in her eyes told me everything. In front of us stood Pifa. I knew her for a long time as the saleslady from the fabric store. Her blond hair peeked through the scarf that covered her head, and she was trembling extensively. Without thinking too much, we hoisted her onto the wagon and continued on our way. The story that I heard from her I will never forget in my life. This has stayed with me all my days, in spite of the fact that I went through many hardships afterward.

She was among those who had been assembled at the time of the second deportation, and the Germans had taken them, as I already mentioned above—for the purpose of a final annihilation—to the ravine, to the open grave where they were all shot by a machine gun. She herself got hit with a bullet. The mass grave then got covered with earth. Meanwhile, night fell. It seems that she was lying on top, and being that she had only gotten wounded (the bullet entered through her mouth and exited under her chin), she came to after a while from her faint, shook the earth off from herself, and dragged herself out of the grave. And now, here she stood in front of us, wounded and bleeding. And this is how we discovered this woman who arose from the dead. In spite of the great danger, we brought her to the ghetto in Kraków, where she received treatment and lived. However, did she survive all the rest of her hardships, troubles, and sorrows during the two and a half years that the war continued? I wasn't able to discover whether her luck held out.

Very little of the underground's activities were of such strategic importance as to affect the course of the war. We limited ourselves to terrorist activities or sudden attacks on the SS or the Gestapo. The majority of the Poles didn't come in droves to the ranks of the underground. This was not a movement on a national scale. The loss of their liberty did not matter to the Polish nation as a whole. The Poles were accustomed to living under the rod. In addition to this, the Germans had implemented and were carrying out all that the anti-Semitic Poles had schemed to do in the depths of their hearts. Now, many of them could enjoy the abandoned possessions that were left in their hands after the Jews were driven away or put to death.

The underground activities continued their course. On the night of December 4, 1943, we bombed the steel railway in Płaszów that the German army used to transport military supplies to the Russian front. This was the most important mission, because we wanted to disrupt these supply lines, even if only for a few days. This same dark night, a battle broke out between us and the Germans. We lost four of our people, and my cousin and I were captured alive.

Of course, we were captured as members of the Polish underground. After the first beatings, we were brought to the well-known jail in Kraków on Montelupich Street.

There we were put into cells that were designated for those awaiting death. The question of when we would be executed depended only on when they would conclude their investigation. It should be known that the interrogations conducted by the Gestapo of prisoners who belonged to the underground fighting against the Germans wasn't a simple matter. Those interrogated had to go through such torture that even Ashmedai [the king of demons] could not even begin to imagine. For the duration of months, day in and day out, they took us from the Montelupich jail to be interrogated at the Gestapo headquarters that was located on Pomorska Street. In our defense, we claimed that we were not members of the underground at all and had absolutely no connection to them. All we had done was just steal some coal (this is what the prepared agreement in the underground was). And in spite of the beatings, tortures, and the constant hunger, I did not break down, and I did not reveal my identity or the identity of my friends in the underground. The results of these interrogations are apparent on my body to this very day.

I knew that my final verdict would be death. I just prayed that my stay would be short. It cannot be put into words, the emotions of one who is sentenced to die. The first few days are especially difficult. Thoughts of imminent death fill the brain without letup, not even for a fraction of a second. After that comes apathy to all one's surroundings, even to those cellmates who are sentenced to death like yourself. I was totally starving yet unable to swallow any food. What more could I expect in this situation? The interrogators were waiting for other convicted prisoners so that they could execute us all at one time.

On May 24, 1944, my cell opened, and my name was called. How I came down to the yard I do not know. I only remember that I found myself standing, the last one near the wall, my hands up and my knees trembling and leaning against the wall. This is how we stood for two and a half hours, until a car arrived. The women were ordered to go inside and bend down so that they couldn't be seen from the window. And they loaded us into the car, laying one on top of the other. Since I was the last one in, I was on top of the pile. The car moved and traveled through the streets of Kraków, which were familiar to me. They transferred us to the camp in Płaszów and took us up to the hill of Hujara Górka.[1]

Exactly at seven o'clock, I was ordered to go down and move forward to the ditch that was to be our grave, apparently my final resting place on this earth. I do not know what the thoughts of others who are sentenced to death are, but as for myself, I only know that one doesn't take stock of one's life in these last final minutes. Heat and choking in the throat and the blurring of all the senses—and the senses die even before the body does—one functions only from inner forces over which a person has no control.

Surrounded by the SS and the Ukrainians, led by the "*Hauptsturmführer*" [captain] the well-known Heinrich, we jumped into the ditch.[2] We started getting undressed, and Heinrich was going from one to the next and asking each one his profession. I was in the middle of disrobing when he came to me, and for some reason that until today I do not understand, I disclosed the fact that I was a Jew and that my trade was boot making. It is

---

[1] The hill [*górka*] was named for SS *Oberscharführer* [senior squad leader] Albert Hujar, an assistant to Amon Goeth.
[2] The head of the camp at Płaszów was *SS Hauptsturmführer* [captain] Amon Goeth. Perhaps Heinrich was the *SS Hauptscharführer* [master sergeant] Heinrich, a lower-ranking SS man.

strange that all through the years I had concealed my Jewish origins, since I operated in the Polish underground. And here, as I was standing at death's doorstep, in the last few seconds of my life, I divulged this secret that had been hidden within me until then. I believe that an inner drive that a person does not control dictates to him what to do in this critical moment. I wanted to die as a Jew. And here a miracle occurred. When Heinrich heard that I was a bootmaker, he told me to get out of the ditch. The fact is that this mistake saved my life. By profession I am a tailor, which in German is *Schäftenmacher*. But I didn't know how to say this in German, and at that moment, I told him *Stiefelmacher* (bootmaker). This is just a play on words, but here it was a game of life and death. The word *Stiefelmacher* was the thing that saved my life.

I was unable to climb out of the ditch by myself. A Ukrainian took hold of my arm and pulled me out into the car. After a few seconds, the sound of many weapons was heard, a command was given to fire, and thirty-five people were murdered. The only one that was saved was the *Stiefelmacher,* who was returned from the field of death to Helclów Street in Kraków, to the workshops of the Gestapo.

In these Gestapo workshops, all the very best Jewish craftsmen selected from Kraków were concentrated together, including seamstresses, tailors, shoemakers, stitchers, etc. They were busy producing orders for the Gestapo members and their families. This is where I was stationed, a blond lad swollen from hunger, beaten, and in shock, disoriented, with the look of a crazed man. For a number of hours, not even one person approached me, since they suspected that perhaps I was sent as a spy to see what was going on. It couldn't be otherwise, they thought to themselves, that a Polish gentile from the underground should now be revealed as a Jew. The roll offered to me by Mr. Jozek Szulimowicz, the only person who dared come close to me, couldn't find its way to my stomach, and despite the tremendous hunger I was suffering from, I could not swallow it. It got stuck in my throat. Only after some time, I tried swallowing some soup that remained in the pot. At dusk, Mr. Dawid Garten returned. He was the administrator of this division, a Jew who was a shoemaker from Kraków, and he asked me my trade. I told him, of course, that I was a tailor and not a bootmaker. And when the truth of the matter was revealed to the *Hauptsturmführer*, Mr. Dawid Garten put in much effort to train me as a bootmaker. And with this, he saved my life a second time.

I remained among these craftspeople about half a year. Slowly, slowly, the suspicions about me started lifting, and my appearance as a human being gradually returned. I worked during this time as a bootmaker. The Jews and their families who were on Helclów Street seemed to be, more or less, living under favorable circumstances in comparison to the people on the outside. The Kraków ghetto was liquidated, and thousands of the ghetto's citizens were killed and murdered on the spot. The largest concentration of Jews was in the Płaszów camp, which was truly hell on earth. During the time that I was in the workshop, it became clear to me that if I succeeded in establishing contact with the people in the PPS underground, they might make an effort to save me. However, my workmates' initial suspicions weren't yet totally alleviated, and they wouldn't allow me to go out to the city (understandably, even under guard), since I might run away. They did consent to take a letter from me and forward it to my Polish friends.

As is the custom of the underground, they assigned two lads to take me out of the workshop and whatever happened would happen. They took advantage of the Polish

nursing home that was located in the basement of a building at the side entrance of
Helclów Street, and here they made contact with me. I was again armed with a revolver
and bullets, and I started planning my escape. To my sorrow, this didn't happen.
Suspicion did its work. They revealed their doubts about me to the Germans who decided
to get rid of me. This time a Gestapo agent, dressed in civilian clothes, invited me to
accompany him. It seems as though he was pressed for time, and when we stood in front
of the exit gate on Montelupich Street, he asked an SS person for information about
whether people were being sent to the camp. When he received an affirmative answer, he
hurried to leave me in the care of the person who had given the information and left. And
sure enough, very early in the morning, they sent out a group of Poles to Auschwitz. I
joined them as a Pole. Actually this was the irony of my fate.

This happened during the summer of 1944. The Russian armies, after they had
succeeded in breaking through the eastern front, made rapid advances to the west. The
Auschwitz concentration camp was liquidated of its prisoners, and this is how I arrived,
after a long and arduous trip, filled with countless great sorrows and tribulations, on the
other side of the Flossenburg camp to the camp at Crawinkel, which was not far from
Buchenwald. This was a very special camp indeed. Special in that not a soul survived
who could stand as a witness to what actually took place there.

Thousands of people found their deaths daily, some by starvation, some from the
plague of typhus,[1] and some through the murderous Nazis. My luck was to contract
typhus. When I felt my temperature rising, I hurried to the hospital, even though I was
well aware that every three hours they emptied out the sick rooms. The patients who were
unconscious, while they were still alive, were thrown into the city dumpster. It is
realistically impossible to comprehend. Can a person actually believe such a phenomenon
in history, such incredibly unbelievable atrocities, sick people being thrown into the
garbage dump?

I presented myself to the Polish doctor who knew me as an activist in the
underground, and I appealed to him, "Save me, Doctor!" I cried. And immediately after
he accepted me into the sick room, I lost consciousness. I do not know what happened to
me after that, how long I was unconscious and how I overcame this condition, and,
generally, how I arrived at the shower in Buchenwald. All this was hidden from my
awareness.

I came to for a moment due to a stream of cold water in the shower at Buchenwald.
Somebody threw a blanket over me, and again I sank into a deep sleep. I was beset by
dreams and visions of many strange and unusual scenes. After them came momentary
flashes of full awareness and again the sinking into a hallucinatory sleep. This repeated
itself again and again. When I finally regained full consciousness, I was lying on a bed
and under the care of a German nurse—this was already after the end of the war.

I recovered from the typhus, but then its complicated aftermath began. My feet had
contracted polio. I will never forget the treatment and unyielding perseverance of the
people who cared for me in order to put me back on my feet. And so, my young body
gradually overcame the polio, and I slowly, slowly regained my health.

---

[1] The word typhus is used in Poland for both typhus (spotted fever) and typhoid fever. The more
common of these diseases was typhus, spread by lice, which was rampant in ghettos and camps.

My Return to Działoszyce

With stumbling feet and a weakened body I returned to my town, looking for my dear ones. I had just disembarked from the train, when an old lady warned me with these words, "Don't venture into town. Escape. They're killing Jews." I continued on a side road to our empty house. I didn't go in. People of the anti-Semitic AK (Armia Krajowa) [the Home Army] surrounded and grabbed me. Here my merits served me well, the merit of my being a member of the Polish underground. I was ordered to leave the town immediately. Otherwise, they threatened, the Poles would complete the murdering that the Germans had started. And then I left Działoszyce, it seems—forever.

Translated from the Hebrew by Rochel Semp

The Deportations from Działoszyce, Skalbmierz, and Miechów
(pp. 304–6)

Abraham Tennenbaum

Many, many years have passed since that sad Thursday, 21 Elul 5702—September 3, 1942, the day of the first deportation of Jews from the towns of Działoszyce, Skalbmierz, and Miechów.

Approximately 20,000 Jews lived at that time in these three towns, among them great scholars and well-known Zionists. Ever since the German occupation of the region of Miechów on September 7, 1939, the Jewish inhabitants suffered cruelly from the decrees of Hitler.

To get some idea of the condition of Jews at that time, it is worthwhile to note just what the murderers carried out in Działoszyce.

A group of five armed SS men violently broke into the home of the town rabbi, Reb Lejzor Epsztajn, a man in his sixties with a large family. The excuse was that a "comrade" of theirs had been shot and killed, and they needed to search for firearms (meaning gold). While they were searching, they subjected the rabbi and his family to murderous blows. Then they went into the neighboring room, which served as a *bes hamedresh*, and there they cut up the Torah books with their bayonets, ostensibly to see if there were any arms hidden in the books. After their search, they cut one of his [the rabbi's] side-locks and half of his beard sideways, turned his coat inside out, and dragged him around town for a few hours.

This happened on one uneventful day out of the 810 days that brought many other such, and even worse, "scenes." But despite all the sorrows and pains during those twenty-seven months, the German's beastly instincts could not destroy the Jewish hope of a better tomorrow, because everyone was still in his own home with his own family.

The situation changed, however, at the beginning of 1942. For the beasts and their cohorts, it was no longer enough to rob people of their fortunes, work people mercilessly, and beat innocent people in murderous rages. The smallest offense by a Jew caused him to be shot.

The people who carried out these atrocities and were responsible for them were the Germans: Beyerlein (the Gestapo chief), Schmidt, Kozak (a deputy), Ritinger, Facht, Dachauer, Schubert, Robert, and Bibi; the *Volksdeutsche* [Polish citizens who were ethnic Germans]: Kowalski, Mucha, and Górniak (the work overseer); and the Poles: Madejski, Kamerdyniak (policeman), and others.

Thus passed long dark days and weeks from January 1942 until August 25, 1942, the day on which Beyerlein and Schmidt decreed that by three o'clock the following morning, enormous sums of money and gold had to be contributed in all the towns.

This decree brought despair among the people, because it was not the first contribution demanded from the Jews. But by then a great many people understood the irony of their fate: it was a prologue to the "dance of demons."

"I will not pay for the murder of my wife and children." This was the sacred and sorrowful cry of my father, *hi"d* [may God avenge his blood]. When the officials came to our house to demand the sum he had been assessed to contribute, he took all his money and jewelry and sent them up in smoke.

While everyone became aware that the ground under their feet was burning, the *Judenrat* continued to carry out the German decrees in Miechów and in Działoszyce.

I witnessed the final terrible tragedy in Skalbmierz. On Wednesday, September 2, 1942, in the evening, there suddenly appeared in town dozens of light and heavy armored SS personnel and gendarmerie. Led by Kozak and Dachauer, hundreds of armed Polish policemen circled the town in a few minutes with a large group of *Junacy* (Polish youth work brigade) carrying spades and axes on their backs.

This horror scene brought together a mass of strangers and Polish neighbors, and thus our family also sought refuge in the house of our neighbor, Rogowski. A frightful silence reigned in the whole house. It was broken by the heart-rending cry of a small child, and by a brief burst of machinegun fire from the street. Later, we heard that two members of the *Judenrat* had been the victims of this shooting outburst: Szyja Moher and Aron Lida.

In the morning around 6:00 AM, the regular soldiers, together with the SS and the gendarmerie, who had been drinking all night long, ran to all the Jewish homes and gave orders that within fifteen minutes everyone should appear at the market square in the center of town, carrying no more than fifteen kilograms of bundles with them. The sick and the old, who could not get ready so quickly, were shot in their homes. By 7:00 AM, all Jews were assembled in the square. There the murderers left them standing for hours.

In the afternoon, the requisitioned farmers' wagons arrived to take the young people to Miechów. The old and the sick were led by the SS gang to the outskirts of the town and shot there. The same fate befell the Jews in Działoszyce, but at the hands of a different SS gang, under Schmidt and Beyerlein. There, too, thousands of sick or old people were led out into the valley outside of town and shot there.

When our transport from Skalbmierz reached Miechów about 8:00 PM on Thursday, we found the Jews from Działoszyce already there, and by early Friday morning, the people from Miechów had arrived and assembled in the square near the train station where we were. On Friday evening, the murderers again carried out their selection. Around 2,000 young and healthy men were separated out, and later, in groups of one hundred, they were sent to various work camps. Older and weaker people, as well as the women and children, in total about 18,000 people, were pushed by the sadistic German executioners with the butt ends of their guns and penned up in hermetically sealed wagons; and then they were taken to a place from where no one can ever return... ever...ever.

Translated from the Yiddish by Zulema Seligson

My Own Experience in the Holocaust (Pages 307–23)

Dov Bejski

For years I have tried to put the war years out of my mind, but in vain. I shall never forget the wise eyes of my father and the tears of my mother when they said farewell to me in that meadow near Miechów. And I shall always bear in mind the community of Działoszyce and how plain and simple Jews lived there, serving God and struggling for a living. They lived in their faith and perished as martyrs to hallow the Name of God. Let us always bear them in mind at least.

The Expulsion

Rumors had been spreading for several weeks, but when the survivors of the Wolbrom expulsion reached Działoszyce, it was clear that we were on the list and our time would come soon. And come it did. The town was cordoned off on September 1, 1942.

(About a year earlier, leaders of the Zionist youth movements had discussed the establishment of an underground resistance movement. They had been: the brothers Szlama and Chaim Kaczka, the brothers Josek and Szlama Szulimowicz, Moszek Kamelgarten, Eliasz Zylber, my brother Moshe, Masza Rożenek, Mordka Rożenek, Alter Frydman, and myself. But we never succeeded in obtaining arms in spite of all our efforts. There was no Polish underground in the region at the time, and so we had to bow before the situation.)

On September 2,[1] all Jews, men, women and children, were summoned to the market in the early hours of the morning. After a heart-rending night, they all appeared with their bundles on their backs. We were driven into line savagely by the SS men. Those unable to walk were told to get onto the waiting carts, and so the lines were emptied of old folk. The carts vanished, but not in the direction of the railway. Then the remainder were marched off in lines, families together, with the SS and Gestapo men on either side, their weapons ready.

On the Way to the Camps

We were all concentrated in a spacious meadow near Miechów, together with the Jews of Skalbmierz and the vicinity. Bread and water were supplied by the Jews of Miechów for their brethren. Next day, they joined us. Then we were ordered to line up again, and the young people capable of hard work were separated. My two brothers and I stood together. I took a last look at my parents and my sister Rachel, weeping and waving farewell. And 1500 to 2000 young men of Działoszyce, Skalbmierz, and the vicinity were marched off to the railway trucks and crushed together in them, while the train moved off.

This chapter is reprinted from pp. 25–31 of the English section of the original Działoszyce Yizkor Book, with minor changes.
[1] While the *Aktion* began on September 2, the deportations occurred on September 3, 1942.

At the Prokocim Camp

This camp was in a Kraków suburb, and in it, we found young men from the small surrounding villages and a few from our own town who warned us what to expect. In the morning, they marched to work while we were lined up and surrounded by Ukrainian guards (Russian prisoners-of-war who had agreed to join the Germans). The camp commander ordered us to hand over all our belongings of every kind, except for twenty-five *złoty* each. After this was done, he searched the pockets of one man at random, found some money, and shot him in the head. Now indeed everybody gave up whatever they had hidden away. That single casual murder by the camp commander, Müller, told us what we had to expect. But at first, it was possible to get in and out of the camp without difficulty, and many escaped. Some went back to Działoszyce when they heard that survivors were gathering there again. They were all exterminated two months later and buried in a common grave in the valley behind the Jewish cemetery. But we three used the opportunity to get away from the camp and, with the aid of a cousin, moved into a camp in Kobierzyńska Street in Kraków.

The Richard Strauch Firm

The men in this camp worked for the above firm, which was owned by Germans and engaged in drainage works; they built canals and embankments on the River Vistula. Jews from Działoszyce and Prosowice worked for them. The work was very hard, and conditions were very difficult. We had never done physical work before, but now we had to dig for thirteen to fourteen hours a day. It was very difficult at first, but in due course, we became excellent laborers. Like all our townsfolk in this camp, we were consumed with anxiety about the fate of our families. Our other concern was how to fill our stomachs. We received a chunk of bread in the morning and watery soup for lunch, but it was entirely insufficient for the work we were doing. Luckily, this camp and the one to which we were sent afterward were not surrounded with barbed wire or strictly guarded, though we were forbidden to leave the area. This did not prevent us from getting out, selling odds and ends we still had, and buying food the next day while at work. Indeed, we only knew what a labor camp really was when we were all concentrated at Płaszów.

At this time, winter 1942, there were still more than 20,000 Jews in the Kraków ghetto. They all tried to be productive workers in the workshops that were being hastily established. (Actually our own synagogue had been transformed into an excellent clothing factory a year earlier, working for the German army. But it made no difference when the expulsion orders were issued.)

We thought that our situation was very harsh; yet we had no idea of what lay in store for us when we were all concentrated in the camp on Jerozolimska Street in Płaszów.

The Płaszów Camp

When we were transferred there at the end of 1942 or early in 1943, the camp on the former cemetery grounds was being enlarged to facilitate the liquidation of the Kraków ghetto. We ourselves had to work outside, in the municipal gasworks for light and cooking. The camp arose at 4:00 AM, and after a long roll call, we were marched out under armed guard. All day long we had to shovel coal, returning in the evening under armed guard again. Those who worked outside were far better off than those in the camp, for we did not see the horrors perpetrated all day long as they did. At this period, the camp commander was Scharführer [squad leader] Müller. The regime was unbearable, the food was less than insufficient, the housing conditions were inhuman. Hundreds were crowded into one hut with three tiers of boards for sleeping. Upon our return, a second roll call was held, and we were usually sent off to work again, this time within the camp. We dragged broken headstones, rocks, boards, hut sections, etc., all at double time and under SS supervision. Anyone thought to be slack at work received dozens of lashes on his naked body. Some of our townsfolk and others were shot and killed.

The Kraków ghetto was liquidated on March 13, 1943, and all the Jews, both living and dead, were brought to Płaszów, since several thousand were shot during the *Aktion* [roundup and deportation] and their bodies were brought along. On our way back from the gasworks, we saw these bodies lying with the blood running into the roadway. The camp inmates buried them all in a huge collective grave, naturally first removing their bloodstained and bullet-riddled clothes. (When the camp was liquidated, these bodies were removed and burned, their gold teeth being first removed by German prisoners who were then in the camp. The fires burned for weeks on end.)

In February 1943, a new commander, SS Oberscharführer [Staff Sergeant] Amon Goeth, arrived with a large group of SS officers. Goeth was a giant with a rigid face. Upon his arrival, working conditions were worsened and hours lengthened, collective punishment became more frequent, torture and death were daily events. Groups passing one another on different work shifts reported the daily number killed. In any case, all outside work soon ceased, cutting off the possibility of contact with Polish workers who had sometimes slipped us a little food for those in the camp, in spite of orders. (If anyone was found with food, the whole group was punished, the mildest punishment being whipping with the victim counting each blow. I myself was lashed twenty-five times on several occasions and fifty times once. Of course, we had to go back to work immediately.) Being sent in a punishment squad on night work in the quarry within the camp was worse. Then there was a punishment cell of twenty inches by twenty inches where the prisoner had to stand twenty-four or forty-eight hours. Men were sometimes hung by the hands from a wall for several hours, being lowered only when they fainted. Cold water was then poured over them, and then they were sometimes hung afresh.

Any SS man could impose any of these punishments whenever he felt like it. On occasion a group returning from work would be shot either in whole or in part. Every inmate of Płaszów Camp faced death at any moment. I remember those cases in which all 20,000 inmates of the camp were summoned to watch public executions. Thus on Yom Kippur 1943, the SS men took fifty men from the barracks and shot them. Another time Engineer Krautwirt and a boy aged fifteen were publicly hung. The rope broke, and the boy fell but was hung again till he died. The engineer cut his wrists and was hung up bleeding. Meanwhile, SS men whipped the inmates to compel them to watch. I cannot understand to this day why not one of us broke the ranks in revolt, even knowing that it meant certain death on the spot.

When bread was found in an office worker's drawer, all the office workers were sent to the shooting range and killed.

Work outside stopped in the middle of 1943, and my group was put to building, road-making, building barracks, leveling ground, etc. in the camp, at the risk of our lives. When a German was seen approaching, a signal was given so that we should all speed up. Goeth would stand at his window with a rifle and shoot down Jews working outside his house. In the workshops established within the camps, the foremen and managers had to be able to state just where every man was at any moment. Otherwise, all those in the workshops were liable to receive collective punishment.

Food consisted of a portion of poor-quality bread and a tasteless drink called coffee twice a day, and a thin soup at noon and irregular intervals with occasional fat or some other spread. Naturally some of the hungry people tried to steal into the kitchen to beg for something more. For a while, Szyja Wdowiński worked there and would get something for those from Działoszyce who could reach him. Those caught were usually shot and killed on the spot. Work that was judged of poor quality was also punished, usually by death.

There was also a special camp prison that was usually kept for Jews who were caught with Aryan papers [attesting that the person was a non-Jew]. Few people came out alive. I remember how Goeth brought a Jew named Olmer of Miechów and set his dogs on him. They tore him to death.

Main danger spots were the kitchen, as already told, and the women's camp to which approach was absolutely forbidden. Still, men stole there to meet wives, sisters, and daughters and get news from them or give them some morsel of food, no matter how great the risk.

The punishments were: *group whipping* at special parades; *night work* after the exhausting regular day's work was over, when part or all the camp were called out to drag great loads up the hill to the new area, carrying great stones on their backs for two or three kilometers in rain and cold; or *the stone railway*, a narrow-gauge railway constructed from the camp quarry uphill for two kilometers. Little carriages were loaded with stones quarried by a punishment squad, to which I belonged for some time. The carriages were dragged along by teams of women who were harnessed to them and who had to pull them uphill. They wore wooden clogs that slipped in the mud or snow and had to work under all weather conditions.

In 1943, we practically all still had warm clothing, but this was taken away in 1944 and replaced by the familiar concentration camp garb of blue and grey stripes and thin material, so that we all suffered from the cold. There was a small enclave of Polish prisoners, and at times, there were more than 25,000 of them in the camp. Prisoners were also sent from Płaszów to Mauthausen, Flossenburg, Buchenwald, Auschwitz, Gross-Rosen, etc. There must have been 1000–1200 people from Działoszyce at this time.

Early in May 1944, we were all paraded and ordered to strip naked. An SS Hauptsturmführer [Captain] was there, reportedly named Blanke. All inmates were run before him, and he sent them right or left—to which side the old, weak and defective, or juvenile were sent. Two days later, they were separated, placed on goods wagons [boxcars], and joined by the 250 children in the camp. The outcry was stifled by SS guns pointed at us all, and loudspeakers played lullabies. More than 1200 adults and 250 children were taken to Auschwitz and the death chambers. One boy of twelve or thirteen named Jerzy Spiro managed to escape and hid all day in the cesspit at the latrine, with only his head uncovered. I do not know whether he survived the war.

Individuals were shot on the spot, anywhere and everywhere in the camp. For group executions, the victims were conducted to a special hill, called Hujar Hill, named after the executioner. There they had to prepare wood and lie down on it. Then they were shot and their bodies burned. Jews caught living as Aryans were killed there, also Polish partisans. These were brought direct in closed cars.

The Płaszów Camp was liquidated in mid-October 1944 when the Russians neared Kraków. With about 1200 others, I was taken to the Gross-Rosen Camp in Germany. About one hundred men were forced into each goods wagon, and the train journey took three days. There was no possibility of sitting, and we had food for less than a day. The only sanitary provision was a pail in each wagon, which was closed from the outside. The treatment in Gross-Rosen was even worse than in Płaszów, but after a short stay, we were transferred to a branch camp at Brinnlitz in Czechoslovakia where the Russians released us on May 8, 1945, at the end of the war.

We Jews of Działoszyce were only a small handful among the millions who were slain. Let us never forget them.

All Alone In Hiding (pp. 324–28)

Eliyahu Rozdział (Raziel)

I was a boy of eight when they announced the deportation of the Jews of Działoszyce by the Germans. We were six children in my parents' home when our parents gathered us together and we started our wanderings, traveling to farms in order to find a hiding place. The going was extremely difficult for us, since we were laden full of bundles and household items. After a march of very many hours, we arrived at a farmer's home near the village of Dębiany. It seems that it had been agreed beforehand between my father and this gentile there that he would give our entire family a hiding place. We were put into a pile of straw in the yard. In the beginning of our stay, the farmer and his wife supplied us with our needs and fed us all types of food. All of this was done, of course, for substantial sums of money. However, after a while, when our money ran out, the farmer demanded clothing and other things from us for the food.

After a certain time, news arrived from town that Jews were allowed to return. Of course, we also returned home. We found a ruined house without furniture and without essential household items. However, we somehow started to reorganize ourselves anew. And here again came a deportation, but this time, it was the last and final eviction…

Like the time before, we escaped again to one of the farms near Stradów, and there we hid at the home of a gentile for a very short time. The gentiles' fear of the Germans escalated and increased time after time, until it was very difficult to find a villager who would be willing to take us into his house, even for payment of money. Thus started our wanderings in open fields, in caves, in bundles of straw, and any other place where we could find some hiding place. In the beginning, we lived on the food that we bought from the gentiles in the area. My father was known in the entire area, since he was always traveling among the farmers as a wheat merchant, and the villagers had full confidence in him. I would like to note that the gentiles, due to the cessation of business during the war, were left owing my father large amounts of money, and they now wanted to cut off all contact with my father's family and close their eyes to our difficult predicament.

The first tragic incident happened on March 16, 1943, at night. My mother and five of us children sat in a hole two kilometers from the farm in Stradów. That evening my father had gone out, and with him, my eldest brother, to bring food from the farm. Suddenly, a few youths appeared, probably inhabitants of the farm, armed with weapons and, without notice or warning, started shooting into the hole at us. In this ambush, my mother and one of my brothers, of blessed memories, were killed. The minute this gang saw from afar that two people were approaching, they got scared and ran away. Their flight saved the rest of us remaining in the hole. Afterward, it became clear to us that these two people were my father and brother, who were returning from the farm. This incident took place late at night, and my father didn't even get to hear the cries of his children. The remaining children were taken out of the hole, and my mother and brother who had been shot were buried on the spot, right in this hole.

We immediately transferred to a more distant place and temporarily hid in wooded areas. So began our wanderings from one place to the next—and a place that served as a cover by night couldn't hide us by day—until another very bitter anguished day arrived for us. On Monday, July 18, 1943, when we emerged at dawn from our hiding place in the area of a village, we were surrounded by German soldiers and the Polish police. We ran away from the place, but they pursued us and caught my father, *z"l*, and two of my younger brothers and also my sister.

My eldest brother and I escaped in different directions. Neither of us knew about the other, and neither knew what had happened to the rest of the family.

That same evening, when each of us had run out of breath, we met by chance on the edge of the woods. This meeting was very emotional. We looked forward to the moment when we would find out what happened to our loved ones.

The next day in the evening, we went to the home of a gentile. Perhaps we might find out from him what had happened on this cursed day. We heard that our father with his three children were caught by the Germans and brought into Działoszyce. After a few more days, we heard that, together with other Jews caught hidden in farms owned by gentiles, they had been taken out to be murdered in the ravine behind the town.

The two of us continued our wanderings. During the day, we hid from the Germans, and at night, we would come out to look for food to break our fast. After much searching, we found a hiding place at a farm in Stradów, underneath a wheat granary of the property owners.

In this spot, we lay many months. One of us used to stealthily go out several times in the hours of darkness and bring back something to eat. In this manner, we were able to live, and we continued lying underneath this wheat granary.

The place was very low, about sixty centimeters under the wooden floor and the earth. We could not sit in any manner and also could not stand. We could only lie in one of three positions—on our backs, on our stomachs, or on our sides.

After we had been in hiding for a few months in this same place, my brother and I came out one evening, on May 11, 1944, to the center of Stradów to obtain food for a while. While we were walking, we met up with two lads from the village whom we had known for some time. When they saw us, they stopped to chat with us about this and that. Suddenly, two shots were fired from the side, and my eldest brother fell dead on the spot.

And so, I remained totally alone in this stormy and murderous world. Right after my brother was murdered, I ran into a yard and into an outhouse that was standing in the yard, and I sat down inside. I sat on the cover of the toilet, trembling and shivering from fright that they might catch me. Suddenly, the door opened, and a man asked me if I had seen someone running. From excitement I couldn't respond, and the man disappeared just the way he came. After I sat a quarter of an hour in this outhouse, I realized that this would be of no help. I went down into the latrine and exited from it on the other side. Crawling approximately 400 meters, I arrived at a burned-out barn that the farmers had filled with straw. I bore deeply into the straw, and I lay there the entire night and also the next day.

After a while people started coming into this yard and into the barn where I was lying. I heard them tossing bundles of straw from one place to another, hoping to find me. It seems that it was clear to them that I could not have escaped very far. The next day, at dusk, the farmer's wife went to take down bundles of hay for the morning, and while doing so, she bumped into my arm. I became frightened but decided to dig in deeper.

After a while, when it became dark, she appeared again, saw me, since I had come up to breathe some fresh air, and told me, "Now it is dark outside, and you can escape." I didn't reply, as though I did not exist. I lay in this place another two days without food or water. Actually, the only thing I ate was straw. And after two days, I left there at night and departed from this village.

I went out to a place still further and found a hiding place in an isolated bundle of straw in a field. I hid there during the daytime, and at night, I would go out to search for food. How did I do this? I would search for a yard in the village that didn't have a dog. I would enter the barn and suck out milk from a cow's udders. And for my provisions along the way, I took some of the mixture of potatoes and porridge in the pig's pen. This food would sour after several hours and was not fit for consumption in normal times even for pigs. However, having no choice, I ate it with much gusto, since nothing else came my way in those days.

As time passed by, I saw that I would not be able to continue in this manner any longer. I decided to return to the hiding spot under the wheat granary where I had hidden together with my brother a few months earlier.

That evening, I snuck into the shack of a gentile and took out a whole loaf of bread, weighing approximately six kilograms. I also took along two empty sacks and two single socks, and again I hid under the flooring of the granary.

I didn't know what was awaiting me and how long I would have to remain there; I was all alone, isolated from people and from God. Twice daily, the wagoners would come into this warehouse and would take seeds or hay for their horses. From the conversations that they would conduct among themselves, I was aware of what was happening in the world. Naturally, all this didn't help me much, since I had no one to exchange a word with regarding the situation.

I lay in this spot during many months and took small slices from the bread so that it would last me a longer time. During this time, the bread got covered with mold. In the beginning, I would take off small pieces of mold from the bread and bury them in a small hole that I dug near me. And this is how I saved food for the longer duration.

A long time elapsed, and the bread was completely gone. I had no other choice but to take out of the earth the moldy bread that I had previously buried. I shook it out well from the mold, and I ate the spoiled food, which actually tasted like a delicacy in my mouth.

I took apart the two socks that I had stolen, and they served as sewing threads. From the sacks, I sewed a shirt and pants, as best as I could, and with the remaining pieces I covered my feet. I did not possess shoes, and winter was outside the walls.

After a certain time, members of the AK [*Armia Krajowa*—Home Army] started living in the yard. Of course, I did not know what these armed people were all about. Only from the conversations that the wagoners conducted, I understood that these people were my enemies and that they posed great danger and threat to me.

During this time, I reached a situation where I had to go out of my hiding place and look for food; otherwise, I would have died from starvation. Thirst didn't bother me, since once a week, I would bring in water from the water they gave the cows in the area nearby.

The moment I went out in order to look for food and tried standing on my feet, I immediately fell backwards. It became clear that my legs were not responding to orders. After lying so long, my muscles had weakened, and, having no choice, I started crawling on all fours.

In an area further from the place, I found a field planted with beets for animals. I collected some of them. Some I ate on the spot, and the rest I shoved into my pants and started going back to my hiding place.

When I was about 200 meters from my place, I suddenly heard someone yelling, "Stop!" I remained motionless on the ground, and the AK people there started searching the entire area with flashlights, looking for me.

This is how I lay for several hours. After that, I turned around and started to crawl in the opposite direction from my hiding place. I arrived at a road and found two sticks that helped me walk and distance myself from the pursuers until I arrived at a haystack. For approximately two weeks, I hid there, and with me were the beets that I had collected in the field.

The winter started tormenting me, and the cold became very intense. Many Germans started circulating in the area, searching for partisans who were situated in the nearby woods. This restricted my movements even more. During the winter, my feet froze due to the extreme cold. The possibility of moving to look for food in order to combat my starvation was next to impossible. In this condition, without any possibilities and the constant starvation, I noticed that the army front was approaching closer to the area.

*

On Friday, January 12, 1945, many airplanes appeared in the sky, and long lines of disorganized German soldiers, some even without carrying arms, were running away toward the west. The big retreat of the Germans had begun.

That day the area I was in got shelled by machine guns of the German army and also bombed by Russian planes. Of course, I myself had no idea what world I was in, and I didn't understand anything of what was happening in the area around me.

The next day, Shabes, everything quieted down. None of the soldiers nor anyone else could be seen.

Sunday morning, a day of rest for the gentiles, the people from the area flocked to their local churches in the nearby village. Suddenly, I noticed that on the nearby road there were rows and rows of soldiers, horses dragging canons, and so on, on all the roads and side roads. At first I could not distinguish who the marching soldiers were, and, instinctively, I picked up my feet and, with the support of the sticks, staggered as I tried to distance myself from the place that slowly, slowly became filled with a large army.

At a certain moment, I sensed that a few hundred meters away, I was being followed by two soldiers accompanied by a gentile whom I knew well from the area. The gentile yelled at me from afar that I shouldn't run away, that these were Russian soldiers and, coincidentally, Jewish as well. He tried to explain to me that these soldiers wanted to help me. To start with, I didn't believe him, with my bitter previous experiences, and I continued to further myself from them. However, when my strength left me, and they came closer to me, the soldiers picked me up in their arms and brought me to the home of the farmer. To my great surprise, the farmer treated me in an excellent manner, fed me the best foods, and even offered me clothing to wear. I couldn't converse with these soldiers, since they didn't know any Yiddish, and I couldn't speak Russian. The conversations between us were carried on through the gentile who was somewhat familiar with Russian.

The soldiers suggested that I join them. They explained that their unit had its own hospital where they would restore me to health and meet all my needs. Since I had no other options, I agreed to go with them.

When we arrived at the point where they were supposed to find their military unit, it became clear that this unit had already left. So they turned me over to a Jewish army doctor who, to my good fortune, also spoke some Yiddish.

In the evening, the doctor sat down with me and listened to all of the bitter episodes, trials, tribulations, and the torturous journeys that I had experienced throughout the war; a lone youth who lived in constant fear and trepidation from his persecutors and tried to hide in different places. The doctor saw to my complete recovery. The people in the sanitarium took me and washed me off many, many times, again and again, until I was cleansed from all the insects and lice that had adhered to my body in the places of dirt and filth where I had lain for approximately the past two and a half years.

Afterward, they dressed me in an army uniform and took me along with them. However, I couldn't withstand the hardships of this journey as they advanced, and I was forced to take leave of them.

Eventually, I arrived at my town of Działoszyce. There I met some local Jews who had gathered from all sorts of hiding areas. I stayed in the town for two days but could not find a resting place. I started wandering from town to town and from village to village with the slim hope that I would find someone from my family.

While traveling thus, I arrived at a small German town in Lower Silesia. Once, while I was wandering in the town, rows of Russians stopped me and took me into their unit.

After a short interrogation, they verified who I was, and the commander of the place suggested that I stay with them as long as I wished.

I stayed with them a good few months; one day I heard, that in the nearby city of Gliwice, Jews were assembling to go to Eretz Yisroel.

I notified the commander immediately that I had decided to leave this place and go to my homeland, Eretz Yisroel. He gave instructions to supply me with clothing and also to give me some money for the journey's expenses.

I traveled to Gliwice and joined a group of youths making *aliye* [immigration], and, together with them, I went to Eretz Yisroel at the end of 1945. In Eretz Yisroel I entered Kibbutz Gazit, which was in the Lower Galilee, and there I built my stable and permanent home.

Translated from the Hebrew by Rochel Semp

Memories (pp. 329–35)

David (Gustav) Rajzfeld

Before I unfurl my memories of the town of Działoszyce, I would like to relate a story that happened to me in 1942. It was when the Polish General Anders arrived, together with his soldiers, in the Palestine of that time.[1] I had the opportunity to meet in a coffee shop with the Polish consul, Mr. Henryk Rozmarin. When I arrived at the appointed hour, I encountered a stranger who was with him. When this man saw me, he got up from his seat and asked me if, by chance, my name was Rajzfeld, from Działoszyce. He declared on the spot that he had never seen me before in his life and he was sure that I had never seen him either. However, I looked very much like my father, of blessed memory, and the speaker said his father knew my father, *z"l*, very well.

This man was a Catholic from the Działoszyce region by the name of Osuchowski and was from the area around Pierocice, approximately three or four kilometers from the town. This gentile was very happy to meet a person from the vicinity of his hometown and was especially happy to find a person here whose father had been a friend and advisor to his father as well as being this person's friend. The village of Pierocice had been the estate of his forefathers, who were of noble descent. In the presence of Consul Rozmarin, Osuchowski expressed his amazement, and this is what he said:

> In Poland, I was a member of the Endecja, the party of Roman Dmowski's point of view, and the publisher of many nationalist newspapers.[2] I was also an ideologue of the economic war against the Jews, and I was successful to a certain extent in removing Jews from businesses in such areas as wheat, meat, poultry, eggs, milk, and milk products, businesses that were the main staples of livelihood for the Jews, in general, and especially in the smaller towns and villages.

However, Osuchowski stressed that he had never met a Jew like Rajzfeld and never knew any other in his life—such a decent and honest person who behaved justly in all areas of his life. One could not find many others like him.

Consul Rozmarin was very surprised that such a prominent person, with such an influential and high-ranking position in the economic life of Poland, who was so respected and held in such high esteem by the Polish government in London, and one whom so many admired, that this individual should respond in this manner to a Jew living in Eretz Yisroel.

After this initial meeting, I met many more times with Osuchowski during his stay in the Land of Israel. He used to come to my house very frequently, and I entertained the

---

[1] When Germany attacked the Soviet Union in 1941, Polish so-called political prisoners who had been deported from eastern Poland to Siberia between 1939 and 1941 (under Soviet occupation) were released to form an army under Polish General Władysław Anders. This army, known as the Anders Army, left the Soviet Union and came to the Middle East, including Palestine, before becoming part of the British Eighth Army and fighting in Italy.

[2] *Endecja* is derived from the abbreviation of the National Democratic Party [ND-eks], an anti-Semitic party in prewar Poland. Roman Dmowski was the co-founder.

hope that through his connections with Poland and with the village of Pierocice, I might succeed in making contact with my father, brother, and sisters. During the war years, they had come, together with their families, numbering approximately thirty persons, to my father's house in Działoszyce.

To my regret, it is difficult today to ascertain whether Osuchowski succeeded in doing anything on behalf of my family. But the thing he used to emphasize at every opportunity was that since I was the son of Rajzfeld, whom he had known since his youth and who was close to and respected by his parents, this awakened in his heart a degree of closeness toward me as well, and that is why he tried to visit me frequently and also to help me out in any way he could.

And now I will try to refresh my memories of the impoverished town of Działoszyce. I knew almost all of its Jewish inhabitants, beginning in the year 1897, about fifteen to eighteen years before World War I.

I was familiar and knew every street and alleyway; I knew each house, who it belonged to and who lived in it. I am trying to go back to a period that was fifty years ago and more and to compare the present with the past. I recall my good friends with whom I studied, together with whom I went through the different phases in the *kheyder*s, and also the teachers. I am reminded of the people who prayed, some in the *bes hamedresh* [house of prayer] and others in the *beysakneses* [synagogue]. I remember the *shtiblekh* [small Hasidic houses of prayer] of all the many and varied courts of the different *rebbe*s, as well as the Hasidim who used to come during the winter nights to the *bes hamedresh* to learn and teach their students free of charge—which means, to give them a lesson in Talmud.

Until this day I can hear their voices and the singsong of those learning and the pointed arguments of those debating a topic on the Talmud. It is not my intent to single out the praises of the Jews of Działoszyce. After all, that is where I was raised. I am only trying to point out the Jewish experience that existed in those days.

All of the heads of households that I mentioned were modest, honest, and friendly; all of them without any exception, the rich and the poor. What always surprised me was the character and quality of the synagogue in Działoszyce. The building of the synagogue was big and very beautiful looking, and in it were many artistic drawings that had been drawn by a professional artist, such as the pictures of the twelve signs of the Zodiac, the twelve tribes of Israel, the *vitrage* [stained glass], etc. Generally, in this synagogue, only the "common" people prayed: butchers, shoemakers, horse traders, and others.

The higher class of householders prayed in the *bes hamedresh* that was located right near the synagogue. The wealthier people and also the Hasidim prayed in their own *shtibl* [small Hasidic house of prayer] to which they belonged. The *shtibl* was mainly housed in a small room, without bathroom facilities, without hygienic or sanitary accommodations. Not so the synagogue. There, everything was prepared with proper accommodations in the finest manner.

More than once I asked one of the elder congregants, "By whom and when was this beautiful synagogue built?" And no one knew the correct answer to the question. However, one can be certain that this was one of the most beautifully decorated synagogues.

In the same vicinity of the synagogue and the *bes hamedresh* was also a building that contained the *mikve* [ritual bath] and the steam bath. On each Friday, on a weekly basis, most of the men in town would congregate there. I would like to portray the scene in the steam bath. Here no one was embarrassed to disrobe in public, and they would "revive their souls" with a brush and a pail. The brush's purpose was to kill two birds at the same time: to cleanse the body and also to beat it. All the while, the steam that spewed out from the giant stove that was constantly burning flowed generously. The pail served both to pour water on the steam and also to cool off the body after the warm brushing. After all the beating and the sweating and cooling with the pail of water, the men went down and immersed themselves in the cool *mikve* waters. This was truly a revival of the soul.

The cantor of the synagogue also lived in the same building. He was a Jew who was a liturgical musician and whose father, grandfather, and great-grandfather had been cantors. The cantor's sons constituted the choir. The town's choir also included the cantor and the well-known singer Ignacy Mann, who later appeared in Polish and Czech operas. He was born in Działoszyce, and the cantor Reb Szyja Śpiewak was the one who discovered his great talent and sent him into the wide world to learn singing and to become a cantor. In the same house also lived the *gabe* [treasurer/trustee] and *shames* [sexton], and along with them, the tombstone engraver, old Moszele, who was assumed to be at least one hundred years old.

*

I left Działoszyce to go to Łódź even before World War I. For a short while during the war, I would return to the town; however, generally, I didn't have ongoing contact with the town. I used to go to the town only at certain times to visit the gravesite of my mother, *z"l*, and during these infrequent opportunities, I came to realize how much the situation of its Jews had deteriorated.

During my visits to the cemetery, my father, *z"l*, used to point out several graves of my forefathers that were near my mother's grave. One could barely decipher the inscriptions on these tombstones. According to estimates, they must have been standing there a few hundred years in the cemetery. My father also indicated that he had prepared a plot for himself near my mother's burial place. He used to sigh deeply and say, "I don't believe any of my offspring will continue to do so."

As I had mentioned, the town had totally deteriorated. We tried with all our might to convince my father to pick himself up and come with us to Łódź. He wouldn't hear of it, since he felt that his responsibility was to stay in Działoszyce so that he could give support, in a spiritual and material sense, to the Jews in decline. He was attached to his usual place in the *bes hamedresh* that he had inherited from his grandfather's grandfather. All in all, he was very connected in mind, body, and soul to this town and its people.

At a later period, my brother Karol purchased large parcels of fruit-bearing orchards in the [British] Mandate of Palestine. His plan was to get our father—who was a very experienced farmer and also served as an advisor to land owners in the area with farming problems—to change his mind and be willing to come with us to the Land of Israel. Finally, finally, he consented.

When the idea took hold, my father started taking the first steps to make this plan materialize, for instance, selling the house that he had built on the property of his father. (On this land were the homes of his father's forefathers in which they had lived and had established splendid beautiful families). Suddenly, on a certain night, my father saw his deceased father in a dream (he couldn't remember any similar episode in which he had dreamt about his father), appearing before him as a young man full of energy and demanding that he not take this step of abandoning the place of his ancestors. He got up from his sleep in the morning, frightened, agitated, and nervous from this sudden vision. When he could not find any explanation or hint about this strange dream, my father turned to the local rabbi and to his [Hasidic] *rebbe* to ask their advice and counsel. Their advice was to fulfill his obligations to his deceased father and stay in Działoszyce. And so, to my great anguish, my father was shot and murdered, when he was about eighty-one years old, in the ravine near Działoszyce. The German murderers killed him together with the rabbi of the town, along with the elders of the Jewish community.

*

These are the memories that I actually remember from Działoszyce. However, at the start of the horrible war, when the Germans came closer to Łódź, where I lived, the population heard the false Polish propaganda that the Polish army's planes were bombing Berlin. On the fifth day of the war, they announced a call and warning over the radio. Since the Germans were nearing Łódź, all the men who were supposed to serve in the army were ordered to report to their units encamped along the road to Warsaw. I also heeded this command and took along my eldest son on this journey of wandering, since I was afraid to leave him in the area being invaded by the Germans. Also wandering together with me until we arrived in Lwów was my brother Janek and my brother-in law. We found that the Russian army was already there.[1]

In Lwów, I was able to make contact with my wife and daughter, who had remained in Łódź and who had continued to run the factory and my business there in my absence. My single goal was to return as soon as possible to Łódź to my family and to remain together with them in these difficult times ahead.

My wife, as well as my senior office staff, tried to discourage me from fulfilling this idea. Their reasoning was very simple. About one hundred Polish *Volksdeutsche* [ethnic Germans] worked in the factory, and it was difficult to foresee their reaction to my return to Łódź—in spite of the good relations that had always existed between them and me. They therefore expressed their opinion (which coincided with my son's, who was together with me in Lwów) that it would be best that we try in any possible way to reach Romania and from there to find a means of saving them as well.

I took their advice, and in December 1939, I was able to cross over the border to Romania. From there I made contact with my family in Poland, with my brother Karol, who lived in the Land of Israel, and my brother who was younger than he, Judka, and with my sister Ruchel and her family, who had settled a few years before the war in the Land of Israel.

As I mentioned, I arrived with my son in Romania, and from Chernovitz, I made contact through letters with my wife and daughter. As a result, I received a letter from my home in response, and in it was a true and vivid description of the events they were

---

[1] As a result of the secret Molotov-Ribbentrop agreement, the Soviets invaded eastern Poland on September 17, 1939, and occupied Lwów [now Lviv, Ukraine] by September 22.

experiencing during that time. Using the best of the educational talents with which she had been blessed, my daughter wrote as follows:

In the month of January 1940, I was forced to leave Łódź because the Germans established a ghetto for the Jews, which was situated in the predominantly Jewish area of Łódź. We were afraid that this fate would befall us as well, and therefore Mother decided to escape to Warsaw. At that time Warsaw didn't have a ghetto yet, and we were hopeful that we could obtain documents for us to leave Poland. Our cash and jewelry, which we had given to our Catholic housekeeper, were lost, since the Germans had searched her on the road and took everything away.

In Warsaw we were greeted by our agent, Kagan, who took us into his spacious apartment. Also living there at the time was Munia Kwiat with his wife and children, all from the Rotenberg family from the side of my mother, z"l. Although it was difficult to obtain food, we somehow managed. All our efforts to obtain passports and exit permits amounted to nothing. Our only hope is that you will send us, from Romania or Palestine, the formal documents that are necessary so that we can leave Poland and join you.

My daughter wrote further:

During March 1940, a man by the name of Dudi Król arrived from the Land of Israel and brought along with him twenty certificates and train tickets to take us to Trieste. This had been arranged by Mr. Weinberg from the Wagonlit Company [travel agency]. You can well imagine the great happiness and impact that this knowledge made on our family, that we had obtained certificates on their behalf. We informed the entire family that we were in possession of certificates and train tickets for them to Trieste and that there was a man waiting here who is being paid to take care of these arrangements and that everyone is to come to Warsaw. Immediately, they came to us—Uncle Janek with his family, Uncle Mietek with his family, Aunt Róża with her daughters and sons-in-law. They arrived with great expectations for the designated moment to leave cursed Poland.

To my great regret, just then, Grandmother became ill, and Mother was compelled to delay the trip. Meanwhile, the international relations between Italy and the Allies had deteriorated, and it was not possible to make the trip to Trieste. And here another incident which was even worse took place: Mr. Weinberg had been in touch with a Gestapo agent and had given him a substantial sum of money in order for him to accompany us on our journey to Trieste. But when he was informed about this change of plans, he threatened us and extorted all the money we still had with us. Dear Father! We then lost all our hopes of ever being able to escape this hell, and Uncles Janek and Mietek took us to Działoszyce. So then the entire family left—all those who were prepared for the journey—for Działoszyce, to our grandfather. They thought that it would be easier and more secure to live through these difficult times there.

My aunts, Grandfather's daughters—Róża, Szyfra, and Sima—together with their families, went to live with Grandfather and some of them with neighbors. Mother and I took a room—if you can call it that—as second boarders with a poor family. During that time very many Jews arrived in the town, those who were escaping from the ghettos in the large cities, and this caused terrible crowding in living accommodations, and the sufferings were inhuman.

My daughter describes in her letter:

The town of Działoszyce made a depressing impression on me, what with its dirty alleyways, houses, and shacks that seemed to be falling apart, and the complete lack of basic hygienic facilities and accommodations. They were without water, without bathrooms, and without toilets in their apartments. The poverty and primitiveness that was etched on the faces of the inhabitants seemed inconsistent with the fact that you, my dear father, were born and raised in this place. Your aristocratic bearing, your education and knowledge, didn't make it possible to believe that your origins indeed are from this place.

Dear Father! When I am lying on my makeshift bed at night and cannot fall asleep, whether it is because of the hunger pangs that I am suffering or due to the thoughts that are disturbing me—because in my imagination I see you sometimes as a flying eagle and on your shoulders is perched my brother, Alfred. And then I get the disturbing thought: Why aren't my mother and I sitting, like Alfred, under your wings—are you not supposed to protect us as well? Dear Father! The way I see it in Działoszyce, the darkness and grayness, because of the rain, seems like a curse. It seems that in this place the sun never shines. I'm sure that you don't recall any longer the foul dirt and mud in the streets and the great darkness in the alleyways. We don't have anything with which to heat our small room; nor do we own any warm clothing that can keep us warm in this bitter cold. My shoes are torn and worn, and although Grandfather promised to give them to the shoemaker, who is an acquaintance of his, to put on new soles—this is one of the big luxuries in Działoszyce—in the end, they didn't mend my torn shoes. I am lying here and listening to my mother's deep sighs in her sleep. Most of the time she dreams about you and about her son, Alfred. And to be truthful, she does not reveal her anxieties in front of me. I hear how in the next room the rain is dripping, drop after drop, into the room, and I am thinking that very soon the rain will seep into our room as well and will reach my bed. During these moments, I bring forth in my imagination the beautiful mansion of Uncle Król in Łódź and the landscaped garden in the house's yard that grew grapes, pears, and tropical fruits that are very rare in the cold country of Poland. On the other side of the garden was the modern factory, and in it were employed several hundred employees, officials, and clerks. Everyone knew in Łódź that the factory belonging to Uncle Król was one of the most modern establishments in Europe. Not only among the Jewish business people but also among the German enterprises, this establishment was known as one of the biggest manufacturers of silk in Łódź. I can still see the two erect officers dressed in uniforms standing on either side of the entrance to the two gates, two men with very personable appearances, dressed spotlessly and shining till the last button. They used to check with Uncle about anyone who wanted to gain entrance, and only after he gave permission would they allow the person into the mansion. And now I am in a forsaken room in which the rain is coming in through the roof and the cold seeps into my bones. So the situation is very sad and the winter very harsh. Only thanks to Uncles Mietek and Janek, who support us and share with us each piece of bread, do we continue to exist, because otherwise we certainly could not survive. Don't take this, dear Father, as a reproach that you went away and left us alone and destitute. I know that this is the hand of Fate. And I am certain and sure that if only you could, you would have returned to us—since all your wanderings were thought and reasoned out in order to save us. What I wrote above were only impulsive reactions to my dreams, a weakness that a person feels when one is suffering inhumanely and without any solutions.

And here among all these dark happenings taking place, the sun rose a little for me. In these darkened days I met a young man, and so that this shouldn't sound so strange, he is of German culture, since when he was still a young boy, his father took him with him to Germany. There he studied, grew up, and obtained a university degree and only by chance came back during this war to Działoszyce. And this is how I got to know him, and we became soul mates. His name is Jakób Nifkier, and I could write very much about him. Don't make fun of me, dear Father; I believe that mutual love is binding us together. Even though I'm aware that I'm only sixteen and a half years old, this short period of the war has added to all of us, including myself, another few years of experience and maturity. And what I expressed with my poor lips, that we're in love with each other, is not a figment of a childish imagination or self-deception but a simple and real fact. This young man invited me very frequently to visit with his family. And it is interesting to note that in spite of the foul dirt and the mud, and in spite of the dilapidated houses that look as though they are about to collapse, there existed in this family's home a most joyful atmosphere. I started liking not only Jakób but also his surroundings. We have decided to get married. However, this decision was difficult for me to make without your consent and without your physical presence.

Father! Believe me. My talents are insufficient to express the conflicting feelings that I went through in order for me to take this step, to march onto the path of a future life without you and without your accompanying blessings. But as you are well aware, no one can predict what is awaiting them and what tomorrow will bring. For only this reason I have decided, with the consent of my beloved mother and the agreement of my dear grandfather and the other members of the family, to take this very step. And I am very happy that I have chosen such a wonderful partner—honest and decent, a cultured person. I am certain that if you would get to know him up close, you would agree with me and my decision, and you would get to love him like a father loves his son.

My daughter continued further:

In the meantime and during this time, this horrible Shoah descended on the Jews in Działoszyce. The murderous Nazis started to act and, on a nice day, gathered the elders of the town, including the local rabbi and all the prominent citizens—among them also dear Grandfather—and in a most brutal, cruel manner murdered them all in a place that is called the "ravine." It is not my intention to describe and cry here over this horrible scene and the feelings that this murderous action evoked in us all. We also knew that the remaining Jews in Działoszyce would be liquidated in the same manner. The motto became: "Every one should find their own way to save themselves according to their own possibilities and understandings."

After a short while, it was decided at a family meeting with my husband, Jakób, together with my beloved mother, that we escape and hide in one of the villages until this wrath blows over, in other words, until the final deportation. And so we wandered from village to village and from one farmer to the next, constantly accompanied by the combined fear of the Germans and the Poles. Our situation got worse and more critical by the threat posed by the Polish citizens, and in the end, we were forced to return to Działoszyce. To our grief and dismay, we found an empty town. No Jew was left in Działoszyce. Under these circumstances, we could not stay on in the town and decided to wander further. This is how we wandered and got farther away until, on a clear day, we arrived in Kraków. My husband got taken to a labor camp in the vicinity of Kraków, and I, together with my husband's niece, managed to get Aryan documents. In Kraków I tried to establish contact with Mother and the entire family. But to my great disappointment, I could not find their dwelling places, and I didn't know where to search for them. I succeeded in finding Uncle Janek, who was mourning the death of his wife, who had died a natural death. I found Uncle Mietek, as well, and neither of them knew where the Germans had taken their children. I was very careful and cautious not to meet with the uncles too frequently so that people would not notice that I was Jewish. And in the meantime, everyone was smiling at me and behaving nicely toward me because I am pretty and developed like a real woman. The German murderers also follow me, smile at me, and want to get to know me better, since they are sure that I am a German or else a Swedish woman.

For all these reasons, it makes my going out into the street very difficult, since the Germans, together with the Poles, have ganged up on me and want to see me stumble. It seems that I will have no alternative but to enter a labor camp, as my husband is there, and, in addition, I have the desire and patience to share this most difficult and cruel fate together with my husband...

Here I am forced to stop. I am reminded of my daughter's last words in her last letter: "Save us, dear people. We are drowning... The tears are choking me, alas..."

I, also cannot continue any more...

Translated from the Hebrew by Rochel Semp

The Tragedy of Działoszyce (pp. 336–42)

David Gelbart (Baltimore)

The Stawisko

Who in Działoszyce did not know the Stawisko, the only sports center in town? Adults and children, and especially the young people, found a place here where they could play in the summer. Here one could come across a little boy dressed in a long coat and a little Jewish hat swinging a hoop or playing "hide-and-seek" with his friends who that day had decided not to go to *kheyder*. The Stawisko was also where the soccer players gathered. The renowned soccer games between Jewish and Polish teams took place here. The Jewish soccer club Hagibor [The Mighty] had its well-known players, the three Zakon brothers (the carpenters), Jechiel Hupert, Lejbcze Tajtelbaum, and others. Here the Polish Lot [Flight] players, the age-old rivals of the Jewish Hagibor, played also. During the summer, soccer matches between these two clubs brought out the Jewish and Polish population of the town. Often the match ended up with a fight between Jews and gentiles, the Działoszyce roughnecks. The losing team would argue that they were robbed. Here in the Stawisko, a circus that must have lost its way somewhere would once in a while raise its large tent in Działoszyce. The circus was a highlight in the town. Months after it left, there was talk and admiration of the wonders that were performed there.

Here, also, at the Stawisko, more than one boy endured a belting from his father on his bare bottom for skipping *kheyder*. The Stawisko was the sports center for all of the young people in the summer. The place was always in an uproar, and one could hear the shouts from a great distance. In winter, however, the place was covered with snow, asleep, as it were. In the spring and fall, the Stawisko became a large river.

The Inhabitants of the Stawisko

Around the Stawisko there were little houses inhabited by poor people. Mainly these were gentile tradesmen, but there were also a few Jewish families that could be counted on the fingers of one hand. There was the Jasny family, who had a butcher shop. Not far from the slaughterhouse lived the Fajgenblats. And at the edge of the Stawisko lived the Smolarz family. At the other end of the Stawisko lived three Jewish families: the Brener family, Aba Balicki, and my own unforgettable family—Nachum Gelbart, his wife, and children, *z"l*. My father, *z"l*, was not a Działoszycer. He was born in Wolbrom, the son of Chaim and Chanka Gelbart, and spent his childhood there. In 1916 he married Surele, a daughter of Judka and Bajla Zalcman, a granddaughter of the *pachciarz* [lease holder], and they moved to Działoszyce.

The Grain Merchants in Działoszyce

Among other ways of making a living, there was one that was called the grain trade, an honorable trade, but not an easy job. The majority of traders wandered all week from village to village, from one farmer to the next, and bought up whatever they could: grain, large and small beans, dried fruits—especially prunes. When the opportunity arose, they also traded in other products. If one could earn a *zloty* from something, it was worthwhile bringing it back to town on Friday. This was one kind of grain trader. There was another kind of merchant who did not travel out of town. Every day these merchants would stand on the road at the edge of town and wait for the farmers who would come their way. Every farmer brought along a sack of rye and a sack of wheat and the like for the purpose of selling them at the edge of town.

Summer and winter, in rain or snow, the trade was carried on. After all, Jews needed to earn a living. They would often have a falling out with their competitors and insult each other but make up before Yom Kippur. Day in, day out, month after month, the years would pass and the trade continued and Jews made a living.

The third kind of merchants were the wholesalers. They would buy up all sorts of grains, beans, and dried fruits. They warehoused their goods with the growers and sent wagonloads to Będzin, Sosnowiec, and Katowice. The main consignee of my father's goods was the firm Szenberg and Buchweitz in Katowice.

My father, *z"l*, ran the business for years in partnership with his brother-in-law, Lejbl Spokojny. Later he bought out Abuś Granetman's lumber warehouse. A few years before the war broke out, he left Działoszyce. But on the third day after the war started, he packed up and returned to Działoszyce. He sought to earn a living in the old way, but in the meantime much had changed. There were decrees and assessments aplenty. At first, the trade could be carried out legally. Later, the trading of grain was forbidden under penalty of death. But one had to live, so Jews, among them my father, *z"l*, bought grain, had it milled illegally in the village of Łysowiec at Zale Wajnbaum's, and sold the flour in the market square. But this business did not last. Like all the Działoszycers, we sold our jewelry and lived in pain and fear but somehow survived.

The Deportation

Every Jew had to be engaged in productive work for the Germans. Thus it was my fate to work in the grain warehouse where the farmers brought their consignments. The warehouse was near the train station. The manager was Tryliński.

When the town was surrounded by the SS and *Junacy* [youth brigade], I was at work and could not return home. I hid among the sacks together with Baruch Poper. All night long we heard gunfire. Baruch Poper decided to go outside, although I warned him not to go. He went out on the following morning but did not get very far. He was shot to death on his way. I lay hidden until eleven o'clock. I asked Tryliński to take me to the *kolejka* [railway], where I shared the fate of all the other Działoszycers. Together with my parents and sisters I went to Miechów, and I was sent with many other young and strong Działoszyce Jews to Prokocim [labor camp near Kraków], where we were assembled together.

Here began the true martyrdom of the Jews of Działoszyce—hungry and chased like dogs. Just for trying to buy food from a Pole, I had my nose broken by a German with his rifle. The camp was a concentration point for Jews from the entire region: Działoszyce, Skalbmierz, Miechów, Słomniki, etc. The camp was only partially built, and winter was approaching. We worked hard and miserably in the rain and the cold without a flicker of hope, morally broken and full of sorrow at having lost our nearest and dearest. As if they had been enslaved forever, groups of Jews would go to the Kraków ghetto to be free. As I was going to the ghetto with a group of people, I was able to hide and stayed in the ghetto, where there were Jews still living. I heard rumors that there were again Jews in Działoszyce. Home, home—I hurried and rode in a truck to Działoszyce and ran, but there was no home.

Between the Two Deportations

In October 1942, after the first deportation, Działoszyce resembled a graveyard around which the living dead hovered. A few hundred Jews had returned from the fields. They were all people who had hidden and escaped from the camps, broken souls turning every which way in pain and sorrow, remembering what there had been and was no more. It is difficult to revive the past in one's thoughts. The town that had been a ferment of life and joy was now dead. Death ruled at every step. Działoszyce was buried in the ravine, in three long graves. But also the remnants, those who returned, could not stay there long. One week after I came back with great difficulty and went into my house (I had to share what few things of value I found with Jews who, unfortunately, were looking for treasure), Eliasz Zylber (Zusma's son) knocked on my door to tell me that within fifteen minutes all Jews must appear at the market square. Again there was a deportation. Again one had to run, again endure beatings, and what would come of it? I had to make a decision in a hurry. I had fifteen minutes left, and my mind had to work quickly while I was covered with sweat. I decided not to appear, come what may. I would not again go like a lamb to market.

Hiding in Działoszyce

Without thinking too long, I took my possessions and went to the counting house bureau at the Stawisko and hid in the second attic right under the roof, where no one would dream that a person could live and survive. During the day I lay in my sorrow, one Jew in a sea of hatred, and tortured myself with gruesome thoughts. I heard clearly how the Germans and the Poles traded in and sold Jewish dwellings. Jewish possessions, Jewish belongings gathered through generations of parents, grandmothers, and grandfathers were sold for pennies by the bestial murderers. And I had to listen to all of this! I had to be the only witness to the robbery and destruction of all the Jewish possessions. Their souls, their lives they had already taken. What is the value of a few possessions now? "Murder and ye shall inherit." The nights were doubly difficult. I often went out late at night to stretch my bones a bit. The shootings went on night after night, killing Jews whom they would find hiding here and there. I used to ask myself, "How long, David, are you going to hide? How long can you last?" Sooner or later, the bullet would find me also. The decision to leave my hideout came one day when the counting clerks, who were hiding me, told me that my childhood friend Majer Szulimowicz, his wife, and their son Josel had been shot. This I could not abide, and I decided to leave Działoszyce. I no longer looked like a human being—unshaven for two weeks, filthy and lice-ridden. I asked them to send for a Christian acquaintance of mine from Jazdowice. He shaved me, turned me back into resembling a human being. I left my last rucksack with the counting clerks, and by way of Miechów, I started toward Kraków. I went to Kobierzyńska Street, where men from Działoszyce worked in the Strauch factory.

In the Camps with People from Działoszyce

The work on Kobierzyńska Street at the Strauch firm was not easy. We boys from Działoszyce had to suddenly become sewer and canal workers. But compared to what awaited us later, the work was light. However, the Germans did not like the idea of private camps. Slowly, all workplaces were concentrated in Płaszów, near Kraków. The camp was erected at the Jewish cemetery site in Kraków. I worked in the locksmith shop with other people from Działoszyce. The person responsible for the locksmith shop was Jerzyk Spiro of the Dziekanowice Spiros. I will not try to describe the Płaszów camp as others will have already done so, but I want to relate two brief incidents that took place in the locksmith shop.

I want you to know under what conditions the Działoszyce people lived. The work at the locksmith shop was carried on at night also. The SS men often visited us, and every one of the visits involved victims, especially when the head of the camp, Goeth, came, may his name and memory be erased.

Once, late at night, he came and asked the foreman, Jerzyk Spiro, how many workers he had. The dutiful Spiro, not being quite sure of the number, said we were thirty-three and hoped the answer would suffice. The drunken Goeth, may his name be erased, ordered everyone to form three rows and count themselves off. As can be imagined, no one wanted to stand in the front row, and everyone sought a space in the second or third row. As it worked out, I ended up in the front, the seventh person. Hurrying to say my number, I called out "six" at the same time as my companion said "six" (the number "six" was used in the camp as a warning to apply oneself to work whenever an SS man approached). The murderer Goeth knew this and shouted angrily, "You said six," and pulled out his gun. He aimed at me, and, a heavenly miracle, the gun jammed, and he could not fire the bullet. Meanwhile, everyone kept counting, and luckily there were thirty-three of us, just as it had been stated. My ancestral merits stood by me, and I was saved. Two minutes later, a drunken SS man brought out two Jews who had been in the latrine. He said that he had found them near the wire fencing and that they had meant to escape. Goeth shot them on the spot. They were not from Działoszyce, but they were Jews like the rest of us. And where were their ancestral merits, dear Lord? We people from Działoszyce lived through such extraordinary suffering in Płaszów until November 1943. Then we were sent to Kielce. I was there with Zale Wajnbaum and his son Kalman. Six months later, I was sent off again, this time to Birkenau, at Auschwitz.

We knew this would be the end, the end of our pain, particularly as we heard the screams of the gypsies when they were gassed in the gas chambers. They had prepared the "final solution" for us also. We were recorded, everything was taken away from us, and we were being led to the gas chambers when an SS man, who looked like a butcher, came in at the last minute and sent us back to the barracks. Thus we were spared. But, irony of fate! Jews from the Łódź ghetto had already filled our places [in the barracks], so we were then sent to Buna [Auschwitz subcamp], to a chemical factory. Here we suffered air bombardments by British pilots. Many Jews died in the bombing, and I was almost one of them. I was in Buna until January 18, 1945. I was taken away from there when the Russian army stood at the walls.

The March

In the hard winter of 1945, we marched for a whole week, frozen and without food. Only half of us arrived at Gliwice. Here we were loaded onto open railroad wagons and sent to Mauthausen, but this camp was also filled to overflowing, so we were taken farther, to Oranienburg, near Berlin, still without any food. Somewhere, the Red Cross dropped bread for us. Obviously, only the able-bodied could catch the bread. Unfortunately, I no longer had the strength and reacted with apathy to all of this. An acquaintance offered me a piece of bread. In Oranienburg, I worked at the Henkel airplane factory. I was sent from there to Leuenberg, then to Flossenburg and Milldorf. On the way, I caught a bullet from a British airplane that shot at us and, luckily, just hit me in one hand. Our transport was headed for the Tyrol, but we never went. The American soldiers liberated us.

The Moment of Liberation

On a beautiful morning on April 30, 1945, standing in the railroad cars on a siding in a field near Tutzing, we suddenly sensed that the Germans were no longer there. With our last bit of strength, we climbed down and went to beg for food from the local Germans. The civilian population, very frightened, told us that the Americans were there. They suddenly became kind and gave us some food. But now, in the first moments of feeling free, we could not, alas, feel happy. Choking on our tears, we at last felt in our hearts the pain, the great tragedy. We were broken, physically and spiritually. An illness rescued me from the spiritual grief. Typhus rendered me unconscious for four weeks. I did not know who or where I was or what was happening to me, but I survived. However, when I woke up, I had no one near me whom I knew, no friend, no relative, nor anyone from Działoszyce.

Translated from the Yiddish by Zulema Seligson

Jankielówka and its Jews (pp. 343–48)

Chaim Fraiman (New York)

Działoszyce was a special Jewish town, but even more unique was Jankielówka Street. It was a little street, unpaved, with small low hovels, one small house connected to the next one, holding each other up so that, God forbid, they would not fall down. It was enough to catch just a glimpse of the little street, even from afar, to realize that very rich people did not live there. If a wealthy Jew ("wealthy" according to Działoszyce standards) already lived here, he lived in a house built of stone or bricks. Jankielówka was hidden behind the cemetery hill, as if it were seeking help from the merits of its ancestors to alleviate its poverty. When water from the rains or from the snow melting in spring flooded the street, the resulting mud was no small matter. The street's inhabitants, therefore, wore high cowhide boots and, many an autumn, found the street barely passable. More than one poor child became stuck and, unable to pull his foot out, would burst into loud sobs, or they fell and their clothes became covered with the sticky mud.

The street's official name was Garbarska (tannery). It seems that many years earlier, there were tanneries there. I know that Chaim Przybnik's in-laws had been tanners, but by my time, there were no longer any tanneries there. There were tanneries in Działoszyce but in a different area of town, not a very wealthy quarter either. The Jews of Działoszyce did not call the street Garbarska, however, but Jankielówka. It was said that the name came from Symcha Hupert's great-great-grandfather, who was the first inhabitant of the street. According to a different story, its first Jewish inhabitants settled there in the fourteenth century. Supposedly, the gentiles called all Jews Jankiel, and so the name of the muddy street became Jankielówka.

The Inhabitants and Their Occupations

Life for the inhabitants was difficult and meager. Who lived on Jankielówka anyway? There were craftsmen, coachmen, village trekkers, small traders, middlemen, etc. About three out of four Jews there had no income to speak of, worked hard, wandered, and were always sweaty and busy chasing after their daily bread. How they survived from one day to the next, only the Lord knows. They lived from miracles. A hard-earned couple of *złotys* from a farmer was a gift from the Lord or at least from an angel in heaven. It was no small thing, bread for the children. And there was no dearth of children, blessed be the name of the Lord—pretty little girls with long braids and smiling faces, little boys in their long coats and typical round hats, or in shorter outfits with little caps on their heads. They all had happy smiling eyes. Despite their poverty, all the children went to school—in the morning to the Polish public school and afternoons either to *kheyder* or the Yavneh School—and they studied. There were no roughnecks allowed on Jankielówka.

The Flood

Jankielówka had no lack of troubles, but, as the saying goes, "If one complains to the Lord, He sends a plague." And the plague came on a certain Shabes in the year 1936. It was very sunny and very humid, and after the usual Shabes afternoon rest, the sky suddenly became covered by black leaden clouds. It began as a strong rain but ended in a terrible cloudburst that inundated half the town. Since Jankielówka was the lowest point in town, it was completely flooded by water. Our house also suffered, everything in it was damaged, but the worst part was that other people's goods were destroyed. Long after this event, my father could not forget the greater pain of having lost not just his own but the goods of his customers.

Jankielówka Characters

There were notable and interesting characters living on Jankielówka Street. It is possible that any Jewish town in Poland had similar types of people, but to us children they were memorable. Unfortunately, I can no longer remember all of them, but those that I do suffice to form a full picture of Jankielówka.

The first one, Ayzykl, *z"l*, with his yellow nag—who did not know him? We children called his horse "Gilgul." It had always been a sorry nag, a *gilgul* [reincarnation] of previously dead nags, a ruined worn-out mare. He sometimes used to carry small amounts of wood to the *olejarnia* [oil mill] or would make some other short trip, depending on Gilgul's endurance. He lived at Ezryel Klajner's in an attic in great poverty.

Wolf Stempel, *z"l*, a good shoemaker. He made handsome and good shoes for the Jews of Działoszyce, but often too tight. "They will stretch out," he would say. With a house full of children, he lived in stressful conditions.

Szaja Bejski, *z"l*, was a tailor, a quiet and honest Jew. He worked day and night, mostly for the farmers in the area, who knew him and came from far away villages summer and winter to order clothes for their children.

Lejbl Ptasznik, *z"l*, was a jester. Always with a smiling face, he did business with aristocrats. He served as an agent for the Maszkowskis in Łabędź. He bought and sold horses. He had no children, unfortunately, but was very fond of goats. We just had to pick on one of Reb Lejbl's goats, and Jankielówka would erupt. Of course, we children took every opportunity to stir things up, even knocking on Reb Lejbl's shutters at night to tell him the goats had run away. By all means, let it be lively on Jankielówka.

At the very end of Jankielówka lived the Chilewiczes. Once, after a strong downpour, their stable collapsed. Chilewicz was hurt and became lame afterward. The family eventually left Działoszyce and sought its fortune in the big city.

Who was there in Działoszyce who did not know Chaim Aron, *z"l*? A well-known coachman, he took passengers from Działoszyce to Pińczów his whole life. In later times, when he was old, his son, Fajwel, became partners with Ezryel Klajner. And they carried the passengers. Like all Działoszycers, he inherited his trade. On the long stretch to Pińczów, all the gentiles recognized the vehicle and would yell, "Here comes Aylom Baylom!" And Fajwel would curse, just as his father, Chaim Aron, had cursed.

My father, Josek Boruch Frajman, *z"l*, came from Neustadt [Nowy Korczyn], my mother, *z"l*, from Jędrzejów. My father, *z"l*, was a small boy when he came to Działoszyce. He worked in agriculture at my grandparents' in Czajęczyce. He later learned tailoring and lived as a tailor his entire life. He took great care of his shears and suffered from the smoke of the pressing iron. In town it was said he was a good tailor, but unlike the other tailors, like Bencion Bejski, *z"l*, or our neighbor, Szaja Bejski, *z"l*, and other tailors in town who worked for the gentiles in the area, my father's clients were all from among the Jewish population. He clothed the business owners and their children with long coats, *chałat*s [kaftans], and silk fur-lined coats, or he made striped trousers, vests, and jackets for the more progressive ones. He worked very hard, together with his children, toiling from early morning to late at night. He came by his income honestly. Unfortunately, he never experienced any joy. In the year 1941, walking to the judge's to pick up some work, he suddenly felt ill, sat down, and never got up again. He just died without making a sound, like a saint, without suffering. But for us, his children, it was a great heartache, as we became orphans. May his memory be blessed!

Life on Jankielówka Street During the War

The great wave of anti-Semitism that flooded Germany, with the accession of Hitler to power, found fertile soil in Poland. As is well known, Polish anti-Semites were not few. They sucked in their hatred toward Jews with their mothers' milk. The dread that all Jews felt was therefore very great when World War II broke out. Among Jankielówka dwellers, there were political and strategic debates. Great experts could be found on every subject, but an expert who could tell people how to survive the day, where to get a *złoty* for a piece of bread or some hot food for the children during the cold winter days, such an expert was not to be found. The situation became ever more dire; the town authorities forbade us to go out. If a Jew was found outside the town, he was shot on the spot. Many of the inhabitants of Jankielówka had been village trekkers, but the trouble was that now one couldn't go to the villages. And if one could not go, there was no way to earn even a miserable piece of dry bread. The majority of dwellers on Jankielówka lived in poverty and great need, much worse than before the war.

But the real troubles were just beginning. The savage Germans kept raising their assessments. It began with contributions of cash, but it ended, as is well known, with total annihilation. For us in Jankielówka, the troubles began even earlier. At the end of Passover in 1942, the *kehile* [Jewish community council] gave out notices that the men had to report for work in camps far from Działoszyce.[1] We also received a summons that said one of us had to appear. My brother Kalman, *z"l*, the oldest, became the family bread earner after my father's death. And since I was the youngest, but strong, I went with many other young men from Działoszyce to Kostrze [labor camp near Kraków], and here the true martyrdom of Działoszyce youth began. After the deportation, we were joined by many who had run away from Działoszyce, including Nuchim Laskier and his son Moniek. Many people from Działoszyce, particularly the elderly, could not endure the troubles and died, among them also Nuchim Laskier.

It did not take long—a few months—before we heard rumors of the deportation. Worries about the family we had left behind were harrowing. After a brief period of time, I found out the terrible truth. My mother, *z"l*, together with my sisters Frajdla and Małka, *z"l*, and my brother Kalman, *z"l*, ran away into the fields during the deportation, but the police caught them and brought them back to Firemen's Hall. (Szlama [another brother]

---

[1] Even though the author uses the Hebrew term *kehile*, by then, the Jewish community council was under the control of the Germans and called by its German name, the *Judenrat*.

had previously escaped to Russia and, thanks to this, survived.) My mother and my sisters were sent to Majdanek, where they died with other Działoszycers who had been sent there. My brother Kalman, *z"l*, was sent to Prokocim, near Kraków, and there I found him a broken man and took him back with me to Kostrze, where there were a lot of young men from Działoszyce.

The First Death March

It began with the camp in Kostrze, and then came Płaszów, a small hell. After that there was Auschwitz, a large hell. But the serious part for us, the young men from Działoszyce, veterans of the camps, was the march from Auschwitz to Gliwice. Many Działoszyce men perished during this march—shot by the Germans or dropped dead from exhaustion. We Działoszycers helped each other, sharing a stolen potato and still holding together like a family. We stayed with one another, asked for help, yearned with hopes, and daydreamed about our families. I knew what had happened to my mother and sisters, but where was my brother Chaskiel? I found out what his fate was at the end of the war. He was sent in 1944 from Płaszów to Gross-Rosen [Sachsenhausen subcamp], from there to Gusen [Mauthausen subcamp], where he became sick and ended his life in the crematorium. Where are my sister and my brother-in-law, Wolf Szternlicht? He married a month before the deportation and experienced no joy. Thus we dreamed as we marched, chased by animals in the guise of people, condemned to death, some earlier, some later— the question was only—when? We begged for the end to come sooner. Enough pain.

The Second Death March

Marching went on with no end from one camp to the next. And when the Germans finally realized that they had been defeated, we felt it especially through their even greater cruelty. From November 1944 to May 3, 1945, about 95 percent of the Działoszyce men from the camps perished during the march. I myself survived through a strange event. While marching, barely dragging my feet, I often had to carry the gun of a German who was of Hungarian descent. He told me that the Americans were near. We were in Germany. He confided to me that in the morning, we would all be shot. There were only between eighty and one hundred of us Jews. Four hundred had already perished. That night we were penned in a pigsty, but the door was not locked. The German was not paying too much attention, and, slowly, one after the other, those who could still drag their feet began escaping. Those who were left were swollen, exhausted living skeletons, who could not go any farther. My brother Kalman, *z"l*, ran with me and some others toward the woods and from the woods to a German farmer. But here a new peril awaited us. Poles who worked in the farms here in Germany began to scream, "The Jews have arrived!" And again we ran with the fear of death. This was in Bavaria, in Traunstein, on the way to Strasbourg. Here I buried my brother Kalman, *z"l*, with my own hands. He could not endure the pain any longer and died three days after liberation. He survived long enough to hear that the war had ended. I buried my brother Kalman, *z"l*, who had gone through the martyrdom with me for three years, in a Christian cemetery. Two years later, he was given a Jewish burial.

This grave is the only one that I have of my entire family. Year in, year out, my tears run and water this grave, a grave that is a reminder for me of those long years of pain and sorrow, of friends and family who perished and never received a Jewish burial.

Let their memory be blessed forever and ever.

Translated from the Yiddish by Zulema Seligson

Years of Pain (pp. 349–356)

Avraham Chobeh (Chaba)

In the morning hours of September 2, 1942,[1] we were thrown out of our homes and ordered to assemble in the market square, where all the Jewish inhabitants of Działoszyce, a few thousand people in all, had gathered. At first, there was a rumor that a few privileged Jews would be allowed to remain, but later, those rumors turned out to be false, started by the Germans to be used for various purposes, such as to gather money, gold, jewels, and such. This came to light later when they were told to join everyone else. It was then that the Germans announced that those who did not feel strong enough to walk to the railroad should be seated in carts that were prepared for this journey. Around 2,000 people went to the carts, and they were taken to a site near the cemetery, where an enormous pit had already been dug, and there, all of them were shot to death. They covered the pit over while a lot of people were still somewhat alive, and for two days afterward, the communal grave shook with the convulsing and trembling bodies.

They then took the rest of us, under heavy guard, to the train and shipped us off. At a certain place before Miechów, we were taken off the wagons and led to a point of assembly. The whole way was lined with Polish policemen, among whom were also the policemen from our town. If they suspected that someone had brought money, they pulled him out of line, dragged him into the woods, took everything he had, and topped it off with a murderous beating.

At the assembly point, we lay all night on the wet ground in the middle of the field. In the early morning, they brought the Jews of Miechów to where we were. We were all made to line up, and of course we tried to stay together with our families. Then they started making us march under the watch of an SS man who separated the young men from the women, children, and older people. I was holding my eldest son, who was twelve, by the hand, and as I passed the SS man, I tried to walk by him, but he noticed, tore him away from my hand, and placed him with my wife and the two younger children.

Then they led all the able-bodied people to the train and jammed them in, more than a hundred people in each wagon. On the other side, they jammed in the women and children into closed wagons, and we all started together in the direction of Kraków. After several hours of travel, we came to a place not far from Kraków.

The Germans left the cars with the able-bodied men there and sent the cars with the women and children farther on. In all probability, very few of them arrived at their destination. Almost all of them were asphyxiated during the journey in the closed cars.

After a brief time in Prokocim and Kostrze [labor camps near Kraków], we heard the news that in Działoszyce a group of escapees from that town, as well as some Jews from surrounding towns, had returned there. There were some people among us who, without asking any questions, started on their way home immediately. Others, I among them, had doubts and asked many questions. As to whether they would permit us to go, no one had

---

[1] While the *Aktion* began on September 2, the deportations occurred on September 3, 1942.

an answer, but an intermediary intervened, and my brother and I were allowed to leave. For this permission, we paid forty dollars in gold.

Arriving home, we found our house sealed up. During the time we were at the camp, the Poles and the Germans sealed up all the Jewish houses. To go into one's house, one had to pay the *Judenrat* [Jewish council] a large sum of money. Inside the house, I found on the table the unfinished meal of weeks earlier. It broke my heart. Everything in the house had remained untouched.

So that my Christian neighbors would not suspect that I had hidden anything, I broke a window in one room and spread a rumor that while I was gone, I had been robbed. At the same time, I began to create a hiding place in the house with my brother, and we placed all our possessions in it, everything that was still there except for the furniture. According to what I heard, my Christian neighbors indeed suspected that I had made a hiding place, because right after the second deportation, my neighbor Kobrzyński moved into my house so that he would have the time to look for traces of the hiding place by day and by night. He was not successful, and everything remained where it had been until after liberation. I was in the catagory of "one whose work is performed by the hands of others"—the gentile Kobrzyński wound up "watching over" our household possessions.

After sustaining ourselves for a few weeks in town, every day we felt that the situation became more suffocating and unbearable. The ground was burning under our feet. So I decided, on the last Friday before the deportation, to begin by sending my brother to a village farmer with whom I was acquainted. We arranged that in the morning I would also arrive at the farm. At dawn on Shabes, when my house was full of people, acquaintances and strangers alike who slept there, I told them that I was abandoning the house because I had to leave town. And this I did. When I reached the farm, the owner took me straight up to the attic where my brother was. Throughout all this, we did not really think of what we were doing and what the result of it would be. Meanwhile, we stayed in the attic all day. At night, when we finally fell asleep, we suddenly heard someone climbing the ladder, and we were very frightened. There was no reason to fear. It was the farmer, carrying a lantern, who came to tell us that his neighbors had reported him for hiding Jews. Therefore, if we wanted to save our lives, we should run away. This seemed almost impossible to us. First of all, we would not know where to go, and, second, the weather was terrible. It was a cold dark night and raining hard, and the field was covered with mud. We were left for a while perplexed and helpless.

Then I had a sudden idea and made a suggestion to the proprietor that if he wanted to be rid of us quickly, he should grant us a favor for which I would reward him handsomely. He should drive us to another village where I knew another farmer, because we did not know the way to that village nor did we know where that farmer lived. But when we reached that place and I knocked on the door, he should leave and stay out of sight. In this way, the other farmer would not know that anyone else was aware of our coming there. He agreed to our suggestion. The new proprietor took us immediately to the barn, and there among the sheaves of wheat, we slept the first night. In the morning, the man came over to the barn, brought us food, and at the same time let us know that there was a great deal of shooting in our town and that they were assembling all the Jews to send them away. Should they find a Jew after this action, they would shoot him on the spot. It is easy to imagine our deep depression and resignation upon hearing this.

In short, we awaited death every minute. We hid the whole week at this farmer's. On Thursday night, the proprietor came over to the barn to tell us that on the following day, Friday, they were coming to inspect the pigs, and it was possible that they would decide to check out the whole place and might find us. We could imagine what would await us and the farmer. I begged him fervently that he find us another safe hiding place, since it would only be for a matter of a few hours. But he insisted that we had to leave. He wanted us to just go anywhere and return at night. We could not fall asleep the whole night, waiting for the unfortunate day that was coming. We got up quite early and went out, not knowing where to go, death hovering over every step. The hunt for Jews went on without measure; we sought places away from the road to avoid running into Germans or bloodthirsty Poles.

As we were walking, we ran into a farmer who was working in the field. He noticed immediately that we were Jews. He told us that the day before, on Thursday, he was in Działoszyce and saw with his own eyes how Germans and Poles were leading a group of people who had hidden in Abram Rożenek's house, among them the Szulimowicz family, the Zylberberg family, and others. They shot them all in the cemetery, and an hour earlier, in this field where we also now stood, some local farmers found three Jews and killed them on the spot. As it turned out, the proprietor knew the peril we were in, but he wanted to get rid of us in a "humanitarian" way. Thus, this day that we had spent in the open fields, under an open sky, seemed to us a lifetime. I decided to try to get to a neighboring village, where a teacher I knew, who had been a client of mine, lived. Knowing him to be a liberal person and friendly to Jews and thinking he would help me, I told him the reason I was calling on him and asked him to provide us with a hiding place until nightfall. He told me that there were strangers in his house and he could not, therefore, help us. After dragging ourselves here and there for another few hours, we went back to our old refuge in the evening. How disillusioned we became when we saw the expression on the farmer's face when he saw us and when we saw how troubled he was by our return.

During the night, the proprietor invited us to come into the house and declared that for us to remain in the barn throughout the winter would be impossible. He decided to dig a hole in the middle of the field where we could hide until summer. The problem would be when snow fell, because it would be impossible to bring us food without leaving footprints, and the Germans could easily discover us. He then came to the conclusion that we should travel to Kraków as soon as possible. There were many Jews assembled there, he said, and he thought that we should get going as early as Sunday morning. To ride in a wagon was out of the question, a certain death. Seeing in what a situation we found ourselves and with no time to spare for further thought, I asked that he go back to my previous host and ask him, on my behalf, to come and see me. When he returned with the proprietor's wife, I proposed a greater sum of money for her to be our guide to Kraków. She told us she would be ready to do that, but instead of to Kraków, to Kościejów, about ten or fifteen kilometers from Kraków. Her parents lived in Kościejów, and they would take us to Kraków.

On Sunday before dawn, the woman came. We changed into farmers' clothes and left our own belongings. We started on our way. The woman walked a bit ahead of us; in case we were discovered she would not be connected to us. Although we were dressed as farmers, we were very scared the whole way. We walked on side roads only so we would not run into other travelers. Despite this, we ran into people who were coming back from church. They addressed us, "Jews, what are you doing here?" They barred our way, and with our last bit of strength, having nothing to lose, we ran away. After much fright, and worn-out, we arrived in Kościejów at our guide's parents' home. She explained to them who we were and what we wanted. Her parents were completely taken aback. They not only refused to give us any kind of help, they practically threw us out because we were a threat to their lives.

We were in a very perilous and helpless situation. Not seeing any other remedy, we started walking toward Kraków on the main road, because without a guide we could not attempt to use side roads. At last, we arrived in Kraków at night. Knowing that on Kobierzyńska Street there was a work camp run by the Strauch firm, where many Jews worked, some also from our town, we boarded a streetcar and went in the direction of the camp. On the way, a few Gestapo types got on, and we got off at the first opportunity and barely made it out with our lives. We got to Kobierzyńska on foot and went into the aforementioned work camp.

The camp consisted of three rooms. We did not receive a particularly hearty welcome there. The first question we were asked by those who were closest to us was, "Where were you the whole time we have been in the camp?" Only after much wear and tear and invented excuses were we able to buy ourselves into their trust as brothers in misfortune. After we were there for a time, we heard that there was another work camp run by the same firm in Kraków, by the name of *Cementownia* [Cement Works] and that the working conditions were better there. Again I had gotten close to the leaders, who happened to be old acquaintances, but easier working conditions trumped old friendships. I tried every which way to get out of this camp on Kobierzyńska. At last, we were able to go over to the Cement Works, where we worked on cement water pipes. My brother, with some other Jews, worked outside the camp. We were there for a while, and suddenly, out of a clear blue sky, there came a decree that the camp would be closed down and we were to move to Płaszów.

In Płaszów we had a taste of hell. Every day there were new demands, all difficult and unbearable. We were there until May 1944. Then we were sent to Gross-Rosen [Sachsenhausen subcamp]. Life there was dreadful. We had Ukrainian guards who beat us almost to death trying to get whatever we still had with us because, as they said, we were on our way to annihilation.

At the Gross-Rosen camp, we were greeted by an orchestra, and we were led into the camp with music. As soon as we were inside, the musicians were transformed into wild beasts. They put down their instruments and picked up sticks with which they beat everyone with murderous blows. There came an immediate order to undress completely and for those who had money or other items of value to place their possessions on a table, where SS men were sitting who took our names and assured us that we would get our possessions back when we left the camp. I was really afraid to approach the table, so I left my money, almost three hundred dollars, in my clothes. We stood naked like that for many hours in a very cold place. We were then sent to the baths, and there our bodies were shaved completely in a rough way that tore our skin. Nearby was a barrel of sharp disinfectant, which burned like fire, and everyone had to wash the wounds made by the razors in that liquid. Afterward, we went to the showers, and coming out, we found the striped uniforms we were to wear laid out. We had to dress in a great hurry. Tall people had to put on clothes they barely could get into, and short people got clothes they were lost in.

Coming out of the bath, I did not recognize my brother nor did he recognize me. We kept looking but could not find each other.

After a few days in Gross-Rosen, a group of about one hundred men, including us, was sent out in trucks in absolutely inhumane conditions. Barely alive, we arrived at Wüstegiersdorf [Gross-Rosen subcamp] in Lower Silesia.

This camp, and others in the vicinity, were under the supervision of SS *Oberscharführer* Lidke Meyer. The camp commander at that place was an SS man by the name of Schwarz. Compared to the murders we had seen in Gross-Rosen, this place felt like paradise to us, even though they also hanged people here and beat them with murderous blows. Here the pain was milder.

We worked there for a few months. The Russian army was approaching. We received an order at that time that the camp would be liquidated and we would all be sent on our way; we did not know where.

We abandoned the camp in January 1945, and one day later, the Russians marched in there. Each one of us had received half a loaf of bread and a few grams of sugar. We thought we would get such a ration every day, so we ate everything up the first day. But we got nothing during the following thirteen days and had to eat grass and leaves of trees. Many paid with their lives trying to tear some leaves off the trees, and they were shot down.

In short, we endured seventy-seven levels of hell. We made it through the camps of Buchenwald, Flossenburg, and Crawinkel, where more than ninety percent of the transport perished.

Only in May 1945, when we were in Theriesenstadt, were we finally liberated.

Translated from the Yiddish by Zulema Seligson

Under the German Boot (pp. 357–60)

Aszer Rafałowicz

As soon as the war broke out, the Jews of Działoszyce felt the German oppression become tighter and tighter. In the surrounding villages, the Germans oppressed the Jewish inhabitants even harder, and Jews were moving out in great numbers to places where they could still breathe a little more easily. They tried to find even the most distant relatives so as to have a place to which they could escape. Meanwhile, sources of income in Działoszyce became ever scarcer, and the crowding in the houses grew beyond measure. There were people even staying in the *bes hamedresh.* The Germans kept stepping up their decrees. They took all kinds of goods and money from the Jews and completely emptied their stores. They soon instituted forced labor. All men, young and old, were required to dry up swamps, build roads, and do various railroad-related work. Jews hoped at the beginning that these decrees would be temporary measures. In no way could people grasp that the rulers had prepared a plan for annihilation. But the German police soon began to inflict great suffering. A few merchants who were moving goods from one place to another were shot dead. They also shot a butcher who was slaughtering a cow. In short, things were getting worse all the time.

Poverty was immeasurable. Many people walked around all day with nothing to put into their mouths. A few fortunate ones managed to engage in trade and eke out a living for their families.

On a certain day, the skull-emblazoned Gestapo[1] came to town to prepare the inhabitants for deportation. As soon as I saw this, I left my store and ran away. They, the Gestapo men, went to Pincia Formalski's and battered down his door. They took Zalman Formalski and beat him mercilessly with a wooden plank. The suffering was hard and unending, until one day in 1942, on 13 Av,[2] they took twenty-two men from the Rafałowicz family to the community hall and interrogated them as to the whereabouts of a Communist named Herszel Rafałowicz. During all this, I kept thinking that they had the power to do as they wished with us because they were the ones with weapons. We all argued with them that there was no such person in our town.

A week later, on Shabes, there was sudden chaos. Everyone was saying that the deportation was to take place soon. There were also rumors that they were digging pits on the outskirts of town. Suddenly, on Wednesday, when I was at work with twenty other Jews in Sarbia [Szarbia?], where we carried sand for the Racławice Road, we heard that the Jews from Skalbmierz were being evacuated to Działoszyce. We ended our work in great fear, and when we returned to town, the Germans had already surrounded it. I went immediately to my mother's to say good-bye. My brother met me there and told me they had shot Akiba Zyngier, the tinsmith. All night long we heard cries from people who had been gathered from all areas of the town and thrown together by the Germans. My mother

---

[1] Caps worn by the Gestapo had a skull and crossbones insignia on them.

[2] The date 13 Av corresponded to July 27 in 1942. Since the deportation came a week or so later (21 Elul/September 3), this date would more likely have been the 13 Elul.

and my brother's children hid in an alley behind a wall. The Jewish militia promised us they would take them out of the hiding place after the chaos subsided. I myself crawled under the roof of the year-round *suke*. Later, I gathered up my brother and Róża Karmioł, and we all hid there for two or three days. On Friday afternoon, Róża went down to check if we could leave, and she ran into a Christian, Kobzej, who wanted to take her to the police station. Róża managed to turn the shaft of the wagon to the side and escaped. A few hours later, we all left town, and, seeing no alternative, fifteen of us hid in a village. We also stayed for a few days in the fields. We endured all this burdened by great pain and sorrow.

We then heard from the Christians that Jews were again gathering in town. Despite all the peril, we decided to go back. We were gathered together in the courtyard of the town hall. Jewish policemen from the Kraków ghetto were there also. As it turned out, we worshiped there during Yom Kippur. It often happened that when someone needed to go out, he would step on other people, we were that crowded. During Yom Kippur prayers, the cries and sobs reached the seventh heaven. We lamented our fate, our pain and sorrows, not seeing any light at the end, only horrendous darkness. We trembled when we thought about our situation. The misery grew and dragged on, day after day, until the second deportation came, in November.

On a completely dark Sunday evening, the Germans gathered about 600 Jews, took them to the forest of Chodów, beyond Miechów, and there shot everyone to death. We managed to escape, my brother and I, to Słupów. Mother, with another brother, escaped to Podgaje. At night a gentile came and frightened us, telling us we had to leave. Desperate, we ran to the Chroberz forest. When we got there, they told us that a gentile named Krzyształ had killed five members of the Jurysta family. Some time later, Monas Rzeźnik, one of the partisans in our area, caught the murderer and shot him "as a lesson so that others might learn and fear."

Monas and his group of partisans also killed a gentile by the name of Przemysław from Dębowa Zaga [Zagaje Dębiańskie?]. For his "good deeds" collaborating with the Germans, he got his head chopped off. From that time on, the gentile murderers were fearful of Monas Rzeźnik and his partisan comrades, and they relented a bit. They also told us that a train carrying weapons was expected to come through the tunnel, so a few of the young men, such as Wolf Skóra, Moszek Hersz Rozenfrucht, and Binem Skórecki prepared explosives to blow up the tunnel when the weapons train came through, but that did not work out.

In the forests of Chroberz, we came across Jews from Pińczów and from other towns. We built bunkers and hid there for a while until the police came and tried to capture us. We ran away again toward Działoszyce to a village named Słupów. My brother and his children were already there, and my sister-in-law, who originally came from the Grundman family in Miechów, was also with them. In the end, the Gestapo captured them all, around fifty people, and shot them to death in a pit in the fields.

The massacre occurred on 11 Adar 1943 [February 16]. Among them were Abuś Granetman, Jakób Mandelbaum and his wife, Izrael Płatkiewicz and his wife, and Szmul Rafałowicz.

Afterward, there were still nine of us Jews hiding in the home of a gentile, Maciek Konieczny. This gentile man was sheltering a boy, Zelig Frenkel, without being paid a cent. This man was a friend of Israel and one should remember him and praise him, because he did many good deeds for Jews and saved their lives from certain death, putting his own life in peril of death. He was one of the righteous among the gentiles.

The pit we were hiding in was a living grave. It was so low that we could not stand up in it and so narrow that we could not turn around. Very little air came in. It was very difficult. At this man's house there were also Russian partisans in hiding, but in a different pit, at the other end of the courtyard. The man would not allow us to come near the partisans, for our own sake, and did not allow them to come near us. This was on account of conspiracies and for everyone's safety.

On January 22, 1945, we heard the Russian army marching in. It is impossible to imagine our joy when we heard our liberators approaching. At last, after five years of sorrow and persecution, we could breathe more easily. It is possible that the partisans had clandestine ties with the Red Army and knew a few days ahead of time that they would be marching in. Finally, the gentile man brought us together with the partisans, and the joy of liberation enveloped us all.

Translated from the Yiddish by Zulema Seligson

I Fainted—and Was a Free Man (pp. 361–64)

David Rotam (Rotner)

Działoszyce was a small town, and until the outbreak of the war, 95 percent of its inhabitants were Jewish. During the war, the town population increased greatly, and it was practically transformed into a city. This was by no means a natural development but the result of the many Jews escaping from Kraków and other big cities in order to find safety and refuge in Działoszyce. The concentration of the many refugees now in Działoszyce caused tremendous overcrowding. In my grandmother's apartment, where before only two persons had lived, seven were now squeezed in. We did not have any money. My mother was widowed even before I was born. The burden of earning a livelihood fell upon the shoulders of my elderly grandfather. My grandfather, Chaim Szymon Szlamowicz, was then about seventy years old and very religious. The Germans decreed that Jews must shave off their beards; my grandfather, however, totally refused to obey. He covered his beard with a kerchief with the pretext of a toothache and, with this cover-up, would circulate among all the villages in the area. He traded back and forth and did business with all the farmers and managed to bring home basic food supplies to sustain our entire family.

In Działoszyce every Jew was forced to work for three days a week for the Germans. In addition to my own forced labor, I would also substitute for those who did not want to work but had the money to pay for a substitute. I continuously spent time at this type of work and other difficult work until we received an order that the Jews of Działoszyce were to send fifty young men to work in Kraków. I was a refugee in the city, so, understandably, I was put on the list of those to leave. Together with the other men from Działoszyce, we arrived at a company by the name of Richard Strauch, whose business was construction, especially sewers and canals. I worked, along with about fifty others from Działoszyce, in an open camp at 5 Kobierzyńska Street. From time to time, we were also able to visit the ghetto in Kraków that still existed. There I met up with my eldest brother, Gerszon, *z"l* [of blessed memory]. For about a year, we continued working for this same company. Suddenly, there appeared on the small campgrounds the *Ordnungsdienst* [Jewish police], headed by Chilowicz. They piled us into vehicles and took us to the Płaszów concentration camp, a camp that was erected on the grounds of the Kraków cemetery. That's where they had brought the remnants of the Jews after the liquidation of the Kraków ghetto.

In the Płaszów Camp

The commander of the Płaszów camp was Amon Goeth. He was a sadistic, evil, and wicked person, who was always accompanied by a dog named Rolf. When the dog would go through the camp, each prisoner had to greet the dog and say, *"Herr Rolf, Ich melde gehorsam, Heftling Nummer...* (Sir Rolf, I obediently report, prisoner number so and so ...")* In the event that the prisoner didn't make this declaration in front of the dog, the trained dog would knock down its victim and dig his teeth into his throat. This dog had a special trainer who dealt with it, and the rumors in the camp were that the dog got its nourishment from human flesh.

In the Płaszów camp there were 20,000 or more Jews, among them about 2,000 prisoners from Działoszyce. The area of the camp was very large. In the heart of the area was a hill, and next to it, a very deep body of water. Near this hill, they would shoot prisoners of the camp and Jews who had been caught on the Aryan side,[1] as well as Polish insurgents. The corpses would roll down on their own into the deep water. The job of certain groups of Jews was to burn these bodies, but prior to that, they had to extract the gold teeth from the victims. The veterans at this type of work would be exterminated, and a new crew would replace them.

In Płaszów, I first worked on various construction jobs. After I met up with my brother, who was brought to the camp after the liquidation of the ghetto, I was put to work in a shoemaking place, thanks to his efforts. However, because I was not a shoemaker, I couldn't stay in this comfortable place very long. Again I started shifting from one work commando to another and was engaged in grueling work. For quite a while I worked in the commando Westbahn [West railway company]. Our job was to put wooden ties under the steel train tracks, as well as to reinforce them in order to strengthen the ground under the rails. Working along with me in the commando (we worked in groups of twenty-five to thirty men) was a young boy, maybe about sixteen, by the name of Jurek Lokaj. Jurek did not look like a Jew. He was a very nice young lad who was very well liked by everyone. One day, my friend Jurek turned to me and asked me to lend him twenty-five złoty. I thought that perhaps he had the opportunity to buy some food products. Generally, the supervisors weren't too strict with the railway workers for such sins and looked the other way. However, Jurek clandestinely escaped from among the workers and never returned. We only noticed his absence when it was time to return to camp.

We returned to camp, and there was huge chaos. They took attendance and determined that a person was missing in our commando. The commander, Goeth, appeared with his dog. We knew full well that if Goeth and his dog were here together, the situation was not good. Ukrainian guards immediately surrounded us, and Goeth, without saying much, took two people out from every group of five, and they were shot on the spot. I was standing in line in the center of the second row, and this saved me. In this roll call, nineteen people were shot and killed.

The *Ordnungsdienst* Man Who Saved My Life

Once, when I was working on the sewers near the villa of Commander Goeth, I was trying to keep working without stopping. The entire area was swarming with SS officers, and I had to be very careful not to draw attention to myself so they wouldn't have any excuse to single me out. Suddenly, an SS officer by the name of Klags, whom we had nicknamed *Kugelmacher* [pudding maker], because of his habit of kicking the testicles of prisoners, passed by me. Being absorbed in my work, I didn't notice him in time to give him a salute. In a minute, he pulled out his revolver from its case and decided to shoot

---

[1] The "Aryan side" was outside the ghetto where "Aryans" [non-Jews] lived. Jews who tried to live on the Aryan side, even if they had Christian identity papers, were often caught.

me. The Jewish policeman (the *Ordnungsdienst* man) who was supervising me offered that instead of shooting me, he would beat me up himself. He assured him that his beatings would be worse than death. The Jewish policeman lifted his rod and didn't let up on his beatings before he left me bleeding thoroughly. In the end, he hit me once more with the butt of his gun, and out fell eight of my teeth. This operation calmed down the SS officer, and they left me in place unconscious. However, the beating of the *Ordnungsdienst* man, which I will never forget, saved my life.

I remained in Płaszów until 1943. At that time, they assembled about 1500 Jewish prisoners, myself among them, as well as many others from Działoszyce, and sent us to Gross-Rosen. Gross-Rosen was considered in those days as a model camp. They would send delegations and various observers there to show them the inside organization and life in the camp. During these visits, they would play lively music in the form of marches. The horrible atrocities that were administered, not only by the Germans but also by the Poles and Ukrainians, were hidden from everyone's sight. A model of a camp, indeed! To my good fortune, I only stayed in this hell of a camp for two weeks. From there, we were sent to the Buchenwald camp. My eldest brother and I left together. My mother, *z"l*, had not wanted to leave her elderly parents and went to her death together with the rest of the people of Działoszyce.

The road from Płaszów to Gross-Rosen and then to Buchenwald was strewn with torture and pain. I traveled it together with my eldest brother, Gerszon. The fact that we were together eased our ordeal. Being among so many strangers, it was comforting to know that there was a brother and friend near me. In Buchenwald, each of us received a striped uniform, a pair of warm underwear, and an undershirt. However, they told us that we were not allowed to wear the underwear or the undershirt. If anyone were to be caught wearing these undergarments, his sentence would be immediate death. They made inspections twice a day. We were constantly outdoors in freezing cold. One day, the SS officers appeared and ordered us to work. My brother Gerszon decided to declare himself ill and not work. Some instinct motivated me to encourage him to go out to work with me. But due to his great weakness and stubbornness, I was unsuccessful in persuading him to change his mind, and he stayed behind. When I returned, I didn't find my brother alive any longer. During the time we were busy working, they made an inspection in the blocks [barracks] and took out all the sick people who remained. My brother, *z"l*, was also caught in this selection, and he was lost to me forever.

After two weeks, we were sent out of Buchenwald to a new camp, Taucha, that was close to Leipzig, to work in an armament factory, which was a branch of the firm Hasag. We worked in daily twelve-hour shifts. The food given to us consisted of 120 grams of bread, a liter of coffee, and a half-liter of soup. The work was crushing and beyond our strength. Prisoners from all over the world were gathered in this camp. Jews were in the vast majority. In addition, there were also Frenchmen, Poles, Belgians, Gypsies, Ukrainians, and Russians.

We could sense some imminent changes in the air. However, we were totally isolated from the outside world; we had not seen a newspaper or listened to any radio. In spite of all this, we were able to surmise from the behavior of the Germans and from snatches of conversations we overheard during the bombings that something was happening. Our work was often interrupted due to the fact that they could not supply us with the raw materials needed to continue our jobs. Toward the end, the work in Taucha stopped altogether.

In March 1945, the Nazi commander of the camp appeared before us and delivered a short speech telling us that due to the fact that the enemy's planes were bombing arms manufacturing plants without cease, and since he was concerned about us, he had decided to transfer us from Taucha to Dresden. However, since there was no transportation for us, we would have to go by foot. According to his estimate, he said we would be en route for three days. They gave each of us 700 grams of bread, a piece of margarine, and a slice of salami. The journey lasted not three days, as promised, but thirty-three days. We were 1200 persons when we began; the majority succumbed, fell, never to get up again. Anyone who weakened for a second and couldn't keep pace with the march was shot on the spot. We slept in open fields. We had no warm coverings whatsoever for our bodies, and the ground was still covered with melting snow.

While traveling, we ate vegetation that was fit for animals and leftover crops that we found in the fields. I remember walking along the footprints of a horse that had traveled on the road, and I collected, one by one, wheat kernels that had fallen from the sack on his back. I felt that my strengths was leaving me, I was a total *muselman*.[1] According to the situation on the road, I surmised that the Russian and British forces were approaching and freedom was very close. The roads were full of refugees who were escaping by foot to the west. The possessions carried on their backs were very familiar to me. But this time, these refugees were Germans. This sight was the one thing that gave us encouragement and strengthened our resolve to overcome our hardships.

In the meantime, we continued our "death march." The SS men who guarded us were older men who were not fit to serve on the front. The going was very slow. From time to time we were stopped either by the army or by refugees. We had no idea where they were taking us or where the last stop would be. For a quarter of an hour, we would walk, and for half an hour, we would stand, and this was repeated again and again. One day, at dusk, we again stopped on the crowded road. I was the first person in one of the rows of five. I sat down exhausted near the stream on the edge of the road and leaned against a telephone pole. I sat and sat. Around us, it grew dark. Suddenly, the idea popped into my head that I should immediately make an escape.

I started crawling toward the stream. From the stream I continued crawling toward a hill surrounded by trees. I lay transfixed and bewildered, as though in a dream. I heard footsteps growing fainter and fainter. The marchers went on their way. At the end of the marchers rode the Nazi officer on a motorcycle, and alongside him ran his wolf dog. It seems as if the dog noticed me and started barking. The commander shot a few bullets in the direction of the hill where I was hiding. After that, the noise of the motorcycle grew fainter until there was total silence.

Around me there was a deathly silence; everything was empty. The Germans had abandoned their homes and escaped to the west out of fear of the Red Army that was approaching and closing in on them. I stayed in this forest for three days. There I encountered German soldiers who had lost their units, as well as other refugees. They

---

[1] *Muselman* was a term used to describe concentration camp inmates who were on the verge of death from starvation.

asked me what was I doing there, and I told them that I had lost my detachment. They didn't harm me in any way.

After three days I heard horses galloping and human voices from afar. I heard them calling in a language that seemed to be Russian. I recognized it even though I didn't know the Russian language. With my last bit of strength, I crawled toward them. I fainted at the feet of the Russian soldiers. The main thing was that I was a free person. This was on May 8, 1945.[1]

Translated from the Hebrew by Rochel Semp

---

[1] May 8, 1945 was the day the Germans surrendered and the war in Europe was over.

My Life Underground with the German Cannibals (pp. 365–73)

David Wohlgelernter

"I am the man that hath seen affliction by the rod of His wrath," laments the prophet Jeremiah at the destruction of the Temple. I will not exaggerate if I say that whatever was said about that destruction was too mild, too pale, to compare to this last disaster in Europe. No matter how much is told and written, the accounts do not give a clear picture of the great horrendous cruel tragedy and its sad outcome.

Even a person with an exquisite sense of perception cannot describe the frightful nightmare that hovered over every Jewish head, because the one who lived through it himself cannot comprehend how the same beings who called themselves human could have been capable of such beastly deeds.

I am a man who experienced the recent annihilation that the German *Düsseldorfisch* murderous beasts carried out on helpless Jews,[1] at first in the camp, then in the fields and pits and in plain hiding places. I will attempt to draw a few sad pictures that are but a small drop in the great sea of sorrow.

Truly, the "good" done by evildoers is never complete—this is a sad reality that I experienced myself.

The majority of Christians who were willing to let wandering Jews into their stables or barns did it with the idea of extracting their possessions from them, either pleasantly or unpleasantly. They would in no way acknowledge that Jews had a right to live. It was seldom that one of them genuinely meant to save a Jew. There were cases of a Jew giving away his whole fortune of a lifetime to a Christian friend, but as soon as the Christian possessed the fortune, he became a bloodthirsty animal. And when the Jew came to him for a hiding-place, he would murder him in a beastly manner—if not with a bullet, he would chop the Jew's head off while he was asleep.

There were many such instances; the Christians gave the unfortunate Jews an eternal hiding-place… If someone was able to save himself at the home of a Christian, it was only for a few days. Thus one had to wander from place to place. Often Jews hid on Christian properties a bit longer but without their knowledge. They buried themselves in stables in the middle of hay.

In the winter, during great frosts, even if a farmer was willing to take people in, they were still afraid to risk it. One way or another, death was always staring them in the face.

The third winter of my being in hiding, my two brothers (who later perished) and I were on the lookout for a hiding place. We inquired from a farmer who made a living by taking food supplies to other people's houses at night. Such people were taking the risk of hiding Jews on their farms.

This farmer in the village of Dębowiec (in the vicinity of Kielce), whose name was B., welcomed us nicely. But his facial expression was frightening, and his roaring voice made our blood run cold.

---

[1] *Düsseldorfisch* [Düsseldorf-like] is possibly a reference to a speech given by Hitler in Düsseldorf on January 27, 1932, in which he proclaimed Nazi power.

But, as Sholem Aleichem says, "*B'makom sh'eyn ish, iz herring oykh fish* [In a place where there is no man, a herring passes for a fish]." We had no alternative, so we stayed there. The farmer assured us that he would make a hiding place in the barn, but until he managed that, we were to stay in the stable. He gave us a good supper, of a kind that we had not had in months—namely, bread and butter and white coffee with sugar. After the festive supper, he led us into the stable, stayed with us a while and listened to our promises for after the war. He was satisfied and showed us where we were to lie down to sleep.

He took our leave with a friendly smile and locked up the stable. It was not more than five minutes later, as we had barely crawled up to where he had indicated we should sleep, that we heard a tiny knock on a board. We looked around and saw in the deep darkness below us a white figure approaching slowly to our side. We stopped moving the straw around and concentrated all our senses on perceiving what this apparition was, perhaps a chimera. It did not take long, and the white apparition climbed up to where we were.

A shiver went through us. A terrible fear invaded us; we almost passed out. We could not utter a word. Suddenly, a thin voice was heard, and yes, it spoke Yiddish.

"Brother Jews," we heard.

"Who are you?"

"I am also a wandering, miserable Jew," came the answer.

"How did you get here, and how did you know about us?"

"I live here, I have a hole," and then he was silent.

His last words confused us again. We did not understand what he was trying to tell us and thought surely that he was a ghost from a pit, one of the hundreds of martyrs.

The figure watched our silence without surprise and added, "I have a hiding place."

He began to tell us his story, in brief, because he was afraid of someone overhearing. How did he know about us? He overheard, he said. He was with his family. Hearing people coming in so late into the stable, he understood immediately that they had to be Jews.

The Jew told us quietly:

> The main thing is not to give him too much money in order not to arouse his greed. The farmer is always looking for an opportunity to get rid of us, because we pay him a pittance. We don't have any more, and we have been here five months already. Who knows how long we will have to stay here yet? If you like, come to our hole to talk, because it is dangerous to talk here.

Of course, we immediately agreed to what the Jew suggested, because it had been seventeen months since we had seen another Jew. The Jew walked ahead and held one of us by the hand, and we each did the same, one by one, in the dark, until we reached the indicated place.

He knocked three times and a board slid away, which looked no different from the other boards, and it was immediately bolted from the inside.

We had to get down on all fours. First, one stuck one's feet and legs through a very narrow passage (it reminded us of the caves of the Spanish Marranos), and thus moving along, we eventually fell into the pit. There we met another man, his brother-in-law, and his wife and three children. The pit was illuminated by an oil lamp. The whole household consisted of a pallet of straw laid out under a sort of makeshift linen cover that at one time had been white. The people, with not a drop of blood in their faces, with protruding eyes and ears, wished to catch even one word of hope.

We looked around and saw a small sack hanging from the ceiling with something round inside. We asked what it was.

It is bread. We have no shortage of bread, because we don't eat it; we just look at it. Only when someone feels very faint from hunger does he take a piece. When there is no moon, for us it is bright. One can go out and look for something to eat. But when there is a moon shining, for us it is dark, and we have to be stingy with the piece of bread.

The people had no strength left to tell us about their experiences. We asked them if they perhaps knew of other Jews. "Yes," they said, "we know other Jews who are out free." "How can that be?" we asked in amazement.

They are partisans in the woods. Their aim is to avenge the blood of our martyrs. They stand with weapons in their hands to fight against the cursed, strong, and brutal enemy. They have taken care of more than one murderer.

We listened to this with bated breath, not quite believing in the reality of what they were telling us. A fantasy in their desperate Jewish minds, they were giving themselves courage and hope and faith that there were other Jews who had the power and the ability to bring down a murdererous dog.

That's what we thought. But they assured us, in secrecy, that they had themselves seen these Jewish heroes. Actually, they had been visited by them twice.

As soon as they find out about a Jew, they come to help in whatever way they can. The first time, there were eighteen of them who came at night, understandably, riding horses. They brought all kinds of wonderful things and gave us some money, which we are using to help us along even now. The farmer did not lose anything because of them. They spoke to him about what a great deed he was performing and what propects awaited him after the war (this influenced the farmer greatly to treat us kindly).

They are all young, strong, well brought-up young men. They come from various towns—Działoszyce, Pińczów, Wolbrom, and others. They took off their shirts and left them here for us.

The second time, to our heartfelt sorrow, only five of them came. The others had fallen heroically in the village of Pawłowice, near Pińczów. Their hiding place was denounced, and hundreds of Nazi bandits appeared and surrounded the house, and a slaughter ensued.

Four of the murderers were killed and one seriously wounded. But thirteen Jews lost their lives. The rest saved their lives heroically; they sprang down from the roof, and, as they were escaping, they were able to shoot at and kill the four Nazis. It was these survivors who recently came. They brought us good provisions and said that as long as they were alive, they would remember us.

We would not have tired of listening about such Jews forever. As we had no possibility of fighting, it was a great comfort that such Jews existed, whom we would want to join, hand in hand, and together accomplish our sacred duty.

We were happy and fortunate that in the "cemetery" of Dębowiec (the name of the village), there were living Jews; and we rested easier considering that these people had been at the farm for several months already, a sort of proof that one could trust the farmer.

We had a worry, however; the fear that our arrival there would endanger them. We decided, though, that we would stay together and help and support one another.

The farmer did not let on, but once, seeing it might not do any harm, he told us that there were other Jews in the village. We attempted to guess, "Perhaps in your farm, Sir?" He smiled.

From then on, we saw the other Jews openly. We told each other of our pains, heavy personal losses, and bitter experiences. But the main thing was to know what awaited us in the future. Our own experiences were nothing compared to theirs.

Here is what they had gone through:

His name was Chaiml Smolarczyk, from the village of Łabędź (between Działoszyce and Pińczów). From his entire family, he had, thank God, his wife and three children, and his brother-in-law, Zalman Gerszonowicz, and they were sticking together. The worst thing that had happened to them was the last incident. It was when in all the villages there were strong raids and every farmer threw out whatever Jews they were sheltering, fearing for their own lives. Even hiding among the high sheaves of grain did not help, because even there, the murderers found them. They [the murderers] went on for a certain time, sweeping through the grain day after day, and shot whomever they found. Dozens of innocent Jewish souls were murdered and left lying there until after the harvest, when the farmers buried them.

During this time, the previously mentioned Jews walked through the mountains, found a hole there, and stayed four weeks in it. They hardly showed themselves in the village, except at night looking for some water. They grabbed what they could from the fields—beet leaves, beans, carrot tops. This sustained them for several weeks. But their hideout was discovered there also. It was the search for water that gave them away.

One night, after they had gone to sleep, they heard someone trying to enter the cave, although it was well fortified. But the seekers had made a provisional side entrance. There were flashlights shining in their eyes, and they heard wild shouts, "Out, leave everything!"

They had to leave the cave.

They were stripped completely naked, and even the insides of their mouths were checked. Then the bandits went into the cave. Taking advantage of the moment (the murderers did not expect them to run away naked), they escaped. When they realized that the Jews were escaping, they shot in their direction. Happily, no one was badly hurt. One bullet hit Zalman in the back (he showed us where the bullet was; when one touched it, it moved from one place to another).

In that condition, naked, they ran to a farmer they knew, who gave them some clothes. Then, after inquiring further, they were led to this farmer where we now were.

Even then, they had no clothes. They wore torn rags, and their feet were wrapped in rags also. Their faces were pale, not a drop of blood in them, shrunken. They were still young but had aged markedly. Young old people. To this day, they don't know who those people were—German murderers or just plain bandits, robbers.

We spent four weeks in these new quarters, but we had no place to hide. We didn't mind sleeping in the stable, even near an open wall, since, so that no trouble would come, one had to have a hiding place. Meanwhile, one slept wherever one could, though it was a bit cold. Bedding, forget it; our coats covered only half our bodies. We huddled together, the three of us, and the night went by...

But one night, our sleep was interrupted by the loud barking of dogs. We realized it was neither early at night nor near dawn. It was still very dark.

The dogs wouldn't stop their barking. It was not a good sign. Not far away, there must have been strangers, and the dogs sniffed this out immediately.

I could not lie still and moved quietly to the boards that faced the village street. I looked through the grooves but saw no one. The whiteness of the snow gave off sufficient light to notice a person. Everything was quiet. The dogs stopped barking. I lay down again and fell asleep. We were so accustomed to all this, that we paid no attention. Besides, we were ready for whatever might come. Our sleep was again interrupted by steps that we heard below us, in the stable. In a short while, we heard someone trying to climb up to us, but the sound was familiar. Yes, Chaimke was coming. But, why in the middle of the night? Important news, otherwise Chaimke would not have been waking us up. We didn't wait for him to come nearer, but called quietly to him,

"What is the matter, Chaiml?"

"Not bad news, thank God," he answered. "The five Jewish partisans arrived half an hour ago."

We sat up immediately and went toward Chaiml. We wanted to see them at last. "Where are they?"

"They are very tired. Had to walk many kilometers, so they are sleeping now, but their commander stands guard."

Hearing us talking, the Jewish hero, with his weapon in hand, came over to us quickly. In the darkness, he found our hands, embraced us and covered us with warm kisses.

We stood as if electrified. A stream of tears fell without end from our embittered eyes.

We asked him to tell us about their life. He was happy to do so and told us about their collective existence. His own experiences were not to be thought of at this moment; time would not allow it.

Every moment is important. We don't sleep. We've forgotten what it means to undress. But I will tell you some things that will bring you satisfaction.

We have already rid the world of a few murderers or traitors to Jews. The leader of Szyszczyce, Ludwig, who pointed out where eight Jews were hiding, we sent him where the Jews are... I acted as best man at his wedding... When we knocked on his door, he refused to open. He must have sensed the angel of death. So we broke down the door and found him in his bed. We demanded that he show us the way to a second village. He knew what was waiting, so he offered that his son-in-law go instead. "I am afraid" he said. "Why are you afraid?" we asked, "surely you must have sinned greatly." We forced him out of his bed as he was. Seeing death in front of his eyes, he said good-bye to his wife and children. His family did not react, knowing that he deserved the verdict.

As soon as we stepped away from the courtyard, there were some shots heard, and the bandit fell dead. There was a note pinned to his back, listing his guilt and the death sentence, and there he was left. The bestial Działoszyce policeman, Madejski, who made all Jews in that town tremble with fear, is also no longer among the living. The house he built in Książ with Jewish money is now standing orphaned, like us.

In that last battle we fought with the German bandits, where our thirteen comrades perished, I was gravely wounded in my left hand. The bullet went in one way and came out the other. Despite this, I did not lose hold of my gun. On the contrary, I was able to shoot and kill a German beast. He washed himself in his own blood; blood was gushing out before my eyes. That was satisfying blood!

And what comes of that? It is not enough. I am very thirsty for German blood, to cool my soul for my one-year old darling Szymele, my dear wife, my sweet innocent Taubele...

And he choked on these words with tears, but he calmed down and continued:

My treasure! Whom did that little baby hurt? I swear, as long as I live, their blood will not rest, I will not forgive!

Dawn was approaching when his words ended. We saw facing us a proud Jewish fighter, a hero. There was a vengeful flame in his eyes. This is how our old historical heroes must have looked, the Maccabees and the Hasmoneans. We felt like nobodies next to this hero with his great soul. This man lived with a mission—to revenge all innocent Jewish victims so as to allow our near and dear ones to lie in peace in their unknown dark grave pits.

Afterward, the rest of the group appeared. One of them had lost five brothers, heroes in the partisan group, not counting his parents, sisters, and other relatives. The gun is all he had. They could not find recompense except in the automatic pistols which they immersed in the German beasts' blood. "Oh," they said, "If our group had survived, things would have been different. We had already achieved power and strength."

We listened with bated breath and were hypnotized by their vengeful deeds over our bloodthirsty enemies. We bowed before them with respect and awe.

Unfortunately, only one of them survived. My two dear brothers also perished with them, and not at the hands of the German cannibals, but at those of our own Polish murderous *Narodowcy* [Nationalists].

Translated from the Yiddish by Zulema Seligson

In Działoszyce and in the Camps (pp. 374-379)

Majer Zonenfeld

I was born in Działoszyce in 1919 to my parents Mendel and Bajla. My father was a merchant, and I was an only son with four sisters. My oldest sister's name was Róża, and the three younger ones were named Sonia, Hela, and Lola. Until I was sixteen years old, I lived with my parents in Działoszyce. In 1932, I moved to Katowice, and there I worked in different companies.[1] In 1937, I left to go to Łódź, where I worked as a representative for three textile companies from Bielsko: Rapaport, Fisch, and Rotenberg. This continued until the outbreak of the war.

The war found me in Łódź living at 17 Piotrkowska Street. I would like to make note of the fact that from my family that remained in Działoszyce, my oldest sister, Róża, together with her husband, Rolnicki, came to live in Israel, and they are still living there.

In the middle of October 1939, I returned to Działoszyce. In November and December of that same year, the Germans decreed that all Jews must wear arm bands on their sleeves that would identify them as Jews. The *Judenrat* [Jewish council] that had been organized at the beginning of the German occupation was obligated to supply a certain number of Jews for forced labor.

I myself didn't register for labor and occupied myself with any type of business that came my way. Again, I lived with my family. The Germans confiscated my father's entire inventory of textiles along with all his money. They totally destroyed him financially and economically. My father stopped doing business, felt totally useless in the world, and became a broken man.

In 1940, the situation in Działoszyce wasn't at its worst. The Germans mainly occupied themselves with sending hundreds of Jews for forced labor. During that period, the German's luck prevailed on the war front, and their treatment of Jews was reasonable. In certain situations, they had business dealings with Jews. It was only on February 8, 1940, that they forbade Jews to travel on trains.

Prior to the war, the Jewish population in the town amounted to 7,000 inhabitants, and during the war, when the Germans started chasing them out from different places— Kraków, Łódź, Posen [Poznań], and Warsaw—the Jewish population in Działoszyce rose and reached an estimated 12,000 inhabitants. In Działoszyce, there was never a closed ghetto, and because the Germans treated the Jews better here, many many Jews flocked to Działoszyce.

The situation worsened on June 22, 1941, with the advance of the Germans into Russia [Russian-occupied eastern Poland]. After that, the relations of the Germans toward the Jews took a drastic turn for the worse. During that time, the Germans started rounding up Jews and sending them to different concentration camps. The first camp was a fortified establishment in the suburb Kraków-Kostrze, and afterward, Płaszów and Prokocim.

This account is based on testimony given at Yad Vashem.

[1] If he was sixteen in 1932 and twenty-six in 1942, he must have been born in 1916, not 1919.

There was constant gunfire to be heard in the town of Działoszyce. You were not allowed to leave your house after six o'clock in the evening. Only people belonging to the *Ordnungsdienst* [Jewish police] were allowed to be out on the streets after six.

In this regard, I am reminded of the following incident: One evening, at six o'clock, I went out into the garden that surrounded my house in order to get some fresh air. I lit a cigarette, and all of a sudden, I noticed a couple standing under a tree, a man and a woman. At that precise moment, the man made a movement toward me, and I saw a German pointing a gun at me. The girl, who was with him, was Jewish, however, and she held onto his sleeve and prevented him from shooting me. The German put down his revolver and asked me what I was doing outside at this hour. I lied to him and said that being that my father was a religious person, I went outside in order for him not to see me smoking on Shabes. This excuse saved me then from death.

At that time, there were murders occurring under a variety of curcumstances. For instance, in connection with the restrictions against ritual slaughter, a few butchers were murdered, among them a woman. I remember the names of three of the murdered people: Moszek Cudzynowski (nineteen years old), Rachel Cudzynowska (sixty years old), and Pintel [Pinkus?] Drobiarz (sixty years old). Some people were murdered because they left the town to go to neighboring farms in order to buy food. Generally, it was permissible for farmers to bring food products into town and for Jews to buy it. One time, ten Jews (whose origins were from Działoszyce) were captured in Racławice. They brought them to Miechów in order to kill them. They were shot in spite of the great efforts made on their behalf by the *Judenrat*.

In 1941, a census of all the Jews residing in Działoszyce was conducted—men from the ages of twelve to sixty and women from the ages of fifteen to fifty-five. This registration was conducted by a gentile from Silesia by the name of Górniak who supervised the labor force in Kraków. I met this Górniak, who was an architect, in Katowice in 1945. I stopped him and led him to the headquarters of the UB [Urząd Bezpieczeństwa—Security Office]. In the end, he received a jail term with fifteen years of hard labor. Based on the registration that took place, transports were sent to concentration camps—where Jews were subjected to the most horrific imaginable beatings, conditions, and sufferings. This Górniak rounded up one hundred elderly Jews, took them to the cemetery, told them to turn their backs to the gate, held them in suspense for a few minutes, and, in the end, fired ten shots into the air. After this soul wrenching experience, he told them they could go back home.

December 15, 1941, arrived. It was the day on which America declared war on Germany after the invasion of Pearl Harbor. From that day on, terrible troubles for all Jews began. The Germans turned into wild animals. A Jew didn't know how to behave with a German. If he greeted him on the street and removed his hat, he got beaten immediately, since no Jew could be the friend of a German. And if he failed to remove his hat for him, his verdict was death, since this showed total disrespect. In this way, Jews were caught between a rock and a hard place.

The year 1942 arrived. The first decree to emerge was for Jews to hand over all their furs to the authorities (to be used at the Russian front). Those who did not give up their furs were immediately sent to the death camps or killed on the spot. In the beginning of the year, there were widespread rumors that Jews were being sent to the "east," as the

Germans had proclaimed. After that, they transferred all the Jews living in the surrounding villages to Działoszyce. The population of Jews in the town then amounted to approximately 15,000.

In March and April, and until September 3 (on this day they took all the Jews of Działoszyce to the camp at Bełżec), they rushed all the young people off to labor camps.

On August 31, 1942, we received news from the nearby villages about the total banishment and extermination of Jews from their dwelling places, also from Słomniki. Upon hearing this, the entire Jewish population still remaining in Działoszyce gathered together and went to the cemetery, where they beseeched God with prayers and cries to save them from destruction and annhilation.

On September 2, SS officers arrived with the *Junacy* [youth brigade]. They sealed off the entire town, preventing any exit or entry, and announced that all Jews had to present themselves in the market square. In addition to the written order, the SS officers, together with the *Junacy,* strolled along the streets and alleyways of the town, shooting and killing any Jewish passerby found trying to escape from the town.

In the morning, when they had gathered a few thousand Jews in the market square, they brought carts, and in each one, they loaded ten Jews. We, in our innocence, thought that these people would be transported to the train station. Instead, however, the Germans took them to the cemetery, where the *Junacy*, the day before, had dug three huge ditches. In these ditches, 1200 Jews were shot and buried. We were able to determine the number of dead by the amount of clothes that the martyrs had taken off before their deaths. This clothing was later transferred to the synagogue. The Jewish carriage drivers, who had transported the clothing and then returned it to the Germans, were also shot in their carriages. I remember the names of two of them: one was Szmul Goldkorn, and the other, Pałasznicki. As I had been convinced that they would take us all to the train station, I had tried to convince my father that he, too, should get on one of the carts, but he completely refused.

At the same time, the Germans were invading Jewish homes and residences and helping themselves to gold, jewelry, and any other valuable items they found—this in order to cover the expenses of transporting these Jews to the "east." In the market square, at the same time, they started selecting Jews in groups of one hundred in order to take them to the trains. Suddenly, we started hearing gunshots coming from the streets. Dozens of sickly and weak people who had been trying to save themselves by hiding in basements and attics were now being viciously and mercilessly shot to death by the Germans.

After that, we were put into open train wagons, and the train took us to the town of Miechów. When we arrived in Miechów, the police greeted us with murderous beatings. The chief of police, whose name was Redinger, rode on a white horse and directed the entire "action" [roundup and deportation]. At the end, they took us to a large open pasture and surrounded us with many machine guns. All day long, the Jews from the market square kept arriving. After they were all assembled, it became dark, and they used searchlights to illuminate the area. You were not allowed to stand up but had to sit in one place without moving. The earth was damp. This is how they kept us, approximately 12,000 to 15,000 people, until the next morning at seven o'clock. At seven o'clock, we saw a transport of Jews arriving from Miechów, and in their lead was the rabbi of that town who appeared to be carrying a sack on his back. (Our elderly rabbi in Działoszyce, Rabbi Staszewski, about ninety years old, had been murdered in his bed by the Germans. They had entered his room and ordered him to get off his bed, but he refused, saying, "Kill me in my bed. I will not get up," and the Germans fulfilled his request).

After this, they combined us with the Jews from Miechów. Also the Gestapo men from Kraków arrived along with the people in charge of the *Arbeitsamt* [employment office], and they ordered us to get up from our places. They formed us into rows, and the Gestapo selected the younger ones, those still able to work. We all stood with raised hands, and they selected those they wanted by pointing with the sticks in their hands. In this manner they chose 800 young people, who were placed to one side. I stood with my father, mother, and three of my sisters. Before the Germans approached us, my mother gave me all the "treasures" that she had hidden on her body, knowing full well that she and her daughters were going to a certain death. My mother was then sixty years old, my father, sixty-four. I was young then, only twenty-six, and was selected for the work group.

I still managed to see my parents when they were put into the closed railroad wagons. They put us into the open wagons, and at six o'clock, they attached our wagons to the closed ones, and we were on our way.

Our train traveled to Płaszów, but the closed cars continued on to the death camp in Bełżec. In the Płaszów camp, we were under the supervision of the "Vlasovians" (Ukranian soldiers who had surrendered to the Germans near Leningrad).[1] They brought us to the Prokocim camp, which was two kilometers further than the camp in Płaszów. En route, they beat us with whips and smashed bottles on our heads while they ripped off our watches, rings, and anything else that we possessed.

The next morning, they took us out to the camp yard, and in a short while, a Gestapo man by the name of Müller arrived and addressed us with this speech: "You will have it good here. You will have work." This Müller only requested one thing from us, that we should hand over all the money in our possession except for twenty *złoty*, which he would allow everyone to keep. Whoever refused would be shot on the spot. As for myself, I didn't agree to do this. I want to note that one of my sisters, Sonia, had gotten married in 1942 with someone from our town, Izrael Skóra. They took my sister Sonia from the town of Miechów to Bełżec, and her husband was taken to the Prokocim camp. After Müller's speech, my brother-in-law wanted to hand over all of his money, but I, however, stopped him. In the blink of an eye, the Vlasovians came over to us with open suitcases and demanded that we add our money as well. Near us stood a German Jew. On his way over to us, Müller took out a man from the line and asked him, "Do you have more than twenty *złoty* on you?" He answered in the negative. Müller went up to him, put his hand into his coat pocket, and withdrew a one hundred *złoty* bill. He took away the bill and ordered the Jew to sit down in his place. Immediately afterward, Müller shot and killed him on the spot.

The elegant and clean Müller, wearing white gloves on his hands, would perform these murderous acts with ease, as though he was extending his hand to someone.

---

[1] The Vlasovians were Russian soldiers under the command of Russian General Andrey Vlasov; they became collaborators after their surrender to the Germans during the Siege of Leningrad.

Afterward, he addressed the shocked spectators, "Now hand over all that you have in your possession." A very big commotion ensued. People ripped open the soles of their shoes, tore open their sleeves and rid themselves of all the money they possessed. However, my brother-in-law and I, as well as some other young men, hid everything in the dirt, right beneath our feet. The Germans, who suspected that money was hidden in the dirt, combed the entire area afterward. They found some of the money but not all of it. My money was saved, together with that of some others.

I stayed in the camp another few days, and afterward, we decided to escape to the ghetto in Kraków. Our camp was enclosed with barbed wire. A group of eighteen men slipped away from the camp, and we hid among the people marching to work at that time until we were outside the gate. The morning was still dark. Jewish police were supervising the group, and in the dark, no one noticed us. After we entered the [Kraków] ghetto gate, in Zgody Square, we encountered the Jewish police (*Ordnungsdienst*) with the *Junacy*. We bribed them and entered the ghetto.

Inside the ghetto, we started to reorganize, and one of the *Junacy*, who had received a handsome payment from us, got us transferred to Nowy Korczyn (Neustadt), via a boat that was traveling along the Vistula River. The town was located eighty kilometers from Kraków, in the direction of Sandomierz. We were informed that there a Jew was still allowed to breathe.

My brother-in-law stayed in the ghetto. There he heard that the Germans were allowing Jews to settle again in Działoszyce. We only stayed in Nowy Korczyn two or three days, since we also heard the news regarding Działoszyce. Eventually, we reached Działoszyce by foot and discovered some of the things that had happened. After the first deportation of Jews, the Germans had rounded up all the remaining Jews, who were scattered about town, into the synagogue, and a small-scale *Judenrat* was created. Under its control were a few hundred Jews. I did not return to my apartment, since by now a "blue" policeman (a member of *Junacy*) was living there.[1] This policeman looted and stole everything that he found in my apartment. So instead, I lived together with my brother-in-law, whose apartment was untouched, until November 9, 1942. During those nine weeks, the Germans organized "clean up squads" whose purpose was to put in storage all the goods robbed from Jews.

On the night of November 9, we were at a flour mill, one and a half kilometers from town. All of a sudden, we heard shots being fired. We heard that the "action" had begun, and we were determined in our hearts to escape from the town. Not far from the mill was the road to Miechów. Each one of us had a gun and sixty bullets. We harbored no illusions; we knew that our end was near. We remained three days at the mill, and when we left there, we had no choice but to remove our armbands, since we could not venture forth openly as Jews any longer. The director of the mill gave us food to take along for the journey. He was a friend of Moszek Rozenfrucht.

However, we were suddenly seized by fear of the unknown. On the third night, we hid in a nearby stack of straw. The next morning at dawn, the miller, Jan Kałat, found our hiding place and yelled in our direction, "Moszek! Slabonik (the commander of the blue

---

[1] Polish policemen, who wore blue uniforms, were sometimes referred to as "blue" policemen.

police) told me to tell you that you are supposed to go to the cemetery to be killed." We understood that this man, a Silesian, was coming to warn us that we must escape.

We came out of our haystack and from that moment on, we organized our "heroic escape route" among the villages in the area. We entered the first farmer's home. We had money with us, and for a very handsome fee, he let us hide there. This is how we wandered from one village to the next. In each place, we stayed only a very short time, because the farmers were afraid to give us shelter due to their fear of the Germans. After weeks of wanderings from village to village and from house to house, we split into two groups. My brother-in-law and I went in the direction of the village of Sudołek, and we hid with a farmer by the name of Jan Mikuła. Wolf Skóra and Moszek Rozenfrucht were hidden in the village of Łabędź with a farmer by the name of Winnik. After half a year, the Germans killed this farmer together with his family, because he was a "Communist." However, Wolf Skóra and Moszek Rozenfrucht managed to escape and find a hiding place in a bunker. Prior to this, they managed, through this "Communist" farmer, to establish ties with the AL (Armia Ludowa) [People's Army], and entered the forest. There they joined the partisans and fought in the woods until they met their deaths.

My brother-in-law and I spent a long time at Mikuła's in various hiding places. His behavior to us was not consistent. Some of the time he treated us well and provided us with food and other needs. At other times he made believe he didn't know us due to his great fear that the Germans would discover us and burn down his house and murder him together with his family as a punishment. In the end, Mikuła put us in the barn. We dug a hole that was two meters deep, three meters wide, and four meters long. We covered the hole with boards, and on top we put bundles of hay. This is how we lay during the day in the hole, and at night we would venture out in order to breathe some fresh air. One time, a strange man was approaching our hiding place, and Mikuła's son, with great cleverness, managed to detract his uncle from finding us. (This man was the brother-in-law of Mikuła, by the name of Balski). Several times the visits of unwanted people would surprise us near our bunker, but we always managed to escape the danger. During the last weeks, we received horrible food, and Mikuła's relationship with us totally disintegrated.

Our sufferings finally came to an end on January 15, 1945. The Russians arrived, liberated us, and brought us out from darkness unto light and from slavery to redemption.[1]

Translated from the Hebrew by Rochel Semp

---

[1] Language used in the Haggadah to describe the Exodus from Egypt.

During and After the War (pp. 380–87)

Abraham Langer

On September 1, 1939, World War II broke out, and with that, very big troubles began, particularly for Jews. On Friday, German airplanes came and dropped bombs, and on Sunday morning, a neighbor of mine, Symcha Jurysta, *z"l*, along with some other people, went to construct shelters near *Stara Rzeka* [Old River]. A bomb fell, and Symcha became the first casualty in our town. There was great sorrow; he was such a wonderful person, a philanthropist, and also a *dozor* [overseer] of the *gmina* [Jewish community].

The first German decrees were that all Jews must wear armbands with Stars of David on them, they must not walk on the sidewalk, and all men must shave. The Polish police cooperated with the Germans, and they dragged Jews into my barbershop to have their hair cut and their beards shaved.

In 1940, the Germans ordered all single unmarried men and also childless men to report to the [Jewish] community office. They sent off crowded transports of young men. Afterward, men from the *Arbeitsamt* [employment office] came and nabbed everyone they could find on the streets and shipped them off to work camps. Their parents cried and complained, but there was nothing to be done. The Germans conducted searches in merchants' shops and took away wagons full of goods. A peasant girl who had denounced the gravedigger's daughter accompanied the Germans. There were also many Jews who bought the goods that had been taken from the merchants. Everyone's life was in danger, but they did not realize it.

In 1941, the situation became much worse. Every morning, upon arising, we heard bad news. On a certain day, the Germans killed four butchers. They caught them slaughtering a calf. On the following day, they shot two Jews—Hilel Skopicki, *z"l*, and Szulim Aszer Zelikowicz, *z"l*, who had had business dealings with the commissar in charge of Jewish property.

It also happened that some Jews were afraid to keep their goods in their own possession and thus passed them over to others. The informers had their work cut out for them, and the Germans immediately performed searches. Afterward, a commando group from Kazimierz came and began to search private houses. One time they searched the house of our rabbi, Reb Lejzor Epsztajn, *zts"l* [of blessed righteous memory], and found a bag of silver. They forced the rabbi to walk to the market square with the bag on his back and stand there all day, until the community was able to get him released from his punishment. Thus they humiliated everyone. Each day brought new problems.

The Germans gave an order that Jews could not leave town. They could only go up to the highway but not beyond it. Anyone found on the other side would be shot on the spot. There were cases where they killed a number of people at the same time. They also took ten proprietors in the town as hostages and stated that if anything happened to the Germans in town, the hostages would be shot.

One Friday, the Germans blocked off Kraków Street and rounded up all the Jews there. There happened to be about ten people in my barber shop. They took me, my workers, and the ten customers to the town hall. All together there were about eighty of us. The town hall was in Szental's building, and the building had a large shed. They sat us all in the shed. They then led us over the river, near Moszek Beker's bridge. We thought surely that this was the end for us, but a miracle occurred. They led us into the synagogue, and there they took all the single men and sent them away to a work camp. They set us, the married men, free. On another day, the leader came to the community office looking for a young man by the name of Rafałowicz. It seems they did not find him, because he was not in town. They actually gave an order that everyone by the name of Rafałowicz come to the office and also bring with them the young man they were looking for. The Rafałowiczes came, about thirteen people, unfortunately without the young man. The Germans took all of the assembled Rafałowiczes to the Szczotkowice meadow and shot them all to death.[1]

The chairman [of the Jewish community], Moszek Josel Kruk, ran after them and shouted at the Germans, "Let the people go," and one of them turned around pointing his gun at him. He came running into my house, and I hid him.

The Year 1942

The year 1942, the year of the annihilation of the Jews, was the most horrible of all.

During the deportation week, we were still prostrating ourselves on the graves. We beseeched the heavens; day and night people recited psalms, praying that we would all be able to bear our sorrows. According to the decree, we were supposed to present ourselves on Wednesday evening. Meanwhile, on Wednesday afternoon, a whole train full of *Junacy* (Ukranian collaborators of the Gestapo) arrived in town,[2] and they were set to dig large pits the whole night. There were two immediate victims: Izrael Lokaj and Akiba Zyngier. They were shot trying to escape. The orders from the community office were that every hour residents of a different street had to report to the market square with their belongings. All night long, Jews from every street moved toward the market square. The square became overcrowded—from one side, all the way to Chmielowa Street, and on the other side, all the way to the pharmacy. One was not allowed to stand but had to lie down on the ground, like sheep.

In the early morning, many carts arrived. The orders said that old or sick people who could not walk should get onto the carts. Alas, they were all taken behind the cemetery and put to death. The pits had already been prepared. Then came an order to line up everyone with their families. They placed Polish policemen on both sides, with us in the middle. They stood about ten meters apart. There were four Germans in brown uniforms: the district chief [of the Gestapo], Schmidt, and two others on horseback. The district chief was named Beyerlein. We walked in rows, pushed by the police. Whoever could not stay in line or keep up was shot on the spot. We kept hearing shots and screams. The whole way from the market to the train station was full of dead people. The streets were bloodied. It was not the Germans this time who were shooting but the Polish police. I myself heard the German commander order them not to shoot people inside the town. But

---

[1] See chapter by Aszer Rafałowicz,"Under the German Boot," (p.311) for a fuller account.
[2] Abraham Tennenbaum, in "The Deportations from Działoszyce, Skalbmierz, and Miechów," describes this *Junacy* youth brigade as being Polish.

the police commander, called Całowan, with the crooked legs, a dangerous murderer, kept shouting in Polish, "*Tylko strzelać*" (Just shoot). I heard this several times. We, the first transport, were thus hounded until Miechów. There they selected 500 older people, took them into the forest, and shot them. All day long they led the transports. By evening, there were 2,000 dead people in Działoszyce, murdered during the deportation. We lay next to the train in a meadow. The heat was horrendous. Jews from Miechów brought us bread and water, and they lamented, "Who will bring something for us tomorrow?" And they were right. In the morning they brought the Jews from Miechów.

On Thursday, they ordered everyone to take their bags, but this caused great problems, as the bags had gotten mixed up. So some people took two, and others had none. Furthermore, they ordered us to line up by families, and they chose 900 of the strongest (I was among them) and pushed them into nine open wagons, one on top of another, 100 to a wagon. All our families were packed into closed wagons. The train had two locomotives, one in front and one in back. Thus we moved ahead, hearing the whole time the cries of our wives and children in the closed wagons. We left Miechów. Between the railroad cars stood SS men. They gave orders that no one stand up in the wagons and that those who did, or didn't hear the order, would be shot. We arrived in Płaszów at eleven o'clock that night. There, the Ukrainians were waiting for us, in their black uniforms. The nine wagons were detached from the train, and the rest went on to Bełżec. We got down from the train, and the Ukrainians began to push us toward Prokocim over a side road. Along the road they beat us mercilessly and took our watches and our money. It was a dark night, and the dust was terrible. We arrived in Prokocim [labor camp near Kraków] beaten and bloodied, half dead, around two o'clock in the morning. Our boys were already there, having arrived earlier. They brought us food and had us lie down in empty barracks on boards.

Dawn came very soon, and they pushed us out to the inspection area. They pulled out three Jews right there and shot them in front of our eyes. Two were from Miechów, and one, Gutman Richter, *z"l*, from Działoszyce.

The Germans then brought out some barrels and made us put anything we had of value into them. The order was that whoever did not give everything over would be shot like the previous three people. The barrels were filled immediately with various coins and other money—dollars, gold, *złoty*, etc.

As soon as the inspection was over, they rushed us off to work. They took us to Bieżanów. We worked at laying a train track and knocking down the houses that were in the way. This was on the first day of Rosh Hashanah. I did not stay in this camp very long, barely eight days. I had "protection," and they sent me to Kraków, to a camp called "The Waffen-SS and Police of Grzegórzki," where there were 400 Jews.[1]

I was the SS barber and *porządkowy* [orderly]. It was an exceedingly bad camp. There were hangings and shootings.

Every Sunday, Icek Kołatacz, *z"l*, from Działoszyce, drove by with a wagon full of bread that he was carrying to the ghetto, and he would leave me twenty loaves. There were twenty Jews from Działoszyce in the camp. There were some Jews still left in Działoszyce who had hidden there. They were being used to liquidate Jewish possessions.

---

[1] Grzegórzki is a district in Kraków; the camp was on Grzegórzecka Street.

Their gathering place was in my house. Icek Kołatacz drove several times to Kraków to get bread for the ghetto. On the way, he drove by Grzegórzecka Street and never forgot to leave twenty loaves for the people in our camp. Later on, when those who were left in Działoszyce had finished liquidating those possessions, they were themselves liquidated. And also, later on, when they liquidated the ghetto in Kraków, they also liquidated all the camps around Kraków, including ours. The survivors were taken to the large camp Płaszów, on Jerozolimska Street. In this camp I was also the SS barber, thanks to "protection" from my assistant, Dawid Rajsman. He was the barber of the head of the camp, Goeth, and I was the barber of Landesdorfer, Hujar-Stryjewski, Kowalski, and the *Wachtmeister* [guard chief] Glazar. At the Płaszów camp, we suffered greatly.

In my barracks there was a group of seventy people. They often would leave the camp to go to work, One day they found one of them with a loaf of bread, and they shot them all. The situation was horrendous. It is simply too difficult to describe. Every day something new happened. The commander would ride around on a horse and peer through a lorgnette. Whenever he felt like it, he got off his horse and shot people. The camp was known as "Płaszów Hell."

In the meantime, I acquired a new client. He was the head of the community, and his name was Ebner. I shaved him twice a day. He was a very mean man. He always carried a dagger and a revolver. I was once a bit late getting to him, and he punished me—I had to leave Płaszów. I was very happy about this, and on May 1, 1944, there was a transport going to Gross-Rosen, so I went with it. We were about 1,000 men. When we got to the new place, we were welcomed at the gates with music. The inspection area was up a number of steps, so the block elders received us there with such beatings that two Jews fell dead right there. We were bathed and given clothes to wear. I went to work with the barbers. Within a few days, we were sent around to camps near Breslau [now Wrocław]. I reached Wolfsberg and again became the SS barber. I stayed there until the Russians were approaching Breslau. We were evacuated to Bergen-Belsen, then to Stettin [now Szczecin], and from there to Barth and to Rostock. We were liberated by the Russians and the Americans on May 1, 1945.

After Liberation

A few days later, I went to Działoszyce. I found some people in my house: Bencion Czarnocha, Chaim Jurysta, Eli Ostry, and Berisz Jurysta. I took out the possessions that I had hidden. Besides them, the house was occupied by the Dalesubes, the family of the woodcutters.

I would like to describe for you how Działoszyce looked after the war. Half of the houses were in ruins. Groswald's house had disappeared, and all the small dwellings were gone. When I passed by the synagogue, I saw a horse and carriage entering it. I went into the *bes hamedresh* and had a great shock—pictures of Jesus and Mary were hanging there. The guards and the lumbermen were living in the Jewish houses. On Berl Zajfman's balcony stood the district watchman, the storekeeper Koniecki; at Moshe Drobiarz's, was the woodcutter Figiel. The peasants from the villages were living in the houses around the market square. When they saw me, they shouted, "*Abramcze, ty jeszcze żyjesz?*" (Abram, you are still alive?) I went to the town hall to secure documents, and it turned out that the bailiff was the man who was in the labor union, Adamski. His representative was Rak, the shoemaker, with the scar on his face. They gave me whatever I asked them for, and at the same time said, "You want to settle in Działoszyce? We don't advise it." I went out to the market square. It was frightening. There was not a living soul to be seen. The people who were living in my house had many goods there—fabric, clothing, radios, sewing machines, etc. They had come three months earlier than I had and brought the goods from Upper Silesia. I was in Działoszyce for just eight days. I went to Kraków to sell some gold, to have money to give to the Christian woman who was staying in my house. She wanted fifty thousand *złoty* as a dowry for her daughter to get out of my house for half an hour, so that I could recover all that I had hidden before I went to the camps.

During this same night, more trouble came. The AK (Armia Krajowa) [Home Army] attacked my house at midnight. They broke in forcefully and beat us up. They demanded that we give them watches and money. We handed everything over. Then they lined us up against the wall, with one of them watching over us. They brought a horse and wagon and emptied the house out. The wagon was full of radios and sewing machines. They assaulted all the Jewish houses, but in ours it was much worse. One of them gave the order—shoot everyone like dogs. In front of me stood Bencion Czarnocha, Berisz Jurysta, and Eli Ostry. They were shot with a machinegun. They all fell instantly, but they missed me. Bencion was dead. The AKs returned after a while, and I told the wounded to be quiet. But they moaned in their great pain.

The murderers threw a grenade and tore off half of Jurysta's body. As I was trying to stem the flow of his blood, I was hit by a bullet in the toe, but this did me no harm. Early in the morning, the police commander, dressed in civilian clothes, appeared. He was a young gentile from the village of Słupów, a client of mine. He had apparently been notified, and he ordered the wounded to be taken to Miechów. Chaim Jurysta died on the way. Eli Ostry and Berisz Jurysta were taken to the hospital in Kraków. I remained with the dead man, Bencion Czarnocha. In the evening, a delegation led by Dr. Grębowski came and decided to send for a handcart to remove the corpse. Since I was wearing a bloodied shirt, Dr. Grębowski and the notary, Jasieński, both of them clients of mine, sent two suits of clothes, but one was too large, and the other one too small. So I put on the smaller trousers and the large one over a shirt. Until that day, there had been about thirty Jews in Działoszyce who had returned from the camps, but they all ran away. I was left, the only one. With the help of the gentile who had brought the handcart, we laid the corpse in the cart and took it to the cemetery. At the cemetery, I discovered that there were no gravestones left. It was a plowed flat field of grain. One lone grave had remained, that of Hilel Skopicki, *z"l*. I dug a grave next to his for Bencion Czarnocha. Afterward I went to Chmielowa Street and found out that they had also shot Szmul Piekarz, *z"l*, so I buried him also in a Jewish grave.

Meanwhile it had turned dark, and the police wanted me to sleep at their headquarters. I was afraid and went on to Dr. Grębowski's and slept there. In the morning, when I started on my way, I ran into my tenant, who asked me to take everything out of my house. But I did nothing. I walked to the railroad and took the train to Sosnowiec. There I worked as a barber for a while to earn some money. I was there one month.

I will not exaggerate when I say, out of my innermost pain, that when I remember the little town of Działoszyce, my heart bleeds to this day. What dear people perished. My heart cries. How did they deserve such severe punishment, such a tragic end?

Afterward, I went to Germany and worked there for the American army until 1949. From there I made *aliye* to Israel.

Translated from the Hebrew by Zulema Seligson

Digging and Drainage Work

Mass grave of approximately 2,000 Jews killed by the Nazis (photo 1967)

Bunks in concentration camp.
On the right: Benjamin Włoski

Theater in war orphanage

Synagogue—a coal warehouse (photo 1967)

Bes Hamedresh—a kindergarten (photo 1967)

Inside the synagogue (photo 1967)

Synagogue—Crumbling walls (photo 1967)

Northern wall of the synagogue (photo 1967)

View of part of our town (photo 1967)

First memorial in Israel to the memory of our town's martyrs (1951)

Dedication of Torah scroll to Rabbi Yehuda Frankel's synagogue
in memory of our town's martyrs

Ambulance contributed by Działoszyce emigrés in the
United States in memory of our town's martyrs

Działoszyce memorial section of the Martyrs' Forest
in the Jerusalem Hills

Guide to List of Town Residents Who Perished in the Shoah

This guide gives an explanation of how the names listed in the next section were transliterated for the English Edition.

As mentioned in the "Foreword to the English Edition," transliterating names and surnames from one language to another is a difficult task. In the case of Jews from Poland, the names have gone through several language changes over time, making it particularly difficult to ascertain which is the "right" spelling—if one exists.

The policy we adopted for the book and for this list was to spell names (using sources such as indexes of vital records, business directories, and Yad Vashem pages of testimony) as they most probably were in prewar Działoszyce. This was done in order to make it easier for researchers to trace their ancestors back to Poland and find official records there.

Certain Hebrew letters can be transliterated differently depending on the vowel signs and the letters around them. For instance, Aleph may be transliterated "A," "E," or "O," Therefore, in searching through the list of martyrs, one should examine all the different sections of the list in order to avoid missing any relevant names.

As is the custom in Poland, the feminine surname endings "cka" and "ska" have been used for women (Rolnicka, Wdowińska) rather than the masculine surname endings "cki" and "ski" (Rolnicki, Wdowiński). Thus, in such cases, the women's names appear before the men's.

For Hebrew given names such as Elihu, Elimelech, Eliezer, and Menachem, the transliterated form given here is the Yiddish equivalent that was most probably used in Działoszyce—i.e., Eliasz, Mejlech, Lejzor, and Nuchim.

In the original edition, the list of martyrs was in alphabetic order according to the Hebrew alphabet. The list here is in alphabetic order according to the English alphabet.

Fay and Julian Bussgang,
Editors of the English Edition

Town Residents Who Perished in the Shoah, *hi"d*[1]

This list was compiled through a world-wide questionnaire among surviving former residents of Działoszyce. The committee made strenuous efforts to ensure that every single person's name was collected and that no one was forgotten. However, since there is no archive for the community, the only source was our memories, which makes it certain that many people were forgotten. May the memory of those forgotten and missing be blessed forever.[2]

Abramowicz, Perec and Chana (b. [born] Cudzynowska)
Ajzen, Chaim Lejzor, Dwosia, and children Rywka, Szmul Hersz (ritual slaughterer) and
    seven children
Akerman, Majer, Pesela, Kalman, and Sura
Akerman, Zelig and Szajndla
Akurant, Laja, Estera, and Dawid
Alter, Icek, Basia, Simek, and Hela
Altman, Becalel, wife Ruchla, and son Szyja
Ankerman, Mania
Arkusz, Chaja (b. Gerstenfeld), and children Estera and Dawid
Arkusz, Josek and wife Gitla (b. Dziewięcka)
Aspis, Bajla [see Wajnryb][3]
Aspis, Icek and Marjem, Wolf, Szmul, Abram, Bajla
Aspis, Wolf, Szmul, Abram, Bajla, Marjem
Balderman, Abram, wife Pesela (b. Groswald), and children Szmul, Jakób, and Lejzor
Balicki, Abram Lejzor, wife Rela, children Ajdla, Nacha, Lewi, Perec, Mejlech, Chana
Banach, Abram and Laja
Banach, Abram Hersz
Banach, Dawid, wife Bajla, daughter Małka
Banach, Szmul, Kajla, Kopel, and Josek
Bejski, Bencion, wife Sura (b. Ptaśnik), daughter Marjem Ruchla
Bergman, Jakób
Biegacz, Ber, Mote, Bluma, Ruchla, Sura
Biegacz, Jechiel Chaim
Biegacz, Szmaja
Binsztok, Sura [see Kaźmierski]
Biter, Abram Szlama, wife Małka, and children Jakób and Rajzla
Biter, Moszek, Motel, and Laja
Biter, Symcha and wife Estera
Blada, Golda, Abram Szulim, and Jachwet
Blat, Abram Moszek and wife Złata Perla, children Aron, Dobcia, Jonas, Zajnwel, Pola,
    Majer, Sura, Jakób Icek, and Lejzor
Blat, Brajndla, Icek, and Mejlech

---

[1] "*Hi"d*" is an abbreviation for "May the Lord avenge their blood."
[2] This paragraph was translated from the Hebrew by David Goldman.
[3] If a woman's maiden name was included in the listing in the original Yizkor book, she has been listed here also under her maiden name, with a reference to the married name under which she had been originally listed—e.g., [see Wajnryb],

Blat, Hercke, wife Chanka, Bajla and Moszek Chaim
Blat, Mejlech, wife Rywka, and children Motel and Balcia
Blat, Rywka [see Rożenek]
Brandys, Abram, wife Hindela (b. Waga)
Brandys, Kopel and family
Brandys, Lejbuś, wife Chana, and children Moszek, Laja, Rafał, and Szlama
Bratkiewicz, Josek, Sura Mindla
Bratkiewicz, Mordka, Mindla, Zysla, Zelig, Marjem, Witla
Brener, Becalel, Sura, Szlama, Simek
Brener, Binem, Bluma, Icek Chaim, Sura Brajndla, Chaja, Ze'ev Aron
Brener, Sura Brajndla [see Nusbaum]
Brojgies, Alter Wowcze [Wolf], Salka, Rojza
Brojgies, Aron and wife Estera
Brojgies, Berl, wife Fajga, daughters Zysla and Tauba
Brojgies, Chana, and children Berl and Rojza
Brojgies, Tauba [see Secemski]
Brojgies, Tauba, Sura, Motel, Ruchla
Brojgies, Zysla [see Gdański]
Bugajski, Judel and Blima
Bursztyn, Bencion; Bursztyn, Jechiel
Bursztyn, Moszek, wife Chawa (b. Dula), and children Rojza, Szymon, and Cyla
Chaba, Fela, Moszek, Szyja, Jakób
Chaba, Michał, Mindla, Fajwel, Jakób, Marjem, Chana Ruchla
Chaba, Ruchla, Rajzla, Abram Lejzor, Mordka, Dawid, and Aron
Chałupowicz, Chaim, wife Luba (b. Prasa), and daughters
Charmac, Chuna, wife Chawa, children Chaim Dawid, Chana, and Estera
Chęcinski, Efroim and family
Chęcinski, Izrael, Chaja, Szoszana, Moszek, Fajwel, and Majer
Cudzynowska, Chana [see Abramowicz]
Cudzynowska, Chawa, Chaskiel Zachariasz, Josek, Zysel
Cudzynowska, Rywka [see Spokojny]
Cudzynowski, Chaim, wife Szajndla (b. Łataś), children Szymon Eliasz, Lejzor, Bracha
Cudzynowski, Dawid, Małka, Chana, Bracha, Wolf, Zysel Akiwa, Bajla
Cudzynowski, Josek, wife Estera (b. Mendlowicz), and daughter Pola
Cudzynowski, Josek, Zysla, Jachwet, Szymon, Dawid, Laja, Estera
Cudzynowski, Josek, Zysla, Laja, Estera, Dawid, Drezla, Ruchla, Sura, Szmul
Cudzynowski, Mordka Josek
Cukierman, Aron, Abram Jakób
Cukierman, Dawid, Henia
Cukierman, Izrael
Cukierman, Jakób, Chaja, Josek, Witla, Chana
Cukierman, Kalman, wife Mala, and children
Cukierman, Zajdel
Cukierwar, Marjem
Cycowski, Juda Lejbuś, Frymeta, Sura, Rywka, Estera Bajla, Dwojra, Zerach, Mendel,
    Frajda, Henia
Czarkowski, Manela and wife Estera Laja
Czarnocha, Berl, Małka, and family
Czarnocha, Beryl and wife Małka
Czarnocha, Chaja, and three children

Czarnocha, Sender and family

Czarny, Szmul, Ruchla, Laja, Ajdla

Czeska, Dwosia (b. Ptaśnik), Henia, Abram, Sura, Chana, Tauba

Czeska, Sura, children Abram, Chana

Czosnek, Jakób, Chana, Bluma Marjem, Moszek

Czosnek, Jakób, Zelda, Zvi [Hersz], Frania, Cyla, Moszek

Czosnek, Lejzor, Laja, Majer, Bluma, Szmul

Czosnek [see also Hesznik]

Dąbrowska, Tauba, Cypora, Bajla, Benjamin, Chaim Majer, Motel

Dąbrowski, Szlama; Dąbrowska, Ita; Dąbrowski, Benjamin

Dafner, Dawid and family

Dafner, Laja

Drobiarz, Chana Perla, and children Rajzla, Abram Icek, Zvi [Hersz]

Drobiarz, Estera and family

Drobiarz, Gitla, and family Hinda, Estera, Abram Icek, Bluma

Drobiarz, Majer, wife Sura (b. Prasa), and daughters Bluma and Rajzla

Drobiarz, Mordka and family

Dula, Abram, wife Frajdla-Nisza, children Bajla, Chana, Szmul, and Aron

Dula, Chawa [see Bursztyn]

Dula, Cypora (Fajgla)

Dula, Jonatan

Dula, Juda, wife Estera, children Bajla, Wolf, Kalman, Frymeta, and Fela

Dula, Kalman and Chawa

Dula, Lejbuś and Rywka

Dula, Marjem, and daughters

Dula, Mendel and Perla

Dula, Mordka

Dula, Ze'ev [Wolf], wife Mala, and daughter

Dziewięcka, Chawa, and two children

Dziewięcka, Gitla [see Arkusz]

Dziewięcki, Chaim Josek, Nacha, Chendla

Dziewięcki, Efroim, wife, and son

Dziewięcki, Herszel

Dziewięcki, Jekutiel

Dziewięcki, Szlama, wife Sura, and son

Edelist, Chuna, wife Zysla, and children Lejbcia and Mindla

Edelist, Gabriel; Edelist, Estera; Edelist, Dina

Edelist, Jekiel and family, Dwosia, and Sima

Elwing, Jakób and family, *zts"l* [righteous of blessed memory], head of the Skalbmierz Jewish community, president of the local Beit Din [Jewish court]

Epsztajn, Alta, Estera Pajcia

Epsztajn, Eliejzor the Levite, the grand rabbi, direct descendant of the grand rabbi from Neustadt, fifth generation from the author of the *Maor Vashemesh*

Epsztajn, Frymeta, the righteous and renowned wife of the grand rabbi. She was famous for righteous acts. She was the daughter of the grand rabbi, the wondrous teacher, Rabbi Jakób Moszek Safrin from Komarno, fourth generation from the grand rabbi, Ajzykl, the great kabalist of Komarno; son Josek Dawid, grand rabbi of Sokołów, Galicia

Epsztajn, Jonatan

Epsztajn, Rabbi Icek Ajzyk and family from Łódź

Epsztajn, Rabbi Izrael and family, grand rabbi in Łódź

Erlich, Zvi [Hersz] Mordka, Cyna, Rywen, Estera, Gita

Fajgenblat, Itka

Fajner, Josek Kalman Chaim, and sister

Fajner, Necha [see Rajzfeld]

Federman, Jetla

Federman, Wolf and family

Ferenc, Herzl

Fink, Jakób

Fiszler, Dawid, Bajla, Moszek, Chanan, Lejzor

Fiszler, Josek Juda, wife Frajdla Estera, and Szmul

Fiszler, Josek, Frajdla, Mendel Dawid, Perla, Juda, Pinkus

Fiszler, Kalman Szymon, Telcia, Bluma

Fiszler, Pinkus, Bracha, Bajla, Mendel, Szabsia

Flaum, Josek, wife Chaja, daughters Chana and Dina

Florenc, Marjem [see Zyngier]

Frajman, Chaja, Nechama, Izrael

Frajman, Chawa (daughter of Icek Zvi), and children Róża, Chaja, Ruchla, Sura, Ita,
    Frajda Małka, Nuchim, Chaskiel, Kalonymos Kalman

Frajman, Estera, Chana

Frajman, Menachem, Chana, Szlama

Frajman, Mendel, wife Zysla, sons Chaim and Szymon

Frajman, Pinkus, wife, and children Dawid, Lejbl, Abram

Frajman, Purna [Pojra?], and children Abram, Icek, and Szymon

Frajn, Moszek and family

Frajn, Nusyn and family

Frajnd, Alter (ritual slaughterer), Cyrka, Jekiel, Chawa, and daughter Golda

Frenkel, Chaim, wife Rywka (b. Lewkowicz), children Jakób, Majer

Frenkel, Josek Chaim, wife Gitla (b. Jutrzenka), Dawid, Witla, Mala, and Bajla

Frydberg, Icek Majer (ritual slaughterer), wife, and daughter

Frydman, Jonas and family

Frydman, Naftali, Eli, Frajda, Chaim

Frydman, Symcha, Bajla, Chana Brajndla, Rywka, Ruchla, Mirla

Frydrych, Dawid, wife Zlota (b. Łataś), Jenta

Fuks, Icze, wife Chawa (b. Szliwińska), and children

Garbarz, Arysz, wife Bluma, and children Fajgla, Henia, Pesla, Binem, and Hinda

Garfinkiel, Dawid, wife Ruchla (b. Grycman), children Jakób, Anszel, Fania

Garfinkiel, Majer, wife, and children Dwojra and Estera, and son Jechiel

Gdańska, Brajndla, husband, and children Izrael and Dawid

Gdański, Rachmiel, wife Zysla (b. Brojgies), children Sura, Jechiel, Dawid

Gelbart, Nuchim, wife Sura, daughters Frymeta and Rywka

Gelibter, Bajla

Gelibter, Icek and family

Gerszonowicz, Lejb, Izrael, Chana, Henia, Bajla, Moszek, Aron, Dwosia, Jakób, Fajgla

Gersztenfeld, Chaja [see Arkusz]

Gertler, Salomea, and children Leopold, Eugenia, and Jonas

Glajt, Balcia

Glajt, Hersz Lejb, wife Fajgla, and children Laja and Racla

Glajt, Izrael and wife Balcia

Glajt, Pejsach and Golda

Glajt, Szlama, wife Chana, and child Moszek

Glazman, Juda, wife Sura, and daughter Chana
Głodna, Marjem Laja
Goldfrajnd, Frajda
Goldkorn, Herszel and Chawa
Goldkorn, Szmul and wife, and children Szlama Berysz and Ruchla
Goldkorn, Zysla [see Wdowiński]
Gotfryd, Aba, Małka, Josek, Perec
Granetman, Abysz, wife Fajgela (b. Szwimer), children Bajla, Rajza, and Szulim
Grosfeld, Chaja
Groswald, Juda Lejb, wife Ruchla, and children Dawid, Jakób, Nuchim, and Szabsia
Groswald, Pesela [see Balderman]
Grycman, Małka
Grycman, Ruchla [see Garfinkiel]
Gryner, Berl
Gryner, Lejzor, and child Berl
Gryner, Szlama, and children Berl and Chana
Grześ, Laja [see Miller]
Gutenberg, Moszek and Zysla
Halpern, Abram, Chaja Mania, Estera, Perla, Szyja Heszel, Nuchim Majer, Szajndla
Herc, Cyrla [see Rodał]
Hercberg, Pejsach, Genia
Herszlowicz, Abram
Herszlowicz, Abram, Chana, and Hercke
Herszlowicz, Hercke, Fajgla, and sister
Heshnik [Czosnek?], Lejbuś
Honigsberg, Michał, Szlama, Jentla, Kalman, Estera
Horowicz, Gerszon, Małka Laja, Jentla, Frymeta, Chana
Horowicz, Rajzla
Ickowicz, Wolf and family
Iserowski, Moszek Fiszel and Chaja
Izraelowicz, Eliasz, Mindla, Tuwia
Jakubowicz, Kopel, Estera, Jakób
Jakubowicz, Mordka Lejb and family
Jakubowicz, Zyskind, wife, and children
Jasny, Aron, Frymeta, Hinda, Sura, Bajla, Ita, Chaim, Bronia, Mejlech
Jasny, Zvi [Hersz], Sura, Nuchim, Chawa, Hela
Jura, Szmaja and family
Jurysta, Aron and family
Jurysta, Chanandel
Jurysta, Icek, Estera, Mordka, Jakób
Jurysta, Judel and family
Jurysta, Sandel and family
Jurysta, Symcha, wife Szajndla, children Chaim Dawid, Dwojra, Abram Aba, Perla, and Szmul
Jutrzenka, Abram, Mirla, and children
Jutrzenka, Chaim Chaskiel, Naomi, Izrael, Cyrla, Lejbl and family
Jutrzenka, Gitla [see Frankel]
Jutrzenka, Icek, Chana, Pincia, Szulim, Ita
Jutrzenka, Jekiel, wife Cwetela (b. Skrzypek)
Jutrzenka, Michał, wife Rajzla, Naomi and sisters

Jutrzenka, Szmul, Fajgla, Witla, Estera, Moszek

Kac, Kalman

Kac, Moszek

Kac, Paltjel, Mendel, Cypora

Kac, Rywka

Kaczka, Gabriel, wife Laja, children Szlama and Chaim

Kajzer, Chaim, Chawa

Kajzer, Mordka, Cyrla, Berysz, Chana, Chaja, Chawa, Herszel

Kamelgart, Josek, wife Szoszana, children Izrael, Jakób, Moszek, Chana, Michał

Kamrat, Kajla [see Rafałowicz]

Kaźmierska, Sura (b. Binsztok)

Kaźmierski, Abram Aba, wife Gelcia, children Rojza, Cypora, Izrael, Perec, and Jakób

Kaźmierski, Godal, Jekiel

Kaźmierski, Lejzer and family

Kaźmierski, Szlama, Laja

Kińryś, Kalman and Szajndla

Kińryś, Szlama and Estera

Kirszenbaum, Jehudit

Klajner, Szmul, Szyfra

Klajnman, Izrael and family

Klajnman, Jonatan (ritual slaughterer) and family

Klajnman, Mejlech and family

Kminkowski, Moszek and Sura

Kohn, Abram and Rywka

Kołatacz, Ajdla, Jenta, Mania, Sejwa, Dolek

Kołatacz, Cypora [see Wdowiński]

Kołatacz, Icek

Kopeć, Icek, Mania, Josek, Rywka, Kalman

Kopeć, Kalman son of Aba

Kopeć, Nusyn; Kopeć, Bluma; Kopeć, Chawa; Kopeć, Josek; Kopeć, Szyja; Kopeć, Sura

Kopeć, Szewa and children

Kopeć, Szoszana [see Krelman]

Kopeć, Zvi [Hersz]

Koźma, Anszel, wife Mechla (b. Lis), and children Fajgla, Icek, Josek, Joel Berl, Itka, Estera, and Bluma

Koźma, Chaim, and sister Chana Cyrla and their families

Koźma, Icek and family

Koźma, Rabbi Abram Dayan, *zts"l* [righteous of blessed memory], and wife Chaja, and children

Krajcer, Jakób, Tyla, Hadassa, Frymeta, Chana, Izrael, Moszek, Anna, Laja

Krelman, Bluma [see Zalcman]

Krelman, Jachwet [see Ryba]

Krelman, Jakób Zvi [Hersz]; Krelman, Szoszana (b. Kopeć)

Krzesiwo, Henoch, wife Estera, children Gitla, Aron, Jechiel, Hersz, Itla

Krzykacz [see Skrzykacz]

Kulimek, Herszel, Hinda, and children

Kulimek, Mejlech, wife Rywka, and eight children

Kurland, Moryc, Rajza, Lasia, Heniek

Kwalwaser, Mordka, wife Bajla, Rywen, Abram, Josek, Mindzia

Langer, Ajzyk, Wolf

Łataś, Abram, Bluma, Jenta Brajndla
Łataś, Masza, Jenta Serca
Łataś, Szajndla [see Cudzynowska]
Łataś, Złata [see Frydrych]
Łaźniarz, Gitla Tauba
Łaznowska, Małka, Hela and siblings
Lejzorowicz, Benjamin, Jakób, Ze'ev [Wolf], Gita, Fryma
Lejzorowicz, Rywka, Ruchla
Lejzorowicz, Zvi [Hersz]
Leszman, Jakób, wife Mania (b. Ptaśnik), children Dov [Ber], Rojza, Dawid, Gitla, Izrael, Ita
Leszman, Juda, and son Izrael
Lewit, Moszek, Benjamin and family
Lewkowicz, Abram, Chana
Lewkowicz, Aron, wife Chaja Sprynca, children Mindla, Fajgla, Rajzla, Josek, Kalman
Lewkowicz, Dwojra
Lewkowicz, Kajla, and children
Lewkowicz, Rachmiel, Dawid
Lewkowicz, Rywka [see Frenkel]
Lewkowicz, Szmul Jakób, Sura Rajzla, Rojza, Chanandel, Moszek, Herszel, Małka, Bluma, and Dawid
Lewkowicz, Zalman, wife, and five children
Lichtig, Estera [see Pryzant]
Lichtig, Szlama
Lida, Arje Lejbuś, Szoszana, Bluma, Małka
Lida, Chaim Zvi [Hersz], Chaja Sura, Juda Arje, Ze'ev [Wolf], Herzl, Lewi, Dwojra, Menachem Mendel, Izrael
Lida, Chana and family
Lida, Laja and family
Lipman, Mordka, Aszer Lejzor Eli Iser Henoch Aba, Szymon Icek Zelig
Lipman, Mordka, Zelig, Aba, Szymszel, Icek, Eliasz Iser
Lis, Jakób, Fajgla
Lis, Mechla [see Koźma]
Lokaj, Abram and family
Lokaj, Herszel, wife Ruchla, children Izrael, Abram, Rafał, Szajndla
Lokaj, Taubele [see Prasa]
Lublin, Lejb, Sura, Lejzor
Majerczyk, Abram
Majerczyk, Chana and family
Majerczyk, Fajgla [see Spiro]
Majerczyk, Gela
Majerczyk, Marjemcia?
Majerczyk, Moszek Aron, Cyrka, Rywka, Henia, Ruchla
Majerczyk, Naftali, Rywka, Fajgla, Gitla
Majerczyk, Rywka, Gitla
Majtek, Chaim, Szyfra
Majtek, Jakób, Moszek Fiszel
Majtek, Michał, wife Bajla (b. Natansohn), and children
Malc, Chana and family
Malc, Herszel, Rywka, Ruchla, Dawid
Mandelbaum, Dawid and Sonia

Mandelbaum, Jakób, wife Szajndla, and son Herszel
Mandelbaum, Josek Juda, wife Fajgla, and daughter Bajla
Mendlowicz, Estera [see Cudzynowski)
Miller, Herszel, wife Laja (b. Grześ), Bajla, Doba, Szmul, Dwojra, Gitla, Jakób
Minc, Szmerl, Bajla, Hersz Lejb, Fajgla, Chaja
Miodownik, Josek Baruch, Kajla, Izrael, Jechiel, Kalmisz, and Motel
Moher, Herszel, Małka, Bluma, Rajzla, Lejbl, Szlama, Chancia
Moneta, Jakób, wife Zysla (b. Zmyślana), and two children
Morowicki, Izrael, Ruchla, Hinda, Lipa, Benjamin, Rojza, Abram, Bajla, Dawid, Laja
Moszenberg, Aszer, Ruchla, Lejzor, Chaim, Chana
Moszkowicz, Hendel, Gela
Mur, Mania
Nagelblat, Chaim Majer, Genendel, Sura Laja, Gitla, Chana, Frajda, Rywka
Nagelblat, Szmul, Bronia, Icek, Jakób, Gitla
Najman, Brajndla
Natansohn, Abram, Fela, Bajla, Szmul
Natansohn, Bajla [see Majtek]
Natansohn, Judel, Mindla, Balcia, Wolf
Natansohn, Kalman, wife, and daughter
Natansohn, Moszek Fiszel, Mordka, Wolf, Majer
Natansohn, Sura, Mindla, and Bajla
Niemowa, Icek, wife Rywka, children Marjem, Sima, Lejb, Wolf
Nifkier, Wita, Bronia (b. Sztajer), Josek, Nadzia (b. Rajzfeld)
Nożycer, Hercke, wife Sura, and sons Herszel and Max
Nożycer, Lejbuś, Sura, Zysel, Zysma, Judel
Nusbaum, Lejb, Ela, Estera, Sura Brajndla (b. Brener)
Nusbaum, Moszek
Obarzańska, Golda and family
Opozdower, Lejbl, Rywka (b. Warszawiak), and children
Ostry, Chaskiel, wife Chaja (b. Prasa), and children Bracha and Izrael Lejb
Ostry, Mordka, wife Cypora, and children Małka, Abram, Bluma, Ruchla, Estera, and Nusyn
Ostry, Mordka, wife Estera Frymeta, and children Efroim Zalman, Chaja Sura, Laja Chana,
    and Frajdla
Owsiany, Chaim, Gitla, and Szymon
Owsiany, Majer, Rywka, and children
Owsiany, Zalman
Pałasznicka, Dora and family
Pałasznicka, Frania
Pałasznicka, Sura and family
Pałasznicki, Dawid, wife Fajgla (b. Tajtelbaum), and daughter Rojza
Paserman, Hinda
Pasternak, Sala and family
Piekarz, Juda and Sura
Piekarz, Juda, Ruchla
Piekarz, Szmul Joel, Estera, Chana, Juda
Piekarz, Szmul, Rochma, Batszewa, and families
Pilc, Szulim and family
Pińczowski, Benjamin and family
Płatkiewicz, Izrael, Rojza
Płatkiewicz, Jentla

Płatkiewicz, Jeta and family
Polska, Chana [see Żydowąs]
Półtora, Estera [see Rafałowicz]
Pomeranc, Abram and family
Pomeranc, Gitla, Lejbl Arje, Mala
Pomeranc, Izrael
Pomeranc, Moszek Dawid
Potok, Aron, Mala, Abram, Sima
Prajs, Dawid and wife Gita
Prajs, Szmerl, wife Bluma, sons Icek Hersz
Prasa, Chaja [see Ostry]
Prasa, Luba [see Chałupowicz]
Prasa, Sura [see Drobiarz]
Prasa, Szmul Johanan, wife Alta (b. Rafałowicz), children Chaim Symcha, Mordka,
    Bluma, Sura
Prasa, Taubele (b. Lokaj), daughter Rajzela
Profesorska, Dwojra
Profesorski, Alter and family
Pryzant, Jakób, Estera (b. Lichtig), Alte Jechiel
Przędza, Josek, wife Marjem (b. Zmyślana)
Przewoźnik, Josek and Mina
Ptaśnik, Abram and Ita
Ptaśnik, Benjamin, Adela, Chana, Abram Dawid, Estera, Mordka
Ptaśnik, Chana [see Retman]
Ptaśnik, Dwosia [see Czeska]
Ptaśnik, Izrael Szaja, wife Ruchla, son Zysza, daughter Frymcia and daughter
Ptaśnik, Jechiel and Rela
Ptaśnik, Lejbuś and wife
Ptaśnik, Mania [see Leszman]
Ptaśnik, Mordka
Ptaśnik, Mordka, Frymcia, Zvi Herszele
Ptaśnik, Sura [see Bejski]
Ptaśnik, Szmul, and children Róża and Dov [Ber]
Pułka, Moszek, Ruchla
Pułka, Sandel, Gela, Chana
Rafałowicz, Abram; Rafałowicz, Jakób
Rafałowicz, Alta [see Prasa]
Rafałowicz, Chaim, Dawid, Rojza, Gela, and children Tuwia, Szmul Hersz, Alte, Estera
Rafałowicz, Estera (Półtora)
Rafałowicz, Hoiwisz, wife Chanka, children Majer, Abram Zajda
Rafałowicz, Izrael Gabriel, Mordka, Frajda, Dov [Ber], and Sura
Rafałowicz, Jakób, wife Sura
Rafałowicz, Josek, Perec, Abram, Szajndla, Wolf, Rajzla and husband
Rafałowicz, Kajla (Kamrat)
Rafałowicz, Krajndla (Spokojny)
Rafałowicz, Moszek, Chanka, Majer, Zeidel
Rafałowicz, Szmul and Brajna, sons Jechiel and Ze'ev [Wolf]
Rafałowicz, Zalman, wife Chana, children Nuta, Moszek, and Nuchim
Rafałowicz, Zvi [Hersz] and Bajla, children Jechiel and Ze'ev [Wolf]
Rajzfeld, Abram, Moszek, Nachman, Sima, Chaim, Kalman, Luba

Rajzfeld, Beni
Rajzfeld, Chawa; Rajzfeld, Fela; Rajzfeld, Moszek
Rajzfeld, Dov Zvi [Ber Hersz], Necha (b. Fajner), Sura Szajndla, Ninka
Rajzfeld, Icek, Sura, sons Mordka and Szaja
Rajzfeld, Jonas and Ruchla, daughters Necha and Hela
Rajzfeld, Mordka, Perla, and children Szmul and Juda Lejb
Rajzfeld, Moszek, son of Herszel
Rajzfeld, Nadzia [see Nifkier]
Rajzfeld, Necha (daughter of Dawid Gustaw)
Rajzfeld, Ruchla (Rotenberg)
Rajzfeld, Sima (married name Zylberberg), children Necha and Szmul
Rajzfeld, Szyfra, and children Necha, Kalman, Ze'ev [Wolf]
Rajzman, Dov [Ber], Czarna, Zvi [Hersz]
Rakowski, Josek, Chana, Chaim, Jakób Kopel, Frajda, Rajza, Frymeta, Szmul Hersz
Rakowski, Moszek Dawid, Perla, Henia, Cyrla, Jechiel, Josek, Zelda, Frymeta, Izrael
Retman, Chaim, wife Chana (b. Ptaśnik), and child Marjem and children Złata, Gitla, Abram
Retman, Josek
Rodał, Izrael Jakób, Moszek, Icek Juda, Cyrla (b. Herc)
Rolnicki, Eliasz, Ruchla, Chawa, Mira, Frajda, Icek, Marian, Mania
Rolnicki, Ludwik, Julek
Rolnicki, Nusyn, Chaim Aron, Fajgla, Aba
Rotenberg, Ruchla [see Rajzfeld]
Rotner, Chana Sura, Estera, Gerszon, Laja, Chaim
Różany, Josek, wife Marjem, and children Frania, Dawid, Regina, Fela, Wolf
Rozdział, Abram, Bajla, Zysla, Rywka, Zelda, Chana, Szyfra, Dawid, Chaja, Sura, Izrael
Rozdział, Szlama, Ruchla, Berl, Alter, Bluma, Jakób, Mendel
Rozenblum, Joel, wife Mirla, children Abram, Ira, Kalman Icek, Lejbuś Wolf, Szymon,
    Ezriel, Szabsia
Rożenek, Cypora
Rożenek, Dawid, Chana, Jechiel Motel
Rożenek, Estera and children
Rożenek, Fajwel, Mala, Abram, Motel, Szmul
Rożenek, Fajwel, Szraga, wife Rywka (b. Blat), and children Mejlech, Zysla, Marjem, Golda
Rożenek, Marjem
Rożenek, Mordka
Rożenek, Moszek, Kalcia, Mania, Sura, Róża
Rożenek, Szmul, Jeta, Sura, Motel, Frymeta
Rożenek, Wolf, Fajga, Frymcia, Sura, Laja, Mordka
Rozenfrucht, Moszek Hersz and family
Różycki, Pejsach, Machla
Rubin, Estera
Ryba, Chaim Lejb, Chawa
Ryba, Fajwisz
Ryba, Hersz and wife
Ryba, Izrael and family
Ryba, Sender and Jachwet (b. Krelman), Dobcia, Ruchla, Cypora
Ryba, Szmul
Ryba, Zelig, wife Małka, and children Krajndla and Kopel
Ryndhorn, Dawid, Rywka Sura (from Kazimierz)
Ryndhorn, Menasze, Róża, Dawid Kalman (from Kazimierz)

Salomon, Jechiel Dawid, Tauba, Ruchla, Laja, Majer, Josek Lejb, Szmul
Salomon, Jechiel, Tauba, Szmul, Ruchla
Secemska, Tauba (b. Brojgies)
Secemski, Aron Josek and Sura
Secemski, Mendel, Sura, Dawid, Witla, Chana
Skop, Alter and family
Skop, Lejzor and Sura
Skop, Nusyn and family
Skop, Szaja and family
Skop, Wolf and wife, son Jakób and sisters
Skóra, Wolf
Skórecki, Jakób, Hinda, Aron, Marjem, Szmul, Frania, Batia, Helena, Moszek
Skórecki, Josek, Binem, Moszek, Marjem, Chana
Skrzykacz [Krzykacz?], Mendel, Krajndla, Izrael Zysel
Skrzypek, Cwetela [see Jutrzenka]
Słabecka, Mira
Smakolek? [Smuklerz?], Hercel
Smolarczyk, Lejb and family
Śpiewak, Chana and family
Śpiewak, Moszek; Śpiewak, Abram
Spiro family from Dziekanowice
Spiro, Dodek
Spiro, Fajgla (b. Majerczyk); Spiro, Wowek [Wolf]
Spiro, Lolek
Spiro, Moniek
Spokojna, Hinda, Sura, Jakób, Izrael, Fajgla, Wolf, Rywka, Rochcia
Spokojna, Krajndla [see Rafałowicz]
Spokojny, Alter, Sura, and children
Spokojny, Dawid, wife Rywka (b. Cudzynowska)
Spokojny, Josek Lejb, Sima, Abram, Chaim
Spokojny, Mordka, Estera, Dawid, Moszek, Jankiel, Chawa
Staszewski, Moszek
Staszewski, Moszek Jechiel, the rabbinic judge, and family
Staszewski, Rabbi Icek, the Levite, and wife
Staszewski, Symcha
Sternberg, Pejsach and family
Strisower/Strzyżower, Krajndla
Szajnfeld, Lejbuś; Szajnfeld, Ruchla
Szajnker, Frajda
Szaniecki, Abram; Szaniecki, Icek
Szenkier, Abram Moszek, wife Henia, and children Ruchla, Dawid, Pesla, Szymon,
    Chaja, Sura
Szenkier, Jehudit
Szenkier, Tauba
Szental, Abram Josek and family
Szental, Aron and family
Szental, Henoch and family
Szental, Mendel and Broncia
Szklarczyk, Jakób, wife, and children Kalman, Dawid
Szlamowicz, Chawa and family

Szliwińska, Chawa [see Fuks]
Szliwiński, Ajzyk, wife Chancia, and children Nusyn, Chawa, Szmul, Krysa
Szliwiński, Jakób and family
Szliwiński, Nusyn, wife Zysla, and children Sura, Chaja, Jakób, Szaja
Szlomowicz, Abram, wife Ajdla, and children Frajdla Itka, Chaim Dawid,
    Marjem Fajga, Golda
Szlomowicz, Josek and family
Szlomowicz, Lejbuś and family
Szmulowicz, Pinia, and children Berl and Itka
Sznal, Fajgla, Gela
Szor, Icek and family
Szor, Jakób and family
Sztajer, Brona [see Nifkier]
Sztajer, Fela Bronia, Adzia
Sztajn, Dawid, Chaja, and children
Sztajn, Jachwet
Sztajn, Mordka Wolf, wife Hinda, and children
Sztajner, Szlama and Laja
Sztajnfeld, Majer
Sztern, Doba
Szternfinkiel, Moszek, wife Ruchla, and daughters Frania and Sura
Szulimowicz, Chawa and family
Szulimowicz, Josek, wife Taubcia (b. Wajnbaum)
Szulimowicz, Majer, wife Chawa, son Szlama
Szulman, Sura
Szwajcer, Anszel and family
Szwajcer, Bluma
Szwajcer, Dawid
Szwajcer, Fajgla and family
Szwajcer, Icek
Szwajcer, Laja and family
Szwajcer, Ruchla and family
Szwajcer, Szajndla and family
Szwajcer, Zvi [Hersz] Dawid and Zysla
Szwimer, Abram, Bajla, Izrael, Jakób, Bluma, Moszek
Szwimer, Fajgela [see Granatman]
Szwimer, Juda, Fajga, Dov [Ber]
Szwimer, Majer, Henia
Szwimer, Zvi [Hersz], Juda, Ita, Chana
Szydłowska, Temera
Szydłowski, Icek, wife Chana, and children Frajdla and Naftali Chaim
Szydłowski, Jonas
Szydłowski, Nuchim Silman, wife Frajdlela, and daughters Sura and Bracha
Tajchtajl, Josek
Tajtelbaum, Fajgla [see Pałasznicki]
Tajtelbaum, Josek, wife Dwosia, and children Dawid, Genia, and Abram
Targownik, Dawid, and Moszek
Targownik, Josek and wife
Tauber, Chawa; Tauber, Jonas; Tauber, Szulim
Tenenbaum, Joew, Henia

Tenenbaum, Zysman, Gryna, Chaja, Rajzela, Eli, Ester
Tintpulver, Szlama, Dwojra, Berysz, Sala, Abram, Chana, Wolf
Topf, Alter, Chana, Sura
Waga, Hindela [see Brandys]
Waga, Icek Majer and family
Waga, Moszek, wife, and children Abram, Motel, Zalman, and sisters
Waga, Ruchla, and children Zajdel, Chaja, Chaim, Gita, Lejbcia
Wajnbaum, Taubcia [see Szulimowicz]
Wajnbaum, Zale, Tauba, Kalcia
Wajner, Abram; Wajner, Ezryel; Wajner, Moszek
Wajnryb, Bajla (b. Aspis)
Wajnsztok, Izrael, Rajzla, Estera, Sura, Szulim, Ruchla, Majer
Wakszlag, Jakób, wife Cyrka, children Chana, Icek, Menachem Mendel, Naftali, Cyrla Laja
Warszawiak, Abram, Chana, Jakób, Fajgla
Warszawiak, Nuchim, Izrael, Pesela, Jakób, Fajwel, Lejbl, Fajga, Pincia
Warszawiak, Rywka [see Opozdower]
Warszawiak, Symcha Binem, Golda Gelcia
Wdowińska, Chaja, and children Mindla, Mancia, Fajgla, Berl, Gitla, Bluma
Wdowińska, Jentla
Wdowiński, Dawid and wife Gita
Wdowiński, Dawid, wife Hindla, daughters Sala, Bronia, and Mindzia
Wdowiński, Icek, wife Zysla (b. Goldkorn), and sons Dawid and Berysz
Wdowiński, Josek, wife Cypora (b. Kołatacz), and children Dawid, Icek, and Aron
Wdowiński, Szraga, wife Małka, and sons Jakób and Icek
Włoska, Chaja, Ze'ev [Wolf], Nuchim, Jakób, Tauba, Jonas Abram, Laja
Włoski, Ze'ev, Chawa, Nuchim, Jakób, Mnucha, Jonas, Tauba, Abram, Itka, Marjem,
    Henia, Ber
Włowski, Jakób, Nacha, Jehudit, Marjem, Henia, Joel, Mote, Zelda, Małka, Nuchim
Wolberg, Alter Majer, wife, and children Aron, Fisze, and sisters
Wolfowicz, Herman, Małka, Chana, Lejb
Wolgelernter, Chaim, Majer
Zając, Abram Icek, Fajgla, Chendla, Gela
Zalcberg, Symcha, wife Złota, children Alter Wolf
Zalcman, Benjamin, wife Frymeta, and son Alter Michał
Zalcman, Berl
Zalcman, Bluma (b. Krelman)
Zalcman, Juda, Bajla, and Jakób
Zalcman, Mendel Menachem, Szprynca, Michał Jechiel, Chawa, Zvi [Hersz], Estera, Mordka
Zalmanowicz, Alter Jakób, wife Gitla, children Chaja Sura and Szajndla
Złotnik, Frymeta, and children Ajdla, Frajda
Złotnik, Jakób, Chana, Berl, Porja, and children Abram and Icek
Złotnik, Mordka, Josek, Pesla, Moszek, Rajzla, Frymeta, Herszel, Ajdla
Złotnik, Moszek, Frymeta, Abram, Mordka Josek
Złotnik, Rywka, and four children
Zmyślana, Hinda, and son Wolf and family
Zmyślana, Marjem [see Przędza]
Zmyślana, Zysla [see Moneto]
Zmyślany, Moszek and Rywka
Zonenfeld, Mendel, wife Bajla, daughters Szajndla Chanka and Laja
Żychliński, Eli and family

Żydowąs, Herszel, wife Chana (b. Polska), and daughters Estera, Chawa, Masza, Pesia,
    and Szulamit
Żydowąs, Icek and family
Żydowąs, Kajla
Żydowąs, Michał and family
Żydowąs, Wolf and family
Zylber, Abram, Sura, Lejbl and sisters
Zylber, Chaja and family
Zylber, Mendel, wife Sura, and children Dov [Ber], Frajdla, Krajndla, Jakób
Zylber, Zysma and family
Zylberberg, Chaja [sic], wife Sura, and children Rywka, Nusyn, Henia
Zylberberg, Pesla; Zylberberg, Jakób
Zylberberg, Sima [see Rajzfeld]
Zylberberg, Wolf, Frania, Bajla, Arje, Szmul
Zyngier, Anszel and wife Chana
Zyngier, Berl and family
Zyngier, Dawid and Estera
Zyngier, Dawid, wife Chana, and children Olek [Aleksander], Estera
Zyngier, Marjem (b. Florenc) and family
Zyngier, Menasze and family
Zyngier, Moszek, Eliasz, Chana, Rywka, Chaskiel, Sura Laja, Aron, Marjem, Cyla
Zyngier, Nacha

The Organizational Committee and Book Committee
of Działoszyce Emigrés

Dov Bejski
Treasurer

Zvi Yehuda Frankel, *shlit"a*
Chairman

Aryeh Shahar
Secretary

Jakób Chaba

Arje Rolnicki

Moshe Rożenek

Shalom Lida

Izrael Rożenek

David Shlomi

Izrael Zvi Skóra

Loyal members and devoted activists—
Committee members who have passed on
May their memory be a blessing.

Zysman Szeniawski

Zvi Rolnicki

Chaim Szkolnik

Josef Brandys

Thus you shall say to the House of Jacob—
These are the lady activists devoted to goodness and charity
in all aspects of the organization of Działoszyce emigrés.
They are all deserving of a blessing forever.

Tova Avni

Shoshana Rolnicka

Chaja Chaba

Sara Szerer

Bracha Pozner

Działoszyce Landsmanshaft in America

Marvin Laskier
President

Chaim Fraiman
First VP

Hillel Gdański
Second VP

Leo Margolin
Secretary

Harry Schwitzer
Treasurer

Meyer Wakschlag
Third VP

Harry Garber

Shloima Fraiman

Guide to the Index of Names

The original Działoszyce Yizkor Book did not contain an index. Therefore, this Index of Names is an entirely new section, added by the editors of the English Edition to make it possible for readers to find passages in the book most relevant to their families.

In compiling the index, certain conventions were used to facilitate the identification of persons who may have been known by more than one name. Married women are listed in the index under both their maiden name and their married name, for example: 1) Najman, Ester m. [married name] Gertler, and 2) Gertler, Ester b. [born] Najman. The names of people who have changed their names are also listed under both names: 1) Harif, Yosef b. [born] Ostry, and 2) Ostry, Josef aka [also known as] Yosef Harif.

What appears as a surname in the book may have been in reality a nickname, often indicating the person's profession. When this is known or suspected, the surname in the index has a [?] after it. If the real (legal) name is known because of something mentioned elsewhere in the book, a reference is made to the real name. Thus, if a man is mentioned as Moszek Dayan [rabbinic judge], but it could be determined that his real name was Moszek Koźma, he is indexed twice, as follows: 1) Dayan[?], Moszek, see Koźma, Moszek; and 2) Koźma, Moszek aka [also known as] Moszek Dayan. The page numbers referenced are listed only under his real name.

Additional information helping to identify an individual is shown in square brackets; nicknames and alternate names are in parentheses.

As is the custom in Poland, the feminine surname endings "cka" and "ska" have been used for women (Rolnicka, Wdowińska) rather than the masculine surname endings "cki" and "ski" (Rolnicki, Wdowiński). Thus the women with such surnames are alphabetized before the men.

When searching for given names, it must be kept in mind that the same given name may have different forms. For example, diminutives in Yiddish are often expressed by adding "el" or "le/la" [Herszel, Fajgela], while diminutives in Polish may be expressed by adding "ek/ka" [Moszek, Hanka] or "cia/sia" [Pincia, Basia]. The names Chaskiel/Jecheskiel were often used interchangeably, as were Eliahu/Eljia/Eliasz; Icchak/Icek/Icze/Izak; Jakób/Jankiel/Jankief; Jehoszua/Szyja [Joshua]; Jeszaja/Szaja [Isaiah]; Lajb/Lajbele/Lajbuś; Eliezer/Lejzor/Luzer; or Menachem/Nuchim. The same person may have been called a different name under different circumstances or by different people. In addition, Hebrew names and their Yiddish equivalents were often used interchangeably, such as Dov/Ber, Cwi [Tsvi]/Hersz, Arje/Lajb, or Wolf/Ze'ev.

In Polish, letters with diacritical marks are usually alphabetized after those written without diacritics. However, since most readers will not know whether the name is written with or without diacritics, diacritics have been disregarded in alphabetizing this Index.

This Index of Names does not include the memorial list of "Town Residents Who Perished in the Shoah." Their names can be seen on pages 346–59.

Fay and Julian Bussgang,
Editors of the English Edition

Index of Names

_____ , = no surname given

_____ , Abele, 98, 169, 173

_____ , Abram Aba [teacher], 179

_____ , Ajzyk [shoemaker], 151

_____ , Alter Jakób [prayer leader], 61

_____ , Anka, 55

_____ , Arele [*shames*], 55

_____ , Arysz [*shtibl* leader], 61

_____ , Awigdor, 173

_____ , Awramcze [dance master], 136

_____ , Awramcze, 157

_____ , Awramele [village trekker], 83

_____ , Ayzykl [had yellow nag], 302

_____ , Benjamin [Lejbl Jutrzenka uncle], 268

_____ , Ber [*rebbe*], 84

_____ , Berysz [yellow-haired], 193

_____ , Bibi [German], 276

_____ , Chaim Aron [coachman], 302

_____ , Chaim Jechiel [teacher], 96, 165, 168, 180

_____ , Chaim-Ber [shoemaker], 44

_____ , Chaim-Jakób, 169

_____ , Chaskiel [Chaim Cycowski uncle], 147

_____ , Chenandel [watchmaker], 161

_____ , Chune [Little Chunele], 193

_____ , Dawid Binem [Miechów hostel], 62

_____ , Ester [Majer Cudzynowski aunt], 159

_____ , Fajwel [coachman], 302

_____ , Fritz [German, Sankt Valentin], 263

_____ , Gerszon [son of village trekker], 84

_____ , Hersz [the deaf Hersz], 133

_____ , Hersz Mendel [*shames*], 167, 204

_____ , Icekl [gravedigger], 79

_____ , Jakób Lejbele [rabbi of Trisk lineage], 56

_____ , Janek [Rajzfeld uncle], 292–93

_____ , Jankiel [Lejbl Jutrzenka uncle], 265

_____ , Jankiel Święty[?] [village trekker], 84

_____ , Josek Pejsach'l [teacher], 179

_____ , Josel [Yosef Harif uncle], 86

_____ , Judka the Baker, 64

_____ , Kalman Kalonas [teacher], 42

_____ , Laja [wife of storekeeper], 42

_____ , Lejb Icek, 82

_____ , Lejb Wolf [teacher], 179

_____ , Lejbniu [rabbi in Kielce], 172

_____ , Lejbuś [Dina Epsztajn husband], 249

_____ , Magda [servant], 38, 41, 50

_____ , Majerek, 178

_____ , Maszka [tavern keeper], 160

_____ , Mejlech [the Red], 193

_____ , Menasze, 159

_____ , Mendel [Little Mendele], 193

_____ , Mendel [son Radzymin rabbi], 249

_____ , Mendele [had food store], 42

_____ , Mietek [Rajzfeld uncle], 292–93

_____ , Mizer, 185

_____ , Mojsze Lejbele [rabbi of Trisk lineage], 56

_____ , Mordka [owner of warehouse], 44

_____ , Moszek [Batia's], 193

_____ , Moszek [Ester Jutrzenka husband], 254

_____ , Moszek [the Hasid], 161

_____ , Moszek Benjamin [son-in-law of ritual slaughterer], 73

_____ , Moszek Szmul [village trekker], 84

_____ , Moszele [*rebbe* in Lublin], 172

_____ , Moszele [tombstone engraver], 290

_____ , Motele [rabbi of Trisk lineage], 56

_____ , Motele [*rebbe* in Chernobyl], 172

_____ , Nachman of Bratslav [*rebbe*], 84

_____ , Nachman the Baker, 64–65

_____ , Nachumcze [rabbi of Trisk lineage], 56

_____ , Nachumcze [rabbi in Warsaw], 172

_____ , Nusyn the American, 157

_____ , Paweł [*Stubenältester*], 263, 267

_____ , Pejsach'l [*melamed*], 168

_____ , Pesla [Akiba Dayan wife], 177, 181

_____ , Pifa [fabric store], 271

_____ , Przemysław [gentile], 312

_____ , rabbi in Alexandrów, 249

_____ , rabbi in Chęciny, 53, 56–57

_____ , rabbi in Ger, 166

_____ , rabbi in Komarno, 56, 248

_____ , rabbi in Końskie, 249

_____ , rabbi in Miechów, 327

_____ , rabbi in Pińczów, 56, 257

_____ , rabbi in Pokrzywnica, 249

_____ , rabbi in Przecław, 249

_____ , rabbi in Radzymin, 249

_____ , rabbi in Ropczyce, 249

_____ , rabbi in Żarki, 172

_____ , Robert [German], 276

_____ , Róża [Rajzfeld relative], 292

_____, Rywka [Yosef Harif grandmother], 86
_____, Sender [Yellow Joel's], 193
_____, Stefek [pseudonym of Szlama Leszman's cousin], 271
_____, Szymele, the Meshugene, 199
_____, Tall Jekl, 54
_____, Zoszka [Gertler maid], 44–45
_____, Jancze, 249
Adamczyks, 119
Adamski [bailiff], 334
Ajnbinder[?], Lejb, 193, 196
Akerman, Kajla/Klara m. Waks, 155
Aleichem, Sholem, 320
Alter, Grusi, 190
Alter, Josek, 77
Alter, Pincia, 136
Anders, General Władysław, 288
Apter[?], Majerl, 246
Arkusz, Chawa, Estera, Dawid, 201
Arkusz, Motel, 120
Arkusz, Wolf, 120
Aszkiel, 89
Avni, Tova b. Szydłowska, 176, 362
Bachmajer, Wolf, 169
Bajuk, Zelig, 235
Balicki, Aba, 252, 296
Balicki, Aron, 98
Balitzki, Hayyim (Chaim Balicki), 165
Balski [gentile], 330
Banach, Pinkus, 173
Bankier, Abram, 261
Baum, Aron, 92
Baum, F., 134
Baum, Herszel, 105
Becker [German], 223
Beder[?], Wolf, 193
Bejska, Rachel, 278
Bejski [father of Moshe], 230
Bejski, Bencion, 74, 303
Bejski, Dov, 13, 78, 111, 113, 192, 211, 220, 232, 239–40, 278, 360
Bejski, Moshe, 11, 13, 105, 209, 239, 278
Bejski, Szaja, 302–3
Bejski, Uri, 232, 278
Beker[?], Mendel, 193
Beker[?], Moszek, 64, 140, 159, 332
Besht [Baal Shem Tov], 84
Beyerlein [German], 223, 276–7, 332
Bielecki [gentile bar owner], 94
Biter, Becalel, 172

Blady, Kalman, 165
Blanke [Hauptsturmführer], 281
Blat, 64
Blat, Abram Moszek, 59, 61
Blat, Aron, 59
Blat, Baruch, 59, 61
Blat, Jakób Icek, 62
Blat, Josef, 59–60, 62
Blat, Mejlach, 92
Brandys, Izrael, 113
Brandys, Josef, 361
Brandys, Josek, 78, 111, 113, 177
Brandys, Kopel, 105, 168, 180
Brandys, Lejbuś, 92
Brandys, Lola, 242
Bratkiewicz, Josek, 74
Brener, 296
Brener, Binem, 89
Brener, Chaja, 101
Brener, Moszek, 89
Brener, Necha, 78, 111
Brener, Szyja Herszel, 89
Brojgies, Dawid, 85
Brojgies, Mancia, 178
Bułówka[?], Ajzyk (see Mann, Ignacy)
Bursztyn, Bajla/Bella, 78, 111, 115
Bursztyn, Hadassa, 135
Bursztyn, Mejlech, 98
Bussgang, Fay and Julian, 7, 9, 345, 364
Całowan [police commander], 333
Chaba family, 306–10
Chaba, Chaim, 94, 244
Chaba, Chaja b. Szulimowicz, 104
Chaba, Chaja, 159, 362
Chaba, Eliasz, 106
Chaba, Jakób, 360
Chęcińska, Róża, 105, 134
Chęciński, Icek, 98
Chilewicz, 302
Chilewicz, Moszek, 133
Chilowicz [Ordnungsdienst head], 191, 314
Chobeh b. Chaba, Avraham, 244, 306
Cohen, Izrael Meir [rabbi], 125
Cudzynowska, Rachel, 326
Cudzynowski, 144
Cudzynowski, Alter, 159
Cudzynowski, Henoch, 119–20
Cudzynowski, Majer, 159
Cudzynowski, Moszek, 326
Cudzynowski, Zalman, 73, 76

Cukierman, 76, 92, 159
Cukierman, Abram, 96
Cukierman, Moszek, 78
Cukierman, Witla, 105
Ćwik, Mrs., 101
Cycowska, Frymeta b. Lautersztajn, 147
Cycowski, Chaim, 145
Cycowski, Judka Lejbuś, 147
Czarnocha, Bencion, 237, 334–35
Czosnek, Hercka, 74
Czosnek, Lejzor, 120
Czosnek, Szmul, 27
Dąbrowski [Pole from Warsaw], 266
Dąbrowski, Szlama, 265, 267
Dachauer [German], 276–77
Dachauer-Kornhäuser [gendarme], 223
Dalesube [woodcutter], 334
Daum, Menachem, 7
Dayan[?], Abram (see Koźma, Abram)
Dayan[?], Akiba, 177, 180–81, 254
Dayan[?], Kalman [grandfather of Alter
    Horowicz], 184
Dayan[?], Moszek (see Koźma, Moszek)
Dmowski, Roman, 288
Dobia, Władek [pseudonym of Szlama
    Leszman], 269–71
Doński, Herszel, 109
Drobiarz, 92, 135
Drobiarz, Abram Icek, 190–91
Drobiarz, Ezryel, 119–20
Drobiarz, Herszel, 172, 190
Drobiarz, Mordka, 191
Drobiarz, Moshe, 190, 334
Drobiarz, Pintel [Pinkus?], 326
Drobiarz, Rywka m. Kulimek, 191
Drobiarz, Szmul, 191
Drobiarz, Zvi [Hersz], 166
Dubiński, 60
Dula, 217
Dula, Abram, 92
Dula, Fajgele, 239
Dutkiewicz, Perec, 136
Dzierążner[?], Chaim, 193
Dziewięcki, Chaim Josek, 95, 125, 172
Ebner [German], 334
Edelist, Chuna, 74
Edelist, Gabriel, 98
Edelman, Dr., 88
Einhorn, Hercka, 126
Englander, Jechiel, 172

Epsztajn [liquor store], 92
Epsztajn [rebetsn], 197, 248
Epsztajn [rebbe], 210
Epsztajn, Ajzyk, 249
Epsztajn, Altela, 249
Epsztajn, Dinale, 249
Epsztajn, Izrael, 249
Epsztajn, Josek, 249
Epsztajn, Kalman/Kalmus [rebbe in
    Neustadt], 56, 173, 248
Epsztajn, Kalonymus Kalman Halevi [rebbe
    in Kraków], 173
Epsztajn, Lejzor Halevi [rebbe], 56, 79, 173,
    191, 204, 248, 276, 331
Facht [German], 276
Fajgenblat, 296
Federman, Wolf, 167
Figiel [woodcutter], 334
Filipowski [gentile violin player], 136
Fink, Lejb, 120–21
Fiszer, Szyja, 172
Formalski, 230
Formalski, Pinkus/Pincia, 92, 311
Formalski, Szmul, 126
Formalski, Zalman, 311
Fraiman (see also Frajman)
Fraiman, Chaim, 301, 363
Fraiman, Shloima, 363
Frajfeld, Zalman, 258
Frajman, Chaskiel, 120, 140, 304
Frajman, Frajdla, 303
Frajman, Josek Baruch and wife, 302
Frajman, Kalman, 303–4
Frajman, Lejb, 119
Frajman, Małka, 303
Frajman, Szlama, 303
Frajnd, Alter, 253
Frajnd, Chaja m. Jutrzenka, 253, 255
Frajnd, Cylka, 255
Frajnd, Jankiel, 256, 260, 265
Frajnd, Mordka, 256
Frajnd, Motel, 260, 265–68
Frankel, Juda/Yehuda Halevi [rabbi],
    95, 125, 171, 343, 360
Frenkel, Zelig, 312
Frydberg, 180
Frydberg, Icek Majer aka Icek Majer Szu"b
    [shoykhet], 96, 125–26, 172, 180, 203
Frydman [blind comedian], 192
Frydman, Alter, 141, 220, 239, 241, 243, 278

Frydman, Awramcze, 59
Frydman, Chaskiel, 123
Frydman, Josek/Joskele [rabbi], 246, 250
Frydman, Josek Dawid, 182
Frydman, Josek, 123
Frydman, Kalman, 123
Frydman, Mendel, 22, 75, 92
Frydman, Naftali, 183
Frydman, Pifa, 182
Frydman, Szulim, 182
Frydman, Zalman, 120–21
Frydrych, Mejlech, 109–10
Frydrych, Ze'ev [Wolf], 110
Gałązka, 217
Gałązka, Abram, 105
Garber, Harry, 363
Garfinkiel, Josek, 135
Garten, Dawid, 273
Gdański, Hillel, 363
Gelbart, Chaim, 296
Gelbart, Chanka, 296
Gelbart, David, 296
Gelbart, Nachum, 296
Gerszonowicz, Zalman, 322
Gertler, 69, 231
Gertler, Eliasz Gabriel, 37, 39
Gertler, Ester b. Najman, 37–41, 43–44
Gertler, G., 242
Gertler, Izrael Zerach, 36–40 (see also
    Zerachi, Yisrael)
Gertler, Jonas, 37, 39–41, 44
Gertler, Poldek, 212, 265
Gertler, Salomea, 220, 239, 241, 243
Gertler, Shlomo/Szlama, 33, 43, 77, 105,
    212, 220
Gertler, Szymon, 42
Gertler, Szymon-Ze'ev, 41–42
Ginsberg, Aszer, 113
Glajt, Szlama, 121
Glazar [guard chief at Płaszów], 334
Glejzor, Zelig, 35
Goeth, Amon, 191, 251, 280–81, 299, 314, 334
Goldberg, Benjamin, 267
Goldfaden, 111
Goldkorn, 94, 205
Goldkorn, Szmul, 327
Goldwaser, Abram Aba, 168, 174
Goldwaser, Bajla, 119
Goldwaser, Jakób, 168, 181
Gordon, Aaron David, 120, 123

Górniak [work overseer], 276, 326
Gotlieb, Chaim Jakób, 101
Grabski, Władysław, 128
Grandapel, Abele, 53, 173
Granetman, Abuś, 297, 312
Grębowski, Dr., 215, 335
Grodziński, Chaim Ozer, 125
Groswald, 334
Groswald, Jakób, 239
Groswald, Moszek, 60
Grundman, 312
Grundman, Awisz, 55
Gryner, Jakób, 120
Grześ, Zalman, 265
Gustav, David (Rajzfeld), 288
Habalan, Wolf, 167
Harchav[?], Majer, 173
Harif, Yosef b. Ostry, 83
Heinrich [Hauptsturmführer Płaszów], 272
Hercberg, Wolf, 111
Hercyk, 259
Heryk, Noach, 110
Herzl, Theodor, 55, 129
Hilhin [drawings in synagogue], 27
Himmler, Heinrich, 261
Hirszenhorn, Szaja Szmul, 101
Hofman [Judenrat head of labor], 218
Horowicz, Alter, 184
Horowicz, Anszel, 173
Horowicz, Herszel, 105
Hujar-Striewski [German], 334
Hupert, Jakób Wolf, 120
Hupert, Jakób, 119–20
Hupert, Jechiel, 296
Hupert, Mrs., 243
Hupert, Symcha, 301
Jabl'a?, Jakób, 201
Jagoda, Motel, 169
Jakubowicz, 259
Jakubowicz, Zyskind, 74, 98
Jasieński [notary], 335
Jasny, 296
Jurysta, 259, 312
Jurysta, Aron, 98
Jurysta, Berisz, 334–35
Jurysta, Chaim, 237, 251, 334
Jurysta, Moszek, 238
Jurysta, Symcha, 331
Jutrzenka, Abram, 253
Jutrzenka, Chaim Chaskiel, 253

Jutrzenka, Chaja b. Frajnd, 253, 255
Jutrzenka, Dawid, 253
Jutrzenka, Ester, 254
Jutrzenka, Ezriel, 253
Jutrzenka, Fajga, 253
Jutrzenka, Feige-Zipporah, 268
Jutrzenka, Gitel, 253
Jutrzenka, Golda, 253, 255
Jutrzenka, Icek Josek, 253
Jutrzenka, Icze [Icek], 253
Jutrzenka, Jankiel, 253
Jutrzenka, Lejbl aka Aryeh Shahar, 125–26,
    169, 172, 179, 253, 259, 360
Jutrzenka, Mendel, 253
Jutrzenka, Miriam, 268
Jutrzenka, Moszek, 257
Jutrzenka, Shmuel, 268
Jutrzenka, Szmul, 92, 95–96, 125–26, 253
Jutrzenka, Witla, 253–54
Kabziński [gentile store owner], 92
Kac, Abram, 167, 265
Kac, Alter, 181
Kac, Chaim Jakób, 160
Kac, Chaim Szaja, 53, 169, 172, 180
Kac, Fajgele m. Rożenek, 160
Kac, Izrael, 160
Kac, Josef, 175
Kac, Lejzor, 126, 256
Kac, Michał Rachmiel, 160
Kac, Zelda, 160
Kacengold, Salek, 235–36
Kaczka brothers, 141, 220
Kaczka, Chaim, 239, 241, 243, 278
Kaczka, Moszek, 239
Kaczka, Szlama, 239, 241–43, 278
Kagan, 292
Kałat, Jan [gentile miller], 329
Kamelgart, Moszek, 220, 241, 243
Kamelgarten, Josef, 74
Kamelgarten, Moszek, 239, 278
Kamelgarten, Yisrolke, 126
Kamelgericht [Kamelgart?] brothers, 141
Kamerdyniak [Polish policeman], 235, 276
Kampat [Kamrat?], Majer, 74
Karasiński [mayor of Skalbmierz], 258
Karmioł, 109
Karmioł, Chawa b. Rozenfrucht, 64
Karmioł, Hercel, 54, 77, 101
Karmioł, Herszel, 105–6
Karmioł, Mordka, 101, 106

Karmioł, Róża, 312
Kaźmierski, Jakób, 181
Kaźmierski, Jankiel, 126
Kaźmierski, Jekiel, 169
Kazun [bandit], 75–76
Klags [SS officer in Płaszów], 315
Klajner, Chaim, 126, 265
Klajner, Ezryel, 302
Klementynowska, Sura, 101
Klingberg, Moszek, 265
Kobrzyński [gentile neighbor of Chaba], 307
Kobzej [Christian], 312
Kohav, David b. Dawid Stern, 110
Kohl [dance teacher from Kielce], 136
Kohn, Izrael [rabbi in Stopnica], 160
Kołatacz, Abramele, 169
Kołatacz, Herszel, 87
Kołatacz, Icek, 54, 60, 77, 105, 134, 201, 333
Kołatacz, Joel, 56
Kołatacz, M., 135, 139
Kołatacz, Marida, 58
Kołatacz, Masza m. Rozenblum, 58
Kołatacz, Mojszele, 169
Kołatacz, Moszek, 133
Kołatacz, Szlama, 133
Kołatacz, Szymon, 75, 84, 169
Komarner[?], Ajzykl [rabbi in Komarno], 249
Koniarz[?], Moszek, 193
Koniecki [district watchman], 334
Konieczny, Maciek [righteous gentile], 312
Kopeć, Herszel, 60
Kowalski [ethnic German], 276
Kowalski [in Płaszów], 334
Kozak [gendarme], 223, 225, 276–77
Koźma, 74
Koźma, Abram aka Abram Dayan, 165,
    169–70, 172, 181
Koźma, Chaimele, 169
Koźma, Moszek aka Moszek Dayan, 169–70
Krautwirt [engineer], 280
Krelman, Moszek, 141
Krelman, Natan/Nusyn, 120, 122, 140
Król [Rajzfeld uncle], 293
Król, Dudi, 292
Kruk, Icek, 150
Kruk, Moszek Josek, 222, 224, 239, 242, 332
Krycer brothers, 120
Krycer, Jechiel, 150
Krycer, Szyja, 120
Krzykacz, Mendel, 168, 180

Krzyształ [gentile], 312
Książek [town mayor], 244
Książek, Paweł [gentile store owner], 92
Książski, 65
Kulczyński-Ślęzak [gentile bar owner], 94
Kulimek, Mejlech, 191
Kulimek, Rywka b. Drobiarz, 191
Kuzin, 64
Kuzmer, Wolf, 73–74
Kwiat, Munia, 292
Landau, H. [teacher], 101, 168–69, 244
Landau, Izrael Szlama, 96
Landesdorfer [German], 334
Langer, Abraham, 73, 331
Langer, Munia, 110
Laskier, 148
Laskier, Abram Benjamin, 149
Laskier, Marvin, 363
Laskier, Menachem, 148
Laskier, Moniek, 303
Laskier, Moszek, 92, 148–49, 173
Laskier, Nuchim Chaskiel, 149
Laskier, Nuchim, 150, 244, 303
Laskier, Rajzla b. Lorja, 149
Laskier, Surele, 149
Laskowski [non-Jew], 109
Łatacz, Jakób, 120
Łatacz, Michał, 120
Lautersztajn, Frymeta m. Cycowska, 147
Lautersztajn, Symcha, 145, 147
Lazar, Dawid [doctor], 215
Lazar, Dwojra [doctor], 215–16
Lazar, Szymon Menachem, 215
Łaznowski, 35, 89
Łaznowski, Aron, 89
Łaznowski, Szlama, 89
Lechtzier[?], Berele, 193
Leopold [Brynica camp commander], 251
Leszman, Dawid, 135
Leszman, Dov, 135
Leszman, I., 139
Leszman, Jakób/Jankiel, 79, 111, 133–35
Leszman, Szlama ben Jakób, 269
Leszman, Szlama, 269
Lewensztajn, J. M., 109
Lewit brothers, 234–35
Lewkowicz, 35
Lewkowicz, Aron, 90
Lewkowicz, Dawid, 90
Lewkowicz, Herszel, 90

Lewkowicz, Jankiel, 90
Lewkowicz, Michał, 90
Lewkowicz, Szmul, 90, 244
Lida, Aron, 277
Lida, Herszel [rabbi], 165
Lida, Shlomo, 360
Lokaj, 79, 111, 135–36
Lokaj, Abram, 135–36
Lokaj, Izrael, 332
Lokaj, Jurek, 315
London, Fiszel, 109
Lorja, 87
Lorja, Josel, 121
Lorja, Rajzla m. Laskier, 149
Ludwig [gentile leader in Szyszczyce], 323
Madejski [Działoszyce policeman], 276, 323
Majer, Zalman, 53
Majerczyk, Abram, 166, 169, 172
Majerczyk, Bendet, 78, 98
Majerczyk, Szulim, 244
Majtek, 90
Majtek, Michał, 120
Malarz[?], Mendel, 193
Malc, 74
Mandelbaum, Izrael Josek, 125
Mandelbaum, Jakób and wife, 312
Mandelbaum, Josek Judel/Judka, 92, 168
Mann, Ignacy b. Ajzyk Man, 61, 185–86,
     189, 290
Mardyks, Josek, 160
Margolin, Leo, 363
Maszkowski [count in Łabędz], 160, 302
Melamed[?], Heszele, 166, 168, 173, 177, 179
Melamed[?], Hinka [wife of Heszele], 167
Melamed[?], Jakób, 180
Melamed[?], Josek Lejb, 179
Meryn, 65, 148
Meryn, Chaim, 134
Meryn, H., 135, 139
Meryn, Tuwia, 89, 92, 149, 173
Meyer, Lidke [Oberscharführer in
     Wüstegiersdorf], 310
Mikuła, Jan [gentile farmer], 330
Miller, Lejbl, 109
Miller, Manela, 135
Moher, Herszel, 54–55, 78
Moher, Szyja, 277
Moszenberg, Aszer, 74, 97
Moszenberg, Mania, 105
Moszkowski, 27, 35, 60, 64, 66, 88

Moszkowski, Bernard, 88
Moszkowski, Józef, 89
Moszkowski, Marcel, 89
Moszkowski, Zysza, 88
Mucha [German], 218, 276
Mufson, Michel, 55
Müller [German], 260, 279–80, 328
Nagelblat, Herszel, 169, 181
Najman, Brajndla, 38
Najman, Dina, 41–42
Najman, Ester m. Gertler, 37–40
Najman, Henie, 48
Najman, Moszek, 40, 42
Najman, Szlama/Salomon, 48
Najman, Szymon-Ze'ev, 37–39
Najman, Ze'ev [Wolf], 36–37
Niewiadomska, Mrs., 258
Niewiadomski, Witek, 255, 258
Nifkier, Jakób, 294
Nifkier, Moszek, 92
Nifkier, Necha b. Rajzfeld, 292–94
Nowak [Polish farmer], 257
Nożycer, Judka, 111
Olmer [Jew from Miechów], 281
Orbach, Zoszka, 110
Osnat, Bajla, 119
Ostrowski, Moszek Fiszel, 173
Ostry, Chana Ruchl, 83
Ostry, Eli, 334–35
Ostry, Izrael Lejb, 84
Ostry, Izrael Wolf, 83
Ostry, Josef aka Yosef Harif, 83
Ostry, Moszek Ber, 83–85
Osuchowski [Catholic], 288
Owsiany, 35
Owsiany, Chaim, 89
Owsiany, Icze, 89
Owsiany, Szmul, 89
Palarz, 109
Pałasznicki, 327
Pałasznicki, Fajwel, 94
Paszkowski, 87
Peretz, I. L., 55
Piekarski, T., 135
Piekarz, Szmul, 237, 251, 335
Pilarzik [German], 157, 259
Pilc, Szymon, 120–21
Piłsudski, 78
Pińczewski, Benjamin, 74
Pińczowski, Lejzor, 111

Pińczowski, Moszek, 109
Płatkiewicz, 217
Płatkiewicz, Izrael and wife, 312
Płatkiewicz, Jekutiel, 92
Płatkiewicz, Moszek, 255
Płatkiewicz, Rywka, 255
Płatkiewicz, Szymon, 101
Pleszowski, 92
Polak, Abram, 258
Pomeranc, Lejbl, 135
Pomeranc, Moszek Dawid, 22, 31, 53
Poper, Baruch, 297
Potok, Zelig, 90
Pozner, Bracha b. Zając, 151, 362
Prasa, Izrael Juda, 74
Prasznik, Zvi [Hersz], 196
Probolovitzer[?], 193
Profesorski, Abram, 92
Profesorski, Alter, 65
Przędza, Josek, 126
Przenica, Szaja Jonas, 101
Przeworski, 27, 64, 66, 85
Przeworski, Judka, 87
Przybnik, Chaim, 301
Ptasznik, Alter, 61
Ptasznik, Berl, 126
Ptasznik, Dov, 166
Ptasznik, Josek, 121
Ptasznik, Lejbele, 58, 74
Ptasznik, Lejbl [jester], 302
Ptasznik, Lejbuś, 25
Ptasznik, Tuwia, 120–21
Ptasznik, Zysia, 135
Pułka, Chaim, 119
Pułka, Jakób, 120
Pułka, Moshe, 119–20
Rafali [Rafałowicz], M., 52
Rafałowicz, 225, 311, 332
Rafałowicz, Aszer, 311
Rafałowicz, Bluma, 126, 172
Rafałowicz, Herszel, 311
Rafałowicz, Icek, 82
Rafałowicz, Jakób, 57
Rafałowicz, Surele, 58
Rafałowicz, Symcha, 172
Rafałowicz, Szmul, 312
Rajch [supervisor at Schindler Factory], 260
Rajsfeld, Jechiel, 235 (see also Rajzfeld)
Rajsman, Dawid, 334
Rajzfeld, 64, 242 (see also Rajsfeld)

Rajzfeld, Alfred, 293
Rajzfeld, David (Gustav), 288
Rajzfeld, Janek, 291
Rajzfeld, Judka, 291
Rajzfeld, Karol, 61, 290–91
Rajzfeld, Necha m. Nifkier, 292–94
Rajzfeld, Ruchel, 291
Rajzfeld, Róża, 292
Rajzfeld, Sima, 292
Rajzfeld, Szyfra, 292
Rak [shoemaker], 335
Rapaport, Szabtai [rabbi in Pińczów], 126
Rashi, 180
Redinger/Ritinger [German], 223, 276, 327
Retman, Aron, 74
Richter, 92, 231
Richter, Gitma, 136
Richter, Gutman, 333
Rodał, Icek, 264–65
Rodał, Szmul, 82
Rogowski, 277
Rolnicka, Frajdla, 135
Rolnicka, Mira, 239
Rolnicka, Róża b. Zonenfeld, 325
Rolnicka, Shoshana, 133, 362
Rolnicki, 230
Rolnicki, Arje, 92, 132, 360
Rolnicki, Eliasz, 92
Rolnicki, Lejbuś, 108
Rolnicki, Nusyn, 109
Rolnicki, Zvi [Hersz], 361
Rotam b. Rotner, David, 314
Rotenberg, 65, 292
Rotner, David (see Rotam, David)
Rotner, Gerszon, 314, 316
Rotsztajn, Benjamin, 180
Rozdział (Raziel), Eliyahu, 283
Rozen, Josef [rabbi in Dvinsk], 170
Rozenblum, Masza b. Kołatacz, 58
Rozenblum, Motele, 191
Rożenek, Abram, 160, 308
Rożenek, Fajgele b. Kac, 160
Rożenek, Fajwel, 160–61
Rożenek, Golda, 160–61
Rożenek, Hinda, 160–61
Rożenek, Izrael, 160–61, 360
Rożenek, Jojne, 160–61
Rożenek, Marjem, 160–61
Rożenek, Masza, 278
Rożenek, Mejlech, 160–61

Rożenek, Michał, 160–61
Rożenek, Mordka, 278
Rożenek, Moshe, 220, 238–39, 241, 243, 360
Rożenek, Motel, 220, 241, 243, 258
Rożenek, Rywka, 161
Rozenfrucht, Chaim Szlama, 101
Rozenfrucht, Chawa m. Karmioł, 64
Rozenfrucht, Josek, 119
Rozenfrucht, Moszek Hersz, 135, 202, 312
Rozenfrucht, Moszek, 329–30
Rozenfrucht, Szlama, 64–65, 169
Rozenman [teacher], 101
Rozmarin, Henryk, 288
Rubin, Icek/Icze, 32, 74, 120–21, 123, 125, 140
Ryba, Sender, 141
Ryba, Zalman, 111
Rzędowski, 27, 66
Rzeźnik, Monas, 312
Salat, 59
Salomon, Moshe, 187
Schenierer, Sara, 97
Schindler, Oskar, 11, 260
Schmidt [German], 223, 276–77, 332
Schubert [German], 223, 276
Schwarz [commander Wüstegiersdorf], 310
Schwimer, Chaim, 185
Schwitzer, Harry, 363
Shahar, Aryeh (see Leibl Jutrzenka)
Shlomi [Szulimowicz], David, 77, 111, 113, 361
Skop, Jakób, 165
Skopicki, Hilel, 73, 331, 335
Skopicki, Jankiel, 73
Skóra, Dawid, 60, 65, 105, 133
Skóra, Herszel, 74
Skóra, Izrael Dov/Ber, 22, 66, 77, 105, 239
Skóra, Izrael Zvi, 361
Skóra, Izrael, 328
Skóra, Sonia b. Zonenfeld, 325, 328
Skóra, Wolf/Ze'ev, 105, 312, 330
Skórecki, Binem, 312
Skrzypek, Chaim, 265
Skrzypek, Mania, 258
Slabonik [commander of Polish police], 329
Słonimski, Chaim Zelig, 65
Smolarczyk, 92–93
Smolarczyk, Chaiml, 322–23
Smolarczyk, H., 134
Smolarczyk, Moszek, 119
Smolarz family, 296
Sokołów, Nahum, 54

Solny, Abram Lejb, 53
Soloducha, Aron, 157
Soloducha, Chaja m. Włoska, 157
Spievak, J., 108
Śpiewak, Małka, 119
Śpiewak, Moszek, 167, 188–89, 197
Śpiewak, Szyja, 98, 167, 185–189, 198, 290
Śpiewak, Taubela, 188–89
Spiro, 35, 60, 64, 78, 89, 96, 140
Spiro, Dwosia, 65
Spiro, Jerzy, 282, 299
Spiro, Rafał Herc, 65
Spiro, Szyja, 65
Spokojny, Alter, 60, 217
Spokojny, Jakób Szyja, 98
Spokojny, Lejbl, 297
Srebrny, Szyja, 62
Staszewski, Icek Halevi [rabbi], 204, 210
Staszewski, Mordka Icek [town rabbi], 55,
    96, 239, 246, 250, 328
Staszewski?, Berko [son of rabbi], 246
Staszewski?, Skalbmierz rabbi [son of
    Działoszyce rabbi], 246
Stempel, Wolf, 302
Stern, Dawid aka David Kohav, 110
Sternberg, 229
Sternberg, Balcia, 133
Sternberg, Pejsach, 60, 78, 92, 98–99, 170
Stersziwer [Strzyżower?], Mordchele, 246
Steurmark, Dr., 66
Świczarczyk, Izrael, 136
Szac, Izrael Chaim, 54
Szajnfeld, Fajgla, 119
Szaniecki, 235
Szaniecki, Icek, 105
Szapiro, Jehuda Majer [rabbi in Lublin], 170
Szenberg and Buchweitz [Katowice], 297
Szeniawski, Lejbuś, 97
Szeniawski, Zysman, 361
Szenkier, Abram Moszek, 95, 165, 169, 180
Szenkier, Abram, 96
Szenkier, Herszel, 134
Szental, 35, 60, 64–65, 89, 119, 148, 159
Szental, Alter, 64
Szental, Arysz, 64–65, 89
Szental, Dania, 89
Szental, Gerszon, 64, 174
Szental, Henoch, 167, 179
Szental, Mendel, 256
Szental, Moszek, 64

Szental, Szmul, 64, 254, 256
Szerer, Sara, 362
Szereszewska, Pesia, 267–68
Szklarczyk, Jakób, 98
Szklarczyk, Moszek, 59
Szkolnik, Chaim, 361
Szlamowicz, 64
Szlamowicz, Chaim, 251
Szlamowicz, Nusyn, 251
Szlamowicz, Shalom, 250
Sznajder[?], Zyskind, 193
Szpitz, Szmul, 159
Szternfinkiel, Nathan, 78
Szternfinkiel, Ze'ev, 78, 105, 109
Szternlicht, Wolf, 304
Szu"b[?], Icek Majer (see Frydberg, Icek
    Majer)
Szulimowicz, 217, 308
Szulimowicz, Chaim Szymon, 314
Szulimowicz, Chaja m. Chaba, 104
Szulimowicz, Chana, 119
Szulimowicz, Dawid, 115 (see also Shlomi,
    David
Szulimowicz, Fiszel (Malekh), 172, 180
Szulimowicz, Josek, 78, 111, 113, 141, 220,
    239, 241–43, 273, 278
Szulimowicz, Josel, 298
Szulimowicz, Majer, 92, 298
Szulimowicz, Mrs. Majer, 298
Szulimowicz, Szlama, 220, 241, 278
Szwajcer, 92
Szwajcer, Moszek, 78
Szwimer, 35, 60, 89
Szwimer, Chaim, 75, 87
Szwimer, Dawid, 87
Szwimer, Szulim, 87
Szydłowska, 109
Szydłowska, Tova m. Avni, 176, 362
Szydłowski, Naftali, 127, 182
Tajtelbaum, Joska, 92
Tajtelbaum, Lejbcze, 296
Targownik, 98, 229
Targownik, Dawid, 105, 201
Targownik, Josek, 77
Targownik, Moszek, 159
Tauman, 92
Tauman, Josek, 77, 105, 136
Tenenwurcel, Icek, 59
Tennenbaum, Abraham, 276
Topioł, Wolf, 98

Topoler, Hercke, 159
Trunk, Jechiel Isaiah [rabbi], 60
Tryliński [manager of grain warehouse], 297
Tshlenov, 113
Ungier, Kopel, 169, 174, 180
Ungier, M., 134, 139
Ungier, Mordka, 101, 106, 134
Ungier, Motel, 135
Ungier, Szymon, 180
Ussishkin, 113
Vogt [German], 223
Waga, Abram, 126, 169
Waga, Icek Majer, 92, 217
Waga, Moszek, 92, 169, 173
Wajdenfeld, Dov Ber [rabbi in Trzebinia], 170
Wajnbaum, Kalman, 299
Wajnbaum, Zale, 150, 297, 299
Wajnsztajn, Moszek, 125, 150
Wajnsztok, Izrael, 92
Wajntraub [wife of Szulimowicz], 239
Waks, Klara b. Kajla Akerman, 155
Wakschlag, Meyer, 363
Waserman, Izrael Jakób, 74
Wdowińska, Fajgla, 134
Wdowińska, Jentla, 83, 86
Wdowińska, Mindla, 135, 139
Wdowiński, 135, 167, 229
Wdowiński, Abram, 83, 86
Wdowiński, Aron, 78
Wdowiński, Dawid, 27
Wdowiński, Hercke, 86
Wdowiński, J., 134
Wdowiński, Joshua, 98, 101 (see also
    Wdowiński, Szyja)
Wdowiński, Mendel, 92, 133
Wdowiński, Moszek, 78
Wdowiński, Szmul, 133–34, 241, 243
Wdowiński, Szyja, 281 (see also
    Wdowiński, Joshua)
Weinberg, 292
Weissler, 73
Weizmann, 113
Wielopolski, Aleksander [margrave], 66
Winnik [gentile farmer], 330
Włodarczyk, Marian, 234
Włoska Chaja b. Soloducha, 157

Włoska, Taube/ Taubele Jojne's, 157
Włoski, Benjamin, 157, 338
Włoski, Izrael, 157
Włoski, Jojne, 157
Wohlgelernter, Chaim Icek, 246
Wohlgelernter, David, 246, 248, 319
Woźniakowski [gentile, made scenery], 135
Woźniakowski, Władysław, 66
Zając, Abram Icek, 53, 165
Zając, Bracha m. Pozner, 151
Zajfman, Berl, 334
Zakon brothers, 296
Zalc, Chaim Majer [rebbe in Pińczów], 145
Zalc, Eliezer [Admor in Pińczów], 145
Zalc, Pinkus [rebbe in Pińczów], 145
Zalcberg, Alter, 169
Zalcman, Bajla, 296
Zalcman, Judka, 296
Zalcman, Lejbuś, 109
Zalcman, Surele, 296
Zelcer (Pomeranc), Moszek Dawid, 173
Zelikowicz, Szulim Aszer, 331
Zerachi, Yisrael, 36, 51 (see also Gertler,
    Izrael Zerach)
Ziegelschmidt, Majer, 66
Zohn, Henoch, 82
Zohn, Juda Lejb, 82
Zonenfeld, Bajla, 325
Zonenfeld, Hela, 325
Zonenfeld, Lola, 325
Zonenfeld, Majer, 325
Zonenfeld, Mendel, 25, 325
Zonenfeld, Rajzla, 132, 139
Zonenfeld, Róża m. Rolnicka, 105,
    134–35, 325
Zonenfeld, Sonia m. Skóra, 325, 328
Zwoliński [mayor of Działoszyce], 92
Zylber, Abramcze, 165
Zylber, Blumcia, 136
Zylber, Eli, 239
Zylber, Eliasz, 278, 298
Zylber, Ester, 136
Zylber, Zusma, 298
Zylberberg, 308
Zylbersztajn, Kalonymos Kalman, 26
Zyngier, Akiba, 311, 332